F
Ab

Wallace Wang

Apress®

Swift OS X Programming for Absolute Beginners

ISBN-13 (pbk): 978-1-4842-1234-9

ISBN-13 (electronic): 978-1-4842-1233-2

Managing Director: Welmoed Spahr
Lead Editor: Louise Corrigan
Technical Reviewer: Bruce Wade
Editorial Board: Steve Anglin, Louise Corrigan, Jonathan Gennick, Robert Hutchinson,
    Michelle Lowman, James Markham, Susan McDermott, Matthew Moodie, Jeffrey Pepper,
    Douglas Pundick, Ben Renow-Clarke, Gwenan Spearing, Steve Weiss
Coordinating Editor: Mark Powers
Copy Editor: Karen Jameson
Compositor: SPi Global
Indexer: SPi Global
Artist: SPi Global
Cover photograph by Martijn Vroom

Distributed to the book trade worldwide by Springer Science+Business Media New York, 233 Spring Street, 6th Floor, New York, NY 10013. Phone 1-800-SPRINGER, fax (201) 348-4505, e-mail orders-ny@springer-sbm.com, or visit www.springeronline.com. Apress Media, LLC is a California LLC and the sole member (owner) is Springer Science + Business Media Finance Inc (SSBM Finance Inc). SSBM Finance Inc is a Delaware corporation.

For information on translations, please e-mail rights@apress.com, or visit www.apress.com.

Apress and friends of ED books may be purchased in bulk for academic, corporate, or promotional use. eBook versions and licenses are also available for most titles. For more information, reference our Special Bulk Sales–eBook Licensing web page at www.apress.com/bulk-sales.

Any source code or other supplementary material referenced by the author in this text is available to readers at www.apress.com/9781484212349. For detailed information about how to locate your book's source code, go to www.apress.com/source-code/.

This book is dedicated to everyone who always wanted to learn how to program on the Macintosh. You can learn anything you want just as long as you're willing to take the time and believe in yourself.

"Promise me you'll always remember: You're braver than you believe, and stronger than you seem, and smarter than you think."

—Christopher Robin to Winnie the Pooh

Contents at a Glance

Contents

About the Author

Wallace Wang is a former Windows enthusiast who took one look at Vista and realized that the future of computing belonged to the Macintosh. He has written more than forty computer books, including *Microsoft Office for Dummies, Beginning Programming for Dummies, Steal This Computer Book, My New Mac,* and *My New iPad.* In addition to programming the Macintosh and iPhone/iPad, he also performs stand-up comedy, having appeared on A&E s "Evening at the Improv," and having performed in Las Vegas at the Riviera Comedy Club at the Riviera Hotel & Casino. When he is not writing computer books or performing stand-up comedy, he also appears on a local San Diego radio show called "Notes From the Underground" that airs twice a week on a radio station KNSJ (www.knsj.org).

In addition, he enjoys blogging about screenwriting at his site, The 15 Minute Movie Method (www.15minutemoviemethod.com), where he shares screenwriting tips with other aspiring screenwriters who all share the goal of breaking into Hollywood. Some of his other sites include Cat Daily News (www.catdailynews.com) that highlights interesting news about cats, The Electronic Author (www.electronicauthor.com) that focuses on self-publishing, and Top Bananas (www.topbananas.com) that covers the possibilities and application of technology related to Apple and other mobile and wearable computer manufacturers.

About the Technical Reviewer

Bruce Wade is the founder of Warply Designed Inc. (www.warplydesigned.com), a company specializing in using game technology for real-world applications. He has more than sixteen years of software development experience with a strong focus on 2D/3D animation and interactive applications, primarily using Apple technology.

Acknowledgments

Thanks go to all the wonderful people at APress for giving me a chance to write about Swift, my latest favorite programming language for the Macintosh, iPhone, iPad, and Apple Watch.

Additional thanks go to Dane Henderson and Elizabeth Lee (`www.echoludo.com`) who share the airwaves with me on our radio show "Notes From the Underground" (`http://notesfromtheu.com`) on KNSJ.org. More thanks go to Chris Clobber, Diane Jean, Ikaika Patria and Robert Weems for letting me share their friendship and lunacy on another KNSJ radio show called "Laugh in Your Face," (`http://www.laughinyourfaceradio.com`) which combines comedy with political activism and commentary.

A special mention goes towards Michael Montijo and his indomitable spirit that has him driving from Phoenix to Los Angeles once a month for the past fifteen years to meet with Hollywood executives. His cartoon show ideas, "Life of Mikey" and "Pachuko Boy," will one day make it to television because he never gave up despite all the obstacles in his way.

Thanks also go to my wife, Cassandra, and son, Jordan, for putting up with a house filled with more gadgets than actual living people. Final thanks go to my cats, Oscar and Mayer, for walking over the keyboard, knocking over laptops, and chewing on power cords at the most inconvenient times of the day.

Introduction

Whether you're a complete novice looking to get started in programming, someone familiar with programming but curious about learning more, or a seasoned programmer comfortable with other programming languages but unfamiliar with Macintosh programming, this book is for you. Whatever your skill level, this book will help everyone understand how to use Apple's latest programming language, Swift, to create OS X programs for the Macintosh.

Now you may be wondering why learn Swift and why program for the Macintosh? The answer is simple.

First, Swift is Apple's newest programming language designed to make creating OS X and iOS programs faster, easier, and more reliable than before. Previously, you had to use Objective-C to create OS X and iOS apps. While powerful, Objective-C is much harder to learn; more complicated to read and write; and because of its complexity, more prone to introducing errors or bugs in a program.

On the other hand, Swift is just as powerful as Objective-C (actually more powerful as you'll soon see), far easier to learn, and much simpler to read and write while also minimizing common programming errors at the same time. Swift gives you all the benefits of Objective-C with none of the drawbacks. Plus Swift gives you features that Objective-C doesn't offer, which makes Swift a far better programming language to learn and use today and tomorrow. Since Swift is Apple's official programming language, you can be certain learning Swift will lead to greater opportunities now and long into the future.

Second, you may wonder why learn to create Macintosh programs? After all, the hot trend is learning to create iOS apps for the iPhone, iPad, and Apple Watch. If you plan on developing software, you definitely want to use Swift to create iOS apps.

However, learning Swift means understanding the following:

- The principles of programming and object-oriented programming in particular
- The syntax of the Swift programming language
- Xcode's features
- Apple's software development framework (called Cocoa) that forms the foundation of every OS X and iOS program
- The principles of user interface design

Does this sound like a lot to learn? Don't worry. We'll go through each process step by step so you won't feel lost. The point is that to create OS X programs and iOS apps, you need to learn multiple topics, but creating iOS apps poses an additional challenge.

For example, an iOS app needs to respond to touch gestures with one finger, two fingers, swipes, shakes, and motion in addition to adapting to changes when the user flips an iPhone or iPad left, right, upside down, or right side up.

In comparison, a Macintosh program only needs to respond to keyboard and mouse input. That means OS X programs are much simpler to create and understand, which also means that learning Swift to create OS X programs is far easier than learning Swift to create iOS apps.

Best of all, the principles are exactly the same. What you learn creating OS X programs are the exact same skills you need to create iOS apps. The difference is that creating OS X programs is far easier, less confusing, and much less intimidating than creating iOS apps.

Trying to create iOS apps right from the start can be like trying to swim across the English Channel before you even know how to hold your breath underwater.

You don't want to frustrate yourself unnecessarily. That's why it's much easier to learn the principles of iOS app programming by first learning OS X programming. Once you're familiar with OS X programming, you'll find it's trivial to transfer your programming skills to creating iOS apps. By learning to create OS X programs in Swift, you'll learn everything you need to know to eventually create iOS apps in Swift, plus you'll know how to create OS X programs so you can tap into the growing Macintosh market as well.

Following Lucrative Programming Trends

The introduction of a new computer platform has always ushered in a lucrative period for programmers. In the early 80s, the hottest platform was the Apple II computer. If you wanted to make money writing programs, you wrote programs to sell to Apple II computer owners, such as Dan Bricklin did, an MBA graduate student at the time, when he wrote the first spreadsheet program, VisiCalc.

Then the next big computing platform shift occurred in the mid-80s with the IBM PC and MS-DOS. People made fortunes off the IBM PC including Bill Gates and Microsoft, which went from a small, startup company to the most dominant computer company in the world. The IBM PC made millionaires out of hundreds of people including Scott Cook, a former marketing director at Proctor & Gamble, who developed the popular money manager program, Quicken.

Microsoft helped usher in the next computer platform when they shifted from MS-DOS to Windows and put a friendly graphical user interface on IBM PCs. Once again, programming Windows became the number one way that programmers and non-programmers alike made fortunes by writing and selling their own Windows programs. Microsoft took advantage of the shift to Windows by releasing several Windows-only programs that have become fixtures of the business world such as Outlook, Access, and Excel.

Now the world is shifting toward the new computer platform of Apple products running OS X and iOS. Thousands of people, just like you, are eager to start writing programs to take advantage of the Macintosh's rising market share along with the dominant position of the iPhone and the iPad in the smart phone and tablet categories, and the Apple Watch in the wearable computer market.

Besides experienced developers, amateurs, hobbyists, and professionals in other fields are also interested in writing their own games, utilities, and business software specific to their particular niche.

Many programmers have gone from knowing nothing about programming to earning thousands of dollars a day by creating iPhone/iPad apps or Macintosh programs. As the Macintosh, iPhone, iPad, and now the Apple Watch continue gaining market share all over the world, more people will use one or more of these products, increasing the potential market for you.

All this means is that it's a perfect time for you to start learning how to program your Macintosh right now because the sooner you understand the basics of Macintosh programming, the sooner you can start creating your own Macintosh programs along with iPhone/iPad/Apple Watch apps.

What to Expect From This Book

Whether you're a complete novice or a seasoned programmer coming from another programming environment, this book will minimize technical jargon and focus on helping you understand what to do and why.

If you just want to get started and learn the basics of programming in Swift, this book is for you. If you're already an experienced Windows programmer and want to get started programming the Macintosh, this book can be especially helpful in teaching you the basics in a hurry.

If you've never programmed before in your life, or if you're already familiar with programming but not with Macintosh programming, then this book is for you. Even if you're experienced with Macintosh programming, you may still find this book handy as a reference to help you achieve certain results without having to wade through several books to find an answer.

You won't learn everything you need to create your own super-sophisticated programs, but you'll learn just enough to get started, feel comfortable using Xcode, and be able to tackle other programming books with more confidence and understanding. Fair enough? If so, then turn the page and let's get started.

> **Note**   All code in this book was tested using Swift 2 in Xcode 7. If you're using Xcode 6, some features in this book won't work.

Understanding Programming

Programming is nothing more than writing step-by-step instructions for a computer to follow. If you've ever written down the steps for a recipe or scribbled directions for taking care of your pets while you're on vacation, you've already gone through the basic steps of writing a program. The key is simply knowing what you want to accomplish and then making sure you write the correct instructions that will tell someone how to achieve that goal.

Although programming is theoretically simple, it's the details that can trip you up. First, you need to know exactly what you want. If you wanted a recipe for cooking chicken chow mein, following a recipe for cooking baked salmon won't do you any good.

Second, you need to write down every instruction necessary to get you from your starting point to your desired result. If you skip a step or write steps out of order, you won't get the same result. Try driving to a restaurant where your list of driving instructions omits telling you when to turn on a specific road. It doesn't matter if 99 percent of the instructions are right; if just one instruction is wrong, you won't get to your desired goal.

The simpler your goal, the easier it will be to achieve it. Writing a program that displays a calculator on the screen is far simpler than writing a program to monitor the safety systems of a nuclear power plant. The more complex your program, the more instructions you'll need to write, and the more instructions you need to write, the greater the chance you'll forget an instruction, write an instruction incorrectly, or write instructions in the wrong order.

Programming is nothing more than a way to control a computer to solve a problem, whether that computer is a laptop, smart phone, tablet, or wearable watch. Before you can start writing your own programs, you need to understand the basic principles of programming in the first place.

> **Note**   Don't get confused between learning programming and learning a particular programming language. You can actually learn the principles of programming without touching a computer at all. Once you understand the principles of programming, you can easily learn any particular programming language such as Swift.

Programming Principles

To write a program, you have to write instructions that the computer can follow. No matter what a program does or how big it may be, every program in the world consists of nothing more than step-by-step instructions for the computer to follow, one at a time. The simplest program can consist of a single line such as:

```
print ("Hello, world"!)
```

Obviously, a program that consists of a single line won't be able to do much, so most programs consist of multiples lines of instructions (or code) such as:

```
print ("Hello, world!")
print ("Now the program is done.")
```

This two-line program starts with the first line, follows the instructions on the second line, and then stops. Of course, you can keep adding more instructions to a program until you have a million instructions that the computer can follow sequentially, one at a time.

Listing instructions sequentially is the basis for programming. Unfortunately, it's also limiting. For example, if you wanted to print the same message five times, you could use the following:

```
print ("Hello, world!")
print ("Hello, world!")
print ("Hello, world!")
print ("Hello, world!")
print ("Hello, world!")
```

Writing the same five instructions is tedious and redundant, but it works. What happens if you want to print this same message a thousand times? Then you'd have to write the same instruction a thousand times.

Writing the same instruction multiple times is clumsy. To make programming easier, the goal is to write the least number of instructions to get the most work done. One way to avoid writing the same instruction multiple times is to organize your instructions using a second basic principle of programming, which is called a loop.

The idea behind a loop is to repeat one or more instructions multiple times, but only by writing those instructions down once. A typical loop might look like this:

```
for i in 1...5 {
  print ("Hello, world!")
}
```

The first line tells the computer to repeat the loop five times. The second line tells the computer to print the message "Hello, world" on the screen. The third line just defines the end of the loop.

Now if you wanted to make the computer print a message one thousand times, you don't need to write the same instruction a thousand times. Instead, you just need to modify how many times the loop repeats such as:

```
for i in 1...1000 {
  print ("Hello, world!")
}
```

Although loops are slightly more confusing to read and understand than a sequential series of instructions, loops make it easier to repeat instructions without writing the same instructions multiple times.

Most programs don't exclusively list instructions sequentially or in loops, but use a combination of both such as:

```
print ("Hello, world!")
print ("Now the program is starting.")
for i in 1...1000 {
  print ("Hello, world!")
}
```

In this example, the computer follows the first two lines sequentially and then follows the last three lines repetitively in a loop. Generally, listing instructions sequentially is fine when you only need the computer to follow those instructions once. When you need the computer to run instructions multiple times, that's when you need to use a loop.

What makes computers powerful isn't just the ability to follow instructions sequentially or in a loop, but in making decisions. Decisions mean that the computer needs to evaluate some condition and then, based on that condition, decide what to do next.

For example, you might write a program that locks someone out of a computer until that person types in the correct password. If the person types the correct password, then the program needs to give that person access. However, if the person types an incorrect password, then the program needs to block access to the computer. An example of this type of decision making might look like this:

```
if password == "secret" {
    print ("Access granted!")
} else {
    print ("Login denied!")
}
```

In this example, the computer asks for a password and when the user types in a password, the computer checks to see if it matches the word "secret." If so, then the computer grants that person access to the computer. If the user did not type "secret," then the computer denies access.

Making decisions is what makes programming flexible. If you write a sequential series of instructions, the computer will follow those lists of instructions exactly the same, every time. However, if you include decision-making instructions, also known as branching instructions, then the computer can respond according to what the user does.

Consider a video game. No video game could be written entirely with instructions organized sequentially because then the game would play exactly the same way every time. Instead, a video game needs to adapt to the player's actions at all times. If the player moves an object to the left, the video game needs to respond differently than if the player moves an object to the right or gets killed. Using branching instructions gives computers the ability to react differently so the program never runs exactly the same.

To write a computer program, you need to organize instructions in one of the following three ways as graphically show in Figure 1-1:

- Sequentially – the computer follows instructions one after another

- Loop – the computer repetitively follows one or more instructions

- Branching – the computer chooses to follow one or more group of instructions based on outside data

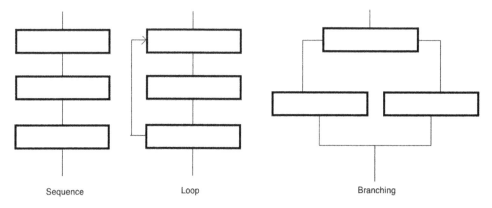

Sequence   Loop   Branching

Figure 1-1. *The three basic building blocks of programming*

While simple programs may only organize instructions sequentially, every large program organizes instructions sequentially, in loops, and in branches. What makes programming more of an art and less of a science is that there is no single best way to write a program. In fact, it's perfectly possible to write two different programs that behave exactly the same.

Because there is no single "right" way to write a program, there are only guidelines to help you write programs easily. Ultimately what only matters is that you write a program that works.

When writing any program, there are two, often mutually exclusive goals. First, programmers strive to write programs that are easy to read, understand, and modify. This often means writing multiple instructions that clearly define the steps needed to solve a particular problem.

Second, programmers try to write programs that perform tasks efficiently, making the program run as fast as possible. This often means condensing multiple instructions as much as possible, using tricks or exploiting little-known features that are difficult to understand and confusing even to most other programmers.

In the beginning, strive toward making your programs as clear, logical, and understandable as possible, even if you have to write more instructions or type longer instructions to do it. Later as you gain more experience in programming, you can work on creating the smallest, fastest, most efficient programs possible, but remember that your ultimate goal is to write programs that just work.

Structured Programming

Small programs have fewer instructions so they are much easier to read, understand, and modify. Unfortunately, small programs can only solve small problems. To solve complicated problems, you need to write bigger programs with more instructions. The more instructions you type, the greater the chance you'll make a mistake (called a "bug"). Even worse is that the larger a program gets, the harder it can be to understand how it works so that you can modify it later.

To avoid writing a single, massive program, programmers simply divide a large program into smaller parts called subprograms or functions. The idea is that each subprogram solves a single task. This makes it easy to write and ensure that it works correctly.

Once all of your separate functions work, then you can connect them all together to create a single large program as shown in Figure 1-2. This is like building a house out of bricks rather than trying to carve an entire house out of one massive rock.

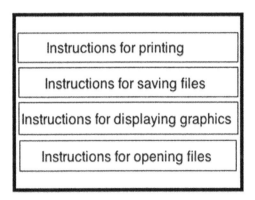

Figure 1-2. Dividing a large program into multiple subprograms or functions helps make programming more reliable

Dividing a large program into smaller programs provides several benefits. First, writing smaller subprograms is fast and easy, and small subprograms make it easy to read, understand, and modify the instructions.

Second, subprograms act like building blocks that work together, so multiple programmers can work on different subprograms, then combine their separate subprograms together to create a large program.

Third, if you want to modify a large program, you just need to yank out, rewrite, and replace one or more subprograms. Without subprograms, modifying a large program means wading through all the instructions stored in a large program and trying to find which instructions you need to change.

A fourth benefit of subprograms is that if you write a useful subprogram, you can plug that subprogram into other programs. By creating a library of tested, useful subprograms, you can create other programs quickly and easily by reusing existing code, thereby reducing the need to write everything from scratch.

When you divide a large program into multiple subprograms, you have a choice. You can store all your programs in a single file, or you can store each subprogram in a separate file as shown in Figure 1-3. By storing subprograms in separate files, multiple programmers can work on different files without affecting anyone else.

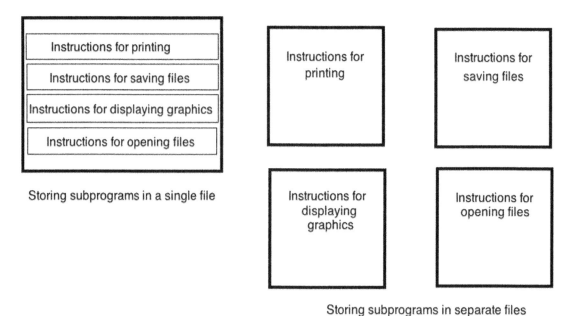

Storing subprograms in a single file

Storing subprograms in separate files

Figure 1-3. You can store subprograms in a single file or in multiple files

Storing all your subprograms in a single file makes it easy to find and modify any part of your program. However, the larger your program, the more instructions you'll need to write, which can make searching through a single large file as clumsy as flipping through the pages of a dictionary.

Storing all of your subprograms in separate files means that you need to keep track of which files contain which subprogram. However, the benefit is that modifying a subprogram is much easier because once you open the correct file, you only see the instructions for a single subprogram, not for a dozen or more other subprograms.

Because today's programs can get so large, it's common to divide its various subprograms in separate files.

Event-Driven Programming

In the early days of computers, most programs worked by starting with the first instruction and then following each instruction line by line until it reached the end. Such programs tightly controlled how the computer behaved at any given time.

All of this changed when computers started displaying graphical user interfaces with windows and pull-down menus so users could choose what to do at any given time. Suddenly every program had to wait for the user to do something such as selecting a menu command or clicking a button. Now programs had to wait for the user to do something before reacting.

Every time the user did something, that was considered an event. If the user clicked the left mouse button, that was a completely different event than if the user clicked the right mouse button. Instead of dictating what the user could do at any given time, programs now had to respond to different events that the user did. Making programs responsive to different events is called event-driven programming.

Event-driven programs divide a large program into multiple subprograms where each subprogram responds to a different event. If the user clicked a menu command, a subprogram would run its instructions. If the user clicked a button, a different subprogram would run another set of instructions.

Event-driven programming always waits to respond to the user's action.

Object-Oriented Programming

Dividing a large program into multiple subprograms made it easy to create and modify a program. However, trying to understand how such a large program worked often proved confusing since there was no simple way to determine which subprograms worked together or what data they might need from other subprograms.

Even worse, subprograms often modified data that other subprograms used. This meant sometimes a subprogram would modify data before another subprogram could use it. Using the wrong data would cause the other subprogram to fail, causing the whole program to fail. Not only does this situation create less reliable software, but it also makes it much harder to determine how and where to fix the problem.

To solve this problem, computer scientists created object-oriented programming. The goal is to divide a large program into smaller subprograms, but organized related subprograms together into groups known as objects. To make object-oriented programs easier to understand, objects also model physical items in the real world.

Suppose you wrote a program to control a robot. Dividing this problem by tasks, you might create one subprogram to move the robot, a second subprogram to tell the robot how to see nearby obstacles, and a third subprogram to calculate the best path to follow. If there was a problem with the robot's movement, you would have no idea whether the problem lay in the subprogram controlling the movement, the subprogram controlling how the robot sees obstacles, or the subprogram calculating the best path to follow.

Dividing this same robot program into objects might create a Legs object (for moving the robot), an Eye object for seeing nearby obstacles, and a Brain object (for calculating the best path to avoid obstacles). Now if there was a problem with the robot's movement, you could isolate the problem to the code stored in the Legs object.

Besides isolating data within an object, a second idea behind object-oriented programming is to make it easy to reuse and modify a large program. Suppose we replace a robot's legs with treads. Now we'd have to modify the subprogram for moving the robot since treads behave differently than legs. Next, we'd have to modify the subprogram for calculating the best path around obstacles since treads force a robot to go around obstacles while legs would allow a robot to walk over small obstacles and go around larger ones.

If you wanted to replace a robot's legs with treads, object-oriented programming would simply allow you to yank out the Legs object and replace it with a new Treads object, without affecting or needing to modify any additional objects that make up the rest of the program.

Since most programs are constantly modified to fix errors (known as bugs) or add new features, object-oriented programming allows you to create a large program out of separate building blocks (objects), and modify a program by only modifying a single object.

The key to object-oriented programming is to isolate parts of a program and promote reusability through three features known as encapsulation, inheritance, and polymorphism.

Encapsulation

The main purpose of encapsulation is to protect and isolate one part of a program from another part of a program. To do this, encapsulation hides data so it can never be changed by another part of a program. In addition, encapsulation also holds all subprograms that manipulate data stored in that object. If any problems occur, encapsulation makes it easy to isolate the problem within a particular object.

Every object is meant to be completely independent of any other part of a program. Objects store data in properties. The only way to manipulate those properties is to use subprograms called methods, which are also encapsulated in the same object. The combination of properties and methods, isolated within an object, makes it easy to create large programs quickly and reliably by using objects as building blocks as shown in Figure 1-4.

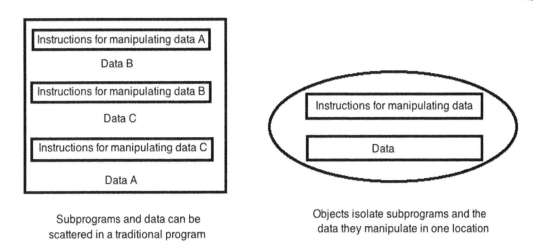

Figure 1-4. *Objects encapsulate related subprograms and data together, hidden from the rest of a program*

Inheritance

Creating a large, complicated program is hard, but what makes that task even harder is writing the whole program from scratch. That's why most programmers reuse parts of an existing program for two reasons. First, they don't have to rewrite the feature they need from scratch. That means they can create a large program faster. Second, they can use tested code that's already proven to work right. That means they can create more reliable software faster by reusing reliable code.

One huge problem with reusing code is that you never want to make duplicate copies. Suppose you copied a subprogram and pasted it into a second subprogram. Now you have two copies of the exact same code stored in two separate places in the same program. This wastes space, but more importantly, it risks causing problems in the future.

Suppose you found a problem in a subprogram. To fix this problem, you'd need to fix this code everywhere you copied and pasted it in other parts of your program. If you copied and pasted this code in two other places in your program, you'd have to find and fix that code in both places. If you copied and pasted this code in a thousand places in your program, you'd have to find and fix that code in a thousand different places.

Not only is this inconvenient and time consuming, but it also increases the risk of overlooking code and leaving a problem in that code. This creates less reliable programs.

To avoid the problem of fixing multiple copies of the same code, object-oriented programming uses something called inheritance. The idea is that one object can use all the code stored in another object but without physically making a copy of that code. Instead, one object inherits code from another object, but only one copy of that code ever exists.

Now you can reuse one copy of code as many times as you want. If you need to fix a problem, you only need to fix that code once, and those changes automatically appear in any object that reuses that code thorough inheritance.

Basically, inheritance lets you reuse code without physically making duplicate copies of that code. This makes it easy to reuse code and easily modify it in the future.

Polymorphism

Every object consists of data (stored in properties) and subprograms (called methods) for manipulating that data. With inheritance, one object can use the properties and methods defined in another object. However, inheritance can create a problem when you need a subprogram (method) to use different code.

Suppose you created a video game. You might define a car as one object and a monster as a second one. If the monster throws rocks at the car, the rocks would be a third object. To make the car, monster, and rocks move on the screen, you might create a method named Move.

Unfortunately, a car needs to move differently on the screen than a monster or a thrown rock. You could create three subprograms and name them MoveCar, MoveMonster, and MoveRock. However, a simpler solution is to just give all three subprograms the same name such as Move.

In traditional programming, you can never give the same name to two or more subprograms since the computer would never know which subprogram you want to run. However in object-oriented programming, you can use duplicate subprogram names because of polymorphism.

Polymorphism lets you use the same method names but replace it with different code. The reason why polymorphism works is because each Move subprogram (method) gets stored in a separate object such as one object that represents the car, a second object that represents the monster, and a third object that represents a thrown rock. To run each Move subprogram, you would identify the object that contains the Move subprogram you want to use such as:

> Car.Move
>
> Monster.Move
>
> Rock.Move

By identifying both the object that you want to manipulate and the subprogram that you want to use, object-oriented programming can correctly identify which set of instructions to run even though one subprogram has the identical name of another subprogram.

Essentially, polymorphism lets you create descriptive subprogram names and reuse that descriptive name as often as you like when you also use inheritance.

The combination of encapsulation, inheritance, and polymorphism forms the basis for object-oriented programming. Encapsulation isolates one part of a program from another. Inheritance lets you reuse code. Polymorphism lets you reuse method names but with different code.

Understanding Programming Languages

A programming language is nothing more than a particular way to express ideas, much like human languages such as Spanish, Arabic, Chinese, or English. Computer scientists create programming languages to solve specific types of problems. That means one programming language may be perfect to solve one type of problem but horrible at solving a different type of problem.

The most popular programming language is C, which was designed for low-level access to the computer hardware. As a result, the C language is great for creating operating systems, anti-virus programs, and hard disk encryption programs. Anything that needs to completely control hardware is a perfect task for the C programming language.

Unfortunately, C can be cryptic and sparse because it was designed for maximum efficiency for computers without regard for human efficiency for reading, writing, or modifying C programs. To improve C, computer scientists created an object-oriented version of C called C++ and a slightly different object-oriented version called Objective-C, which was the language Apple adopted for OS X and iOS programming.

Because C was originally designed for computer efficiency at the expense of human efficiency, all variants of C including C++ and Objective-C can also be difficult to learn, use, and understand. That's why Apple created Swift. The purpose of Swift is to give you the power of Objective-C while being far easier to learn, use, and understand. Swift is basically an improved version of Objective-C, which was an improved version of C.

Each evolution of computer programming builds on the previous programming standards. When you write programs in Swift, you can use Swift's unique features along with object-oriented features. In addition, you can also use event-driven programming, structured programming, and the three basic building blocks of programming (sequential, loops, and branching) when writing Swift programs as well.

Swift, like all computer programming languages, contain a fixed list of commands known as keywords. To tell a computer what to do, you have to keywords to create statements that cause the computer to perform a single task.

Keywords act as building blocks for any programming language. By combining keywords, you can create subprograms or functions that give a programming language more power. For example, one keyword in Swift is var, which defines a variable. One function defined in Swift is print, which prints data on the screen.

You've already seen the print function that prints text such as:

```
print ("Hello, world!")
```

This Swift print function (which stands for print line) works with any data enclosed in its parentheses. Just as learning a human language requires first learning the basic symbols used to write letters such as an alphabet or other symbols, so does learning a programming language require first learning the keywords and functions of that particular programming language.

Although Swift contains dozens of keywords and functions, you don't have to learn all of them at once to write programs in Swift. You just have to learn a handful of keywords and functions initially. As you get more experienced, you'll gradually need to learn additional Swift keywords and functions.

To make programming as easy as possible, Swift (like many programming languages) uses keywords and functions that look like ordinary English words such as print or var (short for variable). However, many programming languages, such as Swift, also use symbols that represent different features.

Common symbols are mathematical symbols for addition (+), subtraction (-), multiplication (*), and division (/).

Swift also uses curly brackets to group related code that needs to run together such as:

```
{
    print ("This is a message")
    print ("The message is done now")
}
```

Unlike human languages where you can misspell a word or forget to end a sentence with a period and people can still understand what you're saying, programming languages are not so forgiving. With a programming language, every keyword and function must be spelled correctly, and every symbol must be used where needed. Misspell a single keyword or function, use the wrong symbol, or put the right symbol in the wrong place, and your entire program will fail to work.

Programming languages are precise. The key to programming is to write:

- As little code as possible
- Code that does as much as possible
- Code that's as easy to understand as possible

You want to write as little code as possible because the less code you write, the easier it will be to ensure that it works right.

You want code that does as much as possible because that makes your program more capable of solving bigger problems.

You want code that's easy to understand because that makes it easy to fix problems and add features.

Unfortunately, these three criteria are often at odds with one another as shown in Figure 1-5.

Write as little code
as possible

Code that does as   Code that's easy
much as possible   to understand

Figure 1-5. *The three, often contradictory, goals of programming*

If you write as little code as possible, that usually means your code can't do much. That's why programmers often resort to shortcuts and programming tricks to condense the size of their code, but that also increases the complexity of their code, making it harder to understand.

If you write code that does as much as possible, that usually means writing large numbers of commands, which makes the code harder to understand.

If you write code that's easy to understand, it usually won't do much. If you write more code to make it do more, that makes it harder to understand.

Ultimately, computer programming is more of an art than a science. In general, it's better to focus on making code as easy to understand as possible because that will make it easier to fix problems and add new features. In addition, code that's easy to understand means other programmers can fix and modify your program if you can't do it.

That's why Apple created Swift to make code easier to understand than Objective-C without sacrificing the power of Objective-C. Despite being more powerful than Objective-C, Swift code can often be shorter than equivalent Objective-C code. For that reason, the future programming language of Apple will be Swift.

The Cocoa Framework

Keywords, functions, and symbols let you give instructions to a computer, but no programming language can provide every possible command you might need to create all types of programs. To provide additional commands, programmers use keywords to create subprograms that perform a specific task.

When they create a useful subprogram, they often save it in a library of other useful subprograms. Now when you write a program, you can use the programming language's keywords plus any subprograms stored in libraries. By reusing subprograms stored in libraries, you can create more powerful and reliable code.

For example, one library might contain subprograms for displaying graphics. Another library might contain subprograms for saving data to a disk and retrieving it again. Still another library might contain subprograms for calculating mathematical formulas. To make writing OS X and iOS programs easier, Apple has created a library framework of useful subprograms called the Cocoa framework.

There are two reasons for reusing an existing framework. First, reusing a framework keeps you from having to write your own instructions to accomplish a task that somebody else has already solved. Not only does a framework provide a ready-made solution, but a framework has also been tested by others, so you can just use the framework and be assured that it will work correctly.

A second reason to use an existing framework is for consistency. Apple provides frameworks for defining the appearance of a program on the screen, known as the user interface. This defines how a program should behave from displaying windows on the screen to letting you resize or close a window by clicking the mouse.

It's perfectly possible to write your own instructions for displaying windows on the screen, but chances are good that writing your own instructions would take time to create and test, and the end result would be a user interface that may not look or behave identically as other OS X or iOS programs.

However, by reusing an existing framework, you can create your own program quickly and ensure that your program behaves the same way that other programs behave. Although programming might sound complicated, Apple provides hundreds of pre-written and tested subprograms that help you create programs quickly and easily. All you have to do is write the custom instructions that make your program solve a specific, unique problem.

To understand how Apple's Cocoa framework works, you need to understand object-oriented programming for two reasons. First, Swift is an object-oriented programming language, so to take full advantage of Swift, you need to understand the advantages of object-oriented programming.

Second, Apple's Cocoa framework is based on object-oriented programming. To understand how to use the Cocoa framework, you need to use objects.

> **Note**   The Cocoa framework is designed for creating OS X programs. A similar framework called Cocoa Touch is designed for creating iOS apps. Because the Cocoa Touch framework (iOS) is based on the Cocoa framework (OS X), they both work similarly but offer different features.

By relying on the Cocoa framework, your programs can gain new features each time Apple updates and improves the Cocoa framework. For example, spell checking is a built-in feature of the Cocoa framework. If you write a program using the Cocoa framework, your programs automatically get spell-checking capabilities without you having to write any additional code whatsoever. When Apple improves the spell-checking feature in the Cocoa framework, your program automatically gets those improvements with no extra effort on your part.

The Cocoa framework is a general term that describes all of Apple's pre-written and tested libraries of code. Some different parts of the Cocoa framework can give your programs audio playing capabilities, graphics capabilities, contact information storage abilities such as names and addresses, and Internet capabilities.

The Cocoa framework creates the foundation of a typical OS X program. All you have to do is write Swift code that makes your program unique.

The View-Model-Controller Design

It's possible to write a large program and store all your code in a single file. However, that makes finding anything in your program much harder. A better solution is to divide a large program into parts and store related parts in separate files. That way you can quickly find the part of your program you need to modify, and you make it easy for multiple programmers to work together since one programmer can work on one file and a second programmer can work on a second file.

When you divide a program into separate files, it's best to stay organized. Just as you might store socks in one drawer and pants in a second drawer so you can easily find what the clothes need, so should you organize your program into multiple files so each file only contains related data. That way you can find the file you need to modify quickly and easily.

The type of data you can store in a file generally falls into one of three categories as shown in Figure 1-6:

- Views (user interface)
- Models
- Controllers

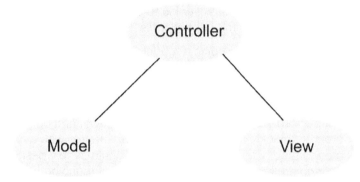

Figure 1-6. Dividing a program into a model-view-controller design

The view or user interface is what the user sees. The purpose of every user interface is to display information, accept data, and accept commands from the user. In the old days, programmers often created user interfaces by writing code. While you can still do this in Swift, it's time consuming, error prone, and inconsistent because one programmer's user interface might not look and behave exactly like a second programmer's user interface.

A better option is to design your user interface visually, which is what Xcode lets you do. Just draw objects on your user interface such as buttons, text fields, and menus, and Xcode automatically creates an error-free, consistent-looking user interface that only takes seconds to create. When you create a user interface using Xcode, you're actually using Apple's Cocoa framework to do it.

By itself, the user interface looks good but does nothing. To make a program do something useful, you need to write code that solves a specific problem. For example, a lottery-picking program might analyze the latest numbers picked and determine the numbers most likely to get picked the coming week. The portion of your code that calculates a useful result is called the model.

The model is actually completely separate from the view (user interface). That makes it easy to modify the user interface without affecting the model (and vice versa). By keeping different parts of your program as isolated as possible from other parts of your program, you reduce the chance of errors occurring when you modify a program.

Since the model is always completely separate from the view, you need a controller. When a user chooses a command or types data into the user interface, the controller takes that information from the view and passes it to the model.

The model responds to this data or commands and calculates a new result. Then it sends the calculated result to the controller, which passes it back to the view to display for the user to see. At all times, the view and model are completely separate.

With Xcode, this means you'll write and store the bulk of your Swift code in files that define the model of your program. If you were calculating winning lottery numbers, your Swift code for performing these calculations would be stored in the model.

You'll also need to write and store Swift code in a controller file. In a simple program, you might have a single view. In a more complicated program, you might have several views. For each view, you'll typically need a controller file to control that view. So the second place you'll write and store Swift code is in the controller files.

In simple programs, it's common to combine a model with a controller in one file. However for larger, more complicated programs, it's better to create one (or more) files for your model and one file for each controller. The number of controller files is usually equal to the number of views that make up your user interface.

Once you've clearly separated your program into models, views, and controllers, you can easily modify your program quickly and easily by replacing one file with a new file. For example, if you wanted to modify the user interface, you could simply design a different view, connect it to your controller, and you'd be done without touching your model files.

If you wanted to modify the model to add new features, you could just update your model files and connect it to your controller without touching your view.

In fact, this is exactly how programmers create programs for both OS X and iOS. Their model remains unchanged. All they do is write one controller and view for OS X and one controller and view for iOS. Then they can create both OS X and iOS apps with the exact same model.

How Programmers Work

In the early days, a single programmer could get an idea and write code to make that program work. Nowadays, programs are far more complicated, and user expectations are much higher so that you need to design your program before writing any code. In fact, most programmers actually don't spend much of their time writing or editing code at all. Instead, programmers spend the bulk of their time thinking, planning, organizing, and designing programs.

When a programmer has an idea for a program, the first step is to decide if that idea is even any good. Programs must solve a specific type of problem. For example, word processors make it easy to write, edit, and format text. Spreadsheets make it easy to type in numbers and calculate new results from those numbers. Presentation programs make it easy to type text and insert graphics to create a slideshow. Even video games solve the problem of relieving boredom by offering a challenging puzzle or goal for players to achieve.

> **Note** The number one biggest failure of software development is not defining a specific problem to solve. The second biggest failure of software development is identifying a specific problem to solve but underestimating the complexity of the steps needed to solve that problem. You have to know what problem to solve and how to solve that problem. If you don't know either one, you can't write a useful program.

Once you have an idea for a problem to solve, the next step is defining how to solve that problem. Some problems are simply too difficult to solve. For example, how would you write a program to write a best-selling novel? You may be able to write a program that can help you write a novel, but unless you know exactly how to create a best-selling novel predictably, you simply can't write such a program.

Knowing a problem to solve is your target. Once you clearly understand your problem, you now need to identify all the steps needed to solve that problem. If you don't know how to solve a particular problem, you won't be able to tell a computer how to solve that problem either.

After defining the steps needed to solve a problem, now you can finally write your program. Generally you'll write your program in parts and test each part before continuing. In this way, you'll gradually expand the capabilities of your program while making sure that each part works correctly.

The main steps you'll go through while using Xcode are:

- Write code and design your user interface
- Edit your code and user interface
- Run and test your program

When your program is finally done, guess what? It's never done. There will always be errors you'll need to fix and new features you'll want to add. Programmers actually spend more time editing and modifying existing programs than they ever do creating new ones.

When you write and edit code, you'll use an editor, which is a program that resembles a word processor that lets you type and edit text. When you design and modify your user interface, you'll use a feature in Xcode called Interface Builder, which resembles a drawing program that lets you drag, drop, and resize objects on the screen. When you run and test your program, you'll use a compiler, which converts (or compiles) your Swift code into an actual working OS X program.

To create an OS X program, you just need a copy of Xcode, which is Apple's free programming tool that you can download from the Mac App Store. With Xcode installed on your Macintosh, you can create your own programs absolutely free just by learning Xcode and Swift.

Summary

To learn how to write programs for the Macintosh, you need to learn several separate skills. First, you need to understand the basic principles of programming. That includes organizing instructions in sequences, loops, or branches; understanding structured programming techniques, event-driven programming, and object-oriented programming.

Second, you need to learn a specific programming language. For the Macintosh, you'll be learning Swift. That means you'll learn the keywords and functions used in Swift along with learning how to write and organize your Swift code in separate files.

Third, you need to know how to use Xcode, which is Apple's programming tool for creating OS X and iOS apps. Xcode lets you write and edit Swift code as well as letting you visually design and modify your user interface.

Fourth, you'll need to learn how to use Apple's Cocoa framework so that you can focus solely on writing instructions that make your program do something unique.

Whether you want to write your own software to sell, or sell your programming skills to create custom software for others, you'll find that programming is a skill that anyone can learn.

Remember, programming is nothing more than problem solving. By knowing how to solve problems using Swift and Xcode, you can create your own programs for the Macintosh much easier and far faster than you might think.

Getting to Know Xcode

To write programs in Swift for the Macintosh, you need to use Xcode. Apple developed Xcode as a professional programming tool that they give away free to encourage everyone to write software for OS X and iOS. Despite being a free program, Xcode is a powerful program used by major companies including Microsoft, Adobe, Google, and even Apple. With Xcode on a Macintosh, you have one of the most powerful programming tools for creating OS X programs and iOS apps.

Although Xcode contains dozens of features specifically for professional programmers, anyone can learn to use Xcode. Xcode's sheer number of features may seem confusing and intimidating at first glance, but relax. To use Xcode, you never need to learn every possible feature. Instead, you can just learn the handful of features you need and ignore all the rest. As you get more experienced, you can gradually learn Xcode's other features. In many cases, you may never use some of Xcode's features at all.

Xcode lets you create an OS X program or an iOS app from start to finish without ever needing another program. Within Xcode you can do the following:

- Create a new project
- Write and edit Swift code
- Design and modify user interfaces
- Manage files that make up a single project
- Run and test your project
- Debug your Swift code

You can download and install Xcode for free through the Mac App Store. On your Macintosh, just click the Apple menu and choose App Store. When the App Store window appears, click in the Search text field in the upper right corner, type **Xcode**, and press Return. Now you can click the button underneath the Xcode icon to download it as shown in Figure 2-1. Since Xcode is a fairly large file, you'll need a fast Internet connection and plenty of space to install it on your Macintosh.

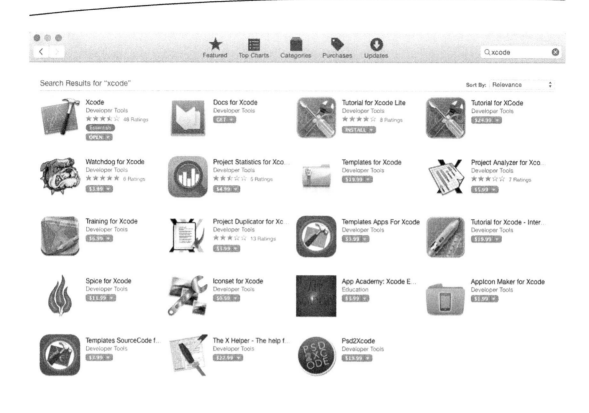

Figure 2-1. When you search for Xcode, it will likely appear in the upper left corner of the App Store window

The four most common parts of Xcode you'll use regularly are:

- The project manager
- The editor
- Interface Builder
- The compiler

A project represents a single OS X or iOS program. In the old days when programs were simple, you could store code in a single file. Now with programs being much larger and complicated, it's far more common to store code in separate files. A collection of files that work together form a single project so the Xcode project manager lets you create, rearrange, and delete the files within a project.

One of the most common types of files every project will contain is a code file, identified by the .swift file extension. Code files are where you can store, edit, and type Swift code. By using Xcode's editor, you can open a code file, copy and paste code, delete code, and write new code to save in that file. An editor basically acts like a simple word processor designed just for helping you write code in the Swift programming language.

Besides code files containing Swift code, every project will also contain a user interface stored in a separate file identified by either the .xib or .storyboard file extension. A simple program might only have a single file containing its user interface, but a more complicated program might have several files containing different parts of the user interface. The feature in Xcode that let you design, create, and modify user interfaces is called Interface Builder.

After you've written Swift code and designed your user interface, you'll need to convert all the files in your project into an actual working program. The process of translating Swift code into a language that the computer can understand (called machine code) is called compiling, so the part of Xcode that does this is called a compiler.

You'll often use these four main parts of Xcode in different order. For example, you may create a project and modify its files using the project manager feature. Then you may use the editor to write Swift code and Interface Builder to design your user interface. Finally, you'll test your program using the compiler. If problems occur, you'll likely go back to the editor or Interface Builder as many times as necessary until your program works right. You may even create new files and rearrange them in the project manager.

Ultimately, there is no single "best or "right" way to use Xcode. Xcode offers features for you to use whenever you need them.

Giving Commands to Xcode

Like many programs, Xcode offers multiple ways to do the exact same task. For example, to open a project, you can choose File ➤ Open or press Command+O. In general, Xcode typically offers three ways to perform common types of commands:

- Use the pull-down menus from the menu bar that appears at the top of the screen

- Press a unique keystroke combination such as Command+O

- Click on an icon that represents a command

Pull-down menus can be convenient to help you find specific commands, but they can be slower and clumsier to use because you have to click on a menu title to pull-down a menu, then you have to click on a command that appears on that menu.

Keystroke combinations are faster and easier, but they force you to memorize cryptic keystroke combinations for commonly used commands. To help you learn which commands have keystroke combinations, look on each pull-down menu, and you'll see keystroke combinations displayed to the right of different commands as shown in Figure 2-2. (Note: Not all commands have keystroke combinations.)

File	Edit	View	Find	Navigate	Ed

New ▶

Add Files to "TestOSXBed"...   ⌥⌘A

Open...   ⌘O
Open Recent   ▶
Open Quickly...   ⇧⌘O

Close Window   ⇧⌘W
Close Tab   ⌘W
Close "AppDelegate.swift"   ^⌘W
Close Project   ⌥⌘W

Save   ⌘S
Duplicate...   ⇧⌘S
Revert to Saved...
Unlock...
Export...

Show in Finder
Open with External Editor

Save As Workspace...
Project Settings...

Create Snapshot...   ^⌘S
Restore Snapshot...

Page Setup...   ⇧⌘P
Print...   ⌘P

Figure 2-2. Keystroke combinations appear to the right of commands on pull-down menus

Keystroke combinations usually include a modifier key plus a letter or function key. The four modifier keys include Command, Control, Option, and Shift as shown in Figure 2-3.

⌘	Command key
^	Control key
⌥	Option key
⇧	Shift Key

Figure 2-3. Symbols used to represent common modifier keys

Clicking on icons to choose a command may be the fastest method of all, but you have to know the command that each icon represents. To help you understand what an icon does, just move the mouse pointer over an icon and wait a few seconds. A tiny window will appear, briefly describing the purpose of that icon as shown in Figure 2-4.

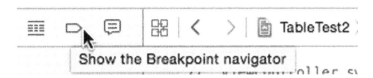

Figure 2-4. Hovering the mouse pointer over an icon displays a brief description of that icon's function

Some people only use pull-down menus, others rely more on icons and keystroke shortcuts, and others use a mix of all three methods. Generally people start with pull-down menus, but when they start using the same commands often, they'll gradually switch to icons and keystroke shortcuts.

Choose whatever method you like but be aware that you almost always have other alternatives. The main point is to get comfortable using Xcode using your preferred method so you can spend more time being creative and less time trying to find the commands you need.

Modifying the Xcode Window

Because Xcode offers so many features, the Xcode window can look cluttered at times. To simplify the appearance of Xcode, you have several options:

- Resize the Xcode window to make it larger (or smaller)
- Close panes to hide parts of Xcode
- Open panes to view parts of Xcode

Like all Macintosh windows, the most straightforward way to resize the Xcode window is to move the mouse pointer over the edge or corner of the Xcode window until the mouse pointer turns into a two-way pointing arrow. Then drag the mouse to resize the window.

A second way to resize the Xcode window is to click on the green dot in the upper left corner of the Xcode window. This expands the Xcode window to take up the full screen and hides the Xcode menu bar at the same time. To exit out of full screen mode, just press the Esc key on the keyboard.

A third way to resize the Xcode window is to choose Window ➤ Zoom. This toggles between expanding the Xcode window to fill the screen while still displaying the Xcode menu bar, or shrinking the Xcode window back to its previous size.

To reduce the amount of information displayed at any given time, Xcode has three panes that you can hide (or open) as shown in Figure 2-5:

- The Navigator pane that displays information about your project

- The Debug Area that lets you search for errors or bugs in your program

- The Utilities pane that lets you customize different items on your user interface

Figure 2-5. Xcode's Navigator pane, Debug Area, and Utilities pane

The Navigator pane displays several icons that let you switch between viewing different types of information. The most common use for the Navigator pane is to let you select a file to open by displaying the Project Navigator. To toggle between hiding and showing the Navigator pane, you have three options:

- Choose View ➤ Navigators ➤ Show/Hide Navigator
- Press Command+0 (the number zero)
- Click the Show/Hide Navigator Pane icon in the upper right corner of the Xcode window as shown in Figure 2-6

Figure 2-6. The Show/Hide Navigator Pane icon

The Debug area is used when you want to check if your program is working correctly. While you're designing your user interface or writing Swift code, you'll likely want to hide this Debug area. To toggle between hiding and showing the Debug area, you have three options:

- Choose View ➤ Debug Area ➤ Show/Hide Debug Area
- Press Shift+Command+Y

■ Click the Show/Hide Debug Area icon in the upper right corner of the Xcode window as shown in Figure 2-7

Figure 2-7. The Show/Hide Debug Area icon

The Utilities pane displays several icons that let you switch between showing different types of information. The most common use for the Utilities pane is to help you design and modify a user interface. To toggle between hiding and showing the Utilities Pane, you have three options:

■ Choose View ➤ Utilities ➤ Show/Hide Utilities

■ Press Option+Command+0 (the number zero)

■ Click the Show/Hide Utilities icon in the upper right corner of the Xcode window as shown in Figure 2-8

Figure 2-8. The Show/Hide Utilities icon

By selectively showing or hiding the Navigator pane, the Debug area, or the Utilities pane, you can make the Xcode window look less cluttered and provide more room for the parts of Xcode that you want to see. To quickly open or hide these three panes, it's usually faster to click on the Show/Hide Navigator, Debug area, or Utilities icons in the upper right corner of the Xcode window.

Creating and Managing Files

Any time you need to create a project (that represents a brand new program) or a file (to add to an existing project), you have three choices:

- Press Command+N
- Choose File ➤ New to display a submenu as shown in Figure 2-9

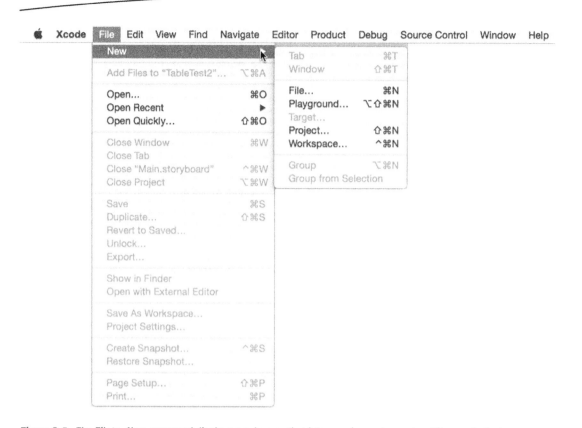

Figure 2-9. *The File ➤ New command displays a submenu that lets you choose to create a File or a Project*

- Right-click on any file displayed in the Navigator pane to display a pop-up menu as shown in Figure 2-10

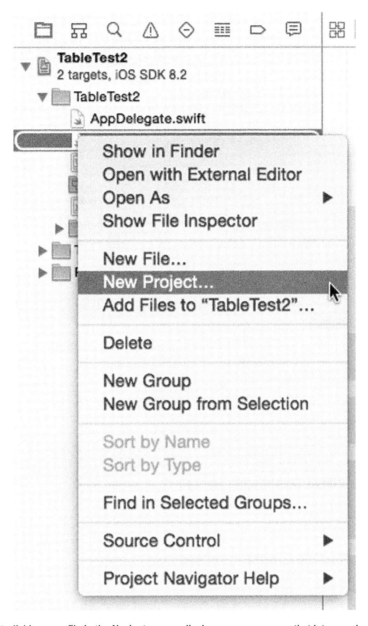

Figure 2-10. *Right-clicking on a file in the Navigator pane displays a pop-up menu that lets you choose to create a File or a Project*

Note   Right-clicking may be disabled on some Macintosh computers. You can simulate a right-click by holding down the Control key while clicking. To turn on right-clicking, click the Apple menu, choose System Preferences, and click on the Mouse or Trackpad icon. Then select the "Secondary click" check box to turn on right-clicking.

When you create a new file, you can choose whether to create a file for an OS X or iOS project. For the purposes of this book, you'll always create files for OS X.

Besides choosing to create a file for OS X, you'll also need to choose what type of file to create. The two most common types of files you'll create will be either files that can hold Swift code (organized under the Source category as shown in Figure 2-11) or files that can hold a user interface (organized under the User Interface category as shown in Figure 2-12).

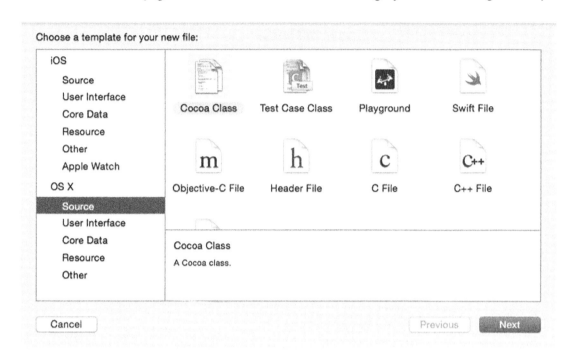

Figure 2-11. *One type of file you can create holds Swift code*

Figure 2-12. *A second type of file you can create holds part of your program's user interface*

When you create a file, that file appears in the Project Navigator. The Navigator pane can actually display several different types of information, but the most common is the Project Navigator, which lists of all the files that make up your project. To open the Project Navigator within the Navigator pane, you have three choices:

▪ Choose View ➤ Navigators ➤ Show Project Navigator

▪ Press Command+1

▪ Click on the Show the Project Navigator icon as shown in Figure 2-13

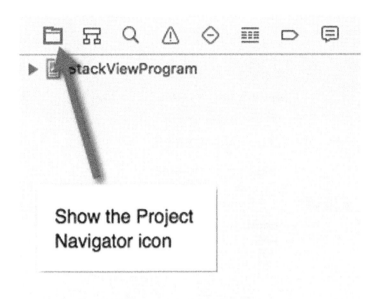

Show the Project
Navigator icon

Figure 2-13. The Project Navigator pane lists all the files that make up a project

The Project Navigator closely resembles the Finder by displaying files and folders. To rename a file or folder, just select it and press Return to edit its name.

To move a file or folder, just drag it with the mouse and drop it in a new location.

To select one or more items, hold down the Command key and click on a file or folder.

Just like the Finder, the Project Navigator lets you organize files into folders. This lets you group related files together and tuck them out of sight so they don't clutter the Project Navigator. To create a folder, click on a file or folder in the Project Navigator and then choose one of the following:

- Choose File ➤ New ➤ Group (or Group from Selection to store one or more selected files in a folder)

- Press Option+Command+N

- Right-click on any file or folder in the Project Navigator, and when a pop-up menu appears, choose New Group (or New Group from Selection to store one or more selected files in a folder)

To delete a file or folder, select a file or folder and then choose one of the following:

- Choose Edit ➤ Delete
- Press the Delete key or Command+Backspace
- Right-click on any file or folder in the Project Navigator, and when a pop-up menu appears, choose Delete

---

Note   When you delete a file or folder, you'll have the option of Remove Reference (which removes a file/folder from a project but does not physically delete it from your Macintosh) or Move to Trash (which removes a file/folder from a project and physically deletes it from your Macintosh).

Perhaps the most important use for the Project Navigator is to let you edit a file in a project. When you click on a file in the Project Navigator, the middle pane of the Xcode window displays the contents of your selected file, which will either hold Swift code or your user interface as shown in Figure 2-14.

Figure 2-14. Selecting a file in the Navigator pane displays the contents of that file

Creating and Customizing a User Interface

The Utilities pane is most often used for creating and customizing your project's user interface. With OS X programs, user interface files may be one of two types:

- .xib files
- .storyboard files

When you create a project, you can choose which type you want to use. In general, .xib files are used for single window user interfaces while .storyboard files are used for multiple windows that are linked to appear in a certain order. It's possible to mix both .xib and .storyboard files to create a user interface or just use .xib or .storyboard files exclusively.

Whether you use .xib or .storyboard files, you'll need to use the Utilities pane for two purposes. First, you'll need to drag and drop items on to your user interface such as buttons, text fields, and pictures. Second, you'll need to customize those user interface items by changing their names, color, or size.

To design a user interface, you start with the Object Library, which appears at the bottom of the Utilities pane as shown in Figure 2-15. To open the Object Library, you can do the following:

■ Choose View ➤ Utilities ➤ Show Object Library

■ Press Control+Option+Command+3

■ Click the Show Object Library icon

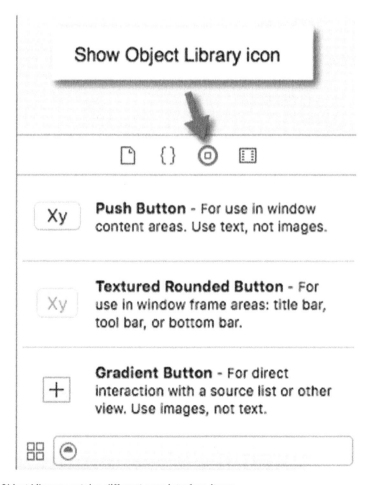

Figure 2-15. *The Object Library contains different user interface items*

To find a user interface item in the Object Library, you can simply scroll up and down the list. However, if you know the name of the item you want, a faster method is to click in the Search field at the bottom of the Object Library window, type all or part of the name of the item you want, and press Return. The Object Library will then show only those items that match what you typed. So if you typed "Button," then the Object Library would only display different buttons you can add to your user interface.

After you have placed one or more items on your user interface, the second step is to customize those items using the Inspector pane. The Inspector pane can display several types of panes but the two most common you'll use to customize user interface items are the:

- Attributes Inspector
- Size Inspector

The Attributes Inspector lets you modify the appearance of an item. The Size Inspector lets you modify the size and position of an item on the user interface.

To open the Attributes Inspector, you can do one of the following:

- Choose View ➤ Utilities ➤ Show Attributes Inspector
- Press Option+Command+4
- Click the Show Attributes Inspector as shown in Figure 2-16

Figure 2-16. The Show Attributes Inspector and Show Size Inspector icons.

To open the Size Inspector, you can do one of the following:

- Choose View ➤ Utilities ➤ Show Size Inspector
- Press Option+Command+5
- Click the Show Size Inspector as shown in Figure 2-16

After opening the Attributes or Size Inspectors, you can then click on a user interface item to modify (such as a button or text field) and then type or choose different options to modify that item's appearance.

The Standard and Assistant Editors

You'll spend most of your time using the editor or Interface Builder. The editor acts like a word processor and lets you type and edit Swift code. Interface Builder acts like a drawing program and lets you drag and drop, resize, and move items on the user interface such as buttons, text fields, and graphics.

To edit Swift code, just click on any file in the Project Navigator pane that contains the .swift file extension. When you click on a .swift file, the contents of that file appears in the middle Xcode pane as shown in Figure 2-17.

Figure 2-17. Clicking on a .swift file displays the Swift code stored in that file

To edit your user interface, just click on any file in the Project Navigator pane that contains the .xib or .storyboard file extension. This displays the contents of that user interface in the middle Xcode pane as shown in Figure 2-18.

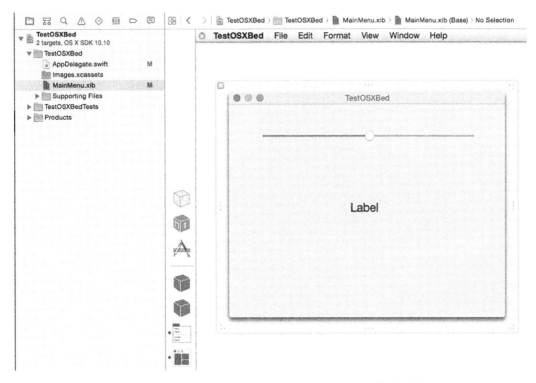

Figure 2-18. Clicking on a .xib or .storyboard file displays the user interface stored in that file

Each time you click on a different file in the Project Navigator pane, Xcode displays the contents of that new file in the middle pane of the Xcode window.

When Xcode displays the contents of a single file in its middle pane, that's called the Standard Editor. However, it's often useful to view the contents of two files side by side. When Xcode displays two file contents side by side, that second file pane is called the Assistant Editor.

The most common reason to open the Assistant Editor is when you have the user interface displayed in the left pane and a Swift file displayed in the right pane as shown in Figure 2-19. The purpose for this is to let you link your user interface to your Swift code.

Figure 2-19. *The Assistant Editor displays two file contents side by side*

When you create a user interface, it's completely independent from your Swift code (and vice versa). That gives you the freedom to replace your user interface with a new user interface without affecting how your Swift code behaves. Likewise, this also lets you modify your Swift code without worrying about affecting your user interface.

In the old days, programmers had to create their user interfaces using code, which meant changing your code often affected your user interface, increasing the chance of errors or bugs in your program. By separating the user interface from your code, Xcode eliminates this problem and helps you create more reliable software.

Initially when you create a user interface, it won't do anything. That's why you need to link some of your user interface items to Swift code that makes the user interface actually work. For example, if your user interface displays a button, clicking on that button won't do anything. You have to write Swift code to tell that button what to do. Then you have to link your button to your Swift code.

That's the purpose of the Assistant Editor. By displaying your user interface next to your Swift code file, the Assistant Editor makes it easy to drag the mouse from your user interface to your Swift code files, creating a link between your user interface and your Swift code.

To open the Assistant Editor, you can choose one of the following:

- Choose View ➤ Assistant Editor ➤ Show Assistant Editor

- Press Option+Command+Return

- Click the Assistant Editor icon as shown in Figure 2-20

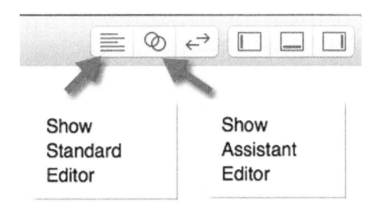

Show Standard Editor   Show Assistant Editor

Figure 2-20. *The Standard and Assistant Editor icons*

To close the Assistant Editor, you have to open the Standard Editor in one of the following ways:

- Choose View ➤ Standard Editor ➤ Show Standard Editor

- Press Command+Return

- Click the Standard Editor icon as shown in Figure 2-20

One problem with using the Assistant Editor is that Xcode displays both file contents in narrow panes. If you prefer seeing two or more files in a wider view, you can display them in separate tabs. This lets you see the contents of each file in the middle pane of Xcode and to simply click on a tab to see a different file's contents.

The drawback of tabs is that you can only see the contents of one file at a time. A second drawback is that you can't see your user interface next to your Swift code so you can't connect user interface items to your Swift code.

To create a tab, choose one of the following:

- Choose File ➤ New ➤ Tab

- Press Command+T

Now you can click on each tab to view the contents of that file. To close a tab, move the mouse over the tab and choose one of the following:

- Click the close icon (it looks like a big X) in the left of the tab

- Right-click on the tab and when a pop-up menu appears, click Close Tab as shown in Figure 2-21

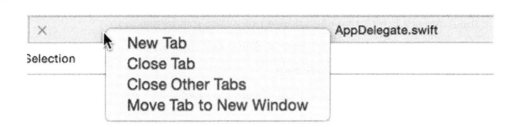

Figure 2-21. Right-clicking on a tab displays a pop-up menu

Running a Program

Typically you'll run your program multiple times to test and make sure it works right. When you run a program, Xcode compiles it into a file that you can distribute to others if you wish. Running a program lets you test your program directly on your Macintosh.

The three ways to run a program are:

- Choose Product ➤ Run

- Press Command+R

- Click the Run icon as shown in Figure 2-22

Figure 2-22. The Run and Stop icons let you test your OS X project

Once your program is running, you can stop it in several ways:

- Choose YourProgramName ➤ Quit where "YourProgramName" is the name of your project

- Click the icon on the Dock that represents your program and press Command+Q

- Click the Stop icon in Xcode as shown in Figure 2-22

If your program has major errors that prevent it from responding to any commands, you can also use the Force Quit command to shut down your program. To use Force Quit, click the Apple menu and choose Force Quit.

When the Force Quit window appears, click on your program's name and then click the Force Quit button to shut it down.

Summary

This chapter introduced you to the major features of Xcode and showed various ways to choose common commands. Don't worry about memorizing or fully understanding everything in this chapter just yet. Think of this chapter as an introduction to Xcode that you can refer back to whenever you have a question.

In the next chapter, we'll actually go through the typical process of creating an OS X program using Xcode. That way you can see the purpose of Xcode's various features that you learned about in this chapter.

Just remember that with Xcode, there are often two or more ways to choose the exact same command, but you don't have to learn all of these different ways. All you have to do is choose the method you like best and ignore the other methods.

As you can see, Xcode offers everything you need to turn your ideas into a fully functional OS X program that you can sell and distribute to others. By learning Xcode, you'll be learning to use the programming tool that professional programmers use to create both OS X and iOS software. The more you use Xcode, the more comfortable you'll get and the less intimidating Xcode's user interface will feel. Pretty soon, you'll be using Xcode like a pro.

Remember, the real key to programming isn't having the best programming tools but knowing how to use them. The more you use Xcode, the more you'll understand how to turn your great ideas into actual working programs. Learning Xcode is your path to writing software for the Macintosh and Apple's many other devices such as the iPhone, iPad, and Apple Watch. By learning Xcode today, you can take advantage of the many lucrative programming opportunities that will be available now and far into the future. Welcome to the world of Xcode!

The Basics of Creating a Mac Program

Whatever type of OS X program you want to create, such as a video game or a custom program for lawyers or stock brokers, you'll always go through the same basic steps. First, you need to create an OS X project. This creates a bare-bones OS X program that includes a generic user interface.

Second, you'll need to customize this generic OS X program in two ways: by adding items to the user interface and by writing Swift code to make the program actually do something.

Third, you'll need to run and test your program. After running and testing your program, you'll likely need to constantly go back and modify your user interface or Swift code to fix problems and add new features. Eventually your program will reach a point where it's complete (for now) and you can ship it. Then you'll repeat these basic steps all over again to add new features once more.

Generally you'll spend more time modifying a program than creating new ones. However, it's useful to create small programs to test out different features. Once you get these smaller, experimental programs working, you can add them to another program. By doing this, you don't risk messing up a working program.

Creating a Project

The first step to creating a program is to create a new project. When you create a project, Xcode gives you the option of choosing different templates, which provides basic functions. All you have to do is customize the template. The four categories of OS X templates are shown in Figure 3-1:

- Application
- Framework & Library

■ System Plug-in

■ Other

Figure 3-1. *The four categories of OS X templates for creating a project*

Most of the time you'll choose a template in the Application category, and the most common template is Cocoa Application, which creates a standard OS X program with pull-down menus and a window.

The other two Application templates are Game (for creating video games) and Command Line Tool (for creating programs that don't need a traditional graphical user interface).

The Framework & Library category is meant to create reusable software libraries. The System Plug-in category is meant to create plug-ins for other type of programs. The Other category is meant for creating programs that don't fit into the other categories.

For the purposes of this book, we'll always use the Cocoa Application under the OS X Application category. The other OS X categories are designed for advanced programmers and won't be covered in this book.

When you create a Cocoa Application project, you'll need to define several items as shown in Figure 3-2:

■ The name of your product

■ The programming language to use (Objective-C or Swift)

■ Whether to use storyboards or not for your user interface

- Whether to create a document-based application

- Whether to use Core Data

Choose options for your new project:

Product Name:	
Organization Name:	Wallace Wang
Organization Identifier:	com.topbananas
Bundle Identifier:	com.topbananas.ProductName
Language:	Swift
	☐ Use Storyboards
	☐ Create Document-Based Application
Document Extension:	super
	☐ Use Core Data

Cancel   Previous   Next

Figure 3-2. Defining a Cocoa Application project

Your product's name is completely arbitrary but should be descriptive since Xcode will store all your files in a folder using your chosen name.

Your organization name and identifier are also arbitrary and are typically assigned from your Apple Developer account. Both of these can also be arbitrary strings if you want, but if you plan on distributing your programs through the Mac App Store, they should be linked to your Apple Developer account.

The Language pop-up menu lets you choose Objective-C or Swift. For the purposes of this book, you always want to choose Swift. Objective-C is a more complicated programming language that Apple still supports, but it's no longer considered Apple's official programming language.

The Use Storyboards check box lets you create a user interface that either consists of a single window (a .xib file) or a series of windows linked together (a .storyboard file). We'll go over both methods for creating a user interface, but unless instructed otherwise, leave the Use Storyboards check box empty. That's because storyboards are more complicated to use.

The Create Document-Based Application means that Xcode creates a Cocoa Application that can open and manage multiple windows, such as the multiple windows available in a word processor. Managing multiple windows is more complicated so leave the Create Document-Based Application check box empty for now.

The Use Core Data check box lets you store data typically for database applications such as saving lists of names and addresses. Leave this check box blank since this is for more advanced OS X programs.

Ready to create your first OS X program? Then follow these steps:

1. Start Xcode. If a Welcome to Xcode screen appears as shown in Figure 3-3, click Create a new Xcode project. If this welcome screen does not appear, choose File ➤ New ➤ Project or choose Window ➤ Welcome to Xcode to display this screen so you can choose Create a new Xcode project. Xcode displays a list of project templates (see Figure 3-1).

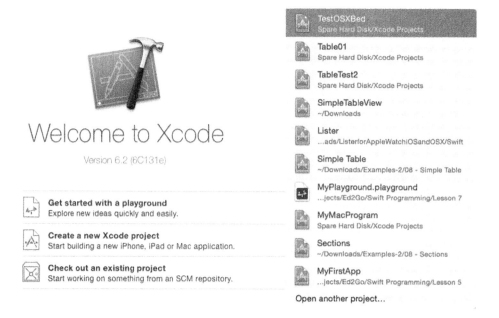

Figure 3-3. The Welcome to Xcode opening screen

2. Click Application under the OS X category. A list of different OS X Application templates appears.

3. Click Cocoa Application and then click the Next button. Xcode now asks for your project name (see Figure 3-2).

4. Click in the Product Name text field and type MyFirstProgram.

5. Click in the Language pop-up menu and make sure Swift appears.

6. Make sure all check boxes are empty and then click the Next button. Xcode now asks where you want to store your project.

7. Click on a folder where you want to store your Xcode project and click the Create button. Congratulations! You've just created your first OS X program. At this point, Xcode just created a generic Macintosh program, but you haven't had to write a single line of Swift code or even design the user interface to create an actual working program.

8. Choose Product ➤ Run, press Command+R, or click the Run icon. Xcode runs your program called MyFirstProgram as shown in Figure 3-4. Notice that the MyFirstProgram displays a menu bar with pull-down menus and a window that you can move or resize on the screen. Because you used the Cocoa Application template, Xcode automatically created all the code necessary to create a generic Macintosh program.

Figure 3-4. The MyFirstProgram running

9. Choose MyFirstProgram ➤ Quit MyFirstProgram. Xcode appears. Keep your MyFirstProgram project open in Xcode for the next section.

Without doing a thing, you managed to create a program that looks and behaves like a typical Macintosh program. Of course, this bare-bones Macintosh program won't do anything interesting until you customize the user interface and write Swift code to make the program do something useful.

Designing a User Interface

When designing a user interface, keep in mind the three purposes for any user interface:

- To display information to the user
- To get data from the user
- To let the user give commands to the program

When you design a user interface, every element must satisfy one of these criteria. Colors and lines might just seem decorative, but they can be useful to organize a user interface so users will know where to find information, how to input data, or how to give commands to the program.

To create a user interface in Xcode, you need to follow a two-step process:

- Use the Object Library to drag and drop items on to your user interface
- Use the Inspector pane to customize each user interface item

To see how to use the Object Library, let's add a label, a text field, and a button to the MyFirstProgram user interface. The label will display text to the user; the text field will let the user type in data; and the button will make the program take the text from the text field, modify it by capitalizing every character, and place the modified uppercase text into the label.

To do this, follow these steps:

1. Make sure your MyFirstProgram project is loaded into Xcode.

2. Choose View ➤ Navigators ➤ Show Project Navigator or press Command+1 to view the list of all the files that make up your MyFirstProgram project.

3. Click the MainMenu.xib file. Xcode displays the user interface. Notice that the actual window of your MyFirstProgram is not visible until you click the MyFirstProgram icon.

4. Click the MyFirstProgram icon that appears in the pane between the Project Navigator and the user interface. This displays the window of the MyFirstProgram user interface as shown in Figure 3-5.

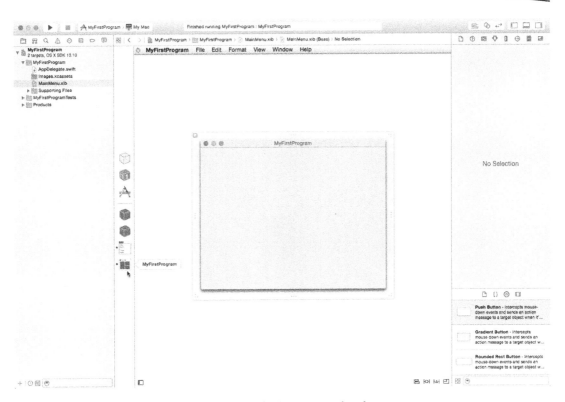

Figure 3-5. The MyFirstProgram icon displays the MyFirstProgram user interface

5. Choose View ➤ Utilities ➤ Show Object Library. The Object Library appears in the bottom right corner of the Xcode window.

6. Drag a Push Button from the Object Library and drop it near the bottom of your MyFirstProgram window. Notice that when you place the button in the middle and near the bottom of the window, blue guidelines appear to help you align user interface items as shown in Figure 3-6.

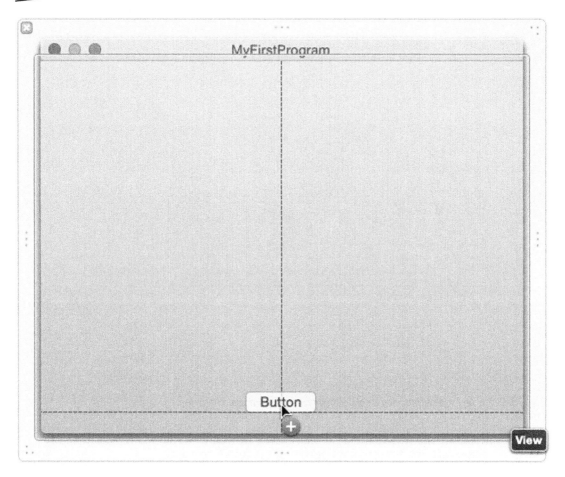

Figure 3-6. Using blue guidelines to place a Push Button near the bottom of the MyFirstProgram window

7. Click in the Search field at the Object Library and type **label**. Notice that the Object Library now only displays label user interface items as shown in Figure 3-7.

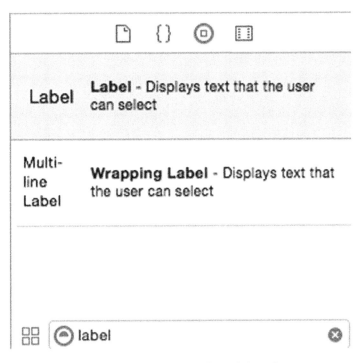

Figure 3-7. Typing in the search field helps you easily find items in the Object Library

8. Drag and drop the label from the Object Library to the middle of your MyFirstProgram window.

9. Click the clear icon (the X in the gray circle) that appears in the right of the Search field at the bottom of the Object Library. The Object Library now displays all possible user interface items.

10. Scroll through the Object Library until you find the Text Field item.

11. Drag and drop the text field above the label so your entire user interface appears as shown in Figure 3-8. (Don't worry about the exact position of each user interface item.)

Figure 3-8. A label, text field, and button on the MyFirstProgram user interface

At this point, you've customized the generic user interface. Now you have to customize each user interface item using the Inspector pane. Through the Inspector pane, you can choose different options for a user interface item, such as typing the exact width of a button or choosing a background color for a text field.

When resizing or moving an item on the user interface, you can either type exact values into the Size Inspector pane, or you can just drag the mouse to resize or move an item. Either way is acceptable but the Size Inspector pane gives you precise control over items. Let's see how to use the Inspector pane to customize our generic user interface.

1. Click on the push button near the bottom of the MyFirstProgram window to select it.

2. Choose View ➤ Utilities ➤ Show Attributes Inspector. The Attributes Inspector pane appears in the upper right corner of the Xcode window as shown in Figure 3-9.

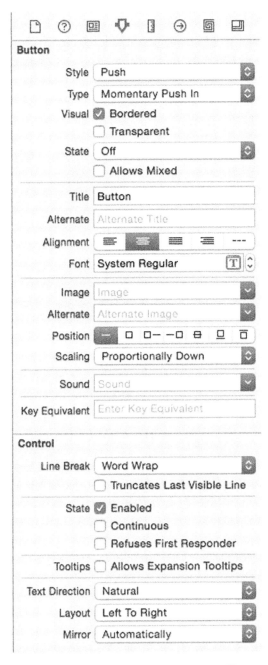

Figure 3-9. *The Attributes Inspector pane lets you customize the appearance of items*

3.   Click in the Title text field that currently displays "Button." Delete
     any existing text in the Title text field, type **Change Case**, and press
     Return. The text on the push button now displays "Change Case."
     However, the button width is too narrow.

4. Choose View ➤ Utilities ➤ Show Size Inspector. The Size Inspector pane appears in the upper right corner of the Xcode window.

5. Click in the Width text field, change the value to 120 as shown in Figure 3-10, and press Return. Xcode changes the width of the push button.

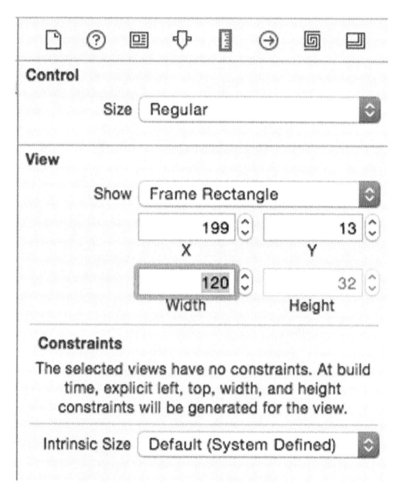

Figure 3-10. The Width text field appears in the Size Inspector pane

6. Click on the label to select it. To modify the size of the label, we'll need to open the Size Inspector pane, which we can do by choosing View ➤ Utilities ➤ Show Size Inspector, but there's a faster method using either keystroke shortcuts or icons.

7. Press Option+Command+5 or just click the Size Inspector icon (it looks like a vertical ruler). The Size Inspector pane appears in the upper right corner of the Xcode window.

8. Click in the Width text field, type 250, and press Return. Xcode widens the width of your label.

9. Click on the text field to select it.

10. Press Option+Command+5 or just click the Size Inspector icon (it looks like a vertical ruler). The Size Inspector pane appears in the upper right corner of the Xcode window.

11. Click in the Width text field, type 250 and press Return. Xcode widens the width of your text field. At this point, all the user interface items appear off center.

12. Drag each item until you see a blue guideline showing that you've centered it in the MyFirstProgram window as shown in Figure 3-11.

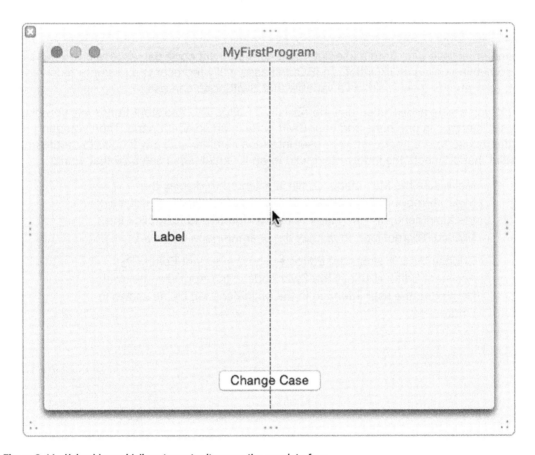

Figure 3-11. Using blue guidelines to center items on the user interface

At this point, you've customized the appearance of your user interface. If you run this program, the user interface will look good but it won't actually do anything. To make a user interface work, you need to finish two more steps:

- Write Swift code
- Connect your user interface to your Swift code

You need to write Swift code to make your program calculate some useful result. You also need to connect your user interface to your Swift code so you can retrieve data from the user interface and display information back on the user interface.

In this example, we'll write Swift code that retrieves text from the text field, changes it to uppercase, then displays the uppercase text back on to the label when the user clicks the Change Case push button.

So we need to write Swift code that converts text to uppercase. Then we need to connect the text field and the label so the Swift code can retrieve data from the text field and put new data on the label.

To send or retrieve data from a user interface item so Swift code can access it, we need to use something called an IBOutlet. An IBOutlet essentially represents a user interface item (such as a label or a text field) as a variable that Swift code can use.

To help you create an IBOutlet, use the Assistant Editor. The Assistant Editor lets you display the user interface in one pane and your Swift code in an adjacent pane. Then you can use the mouse to drag between your user interface items to your Swift code to create an IBOutlet that connects the label or text field to an IBOutlet. Let's see how that works:

1. Make sure the MainMenu.xib file is selected to display the MyFirstProgram user interface window on the screen. (If not, click the MainMenu.xib file in the Project Navigator and then click the MyFirstProgram icon to display the user interface window.)

2. Choose View ➤ Assistant Editor ➤ Show Assistant Editor. The Assistant Editor displays the Swift code in the AppDelegate.swift file next to the user interface in the MainMenu.xib file as shown in Figure 3-12.

Figure 3-12. The Assistant Editor lets you view the user interface and Swift code file side by side

3. Click on the label on your MyFirstProgram window.

4. Hold down the Control key and drag the mouse from the label underneath the @IBOutlet line in the AppDelegate.swift file until you see a horizontal line appear in the Swift code file as shown in Figure 3-13.

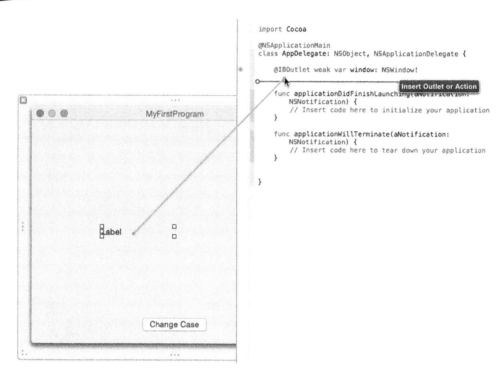

Figure 3-13. Control-dragging creates a connection between a user interface item and your Swift code

5. Release the Control key and the mouse. A pop-up window appears as shown in Figure 3-14.

Figure 3-14. A pop-up window lets you define a name for your IBOutlet

6. Click in the Name text field, type **labelText**, and click the Connect button. (The name you choose should be descriptive but can be anything you want.) Xcode creates an IBOutlet in your Swift file that looks like this:

```
@IBOutlet weak var labelText: NSTextField!
```

7. Click on the text field to select it.

8. Hold down the Control key and drag the mouse from the text field to underneath the IBOutlet you just created until a horizontal line appears in the AppDelegate.swift file.

9. Release the Control key and the mouse. A pop-up window appears.

10. Click in the Name text field, type **messageText**, and click the Connect button. Xcode creates a second IBOutlet in your Swift file that looks like this:

```
@IBOutlet weak var messageText: NSTextField!
```

Let's go over what you just did. First, you created an IBOutlet to represent the label and the text field. The label is now represented by the name "labelText," and the text field is now represented by the name "messageText." Now when your Swift code wants to store or retrieve data from the label or text field, it can just refer to them by the names "labelText" or "messageText."

Second, you created a link between your Swift code and your user interface items. Now your Swift code can send and retrieve data to the label and text field on your program's user interface.

Connecting your user interface to your Swift code is a major step toward making your user interface actually work. However, we need to make the Change Case button do something when the user clicks on it. To do that, we need to create something called an IBAction method.

Where an IBOutlet lets Swift code send or retrieve data from a user interface item, an IBAction method lets a user interface item run Swift code that does something. In this case, we want the user to type text into the text field. Then the program will take that text, capitalize it, and display this capitalized text back into the label.

To do this, we need to know how to do the following:

■ Create an IBAction method

■ Retrieve text from the text field

■ Capitalize all the text retrieved from the text field

■ Store the capitalized text in the label

Storing and retrieving text from a text field and label is similar because both are defined by IBOutlet variables. Let's take a look at what these IBOutlets mean:

```
@IBOutlet weak var labelText: NSTextField!
@IBOutlet weak var messageText: NSTextField!
```

All user interface items in the Object Library are based on class files, which make up the Cocoa framework. In this case, we created two IBOutlet variables called labelText and messageText, which are both based on the NSTextField class file.

If you look up the NSTextField class file in Xcode's documentation, you'll see a long list of all the properties that anything based on the NSTextField can hold. However, you won't find anything that describes the property that holds text.

However, if you remember from Chapter 1, object-oriented programming means that class files can inherit from other class files. In this case, the NSTextField class inherits from another class called NSControl. Looking up NSControl in Xcode's documentation (which you'll learn how to do in the next chapter), you can see that NSControl has a property that holds text called stringValue as shown in Figure 3-15.

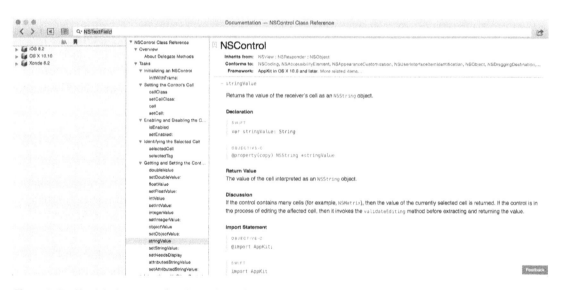

Figure 3-15. Xcode's documentation shows the NSControl property for holding text

To access text stored in the text field, we need to identify the text field by name (messageText) and its property that holds the text (stringValue) such as:

messageText.stringValue

To display text in the label, we need to identify the label by name (labelText) and its property that holds text (stringValue) such as:

labelText.stringValue

Now the next question is how can we capitalize text? Swift stores text in a data type called String, which is based on a class called NSString. (How would you know this? You have to understand the Cocoa framework, which you'll learn more about in Chapter 4.) The NSString class has a method called uppercaseString as shown in Figure 3-16.

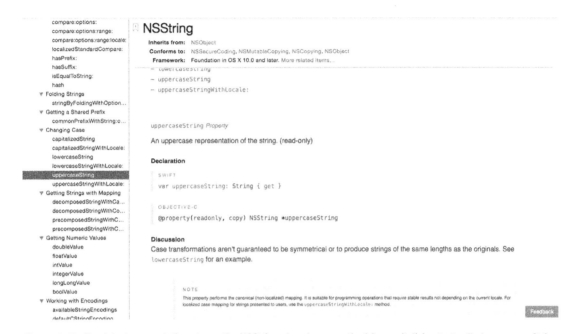

Figure 3-16. Xcode's documentation shows the NSString class has a method for capitalizing text called uppercaseString

To capitalize the text stored in the text field (represented by the IBOutlet name messageText, we just have to apply the uppercaseString method on the IBOutlet's text property like this:

```
messageText.stringValue.uppercaseString
```

This Swift code says take the messageText object (which is the text field on the user interface), retrieve the text it contains (which is in the stringValue property), and apply the uppercaseString method on this text.

Now that we know how to retrieve text from the text field, capitalize it, and store new text back into the label, the last step is to write the code that does all this inside an IBAction method. This IBAction method needs to run each time the user clicks the Change Case button. That means we need to create an IBAction method and link it to the Change Case button.

1. Make sure the Assistant Editor is still open and displays the user interface and AppDelegate.swift file side by side.

2. Click on the Change Case button on your MyFirstProgram user interface to select it.

3. Hold down the Control key and drag the mouse underneath the last IBOutlet until a horizontal line appears as shown in Figure 3-17.

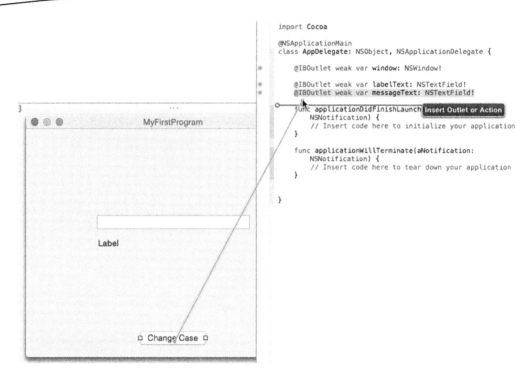

Figure 3-17. *Control-dragging from the button to the AppDelegate.swift file*

4. Release the Control key and the mouse. A pop-up window appears.

5. Click in the Connection pop-up menu and choose Action as shown in Figure 3-18.

Figure 3-18. *Creating an Action connection*

6. Click in the Name text field and type **changeCase**. (The name you choose should be descriptive but can be anything you want.)

7. Click in the Type pop-up menu and choose NSButton as shown in Figure 3-19. Then click the Connect button. Xcode creates an IBAction method that looks like this:

```
@IBAction func changeCase(sender: NSButton) {
}
```

Figure 3-19. Choosing a Type for an IBAction method

At this point, you've created an IBAction method that runs every time the user clicks the Change Case button. Of course, there's no Swift code inside that IBAction, so now we need to type Swift code inside those curly brackets that define the beginning and ending of the IBAction method.

1. Make sure Xcode still displays your user interface and AppDelegate. swift file side by side.

2. Choose View ➤ Standard Editor ➤ Show Standard Editor. Xcode now only shows your MyFirstProgram user interface.

3. Click the AppDelegate.swift file in the Project Navigator. Xcode displays all the Swift code stored in the AppDelegate.swift file.

4. Edit the IBAction changeCase method as follows:

```
@IBAction func changeCase(sender: NSButton) {
    labelText.stringValue = messageText.stringValue.uppercaseString
}
```

5. Choose Product ➤ Run. Your MyFirstProgram runs.

6. Click in the text field of your MyFirstProgram user interface and type **hello, world**.

7. Click the Change Case button. The label displays HELLO, WORLD as shown in Figure 3-20.

Figure 3-20. Running the MyFirstProgram

> 8.   Choose MyFirstProgram ➤ Quit MyFirstProgram. Xcode appears
>   again.

As you can see, you created a simple Macintosh program without writing much Swift code
at all. The Swift code you did write was just a single line that took the text stored in the text
field, changed it to uppercase, and then stored this uppercase text in the label.

Much of the power of Swift comes from relying on Apple's Cocoa framework as much
as possible. That means you have to understand object-oriented programming and how
classes define properties (to store data) and methods (to manipulate data) – and use
inheritance – which you'll learn more about in the next chapter.

The main point is to see how Xcode creates generic OS X programs so you just need to
design and customize the user interface, then write Swift code to make it all work.

Using the Document Outline and Connections Inspector

Before we conclude this short introduction to creating your first Macintosh program, let's
look at two other items that will prove helpful when working with Xcode in the future: the
Document Outline and the Connections Inspector.

The Document Outline lists all the items that make up your user interface. To open or hide the Document Outline, you can do the following as shown in Figure 3-21:

- Choose Editor ➤ Show/Hide Document Outline
- Click the Document Outline icon

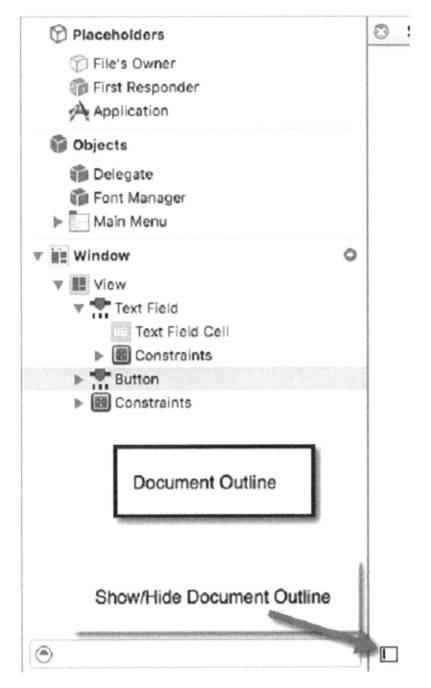

Figure 3-21. *The Document Outline*

The Document Outline makes it easy to select different items on your user interface. In our MyFirstProgram, there's only three items (a label, text field, and button), but in more complicated user interfaces, you could have many more items that could be hidden behind other items or too small to see easily.

If you click on an item in the Document Outline, Xcode selects that item in the user interface (and vice versa) as shown in Figure 3-22.

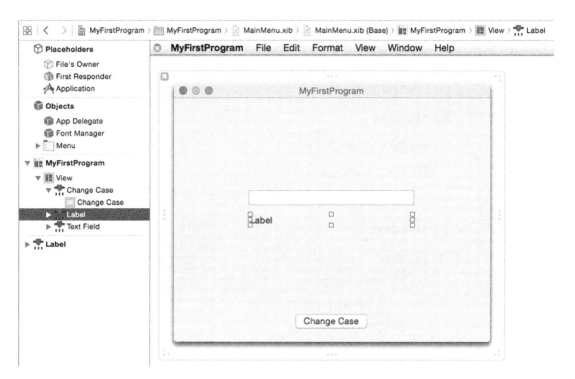

Figure 3-22. Clicking on an item in the Document Outline window selects that item on the user interface

Think of the Document Outline as a fast way to see all the parts of a user interface and select just the items you want.

Once you start connecting user interface items to your Swift code through IBOutlets and IBAction methods, you may wonder what items are connected to which IBOutlets and IBAction methods. To see the connections between IBOutlets/IBAction methods and user interface items, you have two options.

First, you can use the Connections Inspector. Second, you can use the Assistant Editor.

To open the Connections Inspector, first click on any item in the user interface that you want to examine, and then do one of the following to display the Connections Inspector that appears in the upper right corner of the Xcode window as shown in Figure 3-23:

- Choose View ➤ Utilities ➤ Show Connections Inspector
- Press Option+Command+6
- Click the Show Connections Inspector icon

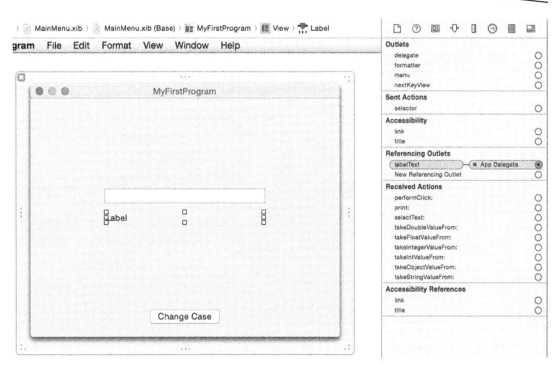

Figure 3-23. The Connections Inspector shows all the connections to the currently selected user interface item

The Connections Inspector shows the Swift file that holds an IBOutlet or the IBAction method connected to the selected user interface item.

> **Note** If you look carefully, the Connections Inspector displays an X to the left of the Swift file that links to the currently selected user interface item. If you click on this X, you can break the link between a user interface item and its IBOutlet or IBAction method.

Another way to see way to see which IBOutlets and IBAction methods are connected to user interface items is to open the user interface (such as clicking on the MainMenu.xib file) and then opening the Assistant Editor.

To the left of each IBOutlet and IBAction method in your Swift file, you'll see a gray circle. When you move the mouse pointer over a gray circle, Xcode highlights the user interface item that's connected to that IBOutlet or IBAction method as shown in Figure 3-24.

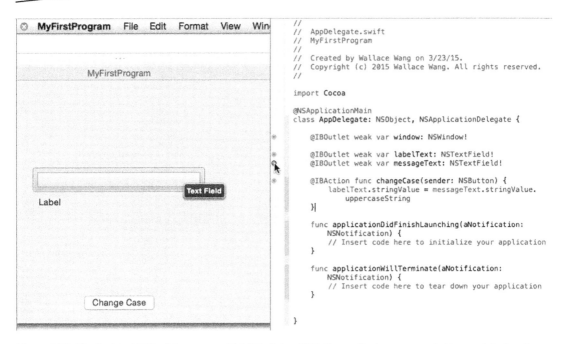

Figure 3-24. The Assistant Editor lets you see which IBOutlet and IBAction methods are connected to user interface items

Summary

Xcode is the only program you need to design, write, and modify your own OS X programs. When you want to create an OS X program, you'll follow the same basic steps:

- Pick a project template to use (typically Cocoa Application)

- Design and customize the user interface

- Connect the user interface items to IBOutlets and IBAction methods

- Write Swift code to make IBAction methods do something

- Run and test your program

To design your user interface, you need to drag and drop items from the Object Library. Then you need to use the Attributes and Size Inspector to customize each user interface item. To help you select user interface items, you can use the Document Outline.

After designing your user interface, you need to connect your user interface to your Swift code through IBOutlets (for retrieving or displaying data) and IBAction methods (to make your user interface do something) using the Assistant Editor.

To review the connections between your user interface items and your Swift code, you can use the Connections Inspector or the Assistant Editor.

Already you can see how the different parts of Xcode work to help you create a program, and we still haven't explored many other Xcode features yet. Perhaps the most confusing part about creating a Macintosh program can be writing Swift code and using methods stored in the class files that make up the Cocoa framework, so the next chapter will explain this in more detail.

As you can see, using Xcode is actually fairly simple once you focus only on those features you actually need and ignore the rest. As we go through each chapter, you'll keep learning a little more about Xcode and Swift programming.

Already you've learned so much about Xcode, and yet you've only just begun.

Chapter **4**

Getting Help

The best way to learn any new skill is to have someone show you what you need to learn. Since that's not always possible, you'll be happy to know that Xcode comes with plenty of built-in help features to make using Xcode less stressful and more enjoyable.

To use Xcode's help, you first need to understand how Swift programs work and how they work with the Cocoa framework. Once you understand how a typical OS X program works and how it relies on the Cocoa framework, you'll be better able to understand how do get the help you need and how you can understand the help you do find through Xcode.

Understanding the Cocoa Framework

When using Xcode, you have to understand that every program you create is based on the Cocoa framework that uses classes that contain various properties and methods. By using these existing classes, you can save time by not writing and testing your own code. Instead, you can just use the existing code in the Cocoa framework that already works. This frees you to spend more time focusing on writing the code that's unique to your particular program.

To use the Cocoa framework, you must understand the principles of object-oriented programming and how objects work. To create an object, you must first define a class. A class contains the actual code that defines properties (to hold data) and methods (to manipulate data stored in its properties). Once you've defined a class, you can define one or more objects based on that class.

Just as a cookie cutter defines the shape of a cookie but isn't the actual cookie, so do classes define an object but isn't an object itself.

The Cocoa framework consists of multiple class files where many class files inherit properties and methods from other class files. When you create an OS X program, you'll typically create objects based on Cocoa framework class files. In fact, every user interface item that you create from the Object Library is based on a Cocoa framework class.

To see what class file each user interface item is based on, let's examine the three-user interface items you created: a label, a text field, and a button:

1. Open the MyFirstProgram project in Xcode.

2. Click on the MainMenu.xib file. Xcode displays your user interface.

3. Choose View ➤ Utilities ➤ Show Object Library. The Object Library appears in the lower right corner of the Xcode window.

4. Click on the Push Button item in the Object Library. A pop-up window appears as shown in Figure 4-1. Notice that this pop-up window tells you the class file (NSButton) of a push button.

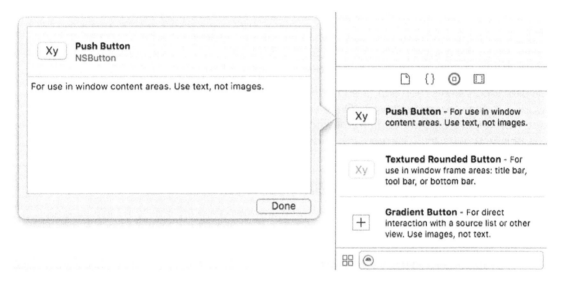

Figure 4-1. *Finding the class file of a Push Button*

5. Click the Done button to make the pop-up window go away.

6. Scroll through the Object Library and click on the Label item. A pop-up window appears as shown in Figure 4-2. Notice that this pop-up window tells you the class file (NSTextField) of a label.

Figure 4-2. Finding the class file of a Label

7. Scroll through the Object Library and click on the Text Field item. A pop-up window appears as shown in Figure 4-3.

Figure 4-3. Finding the class file of a Text Field

By using Xcode's simple help pop-up windows for each item in the Object Library, we've learned the following about our user interface:

▣ Push Button is based on the NSButton class file

▣ Label is based on the NSTextField class file

▣ Text Field is also based on the NSTextField class file

▣ The NSTextField class inherits from (is a subclass of) the NSControl class

Any time you need to find the class file of a user interface item, just click on that item in the Object Library window. To learn what properties and methods we can use for each user interface item, we need to look up all the properties and methods for that particular class. For example, if we want to know what properties and methods we can use for the text field, we have to look up the properties and methods defined by the NSTextField class.

Furthermore, since the NSTextField class inherits from the NSControl class, we can also use any properties and methods defined by the NSControl class. (If the NSControl class inherits from another class, we can use the properties and methods stored in that other class as well.)

Looking Up Properties and Methods in a Class File

Once we know what class a particular user interface item is based on, we can look up its list of properties and methods in Xcode's documentation. There are two ways to do that:

- Choose Help ➤ Documentation and API reference
- Option+click on a class name in your Swift code

Remember when we needed to find the property that stored text in both a label and a text field? Here are the steps we would follow to find this information:

- Identify the class file that each user interface item is based on (NSTextField, which we learned by clicking on that item in the Object Library)
- Look up Xcode's documentation about the NSTextField class file
- If we can't find the information we need in the NSTextField class file, look up the NSControl class file since the NSTextField class inherits all properties and methods from the NSControl class

Looking Up Class Files with the Help Menu

Xcode's menu bar and pull-down menus are usually the most straightforward way to find any command. So the first step is to open Xcode's documentation window, as shown in Figure 4-4, in one of two ways:

- Choose Help ➤ Documentation and API Reference
- Press Shift+Command+0 (the number zero)

Figure 4-4. The Xcode Documentation window

> **Note**   To make the Documentation window less cluttered, click on the Show/Hide Navigator icon.

1. Click in the Search documentation text field at the top of the Documentation window, type **NSTextField**, and press Return. The Documentation window displays information about the NSTextField class.

2. Scroll through the Table of Contents pane to view information about the NSTextField class. If you click on a topic in the Table of Contents pane, the Documentation window displays additional information as shown in Figure 4-5. However, there's nothing in the NSTextField documentation that explains how it stores text. To find that answer, we need to next look in the class that NSTextField inherits from, which is NSControl.

Figure 4-5. Selecting an item in the Table of Contents pane displays information in the right pane

3. Click NSControl that appears to the right of the **Inherits from:** label. Notice that NSTextField inherits from NSControl, which inherits from NSView, which inherits from NSResponder, which inherits from NSObject. To find every property and method available to a label or text field (both based on the NSTextField class), we could exhaustively search each of these class files as well.

4. Click on the Getting and Setting the Control's Value in the Table of Contents pane of NSControl as shown in Figure 4-6. Notice that the property that stores text data in the NSControl class is called stringValue.

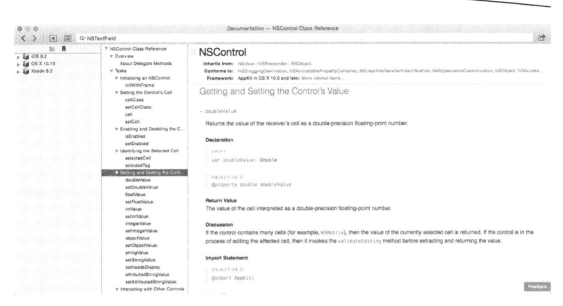

Figure 4-6. The Documentation window lists all the properties in NSControl that stores data

Once we know that we can use the stringValue property to hold text data in the NSControl class, we also know that we can use the stringValue property to hold text data in the NSTextField class. Since both our label and text field are based on the NSTextField class (which we discovered by clicking on them in the Object Library), we know we can access the text data of both the label and text field using the stringValue property.

Looking Up Class Files with Quick Help

Using the Documentation window to look up class files can be handy, but Xcode offers another method called Quick Help. To use Quick Help, you need to move the cursor or mouse pointer over a class file name in a file containing Swift code, then choose one of the following methods:

- Choose Help ➤ Quick Help for Selected Item
- Press Control+Command+Shift+?
- Hold down the Option key and click on a class file name

Quick Help then displays a pop-up window containing a brief description of the selected class file, giving you the option to view the full description in the Documentation window if you choose. To see how Quick Help works using the Option key and the mouse, follow these steps:

1. Make sure the MyFirstProgram is loaded into Xcode.

2. Click the AppDelegate.swift file in the Project Navigator. Xcode displays the contents of the AppDelegate.swift file in the middle pane.

3. Hold down the Option key and move the mouse over the NSTextField word in the IBOutlet. The mouse pointer turns into a question mark as shown in Figure 4-7.

```
import Cocoa

@NSApplicationMain
class AppDelegate: NSObject, NSApplicationDelegate {

    @IBOutlet weak var window: NSWindow!
    @IBOutlet weak var mySlider: NSSlider!
    @IBOutlet weak var myLabel: NSTextField!
```

Figure 4-7. Holding down the Option key turns the mouse pointer into a question mark when hovering over a class file name

4. While holding down the Option key with the mouse pointer over NSTextField, click the mouse. Xcode displays a pop-up window briefly describing the features of the NSTextField class as shown in Figure 4-8.

```
import Cocoa

@NSApplicationMain
class AppDelegate: NSObject, NSApplicationDelegate {

    @IBOutlet weak var window: NSWindow!
    @IBOutlet weak var mySlider: NSSlider!
    @IBOutlet weak var myLabel: NSTextField!
```

Declaration	class NSTextField : NSControl, NSUserInterfaceValidations, NSAccessibilityNavigableStaticText, NSAccessibilityStaticText, NSAccessibilityElement Protocol, NSObjectProtocol
Description	An NSTextField object is a kind of NSControl that displays text that the user can select or edit and that sends its action message to its target when the user presses the Return key while editing.
Availability	OS X (10.10 and later)
Declared In	AppKit
Reference	NSTextField Class Reference

```
}
```

Figure 4-8. Option+clicking on a class file name displays a pop-up window describing that class file

5. Click on NSTextField Class Reference at the bottom of the pop-up window next to the Reference label. Xcode displays the Documentation window listing the NSTextField class file (see Figure 4-5).

Option+clicking is just a way to open the Documentation window without going through the Help ➤ Documentation and Reference API command and typing a class file name.

Browsing the Documentation

Quick Help can display information about specific class files, but what if you know you need information but don't know where to find it? That's when you can spend time browsing through the Documentation window and skimming through the different help topics until you find what you want.

Even if you don't find what you want, chances are good you'll stumble across some interesting information about Xcode or OS X that could come in handy sometime in the future. When browsing through Xcode's documentation, you can look up information specific to iOS, OS X, or Xcode.

If you find something interesting, you can bookmark it. That way you'll be able to find it quickly again later. You can also send information by e-mail or text messaging to share useful information with others.

To browse through the Documentation, follow these steps:

1. Choose Help ➤ Documentation and API Reference. The Documentation window appears.

2. Click the Show/Hide Navigator icon to make sure the Navigator pane appears and lists categories of topics such as iOS, OS X, and Xcode as shown in Figure 4-9.

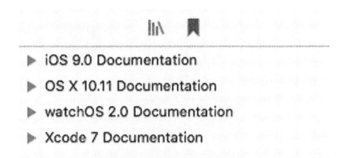

Figure 4-9. The Navigator pane of the Documentation window displays categories of different information

3. Click the gray disclosure triangle that appears to the left of a category such as the OS X or Xcode category. A list of additional topics (with their own gray disclosure triangles) appears. By continuing to click the disclosure triangle of topics, you will eventually find lists of topics that you can click on to view that information as shown in Figure 4-10.

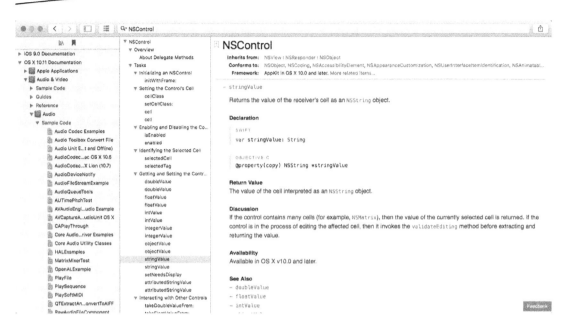

Figure 4-10. Each category lists several other categories of various topics

4.   Click in the Share icon that appears in the upper right corner of the
     Documentation window as shown in Figure 4-11. If you click Email
     Link, the Mail program will load a blank e-mail message with a link to
     that page in the documentation. If you click Add Bookmark, Xcode
     stores that documentation page as a bookmark.

Figure 4-11. The Share icon lets you bookmark a page or share it with others

After you've bookmarked one or more pages, you can view your bookmarks by clicking the
Show documentation bookmarks icon as shown in Figure 4-12. Now you can click on a
bookmark and see that documentation page right away without having to hunt around for it.

Figure 4-12. Viewing bookmarked pages

To delete a bookmark, just right-click over it so a pop-up menu appears. Then choose Delete.

When you want to view the documentation library categories again (iOS, OS X, and Xcode), just click the Browse the documentation library icon as shown in Figure 4-13.

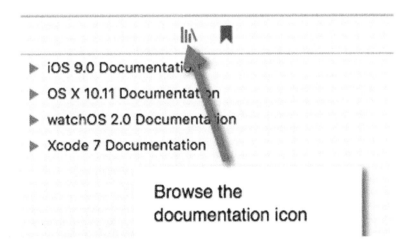

Figure 4-13. The Browse the documentation library icon

Searching the Documentation

Quick Help can display information about specific class files and browsing the documentation can help you explore all the vast information about iOS, OS X, and Xcode. The problem is that Quick Help is only useful for finding information about class files and browsing the documentation can be time-consuming. If you know what you want to find, you can just search for it instead.

When searching for information, type as much as possible to narrow your search results. If you just type a single letter or word, Xcode's documentation will bombard you with irrelevant results.

To see how searching the documentation window works, try the following:

1. Choose Help ➤ Documentation and API Reference. The Documentation window appears.

2. Click in the Search documentation text field and type **text**. A menu of different text results appears that you can click on to get more information as shown in Figure 4-14.

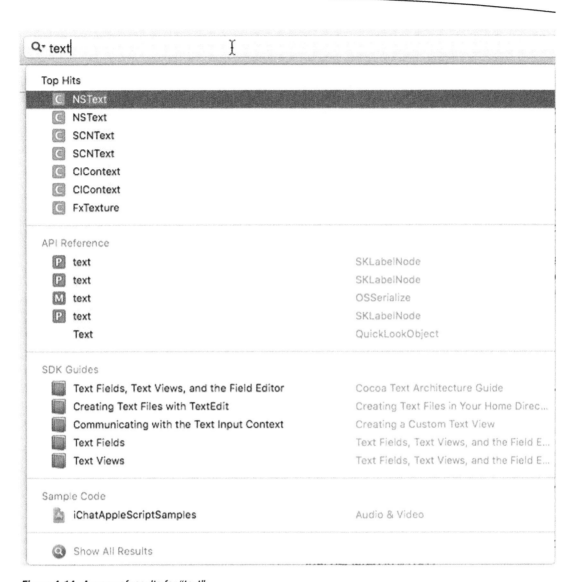

Figure 4-14. A menu of results for "text"

3. Tap the spacebar to create a space after **text**. Notice now the menu
    displays entirely different text results as shown in Figure 4-15.

Figure 4-15. Just adding an extra space after a search term can display a different menu of results

By searching through the documentation, you can find what you need quickly and easily.

Using Code Completion

Back in Chapter 3 when you started typing Swift code, you may have noticed something odd. Each time you typed part of a Swift command, the Xcode editor may have displayed grayed text and a menu of possible commands that match what you partially typed as shown in Figure 4-16.

```
@IBAction func changeCase(sender: NSButton) {
    labelText.integerValue
```

M	Void insertText(insertString: AnyObject)
M	Void insertValue(value: AnyObject!, inPropertyWithKey: String!)
M	Void insertValue(value: AnyObject, atIndex: Int, inPropertyWithKey: String)
V	Int integerValue
M	Void interpretKeyEvents(eventArray: [AnyObject])
V	NSSize intrinsicContentSize
V	Int32 intValue
M	Void invalidateIntrinsicContentSize()

```
}
```

Sets the value of the receiver's cell using an NSInteger value. More...

Figure 4-16. Code completion suggests a likely command you may be trying to type

This feature is called Code Completion and is Xcode's way of helping you type long commands without actually typing every character yourself. When you see grayed out text and a menu, you have three choices:

- Press the Tab key to let Xcode automatically type part of the grayed out text. (You may need to press the Tab key several times to completely select all the grayed out text.)

- Double-click on a command in the pop-up menu to type that command automatically.

- Keep typing.

If you keep typing, Xcode keeps displaying new grayed out text that it thinks you may be trying to type along with a menu of different commands that match what you've typed so far. Let's see how code completion works:

To see how searching the documentation window works, try the following:

1. Make sure your MyFirstProgram is loaded in Xcode.

2. Click on AppDelegate.swift in the Project Navigator pane. The contents of the AppDelegate.swift file appears in the middle Xcode pane.

3. Modify the @IBAction changeCase (sender: NSButton) code by deleting the one line between the curly brackets so it now appears as follows:

```
@IBAction func changeCase(sender: NSButton) {

}
```

4. Move the cursor between the curly brackets of this @IBAction method and type **labelText.s** and notice that grayed out text appears, and a menu of possible commands also appears as shown in Figure 4-17.

```
@IBAction func changeCase(sender: NSButton) {
    labelText.stringValue
M          Void sortSubviewsUsingFunction(compare: CFunctionPointer<((AnyObject!, AnyObject!, UnsafeMutablePointer<Void>) -…
V      String stringValue
V  [AnyObject] subviews
V   AnyClass? superclass
V     NSView? superview
M  AnyObject? supplementalTargetForAction(action: Selector, sender: AnyObject?)
M        Void swapWithMark(sender: AnyObject?)
M        Void swipeWithEvent(event: NSEvent)
}
Sets the value of the receiver's cell using an NSString object. More…
```

Figure 4-17. *Code completion suggests stringValue as a possible command*

5. Tab the Tab key. The first time you tap the Tab key, Xcode types "string."

6. Tap the Tab key a second time and now Xcode types the complete "stringValue."

7. Type **= messageText.stringValue.uppercaseString**. Notice that as you type, Code Completion keeps showing different grayed out text and commands in the pop-up menu.

By using Code Completion, you can type commands faster and more accurately. If you start typing a command and you don't see Code Completion's grayed out text or menu appear, that could be a signal that you mistyped the command. Code Completion is just one more way Xcode tries to make typing code easier for you.

Understanding How OS X Programs Work

To help you better understand what all of Xcode's help documentation means, you need to understand how OS X programs work. In the old days when programs were small, programmers stored all program commands in a single file. Then the computer started at the first command at the top of the file, worked its way down line by line, and stopped when it reached the end of the file.

Today programs are much larger so they're often divided into multiple files. No matter how many files you divide your program into, Xcode treats everything as if it were stored in a single file. Dividing a program into files is for your convenience.

Let's examine your MyFirstProgram line by line so you can understand what's happening. When you view Swift code in Xcode, you'll notice that the Xcode editor color codes different text. These colors help you identify the purpose of different text as follows:

▦ Green – Comments that Xcode completely ignores. Comments are meant to explain something about the nearby code.

▦ Purple – Keywords of the Swift language.

▦ Red – Text strings.

■ Blue – Class file names.

■ Black – Commands.

The very first line tells Xcode to import or include all the code in the Cocoa framework as part of your program. The line looks like this:

```
import Cocoa
```

The next line runs a Swift function that loads your user interface (MainMenu.xib) and creates an object from your AppDelegate class. This basically gets your whole program running as a generic Macintosh program. The line looks like this:

```
@NSApplicationMain
```

The next line defines a class called AppDelegate that is based on the NSObject class and uses the NSApplicationDelegate protocol (which you'll learn about shortly). This line looks like this:

```
class AppDelegate: NSObject, NSApplicationDelegate {
```

The next three lines define IBOutlets that connect this Swift code to the user interface items: the window of the user interface along with the label and text field. The window is based on the NSWindow class (defined in the Cocoa framework) while the label and text fields are based on the NSTextField class. These lines look like this:

```
@IBOutlet weak var window: NSWindow!
@IBOutlet weak var labelText: NSTextField!
@IBOutlet weak var messageText: NSTextField!
```

The next three lines define an IBAction method that's connected to the push button on the user interface. The code takes the text stored in messageText (the text field) and converts it to uppercase. Then it stores the uppercase text into labelText (the label). Both the label and text field are based on the NSTextField class (defined in the Cocoa framework). The lines look like this:

```
@IBAction func changeCase(sender: NSButton) {
    labelText.stringValue = messageText.stringValue.uppercaseString
}
```

The remaining code defines two functions that are empty so they don't do anything. If you typed code inside of these functions, the code would run right after your program started up (applicationDidFinishLaunching) or it would run as soon as your program ended (applicationWillTerminate).

When MyFirstProgram runs, it imports the Cocoa framework and runs to display a generic Macintosh program on the screen that includes your user interface. The applicationDidFinishLaunching function runs, but since it doesn't contain any code, nothing happens. Now the program stops and waits for something to happen.

If the user quits out of the program, the applicationWillTerminate function would run, but since it doesn't contain any code, nothing happens.

When the user clicks the Change Case button, it runs the IBAction changeCase method. The only Swift command in this IBAction method takes the text from the text field (stored in the stringValue property of messageText), capitalizes it, and stores the capitalized text in the label (displayed by the stringValue property of labelText).

Now that you've seen how the MyFirstProgram works, let's look at OS X programming from a more theoretical standpoint. First, creating a program involves using class files defined by the Cocoa framework. When you place items on a user interface, you're using Cocoa framework class files (such as NSTextField and NSButton).

When you define a class in your AppDelegate.swift file, you're also using a class from the Cocoa framework file (NSObject).

A typical OS X program creates objects from the class files in the Cocoa framework and any class files you may define in your Swift files. Objects now communicate with one another in one of two ways:

- Storing or retrieving data from properties stored in other objects
- Calling methods stored in other objects

To store data in an object's property, you have to specify the object name and its property on the left side of an equal sign and a value on the right like this:

```
labelText.stringValue = "Hello, world!"
```

To retrieve data from an object's property, you have to specify a variable to hold data on the left side of an equal sign and the object name and its property on the right like this:

```
let warning = labelText.stringValue
```

To call a method stored in another object, you have to specify the object's name and the method to use like this:

```
messageText.stringValue.uppercaseString
```

This command tells Xcode to run the uppercaseString method on the stringValue property stored in the messageText object.

Setting property values, retrieving property values, and calling methods to run are the three ways objects communicate with each other.

When you create a class, you must define the class file to use such as:

```
class AppDelegate: NSObject
```

This line tells Xcode to define a class called AppDelegate and base it on the class file called NSObject (which is defined in the Cocoa framework).

When you create a class based on an existing class, that class automatically includes all the properties and methods defined by that class. So in the above line of code that defines the AppDelegate class, any object created from the AppDelegate class automatically has all the properties and methods defined by the NSObject class.

Sometimes a class file doesn't have all the methods you may need. To fix this, you can inherit from an existing class and then define a new method in your class. However, if you create a method name that you want other classes to use, a second alternative is to define something called a protocol.

A protocol is nothing more than a list of related method names together but doesn't include any Swift code to make those methods actually do anything. In the code below, the AppDelegate class is not only based on the NSObject class file, but also uses methods defined by the NSApplicationDelegate protocol.

If you open the Documentation window and search for NSApplicationDelegate protocol, you'll see a list of method names defined by the NSApplicationDelegate protocol, such as applicationDidFinishLaunching or applicationWillTerminate as shown in Figure 4-18.

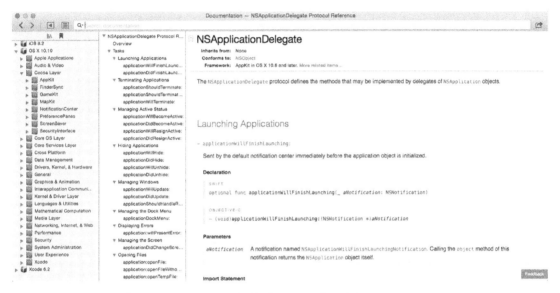

Figure 4-18. The NSApplicationDelegate protocol in the Documentation window

The AppDelegate class inherits properties and methods from the NSObject class and uses the method names defined by the NSApplicationDelegate protocol. Any class based on a protocol must write Swift code to make those protocol methods actually do something. In technical terms, this is known as "implementing or conforming to a protocol."

So the Cocoa framework actually consists of classes and protocols. Classes define objects, and protocols define commonly used method names that different classes may need.

When you write OS X programs, you'll often use both Cocoa framework classes and protocols. When you use a Cocoa framework class, you can use methods that already know how to work such as the uppercaseString method that knows how to capitalize text.

When you use a Cocoa framework protocol, you'll need to write Swift code to make that method actually work. When browsing through Xcode's documentation, keep your eye out for this difference between classes and protocols.

Let's see an example of both classes and protocols in the Xcode documentation window:

1. Make sure your MyFirstProgram is loaded in Xcode.

2. Click on the AppDelegate.swift file in the Project Navigator. Xcode's middle pane displays the contents of that .swift file.

3. Move the cursor in NSApplicationDelegate.

4. Choose Help ➤ Quick Help for Selected Item, or hold down the Option key and click on NSApplicationDelegate. A quick help pop-up window appears as shown in Figure 4-19, explaining how NSApplicationDelegate is a protocol.

```
import Cocoa

@NSApplicationMain
class AppDelegate: NSObject, NSApplicationDelegate {
```

Declaration	protocol NSApplicationDelegate : NSObjectProtocol
Description	The NSApplicationDelegate protocol defines the methods that may be implemented by delegates of NSApplication objects.
Availability	OS X (10.10 and later)
Declared In	AppKit
Reference	NSApplicationDelegate Protocol Reference

```
    func applicationDidFinishLaunching(aNotification: NSNotification) {
        // Insert code here to initialize your application
    }
}
```

Figure 4-19. The NSApplicationDelegate Quick Help pop-up window

5. Click NSApplicationDelegate Protocol Reference. The NSApplicationDelegate protocol reference appears in the Documentation window (see Figure 4-18).

6. Type **NSTextField** in the Search documentation field of the Documentation window and press Return. Notice that the Documentation window explains which classes NSTextField inherits from (the Inherits from: label) and which protocols might be useful when dealing with user interface items (the Conforms to: label) as shown in Figure 4-20.

NSTextField

Inherits from: NSControl : NSView : NSResponder : NSObject
Conforms to: NSUserInterfaceValidations, NSAccessibilityNavigableStaticText, NSUserInterfaceItemIdentification, NSCoding, NSDraggingDestination, NSAnim...
Framework: AppKit in OS X 10.0 and later. More related items...

Figure 4-20. Seeing related classes and protocols

Protocols add methods to a class without the need to create a new class, but you never need to use protocols. When you write programs in Xcode, you'll use Cocoa framework classes and protocols. Then for the unique purposes of your program, you'll likely create your own classes and protocols as well.

When browsing through Xcode's documentation, look for properties and methods in classes before writing your own code. If you don't find the properties and methods you need in one class, look in other classes listed next to the Inherits from: label.

If you need some useful methods, look in the different protocols listed next to the Conforms to: label. Only after you've determined that a property or method doesn't exist in a related class or protocol should you write your own Swift code to do something.

For example, in the MyFirstProgram project, we could have written Swift code to capitalize text typed into the text field. However, it was much easier to just use the existing uppercaseString method instead. That saved us time writing code and debugging it when we could just use proven code in the Cocoa framework instead.

The more you know about the Cocoa framework, the less work you'll have to do writing your own programs. Use Xcode's documentation to help you better understand all the classes and protocols that make up the entire Cocoa framework.

Since the Cocoa framework is so large, don't bother trying to learn everything at once. Just learn what you need and ignore the rest. Gradually the more you use Xcode and write programs, the more likely you'll need and learn the other parts of the Cocoa framework.

The general idea is to rely on the Cocoa framework as much as possible and only write Swift code when you have to. This makes it easy to write reliable software quickly with less effort.

Summary

Learning Xcode can be daunting, so learn it slowly by relying on Xcode's documentation. If you need help in a hurry, use Quick Help to find information about the Cocoa framework classes. If need help on a particular topic, search the documentation.

For those times when you're just curious, browse through Xcode's documentation for iOS, OS X, and Xcode so you can see the vast amount of features available. Through random browsing, you can often learn interesting information about Xcode or writing programs for iOS and OS X.

As you can see, learning to write programs involves learning about Xcode, learning about the Cocoa framework, and learning the Swift programming language. Just take it easy, learn only what you need to know, and gradually keep expanding your knowledge. Through steady progress, you'll learn more and more until one day you'll realize how much you actually know.

Learning to write iOS and OS X programs with Xcode won't happen overnight, but you'll be surprised how much you can learn through steady progress over time. Just practice writing programs and rely on Xcode's documentation available from the Help menu. Before you know it, you'll be capable of writing small programs with confidence, and eventually larger and more complicated ones.

Learning Swift

To write any program, you need to choose a programming language. A programming language lets you define commands for the computer to follow. There's no one "best" programming language because every programming language is meant to solve a specific problem. That means that a programming language may be great at solving certain types of problems, but horrible at solving other types of programs.

With most programming languages, there's a tradeoff between ease of use and efficiency. For example, the BASIC programming language is meant to be easy to learn and use while the C programming language is meant to give you complete control over the computer. By maximizing computer efficiency, the C language is great for creating complicated programs such as operating systems or hard disk utility programs.

Since BASIC was never designed for maximum control over a computer, BASIC would never be used to create an operating system or a hard disk utility program. Since C was designed for maximum computer efficiency, it's difficult for novices to learn and even difficult for experienced programmers to use. The majority of errors or bugs in many programs are due solely to the complexity of the C programming language that confounds even professional programmers with decades of experience.

In the world of Xcode, Apple's official programming language used to be Objective-C, which was a superset of the C programming language and an alternative to the object-oriented C++ language. Unfortunately, Objective-C can still be difficult to learn and even harder to master. By making programming harder than it needs to be, Objective-C makes creating OS X and iOS software difficult for novices and experienced programmers alike.

That's why in 2014, Apple introduced a new programming language called Swift. Swift is meant to be just as powerful as Objective-C while also being much easier to learn. Because Apple will use Swift for both OS X and iOS programming, Swift is now the future programming language for the Macintosh, iPhone, iPad, Apple Watch, Apple TV, CarPlay, and any other future products from Apple.

Since so many people have written programs using Objective-C, there will always be a need for programmers to modify existing Objective-C programs. However, you can always mix Objective-C and Swift in a program. That means over time, there will be less of a need for

Objective-C programmers and more of a need for Swift programmers. If you want to learn the most powerful programming language for writing OS X and iOS programs, you want to learn Swift.

> **Note**   If you're already familiar with Objective-C, you'll notice several ways that Swift makes coding far easier. First, Swift doesn't require a semicolon to end each line. Second, Swift doesn't need asterisks to represent pointers or square brackets to represent method calls to objects. Third, Swift stores everything in a single .swift file in comparison to Objective-C that needs to create an .h header file and an .m implementation file. If you know nothing about Objective-C, just look at any program written in Objective-C and see how confusing the code can be. One look at Objective-C code will make you realize how much easier learning and using Swift can be.

Using Playgrounds

In the old days, programmers had two types of tools to help them learn programming. The first is called an interpreter. An interpreter let you type in a command and then would immediately show you the results. That way you could see exactly what you were doing right or wrong.

The drawback with interpreters was that they were slow and that you couldn't use them to create programs you could sell. To run a program in an interpreter, you needed both the interpreter and the file (called the source code) that contained all your commands written in a particular programming language. Because you had to give away your source code to run programs in an interpreter, others could easily copy your program and steal it. As a result, interpreters were only useful for learning a language but weren't practical for selling software.

The second tool that programmers use to learn programming is called a compiler. A compiler takes a list of commands, stored in a file, and converts them to machine language so the computer can understand them. The advantage of a compiler is that it keeps others from seeing the source code of your program.

The problem with using a compiler is that you have to write a complete program and compile it just to see if your commands work or not. If your commands don't work, now you have to go back and fix the problem. Unlike the interactive nature of an interpreter, a compiler makes learning a programming language much slower and clumsier.

With an interpreter you could write a command and immediately see if it worked or not. With a compiler, you had to write a command, compile your program, and run your program to see if it worked or not.

Interpreters are better for learning while compilers are better for creating software you can distribute to others without giving away your source code. Fortunately, Xcode gives you the best of both worlds.

When you run your program, you're using Xcode's compiler. However, if you only want to experiment with some commands, you can use Xcode's interpreter called a Playground.

Playgrounds let you experiment with Swift code to see if it works or not. When you get it to work, then you can copy and paste it into your project files and compile them to create a working program. By giving you the ability to use both an interpreter and a compiler, Xcode makes it easy to learn Swift and practical for creating programs you can sell or give away to others.

To create a playground, follow these steps:

1. Start Xcode.

2. Choose File ➤ New ➤ Playground. (If you see the Xcode welcome screen, you can also click on Get started with a playground.) Xcode asks for a playground name and platform as shown in Figure 5-1.

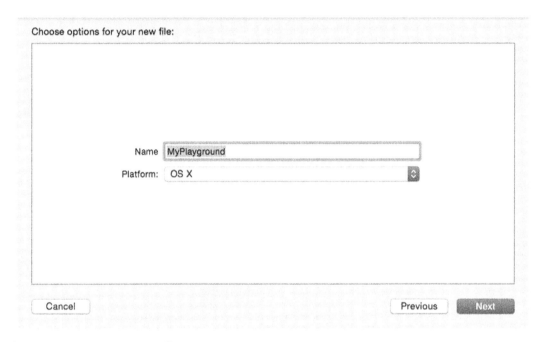

Figure 5-1. Creating a playground file

3. Click in the Name text field and type **IntroductoryPlayground**.

4. Click in the Platform pop-up menu and choose OS X. Xcode asks where you want to save your playground file.

5. Click on a folder where you want to save your playground file and click the Create button. Xcode displays the playground file as shown in Figure 5-2.

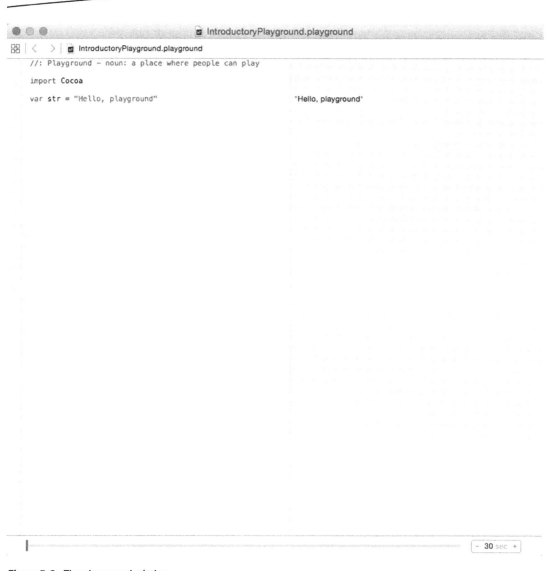

Figure 5-2. The playground window

6. Edit the second line as follows:

```
var str = "This is the Swift interpreter"
```

Notice that the playground window immediately displays the results of your code change in the right margin as shown in Figure 5-3.

Figure 5-3. The playground window displays code changes immediately

Playgrounds let you freely experiment with Swift and access every class in the Cocoa framework without worrying about getting your Swift code to work with a user interface.

Creating Comments in Swift

The simplest commands to type in any programming language are comments. A comment is any text that exists solely for humans to read. In the top of the Playground file, you can see a comment that appears in green that reads:

```
// Playground - noun: a place where people can play
```

Comments let you leave notes about code such as the name of the person who wrote it, the date it was last modified, a description of what the code does and what other files it may depend on, or anything else you think might be useful for you (or another programmer) to read in the future.

If you just need to write a comment on a single line, you can use the // symbols. Anything that appears to the right of the // symbols are comments that the computer completely ignores. Xcode helps identify comments by displaying text in green.

If you need to write a command that spans two or more lines, you can type multiple // symbols in front of each line, but another solution is to define the beginning of a comment with the /* symbols and define the ending of that comment with the */ symbols such as:

```
/* This is a comment that
spans multiple lines */
```

Comments exist for your benefit so feel free to use them whenever you need to write and store crucial information about your code.

> **Note**   One popular use for comments is to temporarily disable Swift code without having to erase it. By disabling one or more lines of Swift code by turning them into a comment, you can see how your program runs as if any commented lines of code were deleted. When you're done testing, you can remove the comment symbols and put your code back in your program without retyping it all over again.

Storing Data in Swift

Every program needs to accept data, manipulate that data somehow, and display that result to the user. To accept data, programs need to store data temporarily in memory. Technically, computers store data in memory addresses, which can be confusing to remember. To make it easier to know where data gets stored, programming languages let you give those memory addresses descriptive names. In Swift, those two choices are called:

- Variables
- Constants

The idea behind both variables and constants is that you define a descriptive name and assign it to hold data such as:

```
str = "This is the Swift interpreter"
```

In the above example, "str" is the descriptive name, and "This is the Swift interpreter" is the data that gets stored. Data can either be a text string or a number such as an integer (3, 12, -9, etc.) or a decimal also known as a floating-point number (12.84, -0.83, 8.02, etc.). At any given time, you can store one chunk of data in a descriptive name, which can be defined as a variable or a constant.

The main difference between a variable and a constant is that you can reuse a variable by storing new data as many times as you want (hence the name "variable"). A constant only lets you store data in it once.

To define a variable, you have to use the "var" keyword like this:

```
var str = "This is the Swift interpreter"
```

To define a constant, you have to use the "let" keyword like this:

```
let str = "This is the Swift interpreter"
```

The first time you store data in a variable or a constant, Swift infers the data type such as:

- Text strings (defined as String)
- Integers (defined as Int)
- Decimal numbers (defined by Float and Double)

Knowing the data type a variable or constant can hold Is crucial because it can only hold one type of data and nothing else. So if you create a variable and store a string in it, that variable can only store strings from now on.

> **Note**   Swift is known as a type-safe programming language because it explicitly defines the type of data each variable or constant can store.

To make it clear what type of data a variable or constant can hold, you can explicitly define the data type such as:

```
var cat: String
var dog: Int
var fish: Float
var snake: Double
```

Based on these data type declarations, the "cat" variable can only store strings, the "dog" variable can only store integers, the "fish" variable can only hold floating-point numbers, and the "snake" variable can only hold double-precision floating-point numbers.

If you try to store the wrong type of data in a variable or constant, Swift won't let you. This is to prevent problems when a program tries to use the wrong type of data. For example, if a program asks the user for how many items to order and the user types in "five" instead of the number 5, the program would have no idea how to do a mathematical calculation on "five," which would cause the program to either crash or work erratically.

> **Note**   Both a Float and a Double data type can hold decimal numbers. The difference is that a Double data type can hold more precise decimal numbers that contain additional decimal places along with smaller and larger values. If you just need to use decimal numbers, use Float since it takes less memory than Double. If you need precise accuracy with decimal numbers, use Double. When Swift infers a decimal number, it infers a Double data type.

Swift gives you three ways to define a variable or a constant:

- ```
  let cat = "Oscar" // Infers String data type
  ```
- ```
  let cat: String = "Oscar"
  ```
- ```
  let cat: String
  cat = "Oscar"
  ```

The first method lets you store data directly into a variable or constant. Based on the type of data you first store, Swift infers the data type as String, Int, or Double (not a Float because a Float stores less precise decimal numbers than Double and Swift assumes you want exact precision).

The second method lets you explicitly declare the data type and store data into that variable or constant. While this can be wordier, it's clear exactly what type of data you want to store.

The third method takes two lines. The first line defines the data type. The second line actually stores the property type of data. This can be handy for variables that may get assigned different data in various parts of your program. You could declare the variable near the top of your file to make it easy to find, then assign data to it later when you need it.
  ```

To see how to declare variables and constants in Swift, follow these steps:

1. Make sure your IntroductoryPlayground file is loaded into Xcode.

2. Modify the Swift code in the playground file as follows:

```
import Cocoa

let cat: String
cat = "Oscar"

cat = "Bo"
```

Notice that when you try to assign new data to a constant that already holds data, you get an error message. Clicking on that warning icon in the left margin displays an error message as shown in Figure 5-4.

```
//: Playground - noun: a place where people can play

import Cocoa

let cat: String
cat = "Oscar"                                              °Oscar°

❶   cat = "Bo"                    ❶ Immutable value 'cat' may only be initialized once
```

Figure 5-4. An error message warns that you cannot store data in a constant more than once

> **Note**   Constants are also called "immutable" because they cannot be changed after you've stored data in them. Variables are called "mutable" because you can constantly change the data that they store. Just remember that variables can only hold one chunk of data at a time. The moment you store new data in a variable, any existing data in that variable gets wiped out.

3. Modify the Swift code in the playground file by changing the constant to a variable (replacing "let" with "var") as follows:

```
import Cocoa

var cat: String
cat = "Oscar"

cat = 42.7
```

Notice that when you try to assign a number to a variable that can only hold strings, you get a warning. Clicking on that warning icon in the left margin displays an error message as shown in Figure 5-5.

```
//: Playground - noun: a place where people can play

import Cocoa

var cat: String
cat = "Oscar"                                              "Oscar"

  cat = 42.7    Cannot assign a value of type 'Double' to a value of type 'String'
```

Figure 5-5. An error message warns that you cannot store the wrong type of data

4. Modify the Swift code in the playground file as follows:

```
import Cocoa

var cat: String
cat = "Oscar"

var greeting = "Hello, "
var period : String = "."

print (greeting + cat + period)
```

Notice that playground displays the results of your Swift code in the right margin as shown in Figure 5-6.

Figure 5-6. The right margin of the playground window constantly shows the result of your code

Typealiases

Declaring variables as data types such as Int, Double, or String only tells you what type of data it can hold, but it doesn't tell you the meaning of that data. For example, if you declared two variables as Int data types, each could hold integers but one variable might represent ages and the other variable might represent Employee ID numbers.

To make the purpose of data types clearer, Swift lets you use something called typealiases. A typealias lets you give a descriptive name to a generic data type name such as:

```
typealias EmployeeID = Int
```

Now instead of declaring a variable as an integer (Int) data type, you could declare it as an EmployeeID data type such as:

```
typealias EmployeeID = Int
var employee : EmployeeID
employee = 192
```

This is equivalent to:

```
var employee : Int
employee = 192
```

Using Unicode Characters as Names

In most programming languages, variables and constants are limited to a fixed range of characters, often excluding foreign language characters. To help make Swift more accessible to programmers comfortable with other languages, Swift lets you use Unicode characters for your variable and constant names.

Unicode is a new universal standard that represents different characters. If you choose Edit ➤ Emoji & Symbols, you can choose from a limited number of characters that you can use instead of or in addition to ordinary letters and numbers as shown in Figure 5-7.

```
import Cocoa

let 😊 = "Happy face"                              "Happy face"
print (😊)                                         "Happy face\n"
```

Figure 5-7. Xcode lets you use special characters as variable or constant names

To see how to use special characters in variable names, follow these steps:

1. Make sure your IntroductoryPlayground file is loaded in Xcode.

2. Delete all the code in your playground except for the "import Cocoa" line.

3. Underneath the "import Cocoa" line, type **let** and press the spacebar.

4. Choose Edit ➤ Emoji & Symbols. A pop-up window appears as shown in Figure 5-8.

```
import Cocoa

let
```

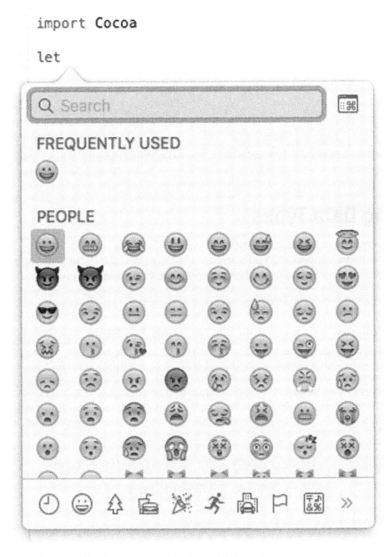

Figure 5-8. *A pop-up window with different categories of special characters*

5. Click on any character that looks interesting. Xcode types that character as your constant name.

6. Type = **"Funny symbol here"** and press Return.

7. Copy the character and paste it in between the parentheses of the print command. Notice that the right margin of the playground window displays the contents of your constant variable as shown in Figure 5-9.

```
import Cocoa

let 😊 = "Funny symbol here"                    "Funny symbol here"
print (😊)                                      "Funny symbol here\n"
```

Figure 5-9. Using a special character as a constant name in Swift code

Special characters can come in handy for displaying actual mathematical symbols instead of spelling them out, or typing variable or constant names in a foreign language. By making variable and constant names more versatile, Swift makes programming understandable for more people.

Converting Data Types

If you have a number stored as an integer and need to convert it to a decimal, or if you have a decimal and need to convert it to an integer, what can you do? The answer is that you can convert one number data type to another just by specifying the data type you want such as:

```
Int(decimal)
```

The Int data type in front tells Swift to convert the number inside the parentheses to an integer. If the number is a decimal, converting it to an integer basically means dropping all numbers after the decimal point, so a number such as 4.9 would be turned into the integer 4.

When Swift converts an integer to a decimal number, it simply tacks on a decimal point with zeroes. So if you converted the integer 75 to a floating-point number, Swift would now store it as 75.0. To see how converting integers to decimals (and vice versa) works, follow these steps:

1. Make sure your IntroductoryPlayground file is loaded in Xcode.

2. Modify the code in the playground file as follows:

    ```
    import Cocoa
    var whole : Int = 4
    var decimal : Double = 4.902

    print (Int(decimal))
    print (Double(whole))
    ```

Notice how Swift turns an integer into a decimal (changing 4 to 4.0) and how it turns a decimal into an integer by dropping every value to the right of the decimal point (changing 4.902 to 4) as shown in Figure 5-10.

```
import Cocoa

var whole : Int = 4                              4
var decimal : Double = 4.902                     4.902

print (Int(decimal))                             "4\n"
print (Double(whole))                            "4.0\n"
```

Figure 5-10. *Changing integers to decimals and vice versa*

Computed Properties

Up until this point, declaring variables and constants, then assigning data to those variable or constants is little different than other programming languages. If you have one variable related to another one, you could do something like this:

```
var cats = 4
var dogs: Int

dogs = cats + 2

print (dogs)
```

Unfortunately, this separates the variable declaration for "dogs" from the actual setting of the value of the "dogs" variable. To keep a variable declaration linked with the code that defines it, Swift offers something called computed properties.

With a computed property, you don't store data directly into a variable. Instead, you define the data type a variable can hold and then use other variables or constants to calculate a new value to store in that variable. This calculation is known as a getter with code that looks like this:

```
var dogs : Int {
    get {
        return cats + 2 // Code to calculate a value

    }
}
```

The above code declares a variable called "dogs" that called only hold integer (Int) data types. Then it encloses code in curly brackets known as a getter (defined by the keyword "get").

You can actually have any amount of Swift code inside the getter's curly brackets, but this example only includes the most important line, which uses the "return" keyword to return a value that gets stored in the "dogs" variable.

In this case, it takes the value stored in the "cats" variable (which must be defined with a value elsewhere in your program), adds 2 to that value, and stores that new value in the "dogs" variable. Change the code in the getter and you change the computed value that gets stored in the "dogs" variable.

Let's see how that works by following these steps:

1. Make sure your IntroductoryPlayground file is loaded in Xcode.

2. Modify the code in the playground file as follows:

```
import Cocoa

var cats = 4

var dogs : Int {
    get {
        return cats + 2 // Code to calculate a value
    }
}

print (dogs)
```

Notice that the right margin of the playground window shows the value of dogs as shown in Figure 5-11.

```
import Cocoa

var cats = 4                                                          4

var dogs : Int {
get {
    return cats + 2 // Code to calculate a value                      6
}
}

print (dogs)                                                        "6\n"
```

Figure 5-11. *The right margin of the playground window shows how the getter portion works*

Getters use code to calculate the value of a variable. A second type of computed property is known as a setter, which runs code that calculates the value of a different variable.

A setter runs every time its variable gets assigned a value. To see how getters and setters work, follow these steps:

1. Make sure your IntroductoryPlayground file is loaded in Xcode.

2. Modify the code in the playground file as follows:

```
import Cocoa

var cats = 4
var dogs : Int {
    get {
        return cats + 2 // Code to calculate a value
    }
```

```
            set(newValue) {
                cats = 3 * newValue
            }
        }

        print (dogs)
        print (cats)
        dogs = 5
        print (dogs)
        print (cats)
```

> **Note**   In the above setter code, "newValue" is actually a default variable that you can omit such as:
>
> ```
> set {
>   cats = 3 * newValue
> }
> ```
>
> If you want to define your own variable name (instead of using the default newValue variable), then you must put that new name within the parentheses like this:
>
> ```
> set (myOwnVariable){
>   cats = 3 * myOwnVariable
> }
> ```

Notice how the value of the cats and dogs variables change when you assign a different value to the dogs variable as shown in Figure 5-12.

```
import Cocoa

var cats = 4                                              4
var dogs : Int {
get {
    return cats + 2 // Code to calculate a value        (2 times)
}
set(newValue) {
    cats = 3 * newValue                                  15
}
}

print (dogs)                                            "6\n"
print (cats)                                            "4\n"
dogs = 5                                                5
print (dogs)                                            "17\n"
print (cats)                                            "15\n"
```

Figure 5-12. The right margin of the playground window shows how the getter and setter code works

Let's go through this code line by line. First, the number 4 gets stored in the "cats" variable. Using the "cats" variable (4) in the getter returns cats + 2 or 4 + 2 (6). So the first print (dogs) command prints 6.

The second print (cats) prints the value of the "cats" variable, which is still 4.

When the "dogs" variable gets assigned the number 5, it runs the setter. The temporary variable "newValue" gets assigned the number 5, which calculates a new value for "cats" as 3 * newValue, which is 3 * 5 or 15. The value of the "cats" variable is now set to 15.

Now the next print (dogs) command runs, using the value of "dogs," which is calculated by the getter. Since the value of "cats" is 15, the getter calculates cats + 2 or 15 + 2, which is 17. So the next print (dogs) command prints 17 and the last print (cats) command prints 15.

> **Note**   Computed properties can run code when assigning a value to a variable. However, use computed properties sparingly since they can make your code harder to understand. Computed properties are most often used for class properties in object-oriented programming. For example, if an object represents a square drawn on the screen, changing the width of the square must also change the height of that square at the same time (and vice versa).

Using Optional Variables

The biggest flaw when you declare a variable is that you can't use that variable until you store data in it. If you try using a variable before it stores any data, your program will fail and crash. To avoid this problem, many programmers initially store "dummy" data in a variable. Unfortunately, such "dummy" data can still be used by a program and cause errors.

To avoid this problem, Swift offers something called optional variables. An optional variable can store data or nothing at all. If an optional variable contains nothing, it's considered to hold a value called nil. By using optional variables, you avoid crashing a program if a variable doesn't contain any data.

To create an optional variable, you just declare a variable and its data type with a question mark like this:

```
var fish : String?
```

The question mark identifies a variable as an optional. You can use optional variables exactly like ordinary variables to store data in them such as:

```
fish = "goldfish"
```

Although storing data in an optional variable is no different than storing data in an ordinary variable, retrieving data from an optional variable requires extra steps. First, you must check if the optional variable even has data in it or not. Once you know that an optional variable contains data, you have to unwrap that optional to get to the actual data by using an exclamation mark such as:

```
print (fish!)
```

To see how optional variables work, try the following:

1. Make sure your IntroductoryPlayground file is loaded in Xcode.

2. Modify the code as follows:

```
import Cocoa

var fish : String?
fish = "goldfish"
print (fish)
print (fish!)
```

Notice that "fish" by itself is actually an optional variable, but when you use the exclamation mark to unwrap it, you access the actual data inside the optional as shown in Figure 5-13.

```
import Cocoa                                    nil
var fish : String?                             "goldfish"
fish = "goldfish"                              "Optional("goldfish")\n"
print (fish)                                   "goldfish\n"
print (fish!)
```

Figure 5-13. Seeing the difference between an optional and the unwrapped data inside an optional

3. Type two additional lines of code underneath:

```
var str : String
str = fish
```

Notice that you can't assign the optional variable "fish" to "str" because "str" can only hold String data types. Instead, you must unwrap the optional variable "fish" and retrieve its actual string content by using the exclamation mark like this:

```
var str : String
str = fish!
```

Before unwrapping optional variables to get to their data, always check to see if the optional variable contains a nil value or a variable. If you try to use an optional variable when it contains a nil value, your program will crash.

To check if an optional variable holds a nil value or not, you have two options. First, you can explicitly check for a nil value like this:

```
if fish != nil {
    print ("The optional variable is not nil")
}
```

This code checks if the "fish" optional variable is not equal to (!=) nil. If an optional variable is not nil, then it must hold a value so then it's safe to retrieve it.

A second way to check if an optional variable has a value or not is to assign it to a constant like this:

```
if let food = fish {
    print ("The optional variable has a value")
    print (food)
}
```

If the optional variable has a value, it stores that value in a constant (or another variable). Now you can access that value through the constant or variable. To see how this works, follow these steps:

1. Make sure your IntroductoryPlayground file is loaded in Xcode.

2. Modify the code as follows:

```
import Cocoa
var fish : String?
fish = "goldfish"

if fish != nil {
    print ("The optional variable is not nil")
    var str : String
    str = fish!
    print (str)
}

if let food = fish {
    print ("The optional variable has a value")
    print (food)
}
```

Notice that you can retrieve the value in an optional variable by unwrapping it with an exclamation mark or storing it in a constant and then using that constant as shown in Figure 5-14.

```
import Cocoa

var fish : String?                                          nil
fish = "goldfish"                                           "goldfish"

if fish != nil {
    print ("The optional variable is not nil")             "The optional variable is not nil\n"
    var str : String
    str = fish!                                            "goldfish"
    print (str)                                            "goldfish\n"
}

if let food = fish {
    print ("The optional variable has a value")           "The optional variable has a value\n"
    print (food)                                          "goldfish\n"
}
```

Figure 5-14. Two ways to access a value stored in an optional variable

Linking Swift Code to a User Interface

Every program needs to store data, and one of the most common ways to store data in a variable is to retrieve data from a user interface. To link a user interface item to Swift code, you need to create an IBOutlet variable.

If you had a text field connected to an IBOutlet variable, anything the user typed in the text field would automatically get stored in the IBOutlet variable. Likewise, anything you store in the IBOutlet variable would suddenly appear in the text field. IBOutlet variables act like a link between your Swift code and your user interface as shown in Figure 5-15.

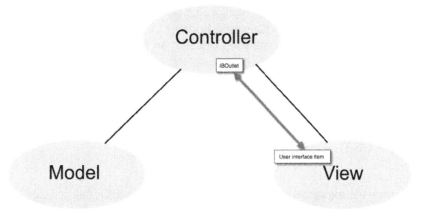

Figure 5-15. IBOutlet variables link your user interface items with Swift code

Since user interface items such as text fields may initially be empty, IBOutlet variables are defined as implicitly unwrapped optional variables defined by an exclamation mark like this:

```
@IBOutlet weak var labelText: NSTextField!
```

If an IBOutlet were a regular variable and connected to an empty text field, your program would risk crashing without any data in the IBOutlet variable.

If an IBOutlet were an optional variable, you could define it with a question mark like this:

```
@IBOutlet weak var labelText: NSTextField?
```

Unfortunately, every time you wanted to access the data stored in this optional variable, you would have to type an exclamation mark. If you accessed this IBOutlet variable multiple times, each time you would have to type an exclamation mark, which can get annoying while making your code look harder to read.

To let you access an IBOutlet variable without typing exclamation marks all the time, it's easier to create an IBOutlet variable as an implicitly unwrapped optional variable, which means that if it holds a value, you can access it without typing the unwrapping exclamation mark.

To see how Xcode creates IBOutlets as implicitly unwrapped optional variables, open the MyFirstProgram project that you created earlier:

1. Make sure your MyFirstProgram is loaded in Xcode.

2. Click on the AppDelegate.swift file in the Project Navigator. Xcode's middle pane displays the contents of that .swift file. Notice that all the IBOutlet variables are declared with an exclamation mark, meaning they're implicitly unwrapped optional variables:

    ```
    @IBOutlet weak var labelText: NSTextField!
    @IBOutlet weak var messageText: NSTextField!
    ```

Also notice that the IBAction changeCase method lets you access the contents of these implicitly unwrapped optional variables without using an exclamation mark.

```
@IBOutlet weak var labelText: NSTextField!
@IBOutlet weak var messageText: NSTextField!

@IBAction func changeCase(sender: NSButton) {
    labelText.stringValue = messageText.stringValue.uppercaseString
    let warning = labelText.stringValue
}
```

3. Replace the exclamation marks at the end of each IBOutlet variable with a question mark like this:

    ```
    @IBOutlet weak var labelText: NSTextField?
    @IBOutlet weak var messageText: NSTextField?
    ```

Notice that Xcode now displays error messages each time you use an IBOutlet variable. That's because you need to unwrap each optional variable with an exclamation mark like this:

```
@IBAction func changeCase(sender: NSButton) {
    labelText!.stringValue = messageText!.stringValue.uppercaseString
    let warning = labelText!.stringValue
}
```

If you define your IBOutlets as regular optional variables (defined by a question mark), then you must unwrap each optional variable with an exclamation mark to access its value.

If you simply define your IBOutlets as implicitly unwrapped optional variables (which Xcode does for you), then you don't need to type an exclamation mark to unwrap the optional variables.

Basically, let Xcode create your IBOutlets as implicitly unwrapped variables (with an exclamation mark) to make typing Swift code easier.

Now you may wonder when should you use an optional variable (defined by a question mark ?) and when should you use an implicitly unwrapped optional variable defined by an exclamation mark !)?

In general, use implicitly unwrapped optional variables for IBOutlets to make it easy to write Swift code without typing exclamation marks all over. If you use implicitly unwrapped optional variables any other time, your variable could contain a nil value and Xcode won't catch any potential errors if you try to use it.

To see the danger of using implicitly unwrapped optional variables, follow these steps:

1. Make sure your IntroductoryPlayground file is loaded in Xcode.

2. Modify the code as follows:

```
import Cocoa

var safe : Int?  // optional variable
var danger : Int!// implicitly unwrapped optional variable

print (danger * 2)
print (safe * 2)
```

Notice that neither integer variable has a value in it, but Xcode cheerfully lets you perform a calculation with a nil value in an implicitly unwrapped optional but flags a possible error with a regular optional variable as shown in Figure 5-16.

```
import Cocoa

var safe : Int?  // optional variable
var danger : Int!// implicitly unwrapped optional variable

print (danger * 2)
print (safe * 2)
            Value of optional type 'Int?' not unwrapped; did you mean to use '!' or '?'?
```

Figure 5-16. Xcode can identify possible problems with undefined optional variables but not undefined implicitly unwrapped optional variables

By making you unwrap optional variables with an exclamation mark (!), Xcode forces you to acknowledge you're using an optional variable so you can remember to check if it has a nil value or not.

Since implicitly unwrapped optional variables let you type the variable name without typing additional symbols, it's much easier to forget you're working with optional variables and check for a possible nil value before trying to use it. Optional variables can't prevent problems, but they can force you to remember you're working with potentially nil values.

Summary

If you're coming from another programming environment, you've already seen numerous ways that Swift differs from other languages. Swift's playground interpreter lets you test your code in a safe environment before copying and pasting it into an actual program. Playgrounds give you the freedom to experiment freely with Swift commands.

You can create single line comments by using the // symbols. You can create multiple line comments by marking the beginning of a comment with the /* symbols and the end of a comment with the */ symbols.

The three most common data types are integers (Int), decimal numbers (Float or Double), and text strings (String). If you need absolute precision with decimal numbers, use Double data types. Otherwise just use Float.

To make data types easier to understand, you can use typealiases, which let you substitute a descriptive name to represent a common data type. To make variable names more flexible, you can use Unicode characters that can represent symbols or foreign language characters.

Storing data in a variable can be as simple as assigning it to a value. Swift also offers computed properties that let you modify a variable or another variable when assigned a new value. Computed properties are far more useful when working with classes and object-oriented programming.

Even more important are optional variables that let you handle nil values without crashing your program. Optional variables are especially important when using IBOutlets to connect Swift code to user interface items such as labels and text fields.

When you create an optional variable (with a question mark), you need to unwrap it to access its actual data (using an exclamation mark).

Variables are crucial for storing data temporarily so you'll use them often. When you start learning about classes and object-oriented programming, you'll use variables for defining properties. Essentially, any time you need to store one chunk of data, you'll declare a variable to hold it.

Manipulating Numbers and Strings

Every program needs to store data temporarily in variables. However, for a program to be useful, it must also manipulate that data somehow to calculate a useful result. A spreadsheet lets you add, subtract, multiply, and divide numbers. A word processor manipulates text to correct your spelling and format text. Even a video game responds to joystick movements to calculate a new position for the player's object such as a cartoon person, airplane, or car. Using data to calculate a new result is the whole purpose of every program.

To manipulate numbers, Swift includes four basic mathematic operators for addition (+), subtraction (-), multiplication (*), division (/), and a remainder operator (%). You can even manipulate strings using the additional operator (+) when you want to combine two strings into one.

Although Swift includes multiple operators for manipulating numbers and text, the Cocoa framework includes plenty of more powerful functions for manipulating numbers and strings. If none of these functions prove suitable, you can always create your own functions to manipulate text and numeric data. By creating miniature programs called functions, you can manipulate data in any way you like and reuse your function as often as necessary.

Using Mathematical Operators

The simplest way to manipulate numbers is to perform addition, subtraction, division, or multiplication. When manipulating numbers, first make sure all your numbers are the same data type such as all integers or all Float or Double decimal numbers. Since mixing integers with decimal numbers can lead to calculation errors, Swift will force you to use all the same data types in a calculation. If all your data isn't the same data type, you'll need to convert one or more data types such as:

```
var cats = 4
var dogs = 5.4

dogs = Double(cats) * dogs
```

In this case, Swift infers that "cats" is an Int data type and "dogs" is a Double data type. To multiple cats and dogs, they must be the same data type (Double), so we must first convert the "cats" value to a Double data type and then the calculation can proceed safely.

When using multiple mathematical operators, use parentheses to define which calculations should occur first. Swift normally calculates mathematical operators from left to right, but multiplication and division occur before addition and subtraction. If you typed the following Swift code, you'd get two different results based solely on the order of the mathematical calculations:

```
var cats, dogs : Double

dogs = 5 * 9 - 3 / 2 + 4      // 47.5
cats = 5 * (9 - 3) / (2 + 4)  // 5.0
```

For clarity, always group mathematical operators in parentheses. The most common mathematical operators are known as binary operators because they require two numbers to calculate a result, as shown in Table 6-1.

Table 6-1. Common mathematical operators in Swift

Mathematical operator	Purpose	Example
+	Addition	5 + 9 = 14
-	Subtraction	5 – 9 = -4
*	Multiplication	5 * 9 = 45
/	Division	5 / 9 = 0.555
%	Remainder	5 % 9 = 5

Out of all these mathematical operators, the remainder operator may need some additional explanation. Essentially the remainder operator divides one number into another and returns just the remainder of that division. So 5 divided by 9 is 0 with a remainder of 5 and 26 divided by 5 would give a remainder of 1.

Prefix and Postfix Operators

When using the addition or subtraction operators to add or subtract 1, Swift gives you two options. First, you can create simple mathematical statements like this:

```
var temp : Int = 1
temp = temp + 1
temp = temp - 1
```

As a shortcut, Swift also offers something called prefix and postfix increment and decrement operators. So if you wanted to add 1 to any variable, you could just do one of the following:

```
var temp : Int = 1
++temp
--temp
```

The ++ or -- operator tells Swift to add or subtract 1 to the variable. When the ++ or -- operator appears in front of a variable, that's called prefix and that means add or subtract 1 to the variable before using it.

If the ++ or -- operator appears after a variable, that's called postfix and that means add or subtract 1 to the variable after using it.

To see how these different increment and decrement operators work, create a new playground by following these steps:

1. Start Xcode.

2. Choose File ➤ New ➤ Playground. (If you see the Xcode welcome screen, you can also click on Get started with a playground.) Xcode asks for a playground name and platform.

3. Click in the Name text field and type **MathPlayground**.

4. Click in the Platform pop-up menu and choose OS X. Xcode asks where you want to save your playground file.

5. Click on a folder where you want to save your playground file and click the Create button. Xcode displays the playground file.

6. Edit the code as follows:

    ```
    import Cocoa

    var temp, temp2 : Int
    temp = 1
    temp2 = temp
    print (++temp)
    print (temp2++)
    print (temp2)
    ```

Notice that the prefix operator (++temp) adds 1 to the variable before using it while the postfix operator (temp--) uses the variable and then adds 1 to it as shown in Figure 6-1.

```
import Cocoa

var temp, temp2 : Int
temp = 1                                              1
temp2 = temp                                          1
print (++temp)                                        "2\n"
print (temp2++)                                       "1\n"
print (temp2)                                         "2\n"
```

Figure 6-1. Seeing how prefix and postfix operators work

Compound Assignment Operators

The increment (++) and decrement (- -) operators let you add or subtract 1 to a variable. If you want to add or subtract a number other than 1 to a variable, you can use a compound assignment operator that looks like this (+=) or (-=).

To use a compound assignment operator, you need to specify a variable, the compound assignment operator you want to use, and then the value you want to add or subtract such as:

```
temp += 5
```

This is equivalent to:

```
temp = temp + 5
```

To see how compound assignment operators work, follow these steps:

1. Make sure your MathPlayground file is loaded in Xcode.

2. Edit the code as follows:

```
import Cocoa

var temp : Int

temp = 2
temp += 57              // Equivalent to temp = temp + 57
print (temp)
temp -= 7               // Equivalent to temp = temp - 7
print (temp)
```

As Figure 6-2 shows, the += compound assignment operator adds 57 to the current value of temp. Then the -= compound assignment operator subtracts 7 from the current value of temp.

```
import Cocoa

var temp : Int

temp = 2                                                          2
temp += 57        // Equivalent to temp = temp + 57              59
print (temp)                                                     "59\n"
temp -= 7         // Equivalent to temp = temp - 7               52
print (temp)                                                     "52\n"
```

Figure 6-2. Seeing how compound assignment operators work

By combining mathematical operators, you can create any type of calculation. However if you need to perform common mathematical operations such as finding the square root or logarithm of a number, it's much simpler and more reliable to use built-in math functions that are part of the Cocoa framework.

Using Math Functions

The Cocoa framework provides dozens of math functions that you can view by choosing Help ➤ Documentation and API Reference. When the Documentation window appears, type **math** and choose math under the API Reference category as shown in Figure 6-3.

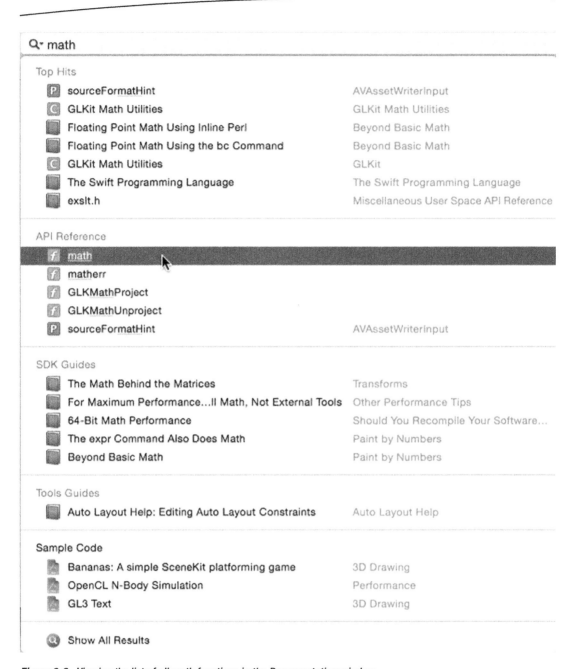

Figure 6-3. Viewing the list of all math functions in the Documentation window

You likely won't need or use all available math functions. Some of the more common math functions include the following:

- Rounding functions
- Calculation functions (sqrt, cbrt, min/max, etc.)

- Trigonometry functions (sin, cosine, tangent, etc.)
- Exponential functions
- Logarithmic functions

Rounding Functions

When you're working with decimal numbers, you may want to round them to the nearest place value. However, there are many ways to round numbers in Swift such as:

- round – Rounds up from 0.5 and higher and rounds down from 0.49 and lower
- floor – Rounds to the lowest integer
- ceil – Rounds to the highest integer
- trunc – Drops the decimal value

To see how these different rounding functions work, create a new playground by following these steps:

1. Make sure the MathPlayground file is loaded in Xcode.

2. Edit the code as follows:

```
import Cocoa

var testNumber : Double

testNumber = round(36.98)
testNumber = round(-36.98)
testNumber = round(36.08)

testNumber = floor(36.98)
testNumber = floor(-36.98)
testNumber = floor(36.08)

testNumber = ceil(36.98)
testNumber = ceil(-36.98)
testNumber = ceil(36.08)

testNumber = trunc(36.98)
testNumber = trunc(-36.98)
testNumber = trunc(36.08)
```

Notice how each type of rounding function works differently with both negative and positive numbers as well as how each function rounds up or down as shown in Figure 6-4.

```
import Cocoa

var testNumber : Double

testNumber = round(36.98)                    37.0
testNumber = round(-36.98)                   -37.0
testNumber = round(36.08)                    36.0

testNumber = floor(36.98)                    36.0
testNumber = floor(-36.98)                   -37.0
testNumber = floor(36.08)                    36.0

testNumber = ceil(36.98)                     37.0
testNumber = ceil(-36.98)                    -36.0
testNumber = ceil(36.08)                     37.0

testNumber = trunc(36.98)                    36.0
testNumber = trunc(-36.98)                   -36.0
testNumber = trunc(36.08)                    36.0
```

Figure 6-4. *Seeing how different rounding functions work*

Calculation Functions

You can combine Swift's four basic mathematical functions (addition, subtraction, division, and multiplication) to create sophisticated calculations of any kind. However, the Cocoa framework includes common types of mathematical functions that you can use so you don't have to create them yourself. Some common calculation functions include:

- fabs – Calculates the absolute value of a number

- sqrt – Calculates the square root of a positive number

- cbrt – Calculates the cube root of a positive number

- hypot – Calculates the square root of (x*x + y*y)

- fmax – Identifies the maximum or largest value of two numbers

- fmin – Identifies the minimum or smallest value of two numbers

To see how these different calculation functions work, follow these steps:

1. Make sure your MathPlayground is loaded in Xcode.

2. Edit the code as follows:

```
import Cocoa

var testNumber : Double
testNumber = fabs(52.64)
testNumber = fabs(-52.64)
```

```
testNumber = sqrt(5)
testNumber = cbrt(5)
testNumber = hypot(2, 3)
testNumber = fmax(34.2, 89.2)
testNumber = fmin(34.2, 89.2)
```

Notice how each type of calculation function works differently as shown in Figure 6-5.

`testNumber = fabs(52.64)`	52.64
`testNumber = fabs(-52.64)`	52.64
`testNumber = sqrt(5)`	2.23606797749979
`testNumber = cbrt(5)`	1.7099759466767
`testNumber = hypot(2, 3)`	3.60555127546399
`testNumber = fmax(34.2, 89.2)`	89.2
`testNumber = fmin(34.2, 89.2)`	34.2

Figure 6-5. Seeing how different calculation functions work

Trigonometry Functions

If you remember from school (or even if you don't), trigonometry is a mathematical field involving angles between intersecting lines. Since trigonometry can actually be handy in the real world, the Cocoa framework provides plenty of functions for calculating cosines, hyperbolic sines, inverse tangents, and inverse hyperbolic cosines. Some common trigonometry functions include:

- sin – Calculates the sine of a degree measured in radians

- cos – Calculates the cosine of a degree measured in radians

- tan – Calculates the tangent of a degree measured in radians

- sinh – Calculates the hyperbolic sine of a degree measured in radians

- cosh – Calculates the hyperbolic cosine of a degree measured in radians

- tanh – Calculates the hyperbolic tangent of a degree measured in radians

- asin – Calculates the inverse sine of a degree measured in radians

- acos – Calculates the inverse cosine of a degree measured in radians

- atan – Calculates the inverse tangent of a degree measured in radians

- asinh – Calculates the inverse hyperbolic sine of a degree measured in radians

- acosh – Calculates the inverse hyperbolic cosine of a degree measured in radians

- atanh – Calculates the inverse hyperbolic tangent of a degree measured in radians

To see how these different trigonometry functions work, follow these steps:

1. Make sure your MathPlayground is loaded in Xcode.

2. Edit the code as follows:

```
import Cocoa

var testNumber : Double
testNumber = sin(1)
testNumber = cos(1)
testNumber = tan(1)

testNumber = sinh(1)
testNumber = cosh(1)
testNumber = tanh(1)

testNumber = asin(1)
testNumber = acos(1)
testNumber = atan(1)

testNumber = asinh(1)
testNumber = acosh(1)
testNumber = atanh(1)
```

Notice how each type of trigonometry function works differently as shown in Figure 6-6.

```
import Cocoa

var testNumber : Double

testNumber = sin(1)                          0.8414709848078965
testNumber = cos(1)                          0.5403023058681398
testNumber = tan(1)                          1.557407724654902

testNumber = sinh(1)                         1.175201193643801
testNumber = cosh(1)                         1.543080634815244
testNumber = tanh(1)                         0.7615941559557649

testNumber = asin(1)                         1.570796326794897
testNumber = acos(1)                         0
testNumber = atan(1)                         0.7853981633974483

testNumber = asinh(1)                        0.881373587019543
testNumber = acosh(1)                        0
testNumber = atanh(1)                        inf
```

Figure 6-6. Seeing how different trigonometry functions work

Exponential Functions

Exponential functions involve multiplication such as multiplying the number 2 by itself a fixed number of times. Some common exponential functions include:

- exp – Calculates e**x where x is an integer
- exp2 – Calculates 2**x where x is an integer
- __exp10 – Calculates 10**x where x is an integer

- expm1 – Calculates e**x-1 where x is an integer

- pow – Calculates x raised to the power of y

To see how these different trigonometry functions work, follow these steps:

1. Make sure your MathPlayground is loaded in Xcode.

2. Edit the code as follows:

```
import Cocoa

var testNumber : Double
testNumber = exp(3)
testNumber = exp2(3)
testNumber = __exp10(3)
testNumber = expm1(3)
testNumber = pow(2,4)
```

Notice how each type of trigonometry function works differently as shown in Figure 6-7.

testNumber = exp(3)	20.0855369231877
testNumber = exp2(3)	8.0
testNumber = __exp10(3)	1,000.0
testNumber = expm1(3)	19.0855369231877
testNumber = pow(2,4)	16.0

Figure 6-7. Seeing how different exponential functions work

Logarithmic Functions

Logarithm functions allow multiplication, division, and addition of large numbers in calculations similar to exponential functions. Some common logarithmic functions include:

- log – Calculates the natural logarithm of number

- log2 – Calculates the base-2 logarithm of a number

- log10 – Calculates the base-10 logarithm of a number

- log1p – Calculates the natural log of 1+x

To see how these different logarithmic functions work, follow these steps:

1. Make sure your MathPlayground is loaded in Xcode.

2. Edit the code as follows:

```
import Cocoa

var testNumber : Double
testNumber = log(3)
testNumber = log2(3)
testNumber = log10(3)
testNumber = log1p(3)
```

Notice how each type of logarithmic function works differently as shown in Figure 6-8.

```
testNumber = log(3)                    1.09861228866811
testNumber = log2(3)                   1.58496250072116
testNumber = log10(3)                  0.477121254719662
testNumber = log1p(3)                  1.38629436111989
|
```

Figure 6-8. Seeing how different logarithmic functions work

Using String Functions

Just as the Cocoa framework provides dozens of math functions, so does it also contain a handful of string manipulation functions. Some common string functions include:

- + -- Concatenates or combines two strings together such as "Hello" + "world," which creates the string "Hello world"

- capitalizedString – Capitalizes the first letter of each word

- lowercaseString – Converts an entire string to lowercase letters

- uppercaseString – Converts an entire string to uppercase letters

- doubleValue – Converts a string holding a numeric value to a Double data type

- isEmpty – Checks if a string is empty or has at least one character

- hasPrefix – Checks if certain text appears at the beginning of a string

- hasSuffix – Checks if certain text appears at the end of a string

When using the + operator to append or combine strings, be careful of spaces. If you omit spaces, then you might get unwanted results. For example, "Hello" + "world" would create the string "Helloworld" without any spaces. That's why you need to make sure you put a space in between words such as "Hello" + "world" to create "Hello world."

To see how these different string functions work, follow these steps:

1. Make sure your MathPlayground is loaded in Xcode.

2. Edit the code as follows:

```
import Cocoa

var text : String = "Hello everyone!"

print (text.capitalizedString)
print (text.lowercaseString)
print (text.uppercaseString)
print (text.isEmpty)
```

```
print (text.hasPrefix ("Hello"))
print (text.hasSuffix ("world"))

var dog : Double
dog = "23.79".doubleValue
```

Notice how each type of string function works differently as shown in Figure 6-9.

```
import Cocoa

var text : String = "Hello everyone!"                    "Hello everyone!"

print (text.capitalizedString)                           "Hello Everyone!\n"
print (text.lowercaseString)                             "hello everyone!\n"
print (text.uppercaseString)                             "HELLO EVERYONE!\n"
print (text.isEmpty)                                     "false\n"
print (text.hasPrefix ("Hello"))                         "true\n"
print (text.hasSuffix ("world"))                         "false\n"

var dog : Double
dog = "23.79".doubleValue                                23.79
```

Figure 6-9. Seeing how different string functions work

Creating Functions

Up until now, all of the functions you've been using to manipulate numbers or strings have been created for you in the Cocoa framework. The basic idea behind a function is that you can use it without knowing how it works. All you need to know is the function name (to call it and make it run) along with any data you might need to pass to the function so it can do something with it (such as capitalizing all the text in a string).

You should always strive to use the built-in functions of the Cocoa framework as much as possible because this lets you create programs by using pretested, reliable code. Of course, the Cocoa framework can't provide every possible function that you may need so you'll eventually need to create your own functions.

The purpose of functions is to simplify code. Rather than include multiple lines of code to calculate the square root of a number, it's much simpler to hide that code in a function and just run or call that function by name. Functions basically replace multiple lines of code with a single line of code known as a function call.

The three types of functions you can create are:

- Functions that do the same thing without accepting any data
- Functions that accept data
- Functions that return values

Remember, functions that accept data can also return values.

Simple Functions Without Parameters or Return Values

The simplest function just consists of a function name such as this:

```
func functionName () {

}
```

By inserting one or more lines of code in between the curly brackets, you can make the function do something such as:

```
func simpleFunction () {
    print ("Hello")
    print ("there")
}
```

To run the code inside a function, you just need to call that function by name such as:

```
simpleFunction()
```

To see how this function works, follow these steps:

1. Start Xcode.

2. Choose File ➤ New ➤ Playground. (If you see the Xcode welcome screen, you can also click on Get started with a playground.) Xcode asks for a playground name and platform.

3. Click in the Name text field and type **FunctionPlayground**.

4. Click in the Platform pop-up menu and choose OS X. Xcode asks where you want to save your playground file.

5. Click on a folder where you want to save your playground file and click the Create button. Xcode displays the playground file.

6. Edit the code as follows:

   ```
   import Cocoa

   func simpleFunction () {
       print ("Hello")
       print ("there")
   }

   var i = 1
   while i <= 5 {
       simpleFunction()
       i = i + 1
   }
   ```

This code defines a simple function that does nothing but print "Hello" and "there." Then it uses a loop (which you'll learn about later) that runs five times and runs or calls the simpleFunction five times as shown in Figure 6-10.

```
import Cocoa

func simpleFunction () {
    print ("Hello")                            (5 times)
    print ("there")                            (5 times)
}

var i = 1                                      1
while i <= 5 {
    simpleFunction()
    i = i + 1                                  (5 times)
}
```

Figure 6-10. Defining and calling a simple function

Without a function, the same Swift code might look like this:

```
import Cocoa

var i = 1
while i <= 5 {
    print ("Hello")
    print ("there")
        i = i + 1
}
```

While this looks simpler, the problem is if you need to reuse this code in multiple parts of a program. That means you'd need to copy and paste the same code in multiple locations. Now if you need to change the code, you'll need to make sure you change that code throughout your program. Miss one copy of your code, and your program may no longer work right.

By storing commonly used code in a function, you store it in one place but can use it in multiple parts of your program. Now if you need to change the code, you just change it in one place and those changes automatically affect multiple parts of your program where you call that function.

Simple Functions With Parameters

Simple functions without parameters can only do the same thing over and over again. Parameters let functions accept data and use that data to calculate a different result. To define a parameter, you just need to define a descriptive name and its data type, much like declaring a variable but without using the "var" keyword such as:

```
func functionName (parameter: dataType) {

}
```

To call a function that defines a parameter, you just need to type the function name followed by the correct number of parameters such as:

```
functionName (parameter)
```

When calling functions with parameters, you need to make sure you pass the correct number of parameters and each parameter is of the correct data type. So if you had a function that accepted a one string parameter like this:

```
func parameterFunction (name : String) {

}
```

You could call this parameter by its name and with one (and only one) string inside parentheses like this:

```
parameterFunction("Oscar")
```

There are three ways a function call can fail:

- If you type the function name wrong
- If you don't list or pass the correct number of parameters
- If you don't list or pass parameters of the correct data type

In this example, the parameterFunction expects one parameter that must be a String data type. If you give parameterFunction zero or two parameters, it won't work. Likewise, if you give parameterFunction one parameter but it's not a String data type, it also won't work.

To see how a function with parameters works, follow these steps:

1. Make sure your **FunctionPlayground** file is loaded in Xcode

2. Edit the code as follows:

```
import Cocoa

func parameterFunction (name : String) {
    print ("Hello, " + name)
}

parameterFunction("Oscar")
```

This Swift program calls parameterFunction and passes it one string parameter ("Oscar"). When the parameterFunction receives this parameter ("Oscar"), it stores it in its name variable. Then it prints "Hello, Oscar" as shown in Figure 6-11.

```
import Cocoa


func parameterFunction (name : String) {
    print ("Hello, " + name)                                "Hello, Oscar\n"
}


parameterFunction("Oscar")
```

Figure 6-11. *Passing a string parameter to a function*

Although this example uses one parameter, there's no limit to the number of parameters a function can accept. To accept more parameters, you would just need to define additional variable names and data types like this:

```
func functionName (parameter: dataType, parameter2 : dataType) {

}
```

Each parameter can accept different data types so you can pass a function a string and an integer such as:

```
func functionName (parameter: String, parameter2 : Int) {

}
```

To call this function, you would specify the function name and its two parameters of the proper data type:

```
functionName ("Hello", 48)
```

If you pass the parameters in the wrong order, the function call won't work such as:

```
functionName (48, "Hello")
```

When passing parameters, always make sure you pass the correct number of parameters and the proper data types in the right order as well.

Functions With Parameters That Return Values

The most versatile functions are those that use parameters to accept data and then return a value based on that data. The basic structure of a function that returns a value looks like this:

```
func functionName (parameter: ParameterDataType) -> DataType {
    return someValue
}
```

The function name is any arbitrary name you want to use. Ideally, make the function name descriptive of its purpose.

The parameter is much like declaring a variable by specifying the parameter name and its data type that it can accept. Parameters are optional but functions without parameters aren't generally useful since they perform the same tasks over and over.

The -> symbol defines the data type that the function name represents.

The return keyword must be followed by a value or commands that calculate a value. This value must be of the same data type that follows the -> symbols.

Suppose you had a function defined as follows:

```
func salesTax (amount: Double) -> Double {
    let currentTax = 0.075 // 7.5% sales tax
    return amount * currentTax
}
```

This function name is salesTax, it accepts one parameter called amount, which can store a Double data type. When it calculates a result, that result is also a Double data type as identified by Double after the -> symbol. The return keyword identifies how the function calculates a value to return.

To see how this function works, follow these steps:

1. Make sure your FunctionPlayground file is loaded in Xcode.

2. Edit the code as follows:

```
import Cocoa

func salesTax (amount: Double) -> Double {
    let currentTax = 0.075
    return amount * currentTax
}

let purchasePrice = 59.95
var total : Double
total = purchasePrice + salesTax(purchasePrice)
print ("Including sales tax, your total is =  \(total)")
```

Notice that this code calls the salesTax function by passing it the value stored in purchasePrice. When you type this code In playground, you'll see the results displayed in the right margin as shown in Figure 6-12. Try changing the values stored in purchasePrice and currentTax to see how it affects the results that this Swift code calculates.

```
import Cocoa

func salesTax (amount: Double) -> Double {              0.075
    let currentTax = 0.075                              4.49625
    return amount * currentTax
}

let purchasePrice = 59.95                               59.95
var total : Double
total = purchasePrice + salesTax(purchasePrice)         64.44625000000001
print ("Including sales tax, your total is =  \(total)")  "Including sales tax, your total is = 64.44625\n"
```

Figure 6-12. *Defining and calling a function*

When a function returns a value, make sure you specify:

- The data type the function represents (-> dataType)

- The value the function name represents (return)

When calling a function that returns a value, make sure the data types match. In the above example, the salesTax function returns a Double data type so in the Swift code, this salesTax function value gets stored in the "total" variable, which is also a Double data type.

Defining External Parameter Names

When a function uses one or more parameters to accept data, you just need to define the parameter name followed by its data type such as:

```
func storeContact (name: String, age : Int) {

}
```

To call this function, you just have to use the function name and give it a string and integer such as:

```
storeContact ("Fred", 58)
```

The problem when passing parameters is that you can only see the data you're passing but may not fully understand what it represents. To solve this problem, Swift lets you create external parameter names that force you to identify the data you're passing to a function.

One way to do this is to create an external parameter name such as:

```
func functionName (externalName internalName: dataType) {

}
```

When you define both an external and internal name for a parameter, you use the external parameter name when passing parameters to a function, but you use the internal parameter name within the function itself. To see how to use external and internal parameter names, follow these steps:

1. Make sure your FunctionPlayground file is loaded in Xcode.

2. Edit the code as follows:

```
import Cocoa

func greeting (person name : String) -> String {
    return "Hello " + name
}

var message : String
message = greeting (person: "Bob")
print (message)
```

This function has an external parameter name of "person" and an internal parameter name of "name." To call this function, you must include the external parameter name "person":

```
greeting (person: "Bob")
```

External parameter names simply make calling a function and passing parameters more understandable.

Using Variable Parameters

When a function accepts parameters, it treats that parameter like a constant. That means within the function, Swift code cannot modify that parameter. If you want to modify a parameter within a function, then you need to create a variable parameter by identifying the parameter with the "var" keyword as follows:

```
func functionName (var parameter: dataType {

}
```

To see how variable parameters work, follow these steps:

1. Make sure your FunctionPlayground file is loaded in Xcode.

2. Edit the code as follows:

```
import Cocoa

func internalChange (var name : String) {
    name = name.uppercaseString
    print ("Hello " + name)
}

internalChange ("Tasha")
```

Within the internalChange function, the name parameter changes. The first line in the internalChange function changes the name parameter into uppercase. However, any changes the internalChange function makes to the name parameter has no effect in any other part of your program. All changes stay isolated within the internalChange function.

If you want to change a parameter and have those changes take effect outside a function, then you need to use inout parameters instead.

Using Inout Parameters

There are two ways to pass data to a function. One is to pass a fixed value such as:

```
sqrt(5)
```

A second way is to pass a variable that represents a value such as:

```
var z : Double = 45.0
var answer : Double
answer = sqrt(z)
```

In this Swift code, the value of z is 45.0 and is passed to the sqrt function. No matter what the sqrt function does, the value of z still remains 45.0.

If you want a function to change the value of its parameters, you can create what's called in-out parameters. That means when you pass a variable to a function, that function changes that variable.

To define a parameter that a function can change, you just have to identify that parameter using the inout keyword such as:

```
func functionName (inout parameter: dataType) {

}
```

If a function has two or more parameters, you can designate one or more parameters as inout parameters. When you identify a parameter as an inout parameter, then the function must change that inout parameter. When you call a function and pass it an inout parameter, you must use the & symbol to identify an inout parameter such as:

```
functionName (&variable)
```

To see how inout parameters work, follow these steps:

1. Make sure your FunctionPlayground file is loaded in Xcode.

2. Edit the code as follows:

    ```
    import Cocoa

    func changeMe (inout name: String, age: Int) {
        print (name + " is \(age) years old")
        name = name.uppercaseString
    }
    ```

```
var animal : String = "Oscar the cat"
changeMe (&animal, age: 2)
print (animal)
```

The changeMe function defines two parameters:

- A string parameter called name and identified as an inout parameter

- An integer parameter called age

The changeMe function must modify the inout parameter somehow, which it does by changing the name parameter to uppercase as shown in Figure 6-13.

```
import Cocoa

func changeMe (inout name: String, age: Int) {
    print (name + " is \(age) years old")          "Oscar the cat is 2 years old\n"
    name = name.uppercaseString                     "OSCAR THE CAT"
}

var animal : String = "Oscar the cat"              "Oscar the cat"
changeMe (&animal, age: 2)                          "OSCAR THE CAT"
print (animal)                                      "OSCAR THE CAT\n"
```

Figure 6-13. Using inout parameters

Calling the changeMe function sends it a String variable called "animal," which holds the string "Oscar the cat." The changeMe function expects two parameters where the first one is an inout parameter. That means calling the changeMe function must meet the following criteria:

- The changeMe function expects two parameters, a string and an integer in that order

- Since the string parameter is an inout parameter, the first parameter must be a variable identified with the & symbol

Before calling the changeMe function, the "animal" variable contains the string "Oscar the cat." After calling the changeMe function, the "animal" variable now contains the string "OSCAR THE CAT." That's because the inout parameter in the changeMe function modified it.

Understanding IBAction Methods

If you remember in Chapter 5, you linked a button from the user interface to your Swift code to create an IBAction method, which is nothing more than a function that looks like this:

```
@IBAction func changeCase(sender: NSButton) {
    labelText.stringValue = messageText.stringValue.uppercaseString
    let warning = labelText.stringValue
}
```

Now that you understand how functions work, let's dissect this line by line. First, @IBAction identifies a function that only runs when the user does something to a user interface item. If you look at the parameter list, you'll see (sender: NSButton), which tells you that when the user clicks on a button, the changeCase function will run the Swift code enclosed within the curly brackets.

The Swift code stored in any IBAction method typically manipulates data somehow. In this case, it converts text from a text field (represented by the IBOutlet variable messageText), converts it to uppercase, and then displays that uppercase text in a label (represented by the IBOutlet variable labelText).

Since it's possible for two or more user interface items to connect to the same IBAction method, the sender parameter identifies which button the user clicked on. Since this IBAction method only connects to one button, the sender parameter is ignored.

IBAction methods are nothing more than special functions linked to items on your user interface. Within any program, you'll likely have multiple IBAction methods (functions) along with any additional functions you may have defined.

In addition, you'll likely use functions defined in the Cocoa framework even if you never see the actual code that makes those functions work. When creating any program, you'll use functions in one form or another.

Summary

The heart of any program is its ability to accept data, manipulate that data, and then return a useful result. The simplest way to manipulate numeric data is through common mathematical operators such as + (addition), - (subtraction), / (division), * (multiplication), and % (remainder). The common way to manipulate strings is through concatenation using the + operator, which combines two strings together.

As a shortcut, you can use the increment and decrement operators to add or subtract 1 from a variable. If you need to add or subtract values other than 1, you can use compound assignment operators instead.

Beyond these basic operators, you can also manipulate data through functions defined by the Cocoa framework. You don't have to know how these functions work; you just have to know they exist so you can use them in your own program by calling these function names. To find function names you can use, you may need to search through Xcode's documentation window.

While there are plenty of functions you can use from the Cocoa framework, you may need to create your own functions as well. Functions typically accept one or more parameters so they can calculate different results.

A function can represent a single value, which means you need to define the data type that the function represents.

At the simplest level, you need to define parameters with a unique name and a data type. To make parameters more understandable, you can create external parameter names, which means you need to identify the parameter name when you pass data to a function.

Normally when a function accepts a parameter, it treats that parameter like a constant that doesn't change in value. However, functions can modify parameters by creating variable parameters using the "var" keyword. Any changes a function makes to a variable parameter stays isolated within that function.

For greater flexibility, functions can also create inout parameters that can modify the value of a parameter. When a function modifies an inout parameter, those changes appear outside of that function.

By defining your own functions, you can make and create libraries of useful code that you can reuse in other parts of your program or even in other projects as well. Functions let you create specific ways to manipulate data for your particular program.

Making Decisions with Branches

After a program receives data, it needs to manipulate that data somehow to return a useful result. Simple programs manipulate data the same way, but more complicated programs need to make decisions on how to manipulate that data.

For example, a program might ask the user for a password. If the user types in a valid password, then the program gives the user access. If the user does not type in a valid password, then the program must display an error message and block access.

When a program analyzes data and makes a decision based on that data, it uses something called Boolean values and branching statements.

Boolean values represent either a true or false value. Branching statements give your program the option of choosing between two or more different sets of commands to follow. Boolean values combined with branching statements give programs the ability to respond to different data.

Understanding Comparison Operators

You can create a Boolean variable by declaring a Bool data type such as:

```
var flag : Bool
```

Bool represents a Boolean data type. Any variable defined as a Bool data type can only hold one of two values: true or false, such as:

```
flag = true
flag = false
```

While you can directly assign true and false to variables that represent Boolean data types, it's far more common to calculate Boolean values using comparison operators. Some common comparison operators are shown in Table 7-1.

Table 7-1. Common comparison operators in Swift

Comparison operator	Purpose	Example	Boolean value
==	Equal	5 == 14	false
<	Less than	5 < 14	true
>	Greater than	5 > 14	false
<=	Less than or equal to	5 <= 14	true
>=	Greater than or equal to	5 >= 14	false
!=	Not equal	5 != 14	true

Note   The equal (==) comparison operator is the only comparison operator that can also compare strings such as "Joe" == "Fred" (which evaluates to false) or "Joe" == "Joe" (which evaluates to true).

Comparison operators can compare values such as 38 == 8 or 29.04 > 12. However, using actual values with comparison operators always returns the same true or false value. What makes comparison operators more versatile is when they compare a fixed value with a variable or when they compare two variables such as:

```
let myValue = 45
myValue > 38          // Evaluates to true

let yourValue = 39
myValue < yourValue    // Evaluates to false
```

When you compare one or more variables, the results can change depending on the current value of those variables. However, when using the equal (==) comparison operator, be careful when working with decimal values. That's because 45.0 is not the same number as 45.0000001. When working with decimal values, it's best to use greater than or less than comparison operators rather than the equal comparison operator.

Understanding Logical Operators

Any comparison operator, such as 78 > 9 evaluates to a true or false value. However, Swift provides special logical operators just for working with Boolean values as shown in Table 7-2.

Table 7-2. Common logical operators in Swift

Comparison operator	Purpose
&&	And
||	Or
!	Not

Both the And (&&) and Or (||) logical operators take two Boolean values and convert them into a single Boolean value. The Not (!) logical operator takes one Boolean value and converts it to its opposite. Table 7-3 shows how the Not (!) logical operator works:

Table 7-3. The Not (!) logical operator

Example	Value
!true	false
!false	true

The And (&&) operator takes two Boolean values and calculates a single Boolean value based on Table 7-4.

Table 7-4. The And (&&) logical operator in Swift

First Boolean Value	Second Boolean Value	Result
true &&	true	true
true &&	false	false
false &&	true	false
false &&	false	false

The Or (||) operator takes two Boolean values and calculates a single Boolean value based on Table 7-5.

Table 7-5. The Or (||) logical operator in Swift

First Boolean Value	Second Boolean Value	Result
true ||	true	true
true ||	false	true
false ||	true	true
false ||	false	false

To see how Boolean values work with comparison and logical operators, create a new playground by following these steps:

1.   Start Xcode.

2.   Choose File ➤ New ➤ Playground. (If you see the Xcode welcome screen, you can also click on Get started with a playground.) Xcode asks for a playground name and platform.

3.   Click in the Name text field and type **BooleanPlayground**.

4.   Click in the Platform pop-up menu and choose OS X. Xcode asks where you want to save your playground file.

5.   Click on a folder where you want to save your playground file and click the Create button. Xcode displays the playground file.

6.   Edit the code as follows:

```
import Cocoa

var x, y, z : Int

x = 35
y = 120
z = -48

x == y
x < y
x > z
y != z
z > -48

// And && operator

(y != z) && (x > z)
(y != z) && (x == y)
(x == y) && (x < y)
(z > -48) && (x == y)

// Or || operator

(y != z) || (x > z)
(y != z) || (x == y)
(x == y) || (x < y)
(z > -48) || (x == y)
```

Notice how the comparison operators evaluate to true or false and how the logical operators (And and Or) take two Boolean values and return a single true or false value as shown in Figure 7-1.

```
var x, y, z : Int                                         35

x = 35                                                    35
y = 120                                                   120
z = -48                                                   -48

x == y                                                    false
x < y                                                     true
x > z                                                     true
y != z                                                    true
z > -48                                                   false


// And && operator

(y != z) && (x > z)                                       true
(y != z) && (x == y)                                      false
(x == y) && (x < y)                                       false
(z > -48) && (x == y)                                     false


// Or || operator

(y != z) || (x > z)                                       true
(y != z) || (x == y)                                      true
(x == y) || (x < y)                                       true
(z > -48)|| (x == y)                                      false
```

Figure 7-1. *Evaluating Boolean values with comparison and logical operators*

Ultimately every Boolean value must be:

- A true or false value

- A comparison of two values that is true or false

- A combination of Boolean values using logical operators that evaluate to true or false

The if Statement

Boolean values are crucial for letting programs make choices. If someone types in a password, a program checks to see if the password is valid. If true (the password is valid), then the program grants access. If false (the password is not valid), then the program blocks access.

To decide what to do next, every program needs to evaluate a Boolean value. Only then can it decide what to do next based on the value of that Boolean value.

The simplest type of branching statement in Swift is an if statement, which looks like this:

```
if BooleanValue == true {

}
```

To simplify this if statement, you can eliminate the "== true" portion so the if statement looks like this:

```
if BooleanValue {

}
```

This shortened version says, "If the BooleanValue is true, then run the code inside the curly brackets. If the BooleanValue is false, then skip all the code inside the curly brackets without running it."

To see how Boolean values work with an if statement, follow these steps:

1. Make sure the BooleanPlayground file is loaded in Xcode.

2. Edit the code as follows:

    ```
    import Cocoa

    var BooleanValue : Bool = true

    if BooleanValue {
        print ("The BooleanValue is true")
    }
    ```

Figure 7-2 shows the results of the if statement running. Change the value of BooleanValue to false and you'll see that the if statement no longer prints the string "The BooleanValue is true."

```
import Cocoa

var BooleanValue : Bool = true                          true

if BooleanValue {
    print ("The BooleanValue is true")                  "The BooleanValue is true\n"
}
```

Figure 7-2. Running an if statement

The if-else Statement

The if statement either runs code or it runs nothing. If you want to run code if a Boolean value is false, you could write two separate if statements as follows:

```
if BooleanValue {

}

if !BooleanValue {

}
```

The first if statement runs if the BooleanValue is true. If not, then it does nothing.

The second if statement runs if the BooleanValue is false. If not, then it does nothing.

The problem with writing two separate if statements is that the logic of your program isn't as clear. To fix this problem, Swift offers an if-else statement that looks like this:

```
if BooleanValue {
    // First set of code to run if true
} else {
    // Second set of code to run if false
}
```

An if-else statement offers exactly two different branches to follow. If a Boolean value is true, then the first set of code runs. If a Boolean is false, then the second set of code runs. At no time is it possible for both sets of code to run in an if-else statement.

To see how Boolean values work with an if-else statement, follow these steps:

1. Make sure the BooleanPlayground file is loaded in Xcode.

2. Edit the code as follows:

   ```
   import Cocoa

   var BooleanValue : Bool = true

   if BooleanValue {
       print ("The BooleanValue is true")
   } else {
       print ("The BooleanValue is false")
   }
   ```

Figure 7-3 shows how the if-else statement works when the BooleanValue is true. Change the BooleanValue to false and see how the if-else statement now runs the second set of code.

```
import Cocoa

var BooleanValue : Bool = true                                    true

if BooleanValue {
    print ("The BooleanValue is true")                "The BooleanValue is true\n"
} else {
    print ("The BooleanValue is false")
}
```

Figure 7-3. Running an if-else statement

The if-else if Statement

An if statement either runs one set of code or it runs nothing. An if-else statement always runs one set of code or a second set of code. However, what if you want a choice of running two or more possible sets of code? In that case, you need to use an if-else if statement.

Like an if statement, an if-else if statement may not run any code at all. The simplest if-else if statement looks like this:

```
if BooleanValue {
    // First set of code to run if true
} else if BooleanValue2 {
    // Second set of code to run if true
}
```

With an if-else if statement, a Boolean value must be true to run code. If no Boolean value is true, then it's possible that no code will run at all. An if-else if statement is equivalent to multiple if statements like this:

```
if BooleanValue {
    // First set of code to run if true
}

if BooleanValue2 {
    // Second set of code to run if true
}
```

With an if-else if statement, you can check for as many Boolean values as you want such as:

```
if BooleanValue {
    // First set of code to run if true
} else if BooleanValue2 {
    // Second set of code to run if true
} else if BooleanValue3 {
    // Third set of code to run if true
} else if BooleanValue4 {
    // Fourth set of code to run if true
} else if BooleanValue5 {
    // Fifth set of code to run if true
}
```

As soon as the if-else if statement finds one Boolean value is true, then it runs the accompanying code trapped within curly brackets. However, it's possible that no Boolean value will be true, in which case no code inside the if-else if statement will run.

If you want to ensure that at least one set of code will run, then you need to add a final else clause to the end of an if-else if statement such as:

```
if BooleanValue {
    // First set of code to run if true
} else if BooleanValue2 {
    // Second set of code to run if true
} else if BooleanValue3 {
    // Third set of code to run if true
} else if BooleanValue4 {
    // Fourth set of code to run if true
} else if BooleanValue5 {
    // Fifth set of code to run if true
} else {
    // This code runs if every other Boolean value is false
}
```

To see how Boolean values work with an if-else statement, follow these steps:

1. Make sure the BooleanPlayground file is loaded in Xcode.

2. Edit the code as follows:

    ```
    import Cocoa

    var BooleanValue : Bool = false
    var BooleanValue2 : Bool = false
    var BooleanValue3 : Bool = false

    if BooleanValue {
        print ("BooleanValue is true")
    } else if BooleanValue2 {
        print ("BooleanValue2 is true")
    } else if BooleanValue3 {
        print ("BooleanValue3 is true")
    } else {
        print ("This prints if everything else is false")
    }
    ```

Notice that because every Boolean value is false, the only code that runs occurs in the final else portion of the if-else if statement as shown in Figure 7-4.

```
import Cocoa

var BooleanValue : Bool = false                              false
var BooleanValue2 : Bool = false                             false
var BooleanValue3 : Bool = false                             false

if BooleanValue {
    print ("BooleanValue is true")
} else if BooleanValue2 {
    print ("BooleanValue2 is true")
} else if BooleanValue3 {
    print ("BooleanValue3 is true")
} else {
    print ("This prints if everything else is false")       "This prints if everything else is false\n"
}
```

Figure 7-4. *Running an if-else if statement with multiple Boolean values*

If you change different Boolean values to true, you can see how the if-else if statement behaves differently by running a different set of code.

With an if-else if statement:

- It's possible that no code will run unless the last part is just a regular else statement

- The program can choose between two or more sets of code

- The number of possible options is not limited to just two options like an if-else statement

Since an if-else if statement checks multiple Boolean values, what happens if two or more Boolean values are true? In that case, the if-else if statement only runs the set of code associated with the first true Boolean value and ignores all the rest of the code as shown in Figure 7-5.

```
import Cocoa

var BooleanValue : Bool = true                               true
var BooleanValue2 : Bool = true                              true
var BooleanValue3 : Bool = true                              true

if BooleanValue {
    print ("BooleanValue is true")                           "BooleanValue is true\n"
} else if BooleanValue2 {
    print ("BooleanValue2 is true")
} else if BooleanValue3 {
    print ("BooleanValue3 is true")
} else {
    print ("This prints if everything else is false")
}
```

Figure 7-5. *Running an if-else if statement with multiple true Boolean values*

The switch Statement

An if-else if statement lets you create two or more sets of code that can possibly run. Unfortunately, an if-else if statement can be hard to understand when there's too many Boolean values to check. To fix this problem, Swift offers a switch statement.

A switch statement works much like an if-else if statement except that it's easier to read and write. The main difference is that instead of checking multiple Boolean values, a switch statement checks the value of a single variable. Based on the value of this single variable, the switch statement can choose to run different sets of code.

A typical switch statement looks like this:

```
switch value/variable/expression {
    case value1: // First set of code to run if variable = value1
    case value2: // Second set of code to run if variable = value2
    case value3: // Third set of code to run if variable = value3
    default: // Fourth set of code to run if nothing else runs
}
```

A switch statement starts by examining a fixed value (such as 38 or "Bob"), a variable that represents data), or an expression (such as 3 * age where "age" is a variable). Ultimately, the switch statement needs to identify a single value and match that value to the first "case" statement it finds. The moment it finds an exact match, it runs one or more lines of code associated with that "case" statement.

To see how Boolean values work with a case statement, follow these steps:

1. Make sure the BooleanPlayground file is loaded in Xcode.

2. Edit the code as follows:

```
import Cocoa

var whatNumber : Int = 3

switch whatNumber {
    case 1: print ("The number is 1")
    case 2: print ("The number is 2")
    case 3: print ("The number is 3")
        print ("Isn't this amazing?")
    case 4: print ("The number is 4")
    case 5: print ("The number is 5")
    default: print ("The number is undefined")
}
```

Because the value of the "whatNumber" variable is 3, the switch statement matches it with "case 3:" and then runs the Swift code that appears after the colon as shown in Figure 7-6. Note that you can store multiple lines of code after the colon and do not need to enclose the code within curly brackets. Change the value of the whatNumber variable to see how it affects the behavior of the switch statement.

```
import Cocoa

var whatNumber : Int = 3                                              3

switch whatNumber {
    case 1: print ("The number is 1")
    case 2: print ("The number is 2")
    case 3: print ("The number is 3")                          "The number is 3\n"
            print ("Isn't this amazing?")                      "Isn't this amazing?\n"
    case 4: print ("The number is 4")
    case 5: print ("The number is 5")
    default: print ("The number is undefined")
}
```

Figure 7-6. Running a switch statement

> **Note**   Unlike other programming languages such as Objective-C, you do not need to use a break
> command to separate code stored in different "case" statements of the switch statement.

The above switch statement is equivalent to:

```
if whatNumber == 1 {
    print ("The number is 1")
} else if whatNumber == 2 {
    print ("The number is 2")
} else if whatNumber == 3 {
    print ("The number is 3")
    print ("Isn't this amazing?")
} else if whatNumber == 4 {
    print ("The number is 4")
} else if whatNumber == 5 {
    print ("The number is 5")
} else {
    print ("The number is undefined")
}
```

As you can see, the switch statement is cleaner and simpler to read and understand.

When creating a switch statement, you must handle all possibilities. In the above switch statement, the whatNumber variable can be any integer, so the switch statement can explicitly handle any value from 1 to 5. If the value does not fall within this 1 to 5 range, then the default portion of the switch statement handles any other value. If you fail to include a default, then Xcode will flag your switch statement as a possible error. (One exception to this rule is if you use a switch statement with an enum structure, which you'll learn about later in this chapter.) This is to protect your code from possibly crashing if the switch statement receives data it doesn't know how to handle.

This example of a switch statement tries to match a value/variable/expression with exactly one value. However, a switch statement can try matching more than one value. There are three ways a switch statement can check a range of values:

- Explicitly list all possible values, separated by a comma

- Define the starting and ending range of numbers separated by three dots (…)

- Define the starting number and the ending range with two dots and a less than sign (..<)

When a case statement lists all values separated by commas, its code will run only if the switch value/variable/expression exactly matches one of those values. For example, consider the following case statement:

```
switch whatNumber {
    case 1, 2, 3: print ("The number is 1, 2, or 3")
    default: print ("The number is undefined")
}
```

Only if the value of whatNumber is 1, 2, or 3 will its code print "The number is 1, 2, or 3."

Explicitly listing all possible values may be fine for a handful of numbers, but for multiple numbers, it can get tedious to write every possible number. As a shortcut, Swift lets you specify a range. If you wanted to match a number between 4 and 20, the case portion of the switch statement might look like this:

```
switch whatNumber {
      case 4...20: print ("The number is between 4 and 20")
      default: print ("The number is undefined")
}
```

In this case, whatNumber could be 4, 20, or any number in between. The three dots signify a range that includes the starting and ending number of the range (4 and 20).

Swift can also check a half range that consists of two dots and a less than symbol such as:

```
switch whatNumber {
      case 20..<49: print ("The number is between 20 and 48")
      default: print ("The number is undefined")
}
```

This 20..<49 half range matches only if whatNumber is 20, 48, or any number in between. Notice that if whatNumber is 49, it will not match the half range but if whatNumber is 20, then it will match.

To see how all three variations of multiple values works, follow these steps:

1. Make sure the BooleanPlayground file is loaded in Xcode.

2. Edit the code as follows:

```
import Cocoa

var whatNumber : Int = 49

switch whatNumber {
    case 1, 2, 3: print ("The number is 1")
        print ("Isn't this amazing?")
    case 4...20: print ("The number is between 4 and 20")
    case 20..<49: print ("The number is between 20 and 48")
    default: print ("The number is undefined")
}
```

When the value is 49, the switch statement matches nothing so it uses the default portion of the switch statement as shown in Figure 7-7.

```
import Cocoa

var whatNumber : Int = 49                                          49

switch whatNumber {
    case 1, 2, 3: print ("The number is 1")
                  print ("Isn't this amazing?")
    case 4...20: print ("The number is between 4 and 20")
    case 20..<49: print ("The number is between 20 and
        48")
    default: print ("The number is undefined")         "The number is undefined\n"
}
```

Figure 7-7. Running a switch statement that checks for multiple values

Change the value of the whatNumber variable to 2, 12, and 48 to see how the switch statement matches different values.

Using the switch Statement with enum Data Structures

The switch statement is often used to check for specific values such as strings or numbers. However, one common use for switch statements is to work with a data structure called enum (which is short for "enumeration"). An enum data structure lets you create a list of different data with descriptive names such as:

```
enum dog {
    case poodle
    case collie
    case terrier
    case mutt
}
```

The above enum data structure creates a data type called "dog" that can only hold one of four values: poodle, collie, terrier, or mutt. To use an enum data structure, you need to create a variable or a constant such as:

```
var myPet = dog.collie
```

The above code defines a variable called "myPet" and assigns it a value of dog.collie. If you wanted to check the value of the mYpet variable, you could use a switch statement like this:

```
switch myPet {
case .poodle:
    print ("Poodle")
case .collie:
    print ("Collie")
case .terrier:
    print ("Terrier")
case .mutt:
    print ("Mutt")
}
```

To see how the switch statement works with the enum data structure, follow these steps:

1. Make sure the BooleanPlayground file is loaded in Xcode.

2. Edit the code as follows:

    ```
    import Cocoa

    enum dog {
        case poodle
        case collie
        case terrier
        case mutt
    }

    var myPet = dog.collie

    switch myPet {
    case .poodle:
        print ("Poodle")
    case .collie:
        print ("Collie")
    case .terrier:
        print ("Terrier")
    case .mutt:
        print ("Mutt")
    }
    ```

The switch statement only looks to see which possible value, specified by the enum data structure, that the myPet variable holds. Since the value is .collie, the switch statement prints "Collie" as shown in Figure 7-8.

```
import Cocoa

enum dog {
    case poodle
    case collie
    case terrier
    case mutt
}

var myPet = dog.collie                                    .collie

switch myPet {
case .poodle:
    print ("Poodle")
case .collie:
    print ("Collie")                                      "Collie\n"
case .terrier:
    print ("Terrier")
case .mutt:
    print ("Mutt")
}
```

Figure 7-8. *Running a switch statement that checks for multiple values*

Making Decisions in an OS X Program

Using playground files to test out Swift code can be fun and simple because it lets you focus solely on learning how Swift works without the interference of other parts of writing a program. However, eventually you'll need to see how Swift code works outside of your playground file.

In this sample program, the user needs to type an employee ID number and password. The employee ID number must fall within a range of 100 to 150 to be valid. The password must exactly match the string "password" (which isn't a very secure password).

That means we'll be using two comparison operators to check if the name and password are valid. Then we'll use a logical operator to make sure that both are valid.

Create a new OS X project by following these steps:

1. From within Xcode choose File ➤ New ➤ Project.

2. Click Application under the OS X category.

3. Click Cocoa Application and click the Next button. Xcode now asks for a product name.

4. Click in the Product Name text field and type **BranchingProgram**.

5. Make sure the Language pop-up menu displays Swift and that no check boxes are selected.

6. Click the Next button. Xcode asks where you want to store the project.

7. Choose a folder to store your project and click the Create button.

8. Click the MainMenu.xib file in the Project Navigator.

9. Click on the BranchingProgram icon to make the window of the user interface appear as shown in Figure 7-9.

Figure 7-9. Making the window of the user interface visible

10. Choose View ➤ utilities ➤ Show Object Library to make the Object Library appear in the bottom right corner of the Xcode window.

11. Drag two Labels, two Text Fields, and a Push Button on the user interface so it looks similar to Figure 7-10.

Figure 7-10. Creating a basic user interface with labels, text fields, and a push button

12. Click on the top label to select it. Then choose View ➤ Utilities ➤ Show Attributes Inspector. The Attributes Inspector pane appears in the upper right corner of the Xcode window as shown in Figure 7-11.

Figure 7-11. *The Attributes Inspector pane for a label*

13. Click in the Title text field and replace "Label" with "ID." Press Return. Notice that the top label now displays the text "ID." When you change a label's Title property, you change the text that appears on that label. Let's see a second and faster way to change the text on a label.

14. Double-click on the second label. Xcode highlights your chosen label as shown in Figure 7-12.

Figure 7-12. Double-clicking on a label lets you change the text without using the Attributes Inspector pane

15. Type **Password** and press Return. Notice that the second label now displays Password. By double-clicking on a label, you can change text on that label without opening the Attributes Inspector pane.

16. Click on the top text field and choose View ➤ Utilities ➤ Show Size Inspector. The Size Inspector pane appears in the upper right corner of the Xcode window as shown in Figure 7-13.

Figure 7-13. The Size Inspector pane

17. Click in the Width text field and type **250**. Then press Return. Xcode expands with width of the text field.

18. Click on the second text field so handles appear around it. Now drag the far right handle to the right until it aligns with the top text field as shown in Figure 7-14.

Figure 7-14. Aligning a text field using the mouse

19. Release the mouse button. Just as you can modify text on a label by using either the Attributes Inspector pane or double-clicking directly on that label, so can you modify the size of an item through the Size Inspector pane or by resizing that item with the mouse.

20. Double-click on the Push Button to select it and type **Check Password**. Then press Return. Your completed interface should look similar to Figure 7-15.

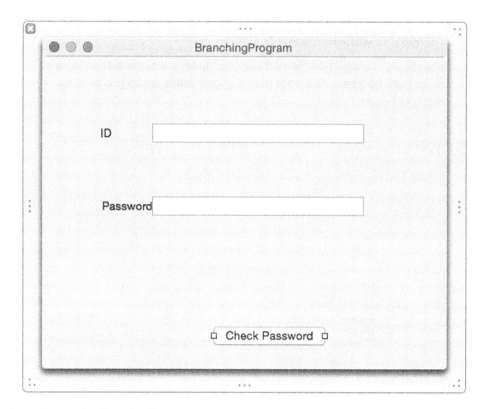

Figure 7-15. The completed user interface

With this user interface, the user will type an ID (an integer) into the ID text field, a password (string) in the Password text field, and then click the Check Password button to see if the ID and password are valid. Once we have a user interface, the next step is to connect the user interface to Swift code using IBOutlets and IBAction methods.

Remember, IBOutlets let you retrieve or display information to a user interface. IBAction methods let the user interface make your program do something.

In this example, we'll need two IBOutlet variables to connect to each text field so we can retrieve the data the user types in. Then we'll need one IBAction method to connect to the Check Password button. That way when the user clicks on the Change Password button, the IBAction method can verify the ID and password.

To connect Swift code to your user interface, follow these steps:

1. With your user interface still visible in the Xcode window, choose View ➤ Assistant Editor ➤ Show Assistant Editor. The AppDelegate. swift file appears next to the user interface as shown in Figure 7-16.

Figure 7-16. The Assistant editor displays the user interface next to the AppDelegate.swift file

2. Move the mouse over the top text field, hold down the Control key, and drag from the top text field to underneath the existing @IBOutlet line in the AppDelegate.swift file as shown in Figure 7-17.

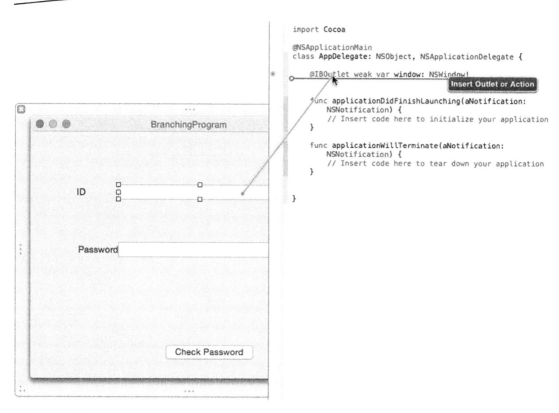

Figure 7-17. *Control-dragging from the top text field to the AppDelegate.swift file*

3. Release the mouse and the Control key. A pop-up window appears as shown in Figure 7-18.

Figure 7-18. *The pop-up window for defining an IBOutlet*

4. Click in the Name text field and type **IDfield** and click the Connect button. Xcode creates an IBOutlet.

5. Move the mouse over the bottom text field, hold down the Control key, and drag the mouse underneath the @IBOutlet line in the AppDelegate.swift file.

6. Release the mouse and the Control key. A pop-up window appears.

7. Click in the Name text field and type **Passwordfield** and click the
    Connect button. Xcode creates another IBOutlet. You should now
    have two IBOutlets that represent the two text fields on your user
    interface:

    ```
    @IBOutlet weak var IDfield: NSTextField!
    @IBOutlet weak var Passwordfield: NSTextField!
    ```

8. Move the mouse over the Check Password push button, hold down
    the Control key, and drag the mouse above the last curly bracket in
    the AppDelegate.swift file as shown in Figure 7-19.

Figure 7-19. *Control-dragging from the push button to the AppDelegate.swift file*

9. Release the mouse and the Control key. A pop-up window appears.

10. Click in the Connection pop-up menu and choose Action to create
    an IBAction method.

11. Click in the Name text field and type **checkPassword**.

12. Click in the Type pop-up menu and choose NSButton as shown in
    Figure 7-20.

Figure 7-20. Defining an IBAction method

13.   Click the Connect button. Xcode creates a blank IBAction method.

14.   Modify the IBAction checkPassword method as follows:

```
@IBAction func checkPassword(sender: NSButton) {
    let validPassword = "password"
    var ID : Int
    ID = IDfield.integerValue
    var myAlert = NSAlert()
    switch ID {
    case 100...150: if (Passwordfield.stringValue == validPassword) {
        myAlert.messageText = "Access granted"
    } else {
        myAlert.messageText = "No access"
        }
    default:
        myAlert.messageText = "No access"
    }
    myAlert.runModal()
}
```

This IBAction method uses a switch statement to check if the user typed an ID that falls within the 100…150 range. If so, then it checks if the user typed "password" in the Password text field. If this is also true, then the switch statement displays "Access granted" in an Alert dialog. If the ID does not fall within the 100…150 range or the Password text field does not contain "password," then the Alert dialog displays "No access."

> **Note**   You may be wondering where stringValue and integerValue came from in the above code. If you look at your IBOutlets, you'll see that each text field IBOutlet is based on the NSTextField class. Look up NSTextField in Xcode's documentation, and you'll see that NSTextField is based on the NSControl class. The NSControl class contains properties such as stringValue and integerValue so that means anything based on NSTextField (such as the IBOutlets that represent the text fields on your user interface) can also use these stringValue and integerValue properties.

15. Choose Product ➤ Run. Xcode runs your BranchingProgram project.

16. Click in the ID text field of your BranchingProgram user interface and type **120**.

17. Click in the Password text field of your BranchingProgram user interface and type **password**.

18. Click the Check Password push button. An Alert dialog appears as shown in Figure 7-21.

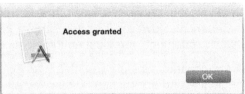

Figure 7-21. *Displaying an Alert dialog*

19. Click the OK button in the Alert dialog to make it go away.

20. Click in the ID text field of your BranchingProgram user interface and type **1**.

21. Click the Check Password push button. Notice that now the Alert dialog displays "No access."

22. Click the OK button in the Alert dialog to make it go away.

23. Choose BranchingProgram ➤ Quit BranchingProgram.

Summary

To respond intelligently to the user, every program needs a way to make decisions. The first step to making a decision is to define a Boolean value, which is either true or false. Boolean values can be calculated through comparison operators or logical operators.

Once you can determine a Boolean value, then you can use that Boolean value to decide which code to follow in a branching statement. The simplest branch is an if statement that either runs a set of code or does nothing at all.

Another branch is the if-else statement, which offers exactly two sets of code to run. If a Boolean value is true, then the first set of code runs. Otherwise the second set of code runs.

If you want to choose between three or more sets of code to run, you can use an if-else if statement. However, it's often simpler to use a switch statement instead. When using a switch statement, you must anticipate all possible values.

A switch statement lets you match an exact value, a range of values (that includes the beginning and ending numbers), or a half range of values (which only includes the beginning number but not the end).

Branching statements combined with Boolean values gives your program the ability to make decisions and run different code based on the data it receives. Branching statements essentially let your program respond intelligently to outside data.

Repeating Code with Loops

The basic goal of programming is to write as little code as possible that does as much as possible. The less code you write, the easier the program will be to understand and modify later. The more your code does, the more powerful your program will be.

One way to write less code is to reuse code stored in functions. A second way to reuse code is through loops. A loop runs one or more lines of code multiple times, thereby eliminating the need to write multiple, redundant lines of code.

For example, if you wanted to print a message five times, you could write the following:

```
print ("Hello")
print ("Hello")
print ("Hello")
print ("Hello")
print ("Hello")
```

This is tedious but it will work. However, if you suddenly decide you need to print a message one thousand times, now you'd have to write that command one thousand times. Not only is typing the same command tedious, but it increases the chance of making a mistake in one of those commands.

A far simpler method is to use a loop. A loop lets you write one or more commands once and then run those commands as many times as you want such as:

```
var counter : Int = 1
while counter <= 5 {
    print ("Hello")
    counter++
}
```

The above loop runs five times and prints "Hello" five times. If we wanted to print "Hello" one thousand times, we could just replace the number 5 with the number 1000. Loops make code easier to write and modify while doing more work at the same time.

The while Loop

The simplest loop in Swift is called the while loop, which looks like this:

```
while BooleanValue {

}
```

Before the while loop does anything, it first checks if a Boolean value is true or false. If it's true, then it runs the code inside its curly brackets once. Then it checks its Boolean value again to see if it's changed to false or if it's still true. The moment this Boolean value becomes false, the while loop stops.

Because the while loop checks a Boolean value before doing anything, it's possible that the while loop may never run any of its code. More importantly, the while loop only runs if its Boolean value is true. That means somewhere inside the while loop's curly brackets, there must be code that eventually changes this Boolean value to false.

If a while loop fails to change its Boolean value from true to false, then the loop will run forever, which is known as an endless loop. An endless loop may crash or freeze your program so it no longer responds to the user or works.

At the simplest level, a while loop's Boolean value can just be true or false such as:

```
while true {

}
```

More commonly, while loops use comparison operators to determine a Boolean value such as:

```
while counter <= 5 {

}
```

As long as "counter <=5" remains true, the while loop will run. The moment "counter <= 5" is no longer true, the while loop will stop.

When using while loops, you need to define the Boolean value before the loop begins (to make sure it's either true or false), and then you must change the Boolean value somewhere inside the while loop (to make sure the while loop eventually stops).

To see how Boolean values work with a while loop, create a new playground by following these steps:

1. Start Xcode.

2. Choose File ➤ New ➤ Playground. (If you see the Xcode welcome screen, you can also click on Get started with a playground.) Xcode asks for a playground name and platform.

3. Click in the Name text field and type **LoopingPlayground**.

4. Click in the Platform pop-up menu and choose OS X. Xcode asks where you want to save your playground file.

5. Click on a folder where you want to save your playground file and click the Create button. Xcode displays the playground file.

6. Edit the code as follows:

```
import Cocoa

var counter = 1

while counter <= 10 {
    print ("Hello")
    counter++
}
```

Note that the "var counter : Int = 1" line defines the variable that the while loop uses to determine a Boolean value (true or false). Also note the "counter++" line inside the while loop. This constantly changes the variable used by the while loop to determine when to stop. By changing the Boolean comparison (counter <=10), you can change how many times the while loop runs as shown in Figure 8-1.

```
import Cocoa

var counter = 1                        1

while counter <= 10 {
    print ("Hello")                    (10 times)
    counter++                          (10 times)
}
```

Figure 8-1. Running a while loop in a playground

When using a while loop, keep in mind the following:

▪ Before the while loop, make sure to define any variables used by the while loop's Boolean value

▪ A while loop may run zero or more times

▪ Inside the while loop, make sure the Boolean value used by the while loop can change to false eventually to avoid creating an endless loop

The repeat-while Loop

As an alternative to the while loop, Swift also offers a repeat-while loop that works almost the same. The only difference is that instead of checking a Boolean value before running, the repeat-while loop checks its Boolean value after it runs.

That means the do-while loop will always run at least once. The structure of a do-while loop looks like this:

```
repeat {

} while BooleanValue
```

Like the while loop, the repeat-while loop also needs code inside its loop that can change its Boolean value from true to false, and it also needs code before the repeat-while loop to initialize any variables that are used to calculate the repeat-while loop's Boolean value.

To see how Boolean values work with a repeat-while loop, follow these steps:

1. Make sure the LoopingPlayground file is loaded in Xcode.

2. Edit the code as follows:

    ```
    import Cocoa

    var counter = 1
    repeat {
        print ("Goodbye")
        counter++
    } while counter <= 10
    ```

Notice that the Boolean value (counter <= 10) determines how many times the do-while loop runs as shown in Figure 8-2. Also note that "counter++" is equivalent to "counter = counter + 1".

```
import Cocoa

var counter = 1                                           1

repeat {
    print ("Goodbye")                            (10 times)
    counter++                                    (10 times)
} while counter <= 10
```

Figure 8-2. *Running a repeat-while in a playground*

Remember, the main difference between the while loop and the repeat-while loop is that the repeat-while loop always runs at least once while the while loop can run zero times.

The for Loop That Counts

Depending on the Boolean value, both the while and repeat-while loop can run multiple times. If your code counts like the previous while and repeat-while loop examples did, then you can specify how many times the loop repeats. However, a while or repeat-while loop could possibly run a different number of times depending in its Boolean value.

For example, a while or repeat-while loop might ask a user to type in a password. If the password is invalid, the loop will ask for a valid password again. Since you never know how many times a user might need to try until typing a correct password, you have no idea beforehand how many times a while or repeat-while loop will run.

That's the purpose of the for loop: to run a fixed number of times. With a for loop you need to define the following:

- A counting variable
- The initial value of the counting variable
- The ending value of the counting variable often defined by a comparison operator
- The increment/decrement value for counting up or down

The structure of the for loop looks like this:

```
for var startingValue; BooleanValue; incrementValue {

}
```

The startingValue needs to define a variable name for counting and an initial value such as I = 1.

The BooleanValue needs to evaluate to a true or false value that uses the variable used for counting, often using a comparison operator.

The incrementValue defines how to count. Counting usually occurs by adding 1, but you can count by larger increments such as by 5 or 10, or even by negative numbers to count backwards. Counting typically uses the increment/decrement operators (such as i++) or the compound assignment operator (such as i += 15).

A typical for loop might look like this:

```
for var i = 1; i <= 10; i++ {

}
```

In this for loop example, the starting value defines a variable called "i" and sets its initial value to 1.

Then the Boolean value is defined by "i <= 10" that uses the counting variable "i".

The increment value is "i++," which simply adds 1 to the value of the "i" variable.

Now this for loop starts counting at 1, keeps repeating the loop and adding 1 to the "i" variable, and stops only when the Boolean value "i <= 10" is no longer true, which occurs when the "i" variable equals 11.

To see how Boolean values work with a for loop, follow these steps:

1. Make sure the LoopingPlayground file is loaded in Xcode.

2. Edit the code as follows:

```
import Cocoa

for var i = 1; i <= 10; i++ {
    print ("Greetings")
}

for var i = 21; i <= 120; i += 10 {
    print ("Greetings")
}
```

Notice that in the second for loop, the initial starting value is not 1 and the increment counter does not add by 1. Yet it still produces the exact same result as the first for loop. You can get as creative as you want with your for loops in choosing a starting value, a Boolean value to stop the loop, and an increment counter. However, it's best to keep for loops as simple as possible so they'll be easy to understand and modify. Figure 8-3 shows the results of the two for loops running.

```
import Cocoa

var counter = 1                             1

for var i = 1; i <= 10; i++ {
    print ("Greetings")                     (10 times)
}

for var i = 21; i <= 120; i += 10 {
    print ("Greetings")                     (10 times)
}
```

Figure 8-3. *Running two identical for loops*

The for-in Statement

A for loop always runs a fixed number of times based on its starting value, its Boolean value, and its increment counter. However, you must specify the Boolean value to make the for loop eventually stop.

Since you may not always know when a for loop should stop based on different data, Swift also offers a for-in loop. The main advantage is that the for-in loop automatically knows how to count so you don't have to specify when to stop.

The structure of a for-in loop looks like this:

```
for countingVariable in listOfItems {

}
```

The countingVariable counts each item in a list of some kind. That list can be a string or an array (which you'll learn about later). The main idea is that a for-in loop automatically knows how to count how many items are in a list.

For example, if you wanted to run a for loop a fixed number of times based on the length of a string, you could do the following:

```
let name = "Oscar"
var nameLength = count(name)

for var i = 0; i < nameLength; i++ {
    print ("Hello")
}
```

In this example, "name" holds the five-character string "Oscar." The "nameLength" variable counts the number of characters in the "name" variable (which is 5). Now the for loop uses the length of the "Oscar" string (5) to determine how many times to run the for loop.

Here's how the equivalent for-in loop looks:

```
for name in "Oscar" {
    print ("Hello")
}
```

Notice how much simpler the for-in loop looks. This for-in loop keeps running based on the number of characters stored in the "Oscar" string, which is 5. Since the for-in loop can automatically count by itself, it reduces the amount of code you need to write while increasing accuracy at the same time.

The for-in loop is especially handy for working with arrays (which you'll learn about later). To see how for-in loops can work, follow these steps:

1. Make sure the LoopingPlayground file is loaded in Xcode.

2. Edit the code as follows:

    ```
    import Cocoa

    let names = ["Oscar", "Sally", "Marty", "Louis"]
    for person in names {
        print (person)
    }
    ```

Figure 8-4 shows how the for-in loop runs four times because the "names" array contains four items. If you add or subtract a name from this array, the for-in loop automatically counts the new number of items in the array.

```
import Cocoa

let names = ["Oscar", "Sally", "Marty", "Louis"]          ["Oscar", "Sally", "Marty", "Louis"]

for person in names {                                       (4 times)
    print (person)
}
```

Figure 8-4. Counting with a for-in loop

Exiting Loops Prematurely

Normally loops run until a Boolean value changes. However, you can prematurely exit out of a loop by using the break command. Normally this loop would run four times:

```
let names = ["Oscar", "Sally", "Marty", "Louis"]
for person in names {
    print (person)
}
```

If you inserted a break command, you could make this loop exit after running only once like this:

```
let names = ["Oscar", "Sally", "Marty", "Louis"]
for person in names {
    print (person)
    break
}
```

This for-in loop would run once, print the name "Oscar," hit the break command, and exit out of the for-in loop. Of course it's rather pointless to put a break command inside a for-in loop to stop it prematurely all the time, so it's more common to use the break command with a branching statement. That way if a certain Boolean value is true, the loop exits prematurely. Otherwise the loop keeps running.

To see how to exit out of the loop prematurely, follow these steps:

1. Make sure the LoopingPlayground file is loaded in Xcode.

2. Edit the code as follows:

   ```
   import Cocoa

   let employees = ["Fred", "Jane", "Sam", "Kelly"]
   for person in employees {
       if person == "Sam" {
           print (person)
           break
       }
       print (person)
   }
   ```

This for-in loop would normally run four times because the "employees" array contains four names. However, as soon as the for-in loop finds the name "Sam," it prints that name, hits the break command, and prematurely exits out of the for-in loop so it only runs twice as shown in Figure 8-5.

```
import Cocoa

let employees = ["Fred", "Jane", "Sam", "Kelly"]          ["Fred", "Jane", "Sam", "Kelly"]

for person in employees {
    if person == "Sam" {
        print (person)                                     "Sam\n"
        break
    }
    print (person)                                         (2 times)
}
```

Figure 8-5. Using the break command to exit out of a loop prematurely

Using Loops in an OS X Program

In this sample program, the computer picks a random number between 1 and 10. Now the user must guess that number as the computer To keep the user from guessing a number outside the range of 1 and 10, the user interface will let the user choose a value from a slider.

Each time the user guesses incorrectly, a label will display a message that the guess is too high or too low. When the user correctly guesses the number, a loop will print a list of each guess and display it in an alert dialog.

Create a new OS X project by following these steps:

1. From within Xcode choose File ➤ New ➤ Project.

2. Click Application under the OS X category.

3. Click Cocoa Application and click the Next button. Xcode now asks for a product name.

4. Click in the Product Name text field and type **LoopingProgram**.

5. Make sure the Language pop-up menu displays Swift and that no check boxes are selected.

6. Click the Next button. Xcode asks where you want to store the project.

7. Choose a folder to store your project and click the Create button.

8. Click the MainMenu.xib file in the Project Navigator.

9. Click on the LoopingProgram icon to make the window of the user interface appear as shown in Figure 8-6.

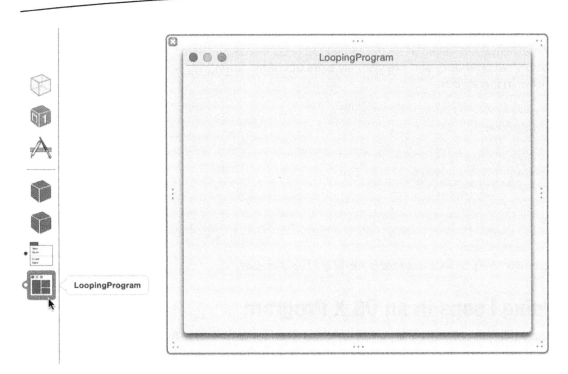

Figure 8-6. Making the window of the user interface visible

10. Choose View ➤ Utilities ➤ Show Object Library to make the Object Library appear in the bottom right corner of the Xcode window.

11. Drag a Horizontal Slider, two Labels, and a Push Button on the user interface and resize them so the user interface looks similar to Figure 8-7.

Figure 8-7. Creating a basic user interface with two labels, a horizontal slider, and a push button

12. Click on the top label to select it. Then choose View ➤ Utilities ➤ Show Attributes Inspector. The Attributes Inspector pane appears in the upper right corner of the Xcode window.

13. Click in the Title text field and type **Guess a number**.

14. Click the Center alignment icon as shown in Figure 8-8.

Figure 8-8. The Attributes Inspector pane for a label

15. Double-click on the bottom label and type **Your guesses =** and then press Return.

16. Double-click on the Push Button, type **Guess**, and then press Return. Your user interface should look like Figure 8-9.

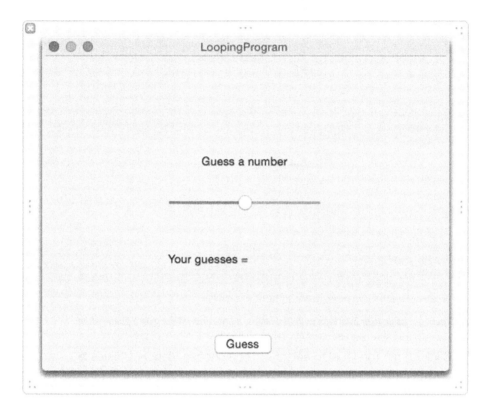

Figure 8-9. The completed user interface

17. Click on the Horizontal Slider to select it and choose View ➤ Utilities ➤ Show Attributes Inspector. The Attributes Inspector pane appears in the upper right corner of the Xcode window.

18. Select the "Only stop on tick marks" check box.

19. Click in the text field directly above the "Only stop on tick marks" check box and type **10**.

20. Click in the Minimum text field and type **1**.

21. Click in the Maximum text field and type **10**.

22. Click in the Current text field and type **5** as shown in Figure 8-10.

Figure 8-10. Changing the Horizontal Slider attributes

With this user interface, the user will use the horizontal slider to choose a number between 1 and 10. If the user guesses a number too high, the label will display "Too High." If the user guesses a number too low, the label will display "Too Low."

Each time the user guesses wrong, the bottom label displays the incorrect guess. When the user guesses the correct number, the top label will display "You got it!"

In this example, we'll need two IBOutlet variables to connect to each label so we can display information on each label. Then we'll need one IBAction method to connect to the Guess button. That way when the user clicks on the Guess button, the IBAction method can check if the user picked the correct number using the horizontal slider.

We'll need to write Swift code that chooses a random number between 1 and 10. Then we'll use a loop to list all the guesses the user made and display those results in an alert dialog.

To connect Swift code to your user interface, follow these steps:

1. With your user interface still visible in the Xcode window, choose View ➤ Assistant Editor ➤ Show Assistant Editor. The AppDelegate. swift file appears next to the user interface.

2. Move the mouse over the top label, hold down the Control key, and drag from the top text field to underneath the existing @IBOutlet line in the AppDelegate.swift file as shown in Figure 8-11.

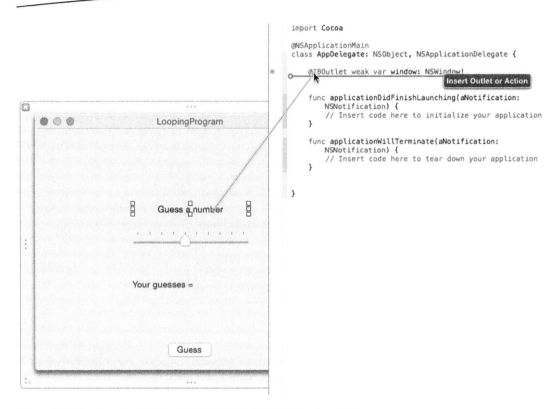

Figure 8-11. *Control-dragging from the top label to the AppDelegate.swift file*

3.   Release the mouse and the Control key. A pop-up window appears
      as shown in Figure 8-12.

Figure 8-12. *The pop-up window for defining an IBOutlet*

4.   Click in the Name text field and type **messageLabel** and click the
      Connect button. Xcode creates an IBOutlet.

5.   Move the mouse over the bottom label, hold down the Control
      key, and drag the mouse underneath the @IBOutlet line in the
      AppDelegate.swift file.

6.   Release the mouse and the Control key. A pop-up window appears.

7. Click in the Name text field and type **guessLabel** and click the Connect button. Xcode creates another IBOutlet.

8. Move the mouse over the horizontal slider, hold down the Control key, and drag the mouse underneath the @IBOutlet line in the AppDelegate.swift file.

9. Release the mouse and the Control key. A pop-up window appears.

10. Click in the Name text field and type **guessSlider** and click the Connect button. Xcode creates another IBOutlet.

11. You should now have three IBOutlets that represent the two text fields on your user interface:

```
@IBOutlet weak var messageLabel: NSTextField!
@IBOutlet weak var guessLabel: NSTextField!
@IBOutlet weak var guessSlider: NSSlider!
```

12. Edit the underneath the IBOutlets so it looks like this:

```
import Cocoa

@NSApplicationMain

class AppDelegate: NSObject, NSApplicationDelegate {

    @IBOutlet weak var window: NSWindow!
    @IBOutlet weak var messageLabel: NSTextField!
    @IBOutlet weak var guessLabel: NSTextField!
    @IBOutlet weak var guessSlider: NSSlider!

    var randomNumber : Int
    var guessHistory : String
    var guessNumber : Int
    var guessArray = [Int]()
    var arrayTotal : Int

    override init () {
        self.guessHistory = ""
        self.guessNumber = 0
        self.guessArray = []
        self.arrayTotal = 0
        self.randomNumber = 1 + Int(arc4random_uniform(10))
        // Int(arc4random_uniform(10)) chooses a random number between 0 and 9,
        so we need to add 1 so it chooses a random number from 1 to 10
    }

    func applicationDidFinishLaunching(aNotification: NSNotification) {
        // Insert code here to initialize your application
    }

    func applicationWillTerminate(aNotification: NSNotification) {
        // Insert code here to tear down your application
    }
```

The IBOutlet variables connect to the items on your user interface.

```
@IBOutlet weak var window: NSWindow!
@IBOutlet weak var messageLabel: NSTextField!
@IBOutlet weak var guessLabel: NSTextField!
@IBOutlet weak var guessSlider: NSSlider!
```

The next five lines declare variables the entire class AppDelegate can use.

```
var guessHistory : String
var guessNumber : Int
var guessArray = [Int]()
var arrayTotal : Int
    var randomNumber : Int
```

When you define variables (called properties) inside a class, you need to give them an initial value. That's the purpose of the override init method:

```
override init () {
    self.guessHistory = ""
    self.guessNumber = 0
    self.guessArray = []
    self.arrayTotal = 0
    self.randomNumber = 1 + Int(arc4random_uniform(10))
    // Int(arc4random_uniform(10)) chooses a random number between 0 and 9, so we need to
    add 1 so it chooses a random number from 1 to 10
}
```

The "self" keyword tells Xcode that all of these variables are defined inside the same class (class AppDelegate). The last line creates a random number between 1 and 10.

The way this entire program works is that it first creates all its variables. Then it runs the override init method to store initial values in these variables.

13. Move the mouse over the Guess push button, hold down the Control key, and drag the mouse above the last curly bracket in the AppDelegate.swift file.

14. Release the mouse and the Control key. A pop-up window appears.

15. Click in the Connection pop-up menu and choose Action to create an IBAction method.

16. Click in the Name text field and type **checkGuess**.

17. Click in the Type pop-up menu and choose NSButton as shown in Figure 8-13.

Figure 8-13. Defining an IBAction method

18. Click the Connect button. Xcode creates a blank IBAction method.

19. Modify the IBAction checkGuess method as follows:

```
@IBAction func checkGuess(sender: NSButton) {
    var userGuess : Int = 0

    // Get guess from horizontal slider
    userGuess = guessSlider.integerValue

    // Store guess in guessArray
    guessArray.append(userGuess)

    if userGuess < randomNumber {
        messageLabel.stringValue = "Too Low"
    } else if userGuess > randomNumber {
        messageLabel.stringValue = "Too High"
    } else {
        messageLabel.stringValue = "You got it!"

        arrayTotal = guessArray.count

        for var i = 0; i < arrayTotal; i++ {
            guessHistory += "Guess \(i+1) = \(guessArray[i])" + "\r\n"
        }
        var myAlert = NSAlert()
        myAlert.messageText = guessHistory
        myAlert.runModal()
    }
    guessLabel.stringValue = guessLabel.stringValue + " \(userGuess)"

}
```

Let's go through this IBAction method so you understand exactly what happens. First, the user needs to use the horizontal slider to pick a number to guess. After choosing a number, the user then needs to click the Guess button, which runs the IBAction method called checkGuess.

The following line declares an integer variable called "userGuess" and sets its value to 0. This line isn't absolutely necessary but it does ensure that the "userGuess" variable has an initial value.

```
var userGuess : Int = 0
```

The next line retrieves the value from the horizontal slider, which is represented by the IBOutlet variable called "guessSlider." To retrieve the integer that the horizontal slider represents, you have to use the integerValue property. This stores the value from the horizontal slider into the "userGuess" variable that we just declared as an integer variable.

```
userGuess = guessSlider.integerValue
```

The next line adds the value stored in the "userGuess" variable into the array called guessArray. This array must be defined earlier in your program.

```
guessArray.append(userGuess)
```

The if-else if statement creates three branches. The first branch runs if the "userGuess" variable is less than the "randomNumber" variable, which must be defined earlier in the program. This displays the text "Too Low" into the label represented by the messageLabel IBOutlet.

```
if userGuess < randomNumber {
    messageLabel.stringValue = "Too Low"
```

The second branch runs if the "userGuess" variable is greater than the "randomNumber" variable. This displays the text "Too High" into the label represented by the messageLabel IBOutlet.

```
} else if userGuess > randomNumber {
    messageLabel.stringValue = "Too High"
```

The third branch runs if the "userGuess" variable is neither less than or greater than the "randomNumber" variable, which means that it must be exactly equal to the "randomNumber" variable. This displays the text "You got it!" into the label represented by the messageLabel IBOutlet.

```
} else {
    messageLabel.stringValue = "You got it!"
```

Then it counts the total number of items stored in the guessArray and puts this value in the "arrayTotal" variable, which must be defined earlier in the program.

```
arrayTotal = guessArray.count
```

Now it uses a for loop to count from 0 to arrayTotal − 1 (i < arrayTotal) and increments by 1 (i++). It creates a string that stores the guess number, such as Guess 1, and the guess that the user chose in the string variable called "guessHistory," which must be defined earlier in the program. Notice that you can print numbers in a string by using the \() characters where a non-string value appears inside the parentheses. This lets you store non-string values in a string without converting them to a string data type first.

Also notice that if you simply typed "Guess \(i)" then the first string would hold the value "Guess 0" as the first guess. To avoid this, we need to add 1 to the current value of i.

Notice that the string also contains the characters "\r\n" at the end. These symbols represent a carriage return and a newline character respectively. These are invisible characters that tell Xcode that if we add more text, it will appear on the next line down.

```
    for var i = 0; i < arrayTotal; i++ {
guessHistory += "Guess \(i+1) = \(guessArray[i])" + "\r\n"
}
```

The code inside the for loop uses a compound assignment operator (+=) to add this string to any existing string stored in the "guessHistory" variable. Because of the "\r\n" characters that create a carriage return and a newline, any new string that gets added will appear on the next line down.

The next three lines create an alert dialog (NSAlert), stores the string from the "guessHistory" variable into the messageText property of the alert dialog, and then displays the dialog to display how many guesses you took and the numbers you chose in each guess as shown in Figure 8-14.

```
var myAlert = NSAlert()
myAlert.messageText = guessHistory
myAlert.runModal()
```

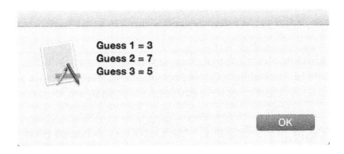

Figure 8-14. The typical results that appear in an alert dialog

The last line of the IBAction method simply stores the user's guesses in the guessLabel IBOutlet, which makes the text appear in the bottom label.

```
guessLabel.stringValue = guessLabel.stringValue + " \(userGuess)"
```

At this point, the program now waits for the user to choose a value in the horizontal slider and click the Guess button.

20. Choose Product ➤ Run. Xcode runs your LoopingProgram project.

21. Click on a value in the horizontal slider to guess a number.

22. Click the Guess push button. If you guess too low or too high, the "Too Low" or "Too High" message appears. Eventually when you guess the correct number, an Alert dialog appears as shown in Figure 8-15.

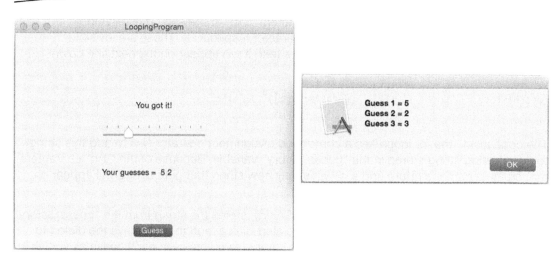

Figure 8-15. *Displaying an Alert dialog*

23. Click the OK button in the Alert dialog to make it go away.

24. Choose LoopingProgram ➤ Quit LoopingProgram.

Summary

Loops let you repeat one or more lines of code by running code until a Boolean value becomes false. A while loop checks a Boolean value first, which means it can run zero or more times. A repeat-while loop checks a Boolean value last, which means it can run one or more times.

A for loop lets you specify how many times the loop can run based on a starting value, a Boolean value, and an increment counting operator. A for-in loop can count items in a list automatically.

When creating a loop, always make sure the loop has a way to end. If a loop never ends, it becomes an endless loop, which will make your program appear to freeze and be unresponsive.

Each type of loop has its advantages and disadvantages, but you can always make each loop duplicate the features of the other loops. If you need to exit out of a loop prematurely, you can use the break command along with an if statement.

Loops give your program the power to do repetitive tasks without requiring you to write duplicate commands. Just make sure that your loops always end eventually and that they run the proper number of times before stopping.

Arrays and Dictionaries

Almost every program needs to accept data so it can manipulate that data and calculate a useful result. The simplest way to store data temporarily is through variables that can store numbers or text strings. However, what if you need to store multiple chunks of data such as a list of names or a list of product numbers? You could create multiple variables like this:

```
var employee001, employee002, employee003 : String
```

Unfortunately, creating separate variables to store related data can be clumsy. What if you don't know how many items you need to store? Then you may create too many or not enough variables. Even worse, storing related data in separate variables means it's easy to overlook the relationship between data.

For example, if you stored the names of three employees in three different variables, how do you know if there isn't a fourth, fifth, or sixth variable containing additional employee names? Unless you keep variables together in your code, it's easy to lose track of related data stored in separate variables.

That's why Swift offers two additional ways to store data: arrays and dictionaries. The main idea behind both data structures is that you create a single variable that can hold multiple items. Now you can store related data in one location and easily find and retrieve it again.

Both arrays and dictionaries are designed to store multiple copies of the same data type such as a list of names (String) or a list of numbers (Int). If you wanted to store a list consisting of different data types such as integers, decimal numbers, and strings, you can declare the array or dictionary to hold AnyObject data types, which can store any type of data.

Using Arrays

You can think of an array as an endless series of buckets that can hold exactly one chunk of data. To help you find data stored in an array, each array element (bucket) is identified by a number called an index. The first item in an array is defined at index 0, the second item is defined at index 1, the third item is defined at index 2, and so on as shown in Figure 9-1.

Figure 9-1. The structure of an array

To create an array, you must define the name of the array and the type of data the array can hold. One way to create an array is like this:

```
var arrayName = Array<DataType>()>()
```

The array name can be anything you wish, although it's best to choose a descriptive name that identifies the type of data the array holds, such as employeeArray. The data type can be Int (integer), String (strings), Float or Double (decimal numbers), or even the name of another data structure. (It's possible to have an array that holds other arrays.)

A second way to create an array is like this:

```
var arrayName = [DataType]()
```

Both of these methods create an empty array. At that point, you'll need to start adding items into that array. If you want to create an array and store it with items at the same time, you'll need to use the arrayLiteral keyword such as:

```
var arrayName = Array<Int>(arrayLiteral: 34, 89, 70, 1, -24)
```

or

```
var arrayName = [Int](arrayLiteral: 34, 89, 70, 1, -24)
```

Both of these commands create an array called "arrayName" that can only hold integers. Then the arrayLiteral keyword followed by the list of integers fills up the array with data. Since you have to define the data type, both of these methods will work with the AnyObject so you can store different types of data in an array.

A shorter and much simpler way to create an array is to define an array name and set it equal to a list of items of the same data type like this:

```
var myArrray = [34, 89, 70, 1, -24]
```

Swift then infers the data type of the array based on the data. This method only works if all items in the array are of the same data type such as all integers or all decimal numbers.

> **Note**   When you declare an array with the "var" keyword, you can add and delete items in that array. If you don't want an array to change, declare it with the "let" keyword like this: `let arrayName = [34, 89, 70, 1, -24]`. An array declared with the "let" keyword can never be modified.

In the previous examples of arrays holding integers, the first number (34) is at index 0, the second number (89) is at index 1, the third number (70) is at index 2, the fourth number (1) is at index 3, and the fifth number (-24) is at index 4. Because arrays count the index numbers starting with 0, Swift arrays are known as zero-based arrays. (Some programming languages count the index of arrays starting with 1 so they're called one-based arrays.)

Adding Items to an Array

Whether an array is empty or already filled with data, you can always add more items to an array by using the append command like this:

```
arrayName.append(data)
```

You must specify the array name to add data to and put the actual data in parentheses. Make sure the data you add is of the proper data type. So if you want to add data to an array that can only hold integers, you can only add another integer to that array.

Instead of using the append command, you can use the addition compound assignment operator to add items to the end of an array like this:

```
arrayName3 += [data1, data2, data3, ... dataN]
```

The += compound assignment operator can add multiple items to the end of an array while the append command only adds one item at a time to the end of an array.

The append command always adds new items to the end of an array. If you want to add a new item to a specific location in an array, you can use the insert and atIndex commands like this:

```
arrayName.insert(data, atIndex: index)
```

With the insert command, you must add data that's the proper data type for that array. Then you must also specify the index number. If you choose an index number larger than the array size, the insert command won't work.

To see how to create an array and add data to it, create a new playground by following these steps:

1. Start Xcode.

2. Choose File ➤ New ➤ Playground. (If you see the Xcode welcome screen, you can also click on Get started with a playground.) Xcode asks for a playground name and platform.

3. Click in the Name text field and type **ArrayPlayground**.

4. Click in the Platform pop-up menu and choose OS X. Xcode asks where you want to save your playground file.

5. Click on a folder where you want to save your playground file and click the Create button. Xcode displays the playground file.

6. Edit the code as follows:

```
import Cocoa

var arrayName = Array<Int>(arrayLiteral: 34, 89, 70, 1, -24)

var arrayName2 = [Int](arrayLiteral: 34, 89, 70, 1, -24)

arrayName.append(2)
arrayName2.append(2)

arrayName.insert(-37, atIndex: 2)
arrayName2.insert(-37, atIndex: 2)
```

Notice how the append and insert commands work differently as shown in Figure 9-2.

```
var arrayName = Array<Int>(arrayLiteral: 34, 89, 70, 1, -24)    [34, 89, 70, 1, -24]

var arrayName2 = [Int](arrayLiteral: 34, 89, 70, 1, -24)        [34, 89, 70, 1, -24]

arrayName.append(2)                                             [34, 89, 70, 1, -24, 2]
arrayName2.append(2)                                            [34, 89, 70, 1, -24, 2]

arrayName.insert(-37, atIndex: 2)                               [34, 89, -37, 70, 1, -24, 2]
arrayName2.insert(-37, atIndex: 2)                              [34, 89, -37, 70, 1, -24, 2]
```

Figure 9-2. Creating arrays in a playground

Deleting Items From an Array

Just as you can add items to an array, so can you also delete items from an array. To remove the last item in an array, you can use the removeLast command like this:

```
arrayName.removeLast()
```

Not only will this delete the last item in an array, but it will also return that value. If you want to save the last item of an array in a variable, you could do something like this:

```
var item = arrayName.removeLast()
```

If you want to remove a specific item from an array, you can identify the index number of that item with the removeAtIndex command like this:

```
arrayName.removeAtIndex(number)
```

So if you wanted to remove the second item in an array, you would specify an index of 1. Like the removeLast command, the removeAtIndex command also returns a value that you could store in a variable like this:

```
var item = arrayName.removeAtIndex(1)
```

If you wanted to remove all items from an array, you can use the removeAll command like this:

```
arrayName.removeAll()
```

To see how to delete items from an array, follow these steps:

1. Make sure the ArrayPlayground file is loaded in Xcode.

2. Edit the code as follows:

```
import Cocoa

var arrayName = [Int](arrayLiteral: 3, 8, 9, 21)
var item = arrayName.removeLast()
print (arrayName)
print (item)

item = arrayName.removeAtIndex(1)
print (arrayName)
print (item)

arrayName.removeAll()
```

Notice how the different commands work when deleting items from an array as shown in Figure 9-3. When specifying index values, you must make sure your index number exists. That means if an array consists of three items, the first item is at index 0, the second is at index 1, and the third is at index 2. So you can remove an item from this array at index values 0, 1, or 2, but any other index number will not work.

```
import Cocoa

var arrayName = [Int](arrayLiteral: 3, 8, 9, 21)          [3, 8, 9, 21]
var item = arrayName.removeLast()                          21

print (arrayName)                                          "[3, 8, 9]\n"
print (item)                                               "21\n"

item = arrayName.removeAtIndex(1)                          8

print (arrayName)                                          "[3, 9]\n"
print (item)                                               "8\n"

arrayName.removeAll()                                      []
```

Figure 9-3. Deleting items from an array

Deleting items from an array physically removes that item from that array. Rather than delete an item from an array, you can also replace an existing item with a new value. All you have to do is specify the index value of the array item you want to replace and assign new data to it like this:

```
arrayName[index] = newData
```

So if you wanted to replace the second item in an array (at index value 1) with new data, you could do the following:

```
arrayName[1] = 91
```

Whatever existing value was stored in the array at index value 1 gets replaced with the number 91. When replacing data, the new data must be of the same data type as the rest of the items in the array such as integers or strings.

Querying Arrays

When you have an array, you might want to know if the array is empty (has zero items stored in it), or if the array does have items, how many items it contains. To determine if an array is empty or not, you can use the isEmpty command that returns a Boolean value like this:

```
arrayName.isEmpty
```

If you want to store this Boolean value in a variable, you could do this:

```
var flag = arrayName.isEmpty
```

If you want to know how many items are stored in an array, you can use the count command like this:

```
arrayName.count
```

If you want to store this integer value in a variable, you could do this:

```
var total = arrayName.count
```

If you just want to access an individual array item, you can copy it from an array and store its value in a variable like this:

```
var item = arrayName[index]
```

This lets you retrieve an item out of an array from a specific index location and store that value in a variable. When retrieving data from an array, make sure you specify a valid index value. So if the array contains three items, the index values would be 0, 1, and 2. That means if you wanted to retrieve the second item in an array (at index 1), you could use this code:

```
var item = arrayName[1]
```

Manipulating Arrays

Two common ways to manipulate an array is to reverse the order of all the items or rearrange the items in ascending or descending order. This simply reverses the order of all items in an array without regard to their actual values such as:

```
arrayName.reverse()
```

When you sort an array in ascending order, the lowest value gets stored in the first item of the array, and the highest value gets stored in the last item of the array. When you sort strings, Swift sorts them in alphabetical order. To sort an array in ascending order, you have two choices:

```
myArray.sort { $0 < $1 }
```

or

```
myArray.sort ()
```

When you sort an array in descending order, the highest value gets stored in the first item of the array, and the lowest value gets stored in the last item of the array. When you sort strings, Swift sorts them in reverse alphabetical order. To sort an array in descending order, use this:

```
myArray.sort { $1 < $0 }
```

To see how sorting an array works, follow these steps:

1. Make sure the ArrayPlayground file is loaded in Xcode.

2. Edit the code as follows:

    ```
    import Cocoa

    var myArray = ["Bob", "Fred", "Jane", "Mary"]

    print (myArray.sort())

    var sortedArray = myArray.sort() { $1 < $0 }
    print (sortedArray)
    ```

Notice that sorting an array changes the position of items based on their content as shown in Figure 9-4.

```
import Cocoa                                                       

var myArray = ["Mack", "Fred", "Sally", "Martha"]                 ["Mack", "Fred", "Sally", "Martha"]

print (myArray.sort())                                            "[Fred, Mack, Martha, Sally]\n"

var sortedArray = myArray.sort() {$1 < $0}                        (7 times)
print (sortedArray)                                               "[Sally, Martha, Mack, Fred]\n"
```

Figure 9-4. Sorting an array

Using Dictionaries

Arrays can be useful for storing lists of related data. The biggest drawback with an array comes when you want to retrieve specific data. Unless you know the exact index number of an item in an array, retrieving data can be cumbersome.

That's the advantage of a dictionary. Unlike an array that just stores data, a dictionary stores two chunks of data known as a key-value pair. The value represents the data you want to save, and the key represents a quick way to retrieve your data.

For example, consider a list of phone numbers. If you stored phone numbers in an array, you would have to retrieve a specific phone number by knowing its exact index value. However, if you stored phone numbers in a dictionary, you could store each phone number (value) with a name (key). Now if you wanted to retrieve a particular phone number, you just search for the key (the person's name).

Regardless of where that data might be stored in the dictionary, you can quickly retrieve a value using a key. That makes retrieving data from a dictionary far easier than retrieving similar data from an array.

Think of a dictionary like an array but instead of storing one chunk of data, you're storing a pair of data (a key and a value). Both the key and the value can be of different data types, but all the keys must be of the same data type and all the values in a dictionary must be of the same data type. However, keys and values can be of different data types. For example, the keys of a dictionary could be of String data types while the values could be Int data types.

To create a dictionary, you must define the dictionary and the data types for both the key and its associated value. One way to define a dictionary is to do this:

```
var DictionaryName = [keyDataType: valueDatatype]()
```

A second way to define a dictionary is to create a list of key:value pairs like this:

```
var DictionaryName = [102: "Fred", 87: "Valerie"]
```

When you directly assign key:value pairs, Swift infers the data type of the key and the value. In this case, the key data type is an integer (Int) and the value data type is a string (String).

Adding Items to a Dictionary

Whether a dictionary is empty or already filled with data, you can always add more items to a dictionary by specifying the dictionary name and its key value, and then assigning a value such as:

```
DictionaryName [key] = value
```

To see how to create a dictionary and add data to it, create a new playground by following these steps:

1. Start Xcode.

2. Choose File ➤ New ➤ Playground. (If you see the Xcode welcome screen, you can also click on Get started with a playground.) Xcode asks for a playground name and platform.

3. Click in the Name text field and type **DictionaryPlayground**.

4. Click in the Platform pop-up menu and choose OS X. Xcode asks where you want to save your playground file.

5. Click on a folder where you want to save your playground file and click the Create button. Xcode displays the playground file.

6. Edit the code as follows:

```
import Cocoa

var DictionaryName = [102: "Fred", 87: "Valerie"]

DictionaryName [120] = "John"
DictionaryName [96] = "Jane"

print (DictionaryName)
```

This Swift code defines a dictionary where the key:value data types are Int:String, which Swift infers from the type of data initially stored in the dictionary.

The next two lines define a key (120) and a value ("John"), which gets stored in the dictionary. Then the other line defines a key (96) and a value ("Jane"), which also gets stored in the dictionary. The last print command lets you see how the dictionary has changed as shown in Figure 9-5.

```
import Cocoa

var DictionaryName = [102: "Fred", 87: "Valerie"]          [102: "Fred", 87: "Valerie"]

DictionaryName [120] = "John"                               "John"
DictionaryName [96] = "Jane"                                "Jane"
                                                            "[120: John, 102: Fred, 87: Valerie, 96: Jane]\n"
print (DictionaryName)
```

Figure 9-5. *Creating a dictionary and adding new key:value data to it*

Retrieving and Updating Data in a Dictionary

Once a dictionary contains key:value pairs, you can retrieve the value by using the key. To do that, you specify the dictionary name and a key. Then you assign this value to a variable such as:

```
variable = DictionaryName [key]!
```

The variable must be the same data type as the value stored in the dictionary. Also notice the exclamation mark, which defines an implicitly unwrapped variable. This exclamation mark ensures that if the key doesn't exist in the dictionary, the nonexistent value does not crash your program.

The following example defines two key:value pairs of data in a dictionary. Then it uses the 87 key to retrieve the value from the dictionary, which is the string "Valeria" as shown in Figure 9-6:

```
var DictionaryName = [102: "Fred", 87: "Valerie"]
var name : String
name = DictionaryName [87]!
print (name)
```

```
import Cocoa

var DictionaryName = [102: "Fred", 87: "Valerie"]              [102: 'Fred', 87: 'Valerie']

DictionaryName[120] = "John"                                  'John'
DictionaryName[96] = "Jane"                                   'Jane'
print (DictionaryName)                                        '[120: John, 102: Fred, 87: Valerie, 96: Jane]\n'

var name : String
name = DictionaryName[87]!                                    'Valerie'
print (name)                                                  'Valerie\n'

DictionaryName.updateValue("Sam", forKey: 87)                 'Valerie'
name = DictionaryName[87]!                                    'Sam'
print (name)                                                  'Sam\n'
```

Figure 9-6. *Retrieving a value with a key and updating an existing key with new data*

Once you've stored a key:value pair in a dictionary, you can always assign a new value to an existing key using the updateValue command like this:

```
DictionaryName.updateValue(value, forKey: key)
```

So if you wanted to update the value stored with the 87 key, you could do the following:

```
DictionaryName.updateValue("Sam", forKey: 87)
```

To see how to retrieve a value from a dictionary using a key and then update a value for an existing key, follow these steps:

1. Make sure the LoopingPlayground file is loaded in Xcode.

2. Edit the code as follows:

```
import Cocoa

var DictionaryName = [102: "Fred", 87: "Valerie"]

DictionaryName [120] = "John"
DictionaryName [96] = "Jane"
print (DictionaryName)

var name : String
name = DictionaryName [87]!
print (name)
```

```
DictionaryName.updateValue("Sam", forKey: 87)
name = DictionaryName [87]!
print (name)
```

Notice that the first time the dictionary retrieves the value associated with the 87 key, it returns the string "Valerie." Then the updateValue command replaces "Valerie" with "Sam" so the next time the dictionary retrieves the value associated with the 87 key, it returns the string "Sam" (see Figure 9-6).

Deleting Data in a Dictionary

Once a dictionary contains key:value pairs, you can delete the value associated with a specific key by using the removeValueForKey command like this:

```
DictionaryName.removeValueForKey(key)
```

The removeValueForKey command removes both the key and the value associated with that key. Note that if you specify a key that doesn't exist in the dictionary, the removeValueForKey command does nothing.

If you want to delete all the key:value pairs in a dictionary, you can just use the removeAll command like this:

```
DictionaryName.removeAll()
```

Querying a Dictionary

Once you store key:value pairs in a dictionary, you can use the following commands to get information about a dictionary:

- ▧ count – counts the number of key:value pairs stored in a dictionary
- ▧ keys – retrieves a list of all the keys stored in a dictionary
- ▧ values – retrieves a list of all the values stored in a dictionary

The count command only needs the dictionary name and returns an integer value that you can assign to a variable such as:

```
var name = DictionaryName.count
```

The keys and values commands need a dictionary name and returns a list of items that you can store in an array such as:

```
let myKeys = Array(DictionaryName.keys)
```

To see how to count and retrieve keys and values from a dictionary, follow these steps:

1. Make sure the DictionaryPlayground file is loaded in Xcode.

2. Edit the code as follows:

```
import Cocoa

var myDictionary = [12: "Joe", 7: "Walter"]

myDictionary.removeValueForKey(7)
print (myDictionary)

myDictionary.removeAll()
print (myDictionary)

myDictionary = [25: "Stephanie", 98: "Nancy"]

print (myDictionary.count)
let myKeys = Array(myDictionary.keys)
let myValues = Array(myDictionary.values)
```

Notice how the removeValueForKey command removes an existing key:value pair while the removeAll command empties the entire dictionary. Also notice how the count command counts all key:value pairs while the keys and values commands return a list of the keys and values respectively as shown in Figure 9-7.

```
import Cocoa                                                           [12: "Joe", 7: "Walter"]

var myDictionary = [12: "Joe", 7: "Walter"]

myDictionary.removeValueForKey(7)                                      "Walter"
print (myDictionary)                                                   "[12: Joe]\n"

myDictionary.removeAll()                                               [:]
print (myDictionary)                                                   "[:]\n"

myDictionary = [25: "Stephanie", 98: "Nancy"]                          [98: "Nancy", 25: "Stephanie"]

print (myDictionary.count)                                             "2\n"
let myKeys = Array(myDictionary.keys)                                  [98, 25]
let myValues = Array(myDictionary.values)                              ["Nancy", "Stephanie"]
```

Figure 9-7. *Deleting dictionary data, counting, and retrieving keys and values*

Using Dictionaries in an OS X Program

In this sample program, the computer creates a list of data stored in a dictionary. Then through the user interface, the user can add new data to the dictionary, delete existing data, or get information about the dictionary.

Create a new OS X project by following these steps:

1. From within Xcode choose File ➤ New ➤ Project.

2. Click Application under the OS X category.

3. Click Cocoa Application and click the Next button. Xcode now asks for a product name.

4. Click in the Product Name text field and type **DictionaryProgram**.

5. Make sure the Language pop-up menu displays Swift and that no check boxes are selected.

6. Click the Next button. Xcode asks where you want to store the project.

7. Choose a folder to store your project and click the Create button.

8. Click the MainMenu.xib file in the Project Navigator.

9. Click on the DictionaryProgram icon to make the window of the user interface appear.

10. Choose View ➤ Utilities ➤ Show Object Library to make the Object Library appear in the bottom right corner of the Xcode window.

11. Drag three Push Buttons, six Labels, and six Text Fields on the user interface and double-click on the push buttons and labels to change the text that appears on them so that it looks similar to Figure 9-8.

Figure 9-8. The user interface of the DictionaryProgram

The Add button will let you type in a key and value in the text fields on the right. The Delete button will let you specify a key to delete its associated value from a dictionary. The Query button will display the total number of items along with the list of keys and values currently stored in the dictionary.

Each text field will need a separate IBOutlet and each push button will need a separate IBAction method, which you'll need to create by Control-dragging each item from the user interface to your AppDelegate.swift file:

1. With your user interface still visible in the Xcode window, choose View ➤ Assistant Editor ➤ Show Assistant Editor. The AppDelegate. swift file appears next to the user interface.

2. Move the mouse over the Add button, hold down the Control key, and drag just above the last curly bracket at the bottom of the AppDelegate.swift file.

3. Release the mouse and the Control key. A pop-up window appears.

4. Click in the Connection pop-up menu and choose Action.

5. Click in the Name text field and type **addButton**.

6. Click in the Type pop-up menu and choose NSButton. Then click the Connect button.

7. Move the mouse over the Delete button, hold down the Control key, and drag just above the last curly bracket at the bottom of the AppDelegate.swift file.

8. Release the mouse and the Control key. A pop-up window appears.

9. Click in the Connection pop-up menu and choose Action.

10. Click in the Name text field and type **deleteButton**.

11. Click in the Type pop-up menu and choose NSButton. Then click the Connect button.

12. Move the mouse over the Query button, hold down the Control key, and drag just above the last curly bracket at the bottom of the AppDelegate.swift file.

13. Release the mouse and the Control key. A pop-up window appears.

14. Click in the Connection pop-up menu and choose Action.

15. Click in the Name text field and type **queryButton**.

16. Click in the Type pop-up menu and choose NSButton. Then click the Connect button. The bottom of the AppDelegate.swift file should look like this:

```
@IBAction func addButton(sender: NSButton) {
}

@IBAction func deleteButton(sender: NSButton) {
}

@IBAction func queryButton(sender: NSButton) {
}
```

17. Move the mouse over the Key text field that appears to the right of the Add button, hold down the Control key, and drag below the @IBOutlet line in the AppDelegate.swift file.

18. Release the mouse and the Control key. A pop-up window appears.

19. Click in the Name text field and type **addKeyField** and click the Connect button.

20. Move the mouse over the Value text field that appears to the right of the Add button, hold down the Control key, and drag below the @IBOutlet line in the AppDelegate.swift file.

21. Release the mouse and the Control key. A pop-up window appears.

22. Click in the Name text field and type **addValueField** and click the Connect button.

23. Move the mouse over the Key text field that appears to the right of the Delete button, hold down the Control key, and drag below the @IBOutlet line in the AppDelegate.swift file.

24. Release the mouse and the Control key. A pop-up window appears.

25. Click in the Name text field and type **deleteKeyField** and click the Connect button.

26. Move the mouse over the Count text field that appears to the right of the Query button, hold down the Control key, and drag below the @IBOutlet line in the AppDelegate.swift file.

27. Release the mouse and the Control key. A pop-up window appears.

28. Click in the Name text field and type **queryCountField** and click the Connect button.

29. Move the mouse over the Keys text field that appears to the right of the Query button, hold down the Control key, and drag below the @IBOutlet line in the AppDelegate.swift file.

30. Release the mouse and the Control key. A pop-up window appears.

31. Click in the Name text field and type **queryKeysField** and click the Connect button.

32. Move the mouse over the Values text field that appears to the right of the Query button, hold down the Control key, and drag below the @IBOutlet line in the AppDelegate.swift file.

33. Release the mouse and the Control key. A pop-up window appears.

34. Click in the Name text field and type **queryValuesField** and click the Connect button.

35. You should now have the following IBOutlets that represent all the text fields on your user interface:

```
@IBOutlet weak var window: NSWindow!
@IBOutlet weak var addKeyField: NSTextField!
@IBOutlet weak var addValueField: NSTextField!
@IBOutlet weak var deleteKeyField: NSTextField!
@IBOutlet weak var queryCountField: NSTextField!
@IBOutlet weak var queryKeysField: NSTextField!
@IBOutlet weak var queryValuesField: NSTextField!
```

At this point we've connected the user interface to our Swift code so we can use the IBOutlets to retrieve and display data on the user interface. We've also created the IBAction methods so the push buttons on the user interface will make the program actually work. Now we just need to write Swift code to create an initial dictionary and then write more Swift code in each IBAction method to add, delete, or query the dictionary.

1. Underneath the IBOutlet list in the AppDelegate.swift file, type the following to create a dictionary where the keys are integers and the values are strings:

```
var myDictionary = [1:"Joe", 2:"Cindy", 3:"Frank"]
```

2. Modify the addButton IBAction method so it takes a value from the Key and Value text fields and adds them to the dictionary as follows:

```
@IBAction func addButton(sender: NSButton) {
    myDictionary.updateValue(addValueField.stringValue, forKey: addKeyField.
    integerValue)
}
```

3. Modify the deleteButton IBAction method so it takes a value from the Key text field and deletes the associates value from the dictionary as follows:

```
@IBAction func deleteButton(sender: NSButton) {
    myDictionary.removeValueForKey(deleteKeyField.integerValue)
}
```

4. Modify the queryButton IBAction method as follows:

```
@IBAction func queryButton(sender: NSButton) {
    queryCountField.integerValue = myDictionary.count

    var keyList = ""

    for key in myDictionary.keys {
        keyList = keyList + "\(key)" + " "
    }
    queryKeysField.stringValue = keyList

    var valueList = ""
    for value in myDictionary.values {
        valueList = valueList + "\(value)" + " "
    }
    queryValuesField.stringValue = valueList

}
```

The myDictionary.count command simply counts the number of key:value pairs in the dictionary and displays that number in the queryCountField IBOutlet.

The first for-in loop goes through each key in the dictionary and stores it in a string called keyList. Then it displays this text string in the queryKeysField IBOutlet.

The last for loop goes through each value in the dictionary and stores it in a string called valueList. Then it displays this text string in the queryValuesField IBOutlet.

The complete contents of the AppDelegate.swift file should look like this:

```
import Cocoa

@NSApplicationMain
class AppDelegate: NSObject, NSApplicationDelegate {

    @IBOutlet weak var window: NSWindow!
    @IBOutlet weak var addKeyField: NSTextField!
    @IBOutlet weak var addValueField: NSTextField!
    @IBOutlet weak var deleteKeyField: NSTextField!
    @IBOutlet weak var queryCountField: NSTextField!
    @IBOutlet weak var queryKeysField: NSTextField!
    @IBOutlet weak var queryValuesField: NSTextField!

    var myDictionary = [1:"Joe", 2:"Cindy", 3:"Frank"]

    func applicationDidFinishLaunching(aNotification: NSNotification) {
        // Insert code here to initialize your application
    }

    func applicationWillTerminate(aNotification: NSNotification) {
        // Insert code here to tear down your application
    }

    @IBAction func addButton(sender: NSButton) {
        myDictionary.updateValue(addValueField.stringValue, forKey: addKeyField.
        integerValue)
    }

    @IBAction func deleteButton(sender: NSButton) {
        myDictionary.removeValueForKey(deleteKeyField.integerValue)
    }

    @IBAction func queryButton(sender: NSButton) {
        queryCountField.integerValue = myDictionary.count

        var keyList = ""

        for key in myDictionary.keys {
            keyList = keyList + "\(key)" + " "
        }
        queryKeysField.stringValue = keyList

        var valueList = ""
        for value in myDictionary.values {
            valueList = valueList + "\(value)" + " "
        }
        queryValuesField.stringValue = valueList

    }
}
```

The Query button works by just clicking on it to display information about the current dictionary contents.

The Add button works by the user typing in a key (integer) and a name (string) into the Key and Value text fields, then clicking the Add button.

The Delete button works by the user typing in a key (integer) and then clicking the Delete button.

After clicking either the Add or Delete button, click the Query button again to see your changes. To see how this program works, follow these steps:

1. Choose Product ➤ Run. Xcode runs your DictionaryProgram project.

2. Click the Query button. The program shows the number of items in then dictionary (3), the list of keys (the numbers 1, 2, and 3), and the list of values ("Joe," "Cindy," and "Frank"). Don't worry about the order of the keys and values. The important point is to see that the order of each key matches up with the correct value such as 1 for "Joe," 2 for "Cindy," and 3 for "Frank."

3. Type 3 in the Key field to the right of the Delete push button and then click the Delete button.

4. Click the Query button. Notice that now the dictionary only contains two items: the keys 1 and 2, and the values "Joe" and "Cindy" as shown in Figure 9-9.

Figure 9-9. Displaying the results after deleting a key:value pair

5. Click in the Key text field to the right of the Add button and type **5**.

6. Click in the Value text field to the right of the Add button and type **Felicia**.

7. Click the Add button.

8. Click the Query button. Notice that the count is now 3 again; the keys are 1, 2 and 5; and the values are "Joe," "Cindy," and "Felicia."

9. Choose DictionaryProgram ➤ Quit DictionaryProgram.

Summary

Arrays and dictionaries are two ways to store lists of related data in a single variable. Arrays make it easy to store data, but retrieving data can be cumbersome since you have to know the exact index value of the data you want to retrieve.

Dictionaries force you to store data with a key, but that key makes it easy to retrieve that data later without knowing the exact location it may be stored in the dictionary.

In the sample OS X program that you created, you also learned how for-in loops can count automatically through a dictionary. By now you should also be getting more comfortable creating user interfaces and seeing which items need IBOutlets and which items need IBAction methods.

Designing programs can occur in three distinct steps. First, create the user interface and customize it. Second, connect your user interface to your Swift file. Third, write Swift code to make your IBAction methods work.

Think of arrays and dictionaries as super variables that can store multiple data in a single variable name. If you only need to save a single value, then use a variable. If you need to store lists of related data, then use an array or a dictionary.

10

Tuples, Sets, and Structures

Variables are good for storing individual chunks of data while arrays and dictionaries are good for storing lists of the same data type. For greater flexibility, Swift also offers additional data structures called tuples and sets.

A tuple lets you store related data in one place that may consist of different data types such as a string and an integer, which could represent a person's name and an employee ID number. A set is similar to an array or a dictionary in letting you store two or more chunks of data that consists of the same data type, such as strings or integers.

To group related data together, Swift also offers structures. With a structure, you can define the data type you want to group together in any combination, such as two strings and a floating-point value. Structures are a way to group different data types together.

Perhaps the biggest advantage of both tuples and structures is when you combine them with other data structures. Instead of creating an array of integers, you could create an array of tuples or an array of structures. This gives you the flexibility to store different data types together and store multiple copies of similar data.

Using Tuples

Suppose you wanted to store somebody's name and age. You could create two separate variables like this:

```
var name : String
var age : Int
name = "Janice Parker"
age = 47
```

Creating two or more separate variables to store related data can be troublesome because there's no connection between the two variables to show any relationship. To solve this problem, Swift offers a unique data structure called a tuple.

A tuple can store two or more chunks of data in a single variable where the separate chunks of data can even be completely different data types such as a string and an integer. Declaring a tuple is just like declaring a variable. The main difference is that instead of defining a single data type, you can define multiple data types enclosed in parentheses like this:

```
var tupleName : (DataType1, DataType2)
```

Just like declaring variables, you have to declare a unique name for your tuple. Then you have to define how many different chunks of data to hold and their data types. Tuples can hold two or more chunks of data, but the more data a tuple holds, the clumsier it can be to understand and retrieve data.

One way to create a tuple is to declare a tuple name and the data types it can hold. The number of data types listed also defines the number of data chunks the tuple can store. So if you wanted to store a string and an integer in a tuple, you could use the following Swift code:

```
var person : (String, Int)
```

Then you could store data in that tuple like this:

```
person = ("Janice Parker", 47)
```

When assigning data to a tuple, make sure you have both the proper data types and the correct number of data chunks. So the following would fail because the person tuple expects a string first and then an integer, not an integer first and then a string:

```
person = (47, "Janice Parker") // This would fail
```

A second way to define a tuple is to simply give it data and let Swift infer the data type such as:

```
var person = ("Janice Parker", 47)
```

If you define a tuple by listing its data types, or if you let Swift infer the data types by the type of data you store, it's not always clear what each chunk of data represents. To make it easier to identify the different chunks of data, Swift also lets you name your data types such as:

```
var person : (name: String, age: Int)
```

or if you want Swift to infer the data types by assigning data directly into the tuple:

```
var person = (name: "Janice Parker", age: 47)
```

Named tuples help clarify what each data chunk represents. In this case, the string represents a name and the integer represents an age.

Accessing Data in a Tuple

Once you've created a tuple and stored data in it, you'll need to retrieve that data eventually. Since a tuple contains two or more chunks of data, Swift offers three ways to retrieve the data you want.

First, you can create multiple variables to access the tuple data as follows:

```
var petInfo = ("Rover", 38, true)

var (dog, number, yesValue) = petInfo
print (dog)
print (number)
print (yesValue)
```

In the first line of code, petInfo is a tuple. that contains three chunks of data: a string ("Rover"), an integer (38), and a Boolean value (true).

The second line of code creates three variables (dog, number, yesValue) and assigns their values to the corresponding data stored in the petInfo tuple. That means dog stores "Rover," number stores 38, and yesValue stores true. The print commands simply print this data out to verify that it retrieved information from the tuple.

To access data from a tuple, you must know the order that the tuple stores data. So if you wanted to retrieve a string from the petInfo tuple, you'd have to know that the petInfo tuple stores names as its first chunk of data, a number as its second chunk of data, and a Boolean value as its third chunk of data.

If you don't want to retrieve all the values stored in a tuple, you can just create a variable to store the data you want and use the underscore character (_) as an empty placeholder to represent each additional value in the tuple that you want to ignore.

That means you still need to know the number of data chunks the tuple holds so you can identify the one chunk of data that you want to retrieve. For example, if a tuple contains three items, you can retrieve the first item like this:

```
var petInfo = ("Rover", 38, true)
var (pet,_,_) = petInfo
print (pet)
```

This would store "Rover" in the pet variable so the print command would print "Rover.".

If you just wanted to retrieve the middle value, you could type the following:

```
var petInfo = ("Rover", 38, true)
var (_,aValue,_) = petInfo
print (aValue)
```

This would store the number 38 into the aValue variable and then the print command would print 38.

The underscore characters act as placeholders that identify data in a tuple that you want to ignore. If you omit the underscore characters, Swift won't know which particular data you want out of a tuple. To retrieve data from a tuple, you must know the number and order of the items that the tuple stores.

A second way to retrieve values from a tuple is to use index numbers where the first element is assigned index number 0, the second element is assigned index number 1, and so on. For example, you might store data in a tuple like this:

```
var petInfo = ("Rover", 38, true)
print (petInfo.0)
print (petInfo.1)
print (petInfo.2)
```

The first item in the tuple is assigned index number 0 so the combination of the tuple name (such as petInfo) followed by the index number lets you directly retrieve a specific tuple value. So petInfo.0 retrieves "Rover," petInfo.1 retrieves 38, and petInfo.2 retrieves true.

A third method for accessing data in a tuple involves using names. To uses this method, you must first assign names to each tuple data. For example, the following Swift code defines two names called "name" and "age":

```
var tupleName = (name: "Bridget", age: 31)
```

Now you can access the tuple data by referencing the tuple name followed by the identifying name for each data like this:

```
print (tupleName.name)   // Prints "Bridget"
print (tupleName.age)    // Prints 31
```

All three methods give you different ways to access data stored in tuples so just use the method you like best. For clarity, naming the specific elements of a tuple makes your code easier to understand but at the sacrifice of forcing you to name your tuple data. The index number method and the multiple variable method may be simpler, but can be less clear and requires you to know the exact order of the data you want to retrieve.

To see how to work with tuples, create a new playground by following these steps:

1. Start Xcode.

2. Choose File ➤ New ➤ Playground. (If you see the Xcode welcome screen, you can also click on Get started with a playground.) Xcode asks for a playground name and platform.

3. Click in the Name text field and type **TuplePlayground**.

4. Click in the Platform pop-up menu and choose OS X. Xcode asks where you want to save your playground file.

5. Click on a folder where you want to save your playground file and click the Create button. Xcode displays the playground file.

6. Edit the code as follows:

```
import Cocoa

var tupleName = (greeting: "Happy Birthday", age: 58, happy: true)

// Method #1
var (message, howOld, mood) = tupleName
print (message)
print (howOld)
print (mood)

var (_,stuff,_) = tupleName
print (stuff)

// Method #2

print (tupleName.0)
print (tupleName.1)
print (tupleName.2)

// Method #3

print (tupleName.greeting)
print (tupleName.age)
print (tupleName.happy)
```

When you try all three methods for accessing values from a tuple, you can see how they all work alike. Tuples make it easy to group related data together in a single variable so you can easily keep related information organized. Then you can choose to retrieve data from a tuple using one of three different methods as shown in Figure 10-1.

```
import Cocoa

var tupleName = (greeting: "Happy Birthday", age: 58, happy:     (.0 "Happy Birthday", .1 58, .2 true)
    true)

// Method #1
var (message, howOld, mood) = tupleName
print (message)                                                  "Happy Birthday\n"
print (howOld)                                                   "58\n"
print (mood)                                                     "true\n"

var (_,stuff,_) = tupleName                                      "58\n"
print (stuff)


// Method #2
                                                                 "Happy Birthday\n"
print (tupleName.0)                                              "58\n"
print (tupleName.1)                                              "true\n"
print (tupleName.2)


// Method #3
                                                                 "Happy Birthday\n"
print (tupleName.greeting)                                       "58\n"
print (tupleName.age)                                            "true\n"
print (tupleName.happy)
```

Figure 10-1. Three different ways to retrieve data from a tuple

Using Sets

Arrays and dictionaries are designed to store lists of the same data types such as a list of strings or a list of integers. The difference between arrays and dictionaries is how you retrieve data. Arrays force you to retrieve data by location using index values. Dictionaries let you retrieve data using a key, but you must define a unique key for each chunk of data you store.

Sets represent another way to store lists of identical data types such as strings or floating-point numbers. One speed advantage of a set is determining if something is stored or not. If you store data in an arrays, you'd have to exhaustively search throughout the entire array to determine if an array stores a particular item. If you store data in a dictionary, you have to know the key stored with that value, or you have to exhaustively search through the dictionary's list of values.

Sets let you quickly determine the following far faster than arrays or dictionaries:

- If an item is stored in a set or not
- If a set contains exactly the same items as another set
- If a set is a subset of another set (contains the same items as a larger set)
- If a set is a superset of another set (contains the same items and more than a smaller set)
- If two sets contain the same items or not

Sets make it easy to compare two different groups of data in ways that arrays and dictionaries can't do as easily.

Creating a Set

To create a set, you can define the name of the set and the type of data the set can hold like this:

```
var setName = Set<DataType>()>()
```

The set name should ideally be descriptive of its contents such as memberSet. The data type can be Int (integer), String (strings), Float or Double (decimal numbers), or even the name of another data structure.

A second way to create a set to define it contents within square brackets and let Swift infer the data type. All data must be of the same data type such as:

```
var setName = Set ([Data1, Data2, Data2 ... DataN])
```

Notice that if you omit the "Set" keyword and the enclosing parentheses, you'll define an array, not a set like this:

```
var thisIsAnArray = [Data1, Data2, Data2 ... DataN]
```

Adding and Removing Items from a Set

With a set, you can add new items at any time, just as long as the new item is the same data type as the existing data. To add an item to a set, just specify the set name, the insert command, and the data you want to add inside parentheses like this

```
setName.insert(data)
```

You must specify the array name to add data to and put the actual data in parentheses. Make sure the data you add is of the proper data type. So if you want to add data to a set that currently holds only integers, you can only add another integer to that set.

If you try to add data that already exists in the set, nothing will happen. That means if a set contains the number 53, you can't add another copy of 53 into that set.

To remove data from a set, you just specify the set name, the remove command, and the data you want to remove enclosed in parentheses like this:

```
setName.remove(data)
```

If you try to remove data that doesn't exist in the set, then the remove command returns a nil value. However if the remove command succeeds in removing data from a set, it returns an optional variable. So if you remove data from a set and store it in a variable like this:

```
var variableName = setName.remove(data)
```

The value stored in the variable can be accessed by using an exclamation mark like this:

```
print (variableName!)
```

If you want to remove all items in a set, specify the set name and the removeAll command like this:

```
setName.removeAll()
```

To see how to create a set and add and remove data from it, create a new playground by following these steps:

1. Start Xcode.

2. Choose File ➤ New ➤ Playground. (If you see the Xcode welcome screen, you can also click on Get started with a playground.) Xcode asks for a playground name and platform.

3. Click in the Name text field and type **SetPlayground**.

4. Click in the Platform pop-up menu and choose OS X. Xcode asks where you want to save your playground file.

5. Click on a folder where you want to save your playground file and click the Create button. Xcode displays the playground file.

6. Edit the code as follows:

   ```
   import Cocoa

   var setOne = Set([2, 45, -9, 8, -34])
   var setTwo = Set<Int>()

   setTwo = [34, 90, -83]

   setOne.insert(65)
   setTwo.insert(-381)

   var temp = setOne.remove(45)
   print (temp)
   print (temp!)
   setOne.removeAll()
   ```

This Swift code creates a set called setOne by storing data directly and letting Swift infer the data types, which are integers. Then it creates a second set called setTwo, defined as holding only integers (Int).

After creating setTwo, the next line stores three integers in that set. The two insert commands store different integers into both setOne and setTwo. When the code removes the number 45 from setOne, it stores 45 as an optional variable in the temp variable. To access the actual value, you have to unwrap the optional variable using the exclamation mark (!).

Finally, the removeAll command empties setOne so it contains nothing as shown in Figure 10-2.

```
import Cocoa

var setOne = Set([2, 45, -9, 8, -34])          {-9, 45, 2, -34, 8}
var setTwo = Set<Int>()                        []

setTwo = [34, 90, -83]                         {-83, 90, 34}

setOne.insert(65)                              {-9, 65, 45, 2, -34, 8}
setTwo.insert(-381)                            {-83, -381, 90, 34}

var temp = setOne.remove(45)                   45
print (temp)                                   "Optional(45)\n"
print (temp!)                                  "45\n"
setOne.removeAll()                             []
```

Figure 10-2. *Creating sets, inserting data in a set, and removing data from a set*

Querying a Set

Once you have a set, you can use the following commands to get information about that set:

- count – counts the number of items in a set
- isEmpty – checks if a set is empty (contains 0 items)
- isSubsetOf – checks if one set is wholly contained within another set
- isSupersetOf – checks if one set contains all the items of another set
- isDisjointWith – checks if two sets have no items in common

Whatever the result of these commands, they never affect the data stored in a set.

The count command returns an integer value and just requires the set name and the count command like this:

```
setName.count
```

You can also assign this value to a variable such as:

```
var total = setName.count
```

The isEmpty command returns a Boolean value of true if a set has zero items in it. Otherwise it returns false. Just specify the set name followed by the isEmpty command like this:

```
setOne.isEmpty
```

The isSubsetOf command checks if one set contains items that are also contained in a second set. Only if this second set contains every item from the first set is it considered a subset.

The isSupersetOf command checks if one set is larger and contains all the same items as a smaller set. Only if this first set is larger and has all its items stored in the second set is it considered a superset.

The isDisjointWith command compares two sets. If they have no items in common, then this command returns true. Otherwise it returns false.

To see how to query a set, follow these steps:

1. Make sure the SetPlayground file is loaded in Xcode.

2. Edit the code as follows:

```
import Cocoa

var mySet = Set(["Fred", "Cindy", "Jody", "Grant"])
print (mySet.isEmpty)
mySet.count
mySet.removeAll()
print (mySet.isEmpty)

var myNewSet = Set(["John", "Oscar"])
var myOtherSet = Set(["John", "Oscar", "Sally"])
var myThirdSet = Set(["Rick", "Vinny"])

myNewSet.isSubsetOf(myOtherSet)
myOtherSet.isSupersetOf(myNewSet)
myNewSet.isDisjointWith(myThirdSet)
```

This code creates a set that holds four strings. It uses the isEmpty command to check if the set is empty (false). Then it counts the set (it has 4 items). Finally, it removes all the items from the set and uses the isEmpty command again to check if the set is empty (true).

The next batch of code creates three different sets called myNewSet, myOtherSet, and myThirdSet, which are filled with different names. Then the isSubsetOf command checks if all the items in myNewSet ["John," "Oscar"]are also in the myOtherSet ["John," "Oscar," "Sally"], which is true.

The isSupersetOf command checks if myOtherSet ["John," "Oscar," "Sally"] contains more items and also contains all the items stored in myNewSet ["John," "Oscar"], which is also true.

Finally, the isDisjointWith command checks if myNewSet ["John," "Oscar"] has nothing in common with myThirdSet ["Rick," "Vinny"], which is also true as shown in Figure 10-3.

```
import Cocoa

var mySet = Set(["Fred", "Cindy", "Jody", "Grant"])          {"Jody", "Cindy", "Grant", "Fred"}
print (mySet.isEmpty)                                        "false\n"
mySet.count                                                  4
mySet.removeAll()                                            []
print (mySet.isEmpty)                                        "true\n"

var myNewSet = Set(["John", "Oscar"])                        {"John", "Oscar"}
var myOtherSet = Set(["John", "Oscar", "Sally"])            {"John", "Oscar", "Sally"}
var myThirdSet = Set(["Rick", "Vinny"])                      {"Rick", "Vinny"}

myNewSet.isSubsetOf(myOtherSet)                              true
myOtherSet.isSupersetOf(myNewSet)                           true
myNewSet.isDisjointWith(myThirdSet)                         true
```

Figure 10-3. Querying a set

Manipulating Sets

When you have two or more sets, you can perform operations on both of sets that creates a third set. Some common set operations include:

- union – combines all items from two sets into a new set

- subtract – removes the items of a second set from a first set to form a new set

- intersect – finds the common items in both sets and stores them in a new set

- exclusiveOr – finds items contained in one set or another, but not items in both sets

Think of the union command like adding two sets together and the subtract command like subtracting one set from another. The union command specifies two set names like this:

```
firstSet.union(secondSet)
```

Think of this as equivalent to firstSet + secondSet where all items from both sets get combined into a third set.

The subtract command specifies two set names, but the order makes a difference such as:

```
thirdSet.subtract(firstSet)
firstSet.subtract(thirdSet)
```

These two commands can give different results depending on the contents of each set. Suppose thirdSet contains {1, 2, 3, 4, 5} and firstSet contains [1, 3, 5, 7]. The thirdSet.subtract(firstSet) command works like this:

```
{1, 2, 3, 4, 5}  thirdSet
[1, 3, 5, 7}     firstSet
```

Both sets contain 1, 3, and 5 so those numbers get eliminated. Take 1, 3, and 5 out of thirdSet and you're left with {2, 4}.

The firstSet.subtract(thirdSet) command works like this:

```
[1, 3, 5, 7}      firstSet
{1, 2, 3, 4, 5}  thirdSet
```

Both sets contain 1, 3, and 5 so those numbers get eliminated. Take 1, 3, and 5 out of firstSet and you're left with {7}.

The intersect command finds items in common between two sets. The exclusiveOr command finds items that are not in both sets. Think of the exclusiveOr command as the opposite of the intersect command.

To see how these four different ways to manipulate sets work, follow these steps:

1. Make sure the SetPlayground file is loaded in Xcode.

2. Edit the code as follows:

```
import Cocoa

var firstSet = Set([1, 3, 5, 7])
var secondSet = Set([2, 4, 6, 8])
var thirdSet = Set ([1, 2, 3, 4, 5])

firstSet.union(secondSet)
secondSet.subtract(firstSet)
firstSet.subtract(secondSet)
firstSet.subtract(thirdSet)
thirdSet.subtract(firstSet)

firstSet.intersect(thirdSet)
firstSet.exclusiveOr(thirdSet)
```

Notice how the subtract command works differently depending on the order you list the two sets as shown in Figure 10-4.

```
var firstSet = Set([1, 3, 5, 7])             {5, 7, 3, 1}
var secondSet = Set([2, 4, 6, 8])            {6, 2, 4, 8}
var thirdSet = Set ([1, 2, 3, 4, 5])         {5, 2, 3, 1, 4}

firstSet.union(secondSet)                    {2, 4, 5, 7, 6, 3, 1, 8}
secondSet.subtract(firstSet)                 {6, 2, 4, 8}
firstSet.subtract(secondSet)                 {5, 7, 3, 1}
firstSet.subtract(thirdSet)                  {7}
thirdSet.subtract(firstSet)                  {2, 4}

firstSet.intersect(thirdSet)                 {5, 3, 1}
firstSet.exclusiveOr(thirdSet)               {7, 2, 4}
```

Figure 10-4. Manipulating sets

Using Structures

Both tuples and sets are built-in features of Swift. Structures are a unique way for you to group different types of data in a single place. With a traditional variable, you can only store one chunk of data at a time. With a structure, you can define two or more chunks of data to store in a single variable. Variables declared inside a structure are called properties.

A structure that stores two chunks of data would look like this:

```
struct structureName {
    var variableName1 : dataType
    var variableName2 : dataType
}
```

Remember, the data type of each variable can be simple data types such as Int, String, or Double, or they can be more complicated data types such as arrays, tuples, sets, or dictionaries.

You can define two or more variables inside a structure where each variable can contain different data types such as a string or an integer. No matter how many properties a structure holds, you must initialize the properties before you can store data in them.

Swift provides three ways to initialize properties. First, you can define an initial value for each property like this:

```
struct structureName {
    var variableName1 : dataType = initialValue
    var variableName2 : dataType = initialValue
}
```

To simplify the property declaration, a second way is to omit the data type and let Swift infer the data type like this:

```
struct structureName {
    var variableName1 = initialValue
    var variableName2 = initialValue
}
```

When you assign an initial value to properties, you can create a variable to represent that structure like this:

```
var variableName = structureName()
```

A third way to initialize structure properties is to create an init function. This means you must create a list of property names and their data types. Then assign values to those properties when you create a variable to represent that structure.

For example, suppose you wanted to store information about a person such as his or her name, e-mail address, and phone number. Instead of creating three separate variables, you could create a single structure like this:

```
struct person {
    var name : String
    var email : String
    var phone : String
}
```

When you create a variable based on this structure, you need to include initial values such as:

```
var workers = person(name: "Sue", email: "sdk@aol.com", phone: "555-1234")
```

Creating a structure involves two parts:

- Create a structure with two or more variables (properties)
- Create a variable to represent that structure and assign initial values to those properties

Storing and Retrieving Items from a Structure

A structure lets you define the type of related data to store. Then you need to create a variable name to represent that structure. Finally, to store in a structure, you need to specify the structure name and the variable name separated by a period like this:

```
structureVariable.variableName = value
```

To retrieve data from a structure, you can assign a variable to a structure's variable like this:

```
var variableName = structureVariable.variableName
```

To see how to create a structure, initialize its properties, and add and retrieve data, create a new playground by following these steps:

1. Start Xcode.

2. Choose File ➤ New ➤ Playground. (If you see the Xcode welcome screen, you can also click on Get started with a playground.) Xcode asks for a playground name and platform.

3. Click in the Name text field and type **StructurePlayground**.

4. Click in the Platform pop-up menu and choose OS X. Xcode asks where you want to save your playground file.

5. Click on a folder where you want to save your playground file and click the Create button. Xcode displays the playground file.

6. Edit the code as follows:

```
import Cocoa

struct pet {
    var name : String = ""
    var age : Int = 0
}

var dog = pet()
dog.name = "Fido"
dog.age = 4

print (dog.name)
print (dog.age)

struct person {
    var name : String
    var email : String
    var phone : String
}

var workers = person(name: "Sue", email: "sdk@aol.com", phone: "555-1234")

let boss = workers.name
print (boss)

workers.name = "Bo"
print (workers.email)
print (workers.phone)
```

The first structure defines initial values for its properties so there's no need for an init function. That's why you can create a variable with empty parentheses like this:

```
var dog = pet()
```

The second structure does not define initial values for its properties, so when you create a variable to represent that structure, you must define initial values.

```
var workers = person(name: "Sue", email: "sdk@aol.com", phone: "555-1234")
```

To store data in a structure, you need to specify the variable name representing the structure followed by the property name as shown in Figure 10-5.

```
import Cocoa

struct pet {
    var name : String = ""                          pet
    var age : Int = 0                               pet
}                                                   pet

var dog = pet()
dog.name = "Fido"
dog.age = 4

print (dog.name)                                    "Fido\n"
print (dog.age)                                     "4\n"

struct person {
    var name : String
    var email : String
    var phone : String
}

var workers = person(name: "Sue", email: "sdk@aol.com",   person
    phone: "555-1234")

let boss = workers.name                             "Sue"
print (boss)                                        "Sue\n"

workers.name = "Bo"                                 person
print (workers.email)                              "sdk@aol.com\n"
print (workers.phone)                              "555-1234\n"
```

Figure 10-5. Creating a structure and retrieving data

Using Structures in an OS X Program

By themselves, structures can only hold a limited number of data. For more flexibility, structures are often combined with other data structures such as arrays. That way you can create an array of structures, which you'll use in this sample program. The program will let you type in multiple names, addresses, and phone numbers, then delete data as well.

1. From within Xcode choose File ➤ New ➤ Project.

2. Click Application under the OS X category.

3. Click Cocoa Application and click the Next button. Xcode now asks for a product name.

4. Click in the Product Name text field and type **StructureProgram**.

5. Make sure the Language pop-up menu displays Swift and that no check boxes are selected.

6. Click the Next button. Xcode asks where you want to store the project.

7. Choose a folder to store your project and click the Create button.

8. Click the MainMenu.xib file in the Project Navigator.

9. Click on the StructureProgram icon to make the window of the user interface appear.

10. Choose View ➤ Utilities ➤ Show Object Library to make the Object Library appear in the bottom right corner of the Xcode window.

11. Drag two Push Buttons, four Labels, and four Text Fields on the user interface and double-click on the push buttons and labels to change the text that appears on them so that it looks similar to Figure 10-6.

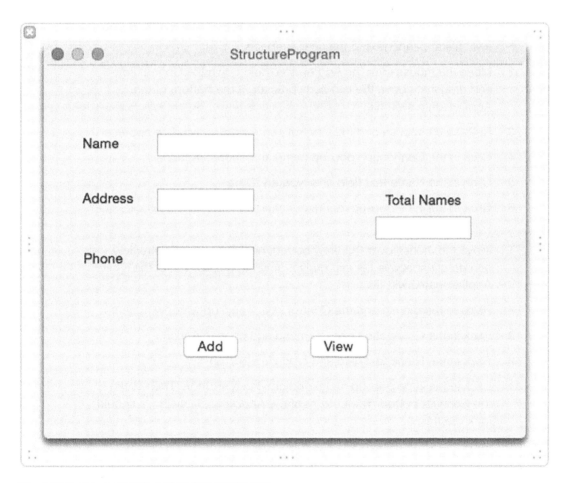

Figure 10-6. The user interface of the StructureProgram

After you type a name, address, and phone number in the appropriate text fields, the Add button will store this information in a structure, and then store this structure in an array. Each time you add another name, address, and phone number, you'll be adding another structure to the array while the Total Names text field constantly lists the total number of structures stored in the array.

The View button removes the last item from the array and displays its contents in an alert dialog so you can verify its contents. Then it displays the new total number of structures in the array.

Each text field will need a separate IBOutlet and each push button will need a separate IBAction method, which you'll need to create by Control-dragging each item from the user interface to your AppDelegate.swift file:

1. With your user interface still visible in the Xcode window, choose View ➤ Assistant Editor ➤ Show Assistant Editor. The AppDelegate. swift file appears next to the user interface.

2. Move the mouse over the Add button, hold down the Control key, and drag just above the last curly bracket at the bottom of the AppDelegate.swift file.

3. Release the mouse and the Control key. A pop-up window appears.

4. Click in the Connection pop-up menu and choose Action.

5. Click in the Name text field and type **addData**.

6. Click in the Type pop-up menu and choose NSButton. Then click the Connect button.

7. Move the mouse over the View button, hold down the Control key, and drag just above the last curly bracket at the bottom of the AppDelegate.swift file.

8. Release the mouse and the Control key. A pop-up window appears.

9. Click in the Connection pop-up menu and choose Action.

10. Click in the Name text field and type **viewButton**.

11. Click in the Type pop-up menu and choose NSButton. Then click the Connect button. The bottom of the AppDelegate.swift file should look like this:

    ```
    @IBAction func viewData(sender: NSButton) {

        }

    @IBAction func addData(sender: NSButton) {
        }
    ```

12. Move the mouse over the Name text field that appears to the right of the Add button, hold down the Control key, and drag below the @IBOutlet line in the AppDelegate.swift file.

13. Release the mouse and the Control key. A pop-up window appears.

14. Click in the Name text field and type **nameField** and click the Connect button.

15. Move the mouse over the Address text field that appears to the right of the Add button, hold down the Control key, and drag below the @IBOutlet line in the AppDelegate.swift file.

16. Release the mouse and the Control key. A pop-up window appears.

17. Click in the Name text field and type **addressField** and click the Connect button.

18. Move the mouse over the Phone text field that appears to the right of the Delete button, hold down the Control key, and drag below the @IBOutlet line in the AppDelegate.swift file.

19. Release the mouse and the Control key. A pop-up window appears.

20. Click in the Name text field and type **phoneField** and click the Connect button.

21. Move the mouse over the Total Names text field that appears to the right of the Query button, hold down the Control key, and drag below the @IBOutlet line in the AppDelegate.swift file.

22. Release the mouse and the Control key. A pop-up window appears.

23. Click in the Name text field and type **totalField** and click the Connect button. You should now have the following IBOutlets that represent all the text fields on your user interface:

    ```
    @IBOutlet weak var window: NSWindow!
    @IBOutlet weak var nameField: NSTextField!
    @IBOutlet weak var addressField: NSTextField!
    @IBOutlet weak var phoneField: NSTextField!
    @IBOutlet weak var totalField: NSTextField!
    ```

At this point we've connected the user interface to our Swift code so we can use the IBOutlets to retrieve and display data on the user interface. We've also created the IBAction methods so the push buttons on the user interface will make the program actually work. Now we just need to write Swift code to create an initial dictionary and then write more Swift code in each IBAction method to add, delete, or query the dictionary.

1. Underneath the IBOutlet list in the AppDelegate.swift file, type the following to create a structure that can hold three strings, a name, address, and phone number; a variable that represents the structure; and an array of structures:

```
struct person {
var name = ""
var address = ""
var phone = ""
}

var employee = person()

var arrayOfStructures = [person] ()
```

2. Modify the addData IBAction method so it takes a value from the Name, Address, and Phone text fields and stores them in the employee structure. Then it stores that structure in an array, displays the total number of array items in the Total Names text field, and clears the Name, Address, and Phone text fields:

```
@IBAction func addData(sender: NSButton) {
    employee.name = nameField.stringValue
    employee.address = addressField.stringValue
    employee.phone = phoneField.stringValue
    arrayOfStructures.append(employee)
    totalField.integerValue = arrayOfStructures.count

    nameField.stringValue = ""
    addressField.stringValue = ""
    phoneField.stringValue = ""
}
```

3. Modify the viewData IBAction method so it takes a value from the Key text field and deletes the associated value from the dictionary as follows:

```
@IBAction func viewData(sender: NSButton) {
    var myAlert = NSAlert()
    if arrayOfStructures.isEmpty {
        myAlert.messageText = "Array is empty"
        myAlert.runModal()
    } else {
        var personData = person()
        personData = (arrayOfStructures.removeLast())
        totalField.integerValue = arrayOfStructures.count
        myAlert.messageText = personData.name + "\r\n" + personData.address +
        "\r\n" + personData.phone
        myAlert.runModal()
    }
}
```

The code inside the viewData IBAction method creates an alert dialog. Then it checks if the array is empty. If so, it displays "Array is empty" in the alert dialog.

If the array is not empty, then it removes the last structure stored in the array, displays the new total number of array items in the Total Names text field, and displays the removed structure data in the alert dialog.

The complete contents of the AppDelegate.swift file should look like this:

```swift
import Cocoa

@NSApplicationMain
class AppDelegate: NSObject, NSApplicationDelegate {

    @IBOutlet weak var window: NSWindow!
    @IBOutlet weak var nameField: NSTextField!
    @IBOutlet weak var addressField: NSTextField!
    @IBOutlet weak var phoneField: NSTextField!
    @IBOutlet weak var totalField: NSTextField!

    struct person {
        var name = ""
        var address = ""
        var phone = ""
    }

    var employee = person()

    var arrayOfStructures = [person] ()

    func applicationDidFinishLaunching(aNotification: NSNotification) {
        // Insert code here to initialize your application
    }

    func applicationWillTerminate(aNotification: NSNotification) {
        // Insert code here to tear down your application
    }

    @IBAction func viewData(sender: NSButton) {
        var myAlert = NSAlert()
        if arrayOfStructures.isEmpty {
            myAlert.messageText = "Array is empty"
            myAlert.runModal()
        } else {
            var personData = person()
            personData = (arrayOfStructures.removeLast())
            totalField.integerValue = arrayOfStructures.count
            myAlert.messageText = personData.name + "\r\n" + personData.address + "\r\n" +
            personData.phone
            myAlert.runModal()
        }
    }
}
```

```
@IBAction func addData(sender: NSButton) {
    employee.name = nameField.stringValue
    employee.address = addressField.stringValue
    employee.phone = phoneField.stringValue
    arrayOfStructures.append(employee)
    totalField.integerValue = arrayOfStructures.count

    nameField.stringValue = ""
    addressField.stringValue = ""
    phoneField.stringValue = ""
}
}
```

To see how this program works, follow these steps:

1. Choose Product ➤ Run. Xcode runs your DictionaryProgram project.

2. Click in the Name text field and type **Bob**.

3. Click in the Address text field and type **123 Main**.

4. Click in the Phone text field and type **555-1234**.

5. Click the Add button. The program shows the number of items in then array (1) in the Total Names text field.

6. Repeat steps 2 – 5 except type the name **Jane**, the address **90 Oak Lane**, and the phone number of **555-9874**. The number 2 appears in the Total Names text field.

7. Click the View button. An alert dialog appears, displaying Jane, 90 Oak Lane, and 555-9874 as shown in Figure 10-7.

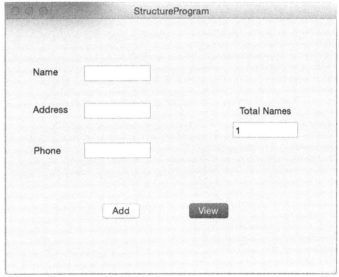

Figure 10-7. An alert dialog showing the last structure added to the array

8. Click OK to make the alert dialog go away.

9. Choose StructureProgram ➤ Quit StructureProgram.

Summary

Tuples are a way to store different data types in a single variable. Like arrays and dictionaries, sets can store lists of the same data type. While arrays are best for storing ordered information and dictionaries are best for fast retrieval of data, sets are best for checking if items belong in a set or not as well as making it easy to manipulate two or more sets.

If you need to store large groups of related data, you could use a tuple, but a tuple gets clumsy with large numbers of data. As an alternative, you can create a structure that lets you define different types of data to hold. Beyond the basic data types (Int, String, Float, and Double), structures also let you hold other data structures such as arrays, dictionaries, or sets. For greater flexibility, you can even put structures in arrays, dictionaries, or sets as well.

In the sample OS X program that you created, you learned how to create a structure and store its data in an array. By now you should be getting comfortable using IBOutlets to display or retrieve data from a user interface, along with creating IBAction methods to make your program actually work.

With tuples, sets, and structures along with arrays and dictionaries, you can combine data structures in a variety of ways to store data in the most flexible way for your particular needs.

Chapter **11**

Creating Classes and Objects

The heart of programming in Swift using Xcode is object-oriented programming. The main idea is to divide a large program into separate objects where each object ideally represents a physical entity. For example, if you were creating a program to control a car, one object might represent the car's engine, a second object might represent the car's entertainment system, and a third object might represent the car's heating and cooling system.

Now if you want to update the part of a program that controls the car's engine, you just have to modify or replace the object that controls that car engine. Objects not only help you better understand how different parts of a program work together, but also isolate code so you can create building blocks to put together larger, more sophisticated programs.

Objects help you visualize your program as separate building blocks that are independent from each other. Before object-oriented programming, programmers divided programs into subprograms, which also acted like miniature building blocks. The main difference between subprograms and objects is that subprograms could access data used by other subprograms. That meant that if you modified one subprogram, you often inadvertently affected other parts of the program. That made fixing errors or bugs difficult and also made modifying programs difficult as well.

With objects, the main idea is to create separate, independent building blocks that work together without affecting each other's data. To keep data isolated, objects use encapsulation. That means an object has its own variables (called properties) and functions (called methods).

Objects can communicate with each other in two ways:

- By storing new values in another object's properties
- By calling another object's methods

Ideally, a program should consist of multiple objects that perform tasks completely independent from each other. That makes it easy to modify a program by replacing one object with an improved version of that object.

Creating Classes

There are two steps to creating an object. First, you have to create a class. Second, you create an object based on that class.

A class looks and works much like a structure (see Chapter 10) where you define a name. Once you've defined a class, you can create one or more objects based on that class. Think of a class as a cookie cutter that defines the shape of cookies, and objects as different type of dough you can define based on the class.

The simplest type of class you can define looks like this:

```
class className {

}
```

To create an object from this class, you just declare a variable, but instead of defining a data type such as Int or String, you define the class name such as:

```
var myObject = className()
```

Of course, a class that contains no code is useless, so the two types of code you can include in a class are variables (known as properties) and functions for manipulate data (known as methods). Creating properties in a class involves creating one or more variables and defining a data type and an initial value such as:

```
class className {
    var name : String = ""
    var ID : Int = 0
    var salary : Double = 0
}
```

Initial values are important because when you create an object based on a class, you don't want uninitialized values that could cause problems if you try to use them.

To define a property, you declare a variable name, a data type, and an initial value. Since Swift can infer data types, you could omit the data type declaration and just assign initial values like this:

```
class className {
    var name = ""
    var ID   = 0
    var salary = 0.0
}
```

Whether you define class properties with a data type or not, you can create an object from this class by just creating a variable name, setting it equal to the class name, and following it with an empty set of parentheses like this:

```
var myObject = className()
```

Both of the previous methods create the same initial values for the class properties. For more flexibility, you can create an initializer method called init. This lets you define initial values each time you create an object from a class. An initializer in a class might look like this:

```
class secondClass {
    var name : String
    var ID : Int
    var salary : Double
    init (name: String, ID: Int, salary: Double) {
        self.name = name
        self.ID = ID
        self.salary = salary
    }
}
```

This initializer method (init) defines a parameter list that accepts three items: a string, an integer, and a double value. Then it stores this information in the name, ID, and salary properties respectively. When a class has an initializer, you must create an object from that class by including the proper number and data type to match the initializer parameter list.

That means creating an object that includes a string, an integer, and a double value in parentheses like this:

```
var secondObject = secondClass (name: "Joe", ID: 102, salary: 120000)
```

Notice that when you include data in the parameter list, you must label each data chunk with the variable name defined in the initializer parameter list. In this case, the three parameter names are name, ID, and salary, so creating an object means identifying the data with those same parameter names.

Accessing Properties in an Object

To access an object's properties, you must specify the object name followed by a period and the property name such as:

```
objectName.propertyName = data
```

You can also assign an object's property values to a variable like this:

```
var person = myObject.name
```

To access properties, you need to specify the object name, a period, and the property name that you want to access such as:

```
print (person.name)
```

> **Note**   When accessing values stored in properties, make sure you specify the object name, not the class name. If you created a "person" object from the "className" class, then you would access properties by specifying the object name (person) and the property name (name, ID, salary) such as person.name or person.ID. You would not access the property value by using the class name such as className.name or className.ID. If you try this, your code will not work.

Just like ordinary variables, an object's properties can only hold one chunk of data at a time. The moment you store new data in a property, it wipes out the previous data.

To see how to create a class and work with an object's properties, create a new playground by following these steps:

1. Start Xcode.

2. Choose File ➤ New ➤ Playground. (If you see the Xcode welcome screen, you can also click on Get started with a playground.) Xcode asks for a playground name and platform.

3. Click in the Name text field and type **ClassPlayground**.

4. Click in the Platform pop-up menu and choose OS X. Xcode asks where you want to save your playground file.

5. Click on a folder where you want to save your playground file and click the Create button. Xcode displays the playground file.

6. Edit the code as follows:

```
import Cocoa

class className {
    var name = ""
    var ID  = 0
    var salary = 0
}

var worker = className()
worker.name = "Bob"
worker.ID = 102
worker.salary = 10

var executive = className()
executive.name = "Robert"
executive.ID = 1
executive.salary = worker.salary * 100
```

```
class secondClass {
    var name : String
    var ID : Int
    var salary : Double
    init (name: String, ID: Int, salary: Double) {
        self.name = name
        self.ID = ID
        self.salary = salary
    }
}

var consultant = secondClass (name: "Joe", ID: 17, salary: 50000)
```

The first class initializes its properties when they're declared. Then it creates an object (worker) based on the class (className). To store data in the worker object, the code specifies the object name (worker) and property name and assigns it a value.

The second class example uses an initializer to define the property values. The init method accepts three chunks of data, a string, an integer, and a decimal (Double) value in that order.

To create an object (consultant) from this second class (secondClass), the parentheses need to include the right number of data in the right order along with the proper data types in addition to displaying a label to identify what the data means as shown in Figure 11-1.

```
class className {
    var name = ""
    var ID   = 0
    var salary = 0
}

var worker = className()                        {name "" ID 0 salary 0}
worker.name = "Bob"                             {name "Bob" ID 0 salary 0}
worker.ID = 102                                 {name "Bob" ID 102 salary 0}
worker.salary = 10                              {name "Bob" ID 102 salary 10}


var executive = className()                     {name "" ID 0 salary 0}
executive.name = "Robert"                       {name "Robert" ID 0 salary 0}
executive.ID = 1                                {name "Robert" ID 1 salary 0}
executive.salary = worker.salary * 100          {name "Robert" ID 1 salary 1000}


class secondClass {
    var name : String
    var ID : Int
    var salary : Double
    init (name: String, ID: Int, salary: Double) {
        self.name = name
        self.ID = ID
        self.salary = salary
    }
}

var consultant = secondClass (name: "Joe", ID: 17,    {name "Joe" ID 17 salary 50000}
    salary: 50000)
```

Figure 11-1. Creating a class file and accessing properties

Computed Properties in an Object

As an alternative to defining fixed values for properties, you can also use computed properties where one property's initial value depends on the value of another property. The simplest way to create a computed property is to define a property name, a data type, and then in curly brackets write code that calculates a value. Finally, use the "return" keyword to define the value to store in the property like this:

```
class shape {
    var height : Int = 5
    var width : Int {
      return height * 2
    }
}
var rectangle = shape()
print (rectangle.height)
print (rectangle.width)
```

This computed property simply takes the value stored in the height property, multiples it by 2, and stores that result in the width property. When you create an object based on the shape class, the initial value of 5 gets stored in the height property and the computed property multiples the height value (5) by 2 to get 10, which it stores in the width property as shown in Figure 11-2.

```
class shape {
    var height : Int = 5
    var width : Int {
      return height * 2                                    10
    }
}

var rectangle = shape()                              {height 5}
println (rectangle.height)                           "5"
println (rectangle.width)                            "10"
```

Figure 11-2. Using computed properties to determine a property's initial value

In this example of a computed property, the value of one property (width) gets the value of another property (height) to determine its own value. In technical terms, this is known as a getter.

Setting Other Properties

Another option is to use what's called a setter. With a setter, defining one property sets the value of another property. Since getters and setters are so similar, they're often used within the same property. That way one property uses a getter to calculate its value from another property, then if you set that property with a value, it can change another property. Defining getters and setters looks like this:

```
class blob {
      var property1 : dataType = value
   var property2 : dataType {
      get {
         return valueHere
      }
      set {
         property1 = valueHere
      }
   }
}
```

In the getter, you always need a "return" keyword to return a value to the property that has the getter. In the setter, you must assign a property to a value. This value can be a fixed value or a calculation that returns a value.

> **Note**   You don't need both a getter and a setter. You can just have a getter, which you can shorten by eliminating the "get" keyword and just enclose code in curly brackets as in the class shape example in the beginning of this section. You can also have just a setter, but you'll need to use the "set" keyword.

In the above example, every time property2 gets assigned a new value, it uses its setter to define a new value for property1.

A setter can also accept a value and use that value to calculate a new result for a different property. To accept a value for a setter, you just need to create a variable enclosed in parentheses and use that value to calculate a result for another property. If you don't create a variable enclosed in parentheses, you can just use the default parameter name of "newValue." The following example shows how to use a setter:

```
class blob {
      var property1 : dataType = value
    var property2 : dataType {
      get {
          return valueHere
      }
      set (newValue) {
          property1 = valueHere based on newValue
      }
    }
}
```

To see how getters and setters work, follow these steps:

1. Make sure your ClassPlayground file is loaded into Xcode.

2. Edit the code as follows:

```
import Cocoa

class shape {
    var height : Int = 5
    var width : Int {
      return height * 2
    }
}

var rectangle = shape()
print (rectangle.height)
print (rectangle.width)

rectangle.height = 20
print (rectangle.width)

class blob {
    var height : Int = 5
    var width : Int = 10
    var area : Int {
        get {
            return height * width
        }
```

```
        set {
            height = 24
            width = 45
        }
    }
}

var cat = blob()
cat.area
cat.area = 129

class anotherBlob {
    var height : Int = 5
    var width : Int = 10
    var area : Int {
        get {
            return height * width
        }
        set (newValue) {
            height = newValue + 10
            width = newValue - 5
        }
    }
}

var CEO = anotherBlob()
print (CEO.area)
CEO.area = 247
print (CEO.height)
print (CEO.width)
```

You can think of a getter and setter as a function that changes other properties. Be careful when using getters and setters, though, since they could cause unexpected behavior if you aren't aware of their existence or how they work. Figure 11-3 shows the result of the above code so you can see how the getters and setters affect properties.

```
class shape {
    var height : Int = 5
    var width : Int {
        return height * 2                                    (2 times)
    }
}

var rectangle = shape()                                      {height 5}
println (rectangle.height)                                   "5"
println (rectangle.width)                                    "10"

rectangle.height = 20                                        {height 20}
println (rectangle.width)                                    "40"



class blob {
    var height : Int = 5
    var width : Int = 10
    var area : Int {
        get {
            return height * width                            50
        }
        set {
            height = 24                                      {height 24 width 10}
            width = 45                                       {height 24 width 45}
        }
    }
}

var cat = blob()                                             {height 5 width 10}
cat.area                                                     50
cat.area = 129                                               {height 24 width 45}



class anotherBlob {
    var height : Int = 5
    var width : Int = 10
    var area : Int {
        get {
            return height * width                            50
        }
        set (newValue) {
            height = newValue + 10                           {height 257 width 10}
            width = newValue - 5                             {height 257 width 242}
        }
    }
}

var CEO = anotherBlob()                                      {height 5 width 10}
println (CEO.area)                                           "50"
CEO.area = 247                                               {height 257 width 242}
println (CEO.height)                                         "257"
println (CEO.width)                                          "242"
```

Figure 11-3. Using getters and setters to modify properties

Using Property Observers

Swift provides two property observers called willSet and didSet. The willSet property observer runs code before a property receives a value. The didSet property observer runs code after a property receives a value.

Like getters and setters, property observers essentially are functions that run when a property gets a new value. The basic structure for a willSet and didSet property observer is identical to the structure for a getter and setter like this:

```
var property : dataType = initialValue {
    willSet {

    }
    didSet {

    }
}
```

The willSet property observer runs code before the property gets a new value. The didSet property observer runs code after the property gets a new value. To see how property observers work, follow these steps:

1. Make sure your ClassPlayground file is loaded into Xcode.

2. Edit the code as follows:

```
import Cocoa

class animal {
    var IQ : Int = 0
    var legs : Int = 0 {
        willSet {
            IQ += 10
        }
        didSet {
            IQ -= 5
        }
    }
}

var pet = animal()
print (pet.IQ)
pet.legs = 4
print (pet.IQ)
```

In this example, the IQ property has an initial value of 0. Notice that when you set the legs property to 4, it immediately runs the willSet property observer code, which increases the IQ property by 10. Then it immediately runs the code in the didSet property observer, which subtracts 3 as shown in Figure 11-4.

```
class animal {
    var IQ : Int = 0
    var legs : Int = 0 {
        willSet {
            IQ += 10
        }
        didSet {
            IQ -= 3
        }
    }
}

var pet = animal()                              {IQ 0 legs 0}
println (pet.IQ)                                "0"
pet.legs = 4                                    {IQ 7 legs 4}
println (pet.IQ)                                "7"
```

Figure 11-4. Using property observers

Creating Methods

A class that simply stores one or more properties can be convenient for grouping related data together. However, what makes object-oriented programming more useful is when objects can also manipulate their own data. To create mini-programs for objects to run, you need to define functions (called methods) inside a class.

You've already seen methods when you've linked push buttons from the user interface to create an IBAction method in the Swift code file. The simplest method inside a class performs the exact same function like this:

```
class countDown {
    var counter = 10
    func decrement() {
        counter--
    }
}
```

This decrement method simply subtracts 1 from the counter property, which has an initial value of 10. To make this method run, you have to specify the object name, a period, and the method name like this:

```
var counter = countDown ()
counter.decrement()
```

This decrement method does the exact same thing every time, which subtracts 1 from the counter property. A more interesting and flexible method would accept data (one or more parameters) to modify the code in the method works such as:

```
class countDown {
    var counter = 10
    func decrement() {
        counter--
    }
    func decrementByValue (step : Int) {
        counter -= step
    }
}
```

The second method, decrementByValue, accepts a single integer that gets stored in a variable called "step." Then it subtracts the value of "step" from the counter property as shown in Figure 11-5.

```
class countDown {
    var counter = 10
    func decrement() {
        counter--                                        10
    }
    func decrementByValue (step : Int) {
        counter -= step
    }
}

var counter = countDown ()                               {counter 10}
counter.decrement()                                      {counter 9}
counter.decrementByValue(3)                              {counter 6}
```

Figure 11-5. Running a method that accepts a value

When a method accepts data, it can also return a specific value. To create such a method, you need to identify the data type the method returns (using the -> symbols) along with the "return" keyword that defines the specific value to return.

So if you wanted to create a method that returns a Float data type, you could define a method such as:

```
class mathBrain {
    var tempValue: Float = 0
    func average (first : Float, second : Float) -> Float {
        return (first + second) / 2
    }
}
```

This method accepts two Float numbers (stored in variables called "first" and "second") and returns a Float value. To call this method, you would specify an object name, a period, the method name, and two numbers that are Float data types.

Notice that this method has two parameters called "first" and "second." When passing the first parameter, you do not need to specify the parameter name ("first") since it doesn't have a # symbol in front of it. However, when passing any other parameters, you must specify the parameter name such as:

```
var math = mathBrain()
var temp : Float = math.average(4.0, second: 9.0)
print (temp)
```

To see how to create a set and add and remove data from it, create a new playground by following these steps:

1. Start Xcode.

2. Choose File ➤ New ➤ Playground. (If you see the Xcode welcome screen, you can also click on Get started with a playground.) Xcode asks for a playground name and platform.

3. Click in the Name text field and type **MethodPlayground**.

4. Click in the Platform pop-up menu and choose OS X. Xcode asks where you want to save your playground file.

5. Click on a folder where you want to save your playground file and click the Create button. Xcode displays the playground file.

6.   Edit the code as follows:

```
import Cocoa

class mathBrain {
    var tempValue: Float = 0
    func average (first : Float, second : Float) -> Float {
        return (first + second) / 2
    }
}

var math = mathBrain()
var temp : Float = math.average(4.0, second: 9.0)
print (temp)
```

The "average" method accepts two parameters, adds them together, and divides by 2. Then it uses the "return" keyword to return this value.

When the average method gets past the numbers 4.0 and 9.0, it returns a value of 6.5, which gets stored in a variable called "temp" as shown in Figure 11-6.

```
class mathBrain {
    var tempValue: Float = 0
    func average (first : Float, second : Float) -> Float
        {
        return (first + second) / 2                      6.5
    }
}

var math = mathBrain()                                    {tempValue 0}
var temp : Float = math.average(4.0, second: 9.0)        6.5
println (temp)                                            "6.5"
```

Figure 11-6. Creating sets, inserting data in a set, and removing data from a set

Using Objects in an OS X Program

Objects can contain any number of properties and those properties can hold simple data types such as integers or strings, or more complicated data types such as tuples, sets, or arrays. An object can also contain one or more methods that typically manipulate the object's properties.

In this sample program, you'll define one class and create two objects based on that class. You'll also see how to store a class in a separate file. Rather than cram everything into a single file, it's easier to store code in separate files.

The two objects will run methods stored in the other object. The user interface will also retrieve values from both object's properties to display in the text field of the user interface.

To learn more about user interfaces, you'll also see how to connect two buttons to a single IBAction method and determine which button the user clicked. As usual, you'll see how to display data in a user interface item through an IBOutlet. To create the sample program, follow these steps:

1. From within Xcode choose File ➤ New ➤ Project.

2. Click Application under the OS X category.

3. Click Cocoa Application and click the Next button. Xcode now asks for a product name.

4. Click in the Product Name text field and type **ObjectProgram**.

5. Make sure the Language pop-up menu displays Swift and that no check boxes are selected.

6. Click the Next button. Xcode asks where you want to store the project.

7. Choose a folder to store your project and click the Create button.

8. Click the MainMenu.xib file in the Project Navigator.

9. Click on the ObjectProgram icon to make the window of the user interface appear.

10. Choose View ➤ Utilities ➤ Show Object Library to make the Object Library appear in the bottom right corner of the Xcode window.

11. Drag two Push Buttons, two Labels, and two Text Fields on the user interface and double-click on the push buttons and labels to change the text that appears on them so that it looks similar to Figure 11-7.

Figure 11-7. The user interface of the ObjectProgram

This user interface will display the number of hit points for two characters: a sheriff and an outlaw. Each time you click either the Sheriff Shoot or the Outlaw Shoot button, an IBAction method will randomly determine if the other character was hit or not. If so, it will also determine how much damage the shot causes, ranging from 1 to 3. Any changes will appear in the text field under the Sheriff or Outlaw label.

The Sheriff Shoot and Outlaw Shoot buttons runs an IBAction method that first determines which button the user clicked: the Sheriff Shoot or the Outlaw Shoot button. To identify which button the user clicked, you'll need to modify a Tag property on each button so the Sheriff Shoot button will have a Tag value of 0 while the Outlaw Shoot button will have a Tag value of 1.

After determining whether the sheriff or the outlaw is shooting, the IBAction method runs the shoot method that randomly determines if the shot hit and the damage it caused, which gets subtracted from the hitPoints property of each object.

The total number of hit points appears in the text field under the Sheriff and Outlaw label. The moment the total number of hit points for either the sheriff or outlaw drops to 0 or less, an alert dialog appears to let you know whether the sheriff or the outlaw died. To connect your user interface to your Swift code, follow these steps:

1. With your user interface still visible in the Xcode window, choose View ➤ Assistant Editor ➤ Show Assistant Editor. The AppDelegate. swift file appears next to the user interface.

2. Move the mouse over the Sheriff Shoot button, hold down the Control key, and drag just above the last curly bracket at the bottom of the AppDelegate.swift file.

3. Release the mouse and the Control key. A pop-up window appears.

4. Click in the Connection pop-up menu and choose Action.

5. Click in the Name text field and type **shootButton**.

6. Click in the Type pop-up menu and choose NSButton. Then click the Connect button.

7. Move the mouse over the Outlaw Shoot button, hold down the Control key, and drag over the existing IBAction shootButton method you just created until the entire method appears highlighted as shown in Figure 11-8.

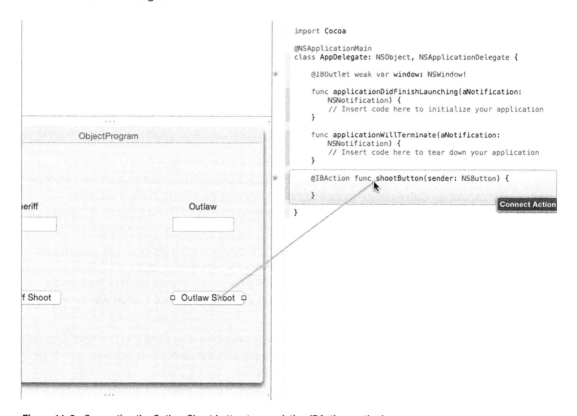

Figure 11-8. Connecting the Outlaw Shoot button to an existing IBAction method

8. Release the mouse and the Control key to connect the Outlaw Shoot button to the existing IBAction shootButton method.

9. Move the mouse over the Sheriff text field, hold down the Control key, and drag below the @IBOutlet line in the AppDelegate.swift file.

10. Release the mouse and the Control key. A pop-up window appears.

11. Click in the Name text field and type **sheriffHitPoints** and click the Connect button.

12. Move the mouse over the Outlaw text field that appears to the right of the Add button, hold down the Control key, and drag below the @IBOutlet line in the AppDelegate.swift file.

13. Release the mouse and the Control key. A pop-up window appears.

14. Click in the Name text field and type **outlawHitPoints** and click the Connect button. You should now have the following IBOutlets that represent all the text fields on your user interface:

```
@IBOutlet weak var window: NSWindow!
@IBOutlet weak var sheriffHitPoints: NSTextField!
@IBOutlet weak var outlawHitPoints: NSTextField!
```

At this point we've connected the user interface to our Swift code so we can use the IBOutlets to display data on the user interface. We've also created a single IBAction method to run when the user clicks on either of the two push buttons. Now we need to change the Tag property of the Outlaw Shoot button.

1. Click on the Outlaw Shoot button to select it.

2. Choose View ➤ Utilities ➤ Show Attributes Inspector. The Attributes Inspector pane appears in the upper right corner of the Xcode window.

3. Scroll down to the View category and change the Tag property to 1 as shown in Figure 11-9.

Figure 11-9. The Tag property at the bottom of the Attributes Inspector pane

Now that we've defined the user interface, the next step is to create a separate Swift file to hold our class, which you can do by following these steps:

1. Choose File ➤ New ➤ File. A dialog appears asking for a template to use.

2. Click Source under the OS X category and then click the Swift File as shown in Figure 11-10.

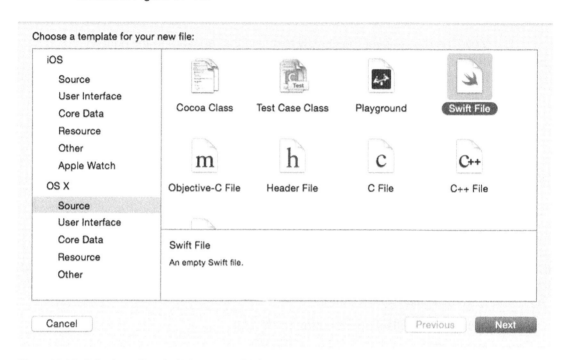

Figure 11-10. *Selecting a file to hold the class definition code*

3. Click the Next button. Xcode asks where you want to store this file and what name you want to give it.

4. Click in the Save As text field and type **personClass**. Then click the Create button. Xcode displays the personClass.swift file in the Project Navigator pane.

5. Click on the personClass.swift file in the Project Navigator pane. Xcode displays the file's contents.

6. Edit The personClass.swift file as follows:

```
import Foundation

class person {
    var hitPoints = 10
    func shoot () -> Int {
        var odds = 1 + Int(arc4random_uniform(3))
        if odds == 3 {
            // Hit, randomly determine damage from 1..3
            return 1 + Int(arc4random_uniform(3))
        } else {
            return 0 // Missed
        }
    }
}
```

This class defines one property called hitPoints, which it initializes with a value of 10. It also defines one method called shoot, which does not accept any parameters but does return an integer value. Inside the shoot method, it calculates a random number from 1 to 3 and stores this value in the "odds" variable.

Next, it checks if the value in "odds" is exactly equal to 3. If so, then it calculates a second random number from 1 to 3 and returns this value. If the value in "odds" is not 3, then the method returns 0.

Now that you've defined a class in a separate Swift file, it's time to actually use that class to create objects, which you can do by following these steps:

1. Click the AppDelegate.swift file in the Project Navigator pane. Xcode displays the contents of the AppDelegate.swift file.

2. Underneath the IBOutlet list in the AppDelegate.swift file, type the following to create two objects based on the person class defined in the personClass.swift file:

```
@IBOutlet weak var window: NSWindow!
@IBOutlet weak var sheriffHitPoints: NSTextField!
@IBOutlet weak var outlawHitPoints: NSTextField!

var sheriff = person ()
var outlaw = person ()
```

3. Modify the applicationDidFinishLaunching method so it displays the initial values of the hitPoints properties of the sheriff and outlaw objects in the text fields on the user interface. These are the two IBOutlets called sheriffHitPoints and outlawHitPoints:

```
func applicationDidFinishLaunching(aNotification: NSNotification) {
    // Insert code here to initialize your application
    sheriffHitPoints.integerValue = sheriff.hitPoints
    outlawHitPoints.integerValue = outlaw.hitPoints
}
```

4. Modify the shootButton IBAction method follows:

```
@IBAction func shootButton(sender: NSButton) {
    if sender.tag == 0 {     // Sheriff shooting
        outlaw.hitPoints -= sheriff.shoot()
    } else {     // Outlaw shooting
        sheriff.hitPoints -= outlaw.shoot()
    }

    sheriffHitPoints.integerValue = sheriff.hitPoints
    outlawHitPoints.integerValue = outlaw.hitPoints

    if sheriffHitPoints.integerValue <= 0 {
        var myAlert = NSAlert()
        myAlert.messageText = "The sheriff died."
        myAlert.runModal()
    } else if outlawHitPoints.integerValue <= 0 {
        var myAlert = NSAlert()
        myAlert.messageText = "The outlaw died."
        myAlert.runModal()
    }
}
```

This code checks the Tag property of the "sender" variable, which identifies which button the user clicked. If the Tag property is 0, then the user clicked on the Sheriff Shoot button so it runs the shoot method in the sheriff object and subtracts the result (a value from 0 to 3) from the outlaw.hitPoints property.

If the user clicked on the Outlaw Shoot button, then the shoot method runs the shoot method in the outlaw object and subtracts the result (a value from 0 to 3) from the sheriff. hitPoints property.

Whatever the result, it then displays the latest values of the hitPoints property from both the sheriff and the outlaw back in the two text fields on the user interface, identified by the sheriffHitPoints and outlawHitPoints IBOutlets.

Finally, if the hitPoints property of either the sheriff or the outlaw falls to 0 or less, then an alert dialog appears to display a message that either the sheriff or the outlaw died. The complete contents of the AppDelegate.swift file should look like this:

```
import Cocoa

class AppDelegate: NSObject, NSApplicationDelegate {

    @IBOutlet weak var window: NSWindow!
    @IBOutlet weak var sheriffHitPoints: NSTextField!
    @IBOutlet weak var outlawHitPoints: NSTextField!

    var sheriff = person ()
    var outlaw = person ()
```

```
func applicationDidFinishLaunching(aNotification: NSNotification) {
    // Insert code here to initialize your application
    sheriffHitPoints.integerValue = sheriff.hitPoints
    outlawHitPoints.integerValue = outlaw.hitPoints
}

func applicationWillTerminate(aNotification: NSNotification) {
    // Insert code here to tear down your application
}

@IBAction func shootButton(sender: NSButton) {
    if sender.tag == 0 {    // Sheriff shooting
        outlaw.hitPoints -= sheriff.shoot()
    } else {    // Outlaw shooting
        sheriff.hitPoints -= outlaw.shoot()
    }

    sheriffHitPoints.integerValue = sheriff.hitPoints
    outlawHitPoints.integerValue = outlaw.hitPoints

    if sheriffHitPoints.integerValue <= 0 {
        var myAlert = NSAlert()
        myAlert.messageText = "The sheriff died."
        myAlert.runModal()
    } else if outlawHitPoints.integerValue <= 0 {
        var myAlert = NSAlert()
        myAlert.messageText = "The outlaw died."
        myAlert.runModal()
    }
}

}
```

To see how this program works, follow these steps:

1. Choose Product ➤ Run. Xcode runs your ObjectProgram project. Notice that the text fields under both the Sheriff and Outlaw display 10, which represents their total hit points. Each time they're hit, their hit point total will drop. The loser will be the character whose hit points drops to 0 or less.

2. Click the Sheriff Shoot button. If the sheriff hit the outlaw, then you'll see the value under the outlaw label drop from 10 to a lower value such as 8. If the sheriff missed, then the number under the outlaw won't change at all.

3. Click the Outlaw Shoot button.

4. Repeat steps 2 and 3 to alternate clicking the Sheriff Shoot and Outlaw Shoot buttons until one character's hit points drops to 0 or less. Then an alert dialog appears as shown in Figure 11-11.

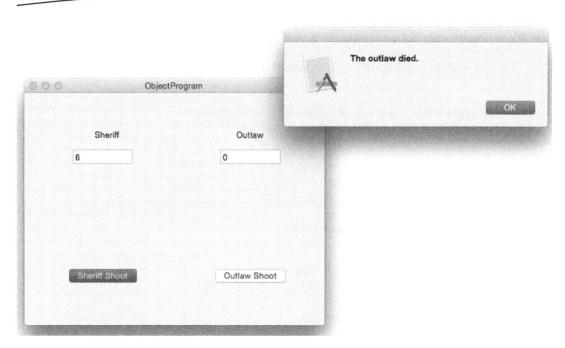

Figure 11-11. When one character's hit point total drops to 0 or less, an alert dialog appears

5.   Click OK to make the alert dialog go away.

6.   Choose ObjectProgram ➤ Quit ObjectProgram.

Summary

Swift programming depends entirely on objects and the principles of object-oriented programming. To create an object, you must first define a class. A class typically consists of one or more variables (called properties) and one or more functions (called methods). Once you've defined a class, you can create an object that represents that class.

Properties in a class always need to be initialized. You can define initial values for every property at the same time you define those properties, or you can create a special initializer method that lets you accept data to define initial values for an object.

Properties can be initialized with a fixed value, or they can be computed based on values of another property. The value of one property can change the value of a different property.

You can create as many objects from a single class as you want. Typically it's best to store class definitions in separate files to keep your code organized. An object-oriented program works by objects sending data to the properties of other objects, or calling methods stored in other objects. By working together, yet being independent, objects make it easy to create reliable and sophisticated programs much faster than before.

Inheritance, Polymorphism, and Extending Classes

In Chapter 11 you learned how objects were created from classes and how classes define properties and methods. To protect its data and methods from other parts of a program, an object isolates or encapsulates its code. Encapsulation is one prime advantage of object-oriented programming because it creates self-contained code that you can easily modify or replace without affecting any other part of a program.

By keeping code as independent as possible from other parts of a program, objects increase reliability. Think of a house built out of playing cards. Remove one card and the whole thing collapses, which is the way most software worked before object-oriented programming.

Objects are like playing cards that you can remove and replace without affecting any other card. Besides encapsulation, object-oriented programming also includes two additional features called inheritance and polymorphism.

The idea behind inheritance is to reuse existing code without physically making another copy of that code. The idea behind polymorphism is that you can replace inherited code without modifying the original code. Through both inheritance and polymorphism, you can reuse existing code, even without understanding how the original code works.

In fact, each time you create a project in Xcode, look at the top of your Swift files and you should see a line that looks like this:

```
import Cocoa
```

This line tells Xcode to use all the classes that Apple has created for you that are stored in the Cocoa framework. In our previous example programs, you used the Cocoa framework to manipulate arrays, sets, and dictionaries. Without the Cocoa framework, you would have to write Swift code to perform these common functions yourself. Not only would this be time consuming, but it would be error prone as well since you would have to write code and then test to make sure it worked.

By simply relying on classes in the Cocoa framework, you can add functionality to your program without writing much code at all. As you get more experienced writing your own classes, you can create useful libraries of your own that you can easily plug into other projects to reuse all your hard work.

Understanding Inheritance

The main purpose of inheritance is to make reusing code easy. In the old days, people reused code by simply making another copy of that code. Now what happens if you find an error (bug) in the code? That means you'll need to fix that bug in every copy of your code. Miss one copy of the faulty code and your program won't work.

Creating multiple copies of the same code causes two problems. First, it wastes space. Second, it makes modifying the code harder with multiple copies of code scattered all over a program. Inheritance fixes both problems.

First, inheritance never makes a copy of code so it never wastes space. Second, since inheritance only keeps one copy of code, you just need to modify one copy of code to have your changes automatically affect every part of your program that relies on that code.

Instead of physically copying code, inheritance basically creates pointers or references to one copy of code. When you create a class, you can simply state its name like this:

```
class className {

}
```

To inherit code from another class, name that other class like this:

```
class className : superClass {

}
```

This code defines a class called "className," which inherits code from another class called "superClass." That means any properties and methods defined in "superClass" automatically work in "className" as well, even though the "className" class is completely empty.

If you peek at any of the OS X sample programs you created in earlier chapters, you may see code that looks like this:

```
class AppDelegate: NSObject, NSApplicationDelegate {
```

This defines a class called AppDelegate, which inherits code from another class called NSObject. (This code also adds additional code to the AppDelegate class through another file called NSApplicationDelegate, which is a file that you'll learn more about later in this chapter.)

To see how to use inheritance with classes, create a new playground by following these steps:

1. Start Xcode.

2. Choose File ➤ New ➤ Playground. (If you see the Xcode welcome screen, you can also click on Get started with a playground.) Xcode asks for a playground name and platform.

3. Click in the Name text field and type **InheritPlayground**.

4. Click in the Platform pop-up menu and choose OS X. Xcode asks where you want to save your playground file.

5. Click on a folder where you want to save your playground file and click the Create button. Xcode displays the playground file.

6. Edit the code as follows:

```
import Cocoa

class firstClass {
    var speed : Int = 0
    var locationX : Int = 3
    var locationY : Int = 5
    func move (X: Int, Y: Int) {
        locationX += X
        locationY += Y
    }
}

class copyCat : firstClass {

}

var kitten = copyCat ()
kitten.speed = 4
kitten.move(4, Y: 8)
print (kitten.locationX)
print (kitten.locationY)
```

This Swift code defines two classes. First, it defines a class (called firstClass) that has three properties (speed, locationX, and locationY) and one method (move). Then it defines a second class (called copycat) that's completely empty, but it inherits all the code from firstClass.

To show that the copyCat class inherits code from firstClass, the Swift code next creates an object called "kitten," which is based on the copyCat class. The kitten object can store data in a speed property and use the move method to change its locationX and locationY properties, yet the copyCat class is completely empty. Figure 12-1 shows the results of running this Swift code in a playground.

```
class firstClass {
    var speed : Int = 0
    var locationX : Int = 3
    var locationY : Int = 5
    func move (X: Int, Y: Int) {
        locationX += X
        locationY += Y
    }
}

class copyCat : firstClass {

}

var kitten = copyCat ()                    {{speed 0 locationX 3 locationY 5}}
kitten.speed = 4                           {{speed 4 locationX 3 locationY 5}}
kitten.move(4, Y: 8)                       {{speed 4 locationX 7 locationY 13}}
println (kitten.locationX)                 "7"
println (kitten.locationY)                 "13"
```

Figure 12-1. Showing how inheritance works

> **Note**   Some programming languages, such as C++, allow one class to inherit from two or more classes, which is known as multiple inheritance. However in Swift, a class can only inherit from only one other class, which is known as single inheritance.

In the above example, the copyCat class inherits three properties (speed, locationX, and locationY) and one method (move) from firstClass. Since the copyCat class didn't define any properties or methods of its own, the copyCat class is basically identical to firstClass.

In actual use, there's no reason for a class to inherit from another class as an exact duplicate. Instead, it's more common for one class (known as the subclass) to inherit from another class (known as the superclass) and then add additional properties and methods of its own.

In this way, the subclass only needs to include the code for these new properties and methods while still having access to all the properties and methods of the superclass. For example, consider the following class:

```
class copyDog : copyCat {
    var name : String = ""
}
```

This class inherits all the code from the copyCat class and adds one new property of its own called "name" that can hold a string. The above class definition that defines a name property and inherits code from the copyCat class is equivalent to the following:

```
class copyDog {
    var speed : Int = 0
    var locationX : Int = 3
    var locationY : Int = 5
    func move (X: Int, Y: Int) {
        locationX += X
        locationY += Y
    }
    var name : String = ""
}
```

Remember, the copyCat class inherited everything from firstClass, which defined the speed, locationX, and locationY properties along with the move method. In comparison, the copyDog class that inherits code from the copyCat class is much shorter and simpler.

Inheritance works like a daisy chain. If class A inherits from class B, but class B inherits everything from class C, then class A inherits everything from both class B and class C. For example, the copyDog class inherits everything from the copyCat class. The copyCat class, in turn, inherits everything from firstClass. That means the copyDog class ultimately inherits everything from both the copyCat class and firstClass as shown in Figure 12-2.

Figure 12-2. Classes inherit everything from previous classes

This daisy chain effect of inheritance is how the Cocoa framework is designed. At its simplest level, there's a basic class called NSObject. A class such as NSResponder inherits everything from NSObject and adds new properties and methods of its own. Another class such as NSView inherits everything from NSResponder and NSObject. When you look up classes in the Cocoa framework in Xcode's Documentation window, you can see this daisy chain link of classes identified by the "Inherits from:" label as shown in Figure 12-3.

⊠ NSControl

Inherits from: NSView : NSResponder : NSObject
Conforms to: NSAnimatablePropertyContainer, NSAccessibilityElement, NSObject, NSAccessibility, NSDraggingDestination, NSCoding, NSAppe...
Framework: AppKit in OS X 10.0 and later. More related items...

Figure 12-3. The Documentation window identifies the superclasses that the currently displayed class inherits from

To see how to use inheritance works between multiple classes, follow these steps:

1. Make sure the InheritPlayground file is loaded in Xcode.

2. Edit the code as follows:

```
import Cocoa

class animal {
    var legs : Int = 0
}

class packAnimal : animal {
    var strength : Int = 100
}

class biped : packAnimal {
    var IQ : Int = 75
}

var snake = animal()
print (snake.legs)

var mule = packAnimal()
mule.legs = 4
mule.strength = 120

var relative = biped()
relative.legs = 2
relative.strength = 55
relative.IQ = 10
```

This code creates three classes: animal (legs property), packAnimal (strength property), and biped (IQ property). Then it creates three objects based on these classes. The first object, snake, is based on the animal class. The second object, mule, is based on the packAnimal class. The third object, relative, is based on the biped class.

Ultimately the relative object contains properties from all three classes, the mule object only contains properties from the animal and packAnimal class, and the snake object only contains properties from the animal class as follows:

Object	Based on these classes	Contains these properties
snake	animal	legs
mule	packAnimal, animal	legs, strength
relative	biped, packAnimal, animal	legs, strength, IQ

The snake, mule, and relative objects contain different properties based on their different classes and the classes that they inherit from as shown in Figure 12-4.

```
class animal {
    var legs : Int = 0
}

class packAnimal : animal {
    var strength : Int = 100
}

class biped : packAnimal {
    var IQ : Int = 75
}

var snake = animal()                        {legs 0}
println (snake.legs)                        "0"

var mule = packAnimal()                     {{legs 0} strength 100}
mule.legs = 4                               {{legs 4} strength 100}
mule.strength = 120                         {{legs 4} strength 120}

var relative = biped()                      {{{...} strength 100} IQ 75}
relative.legs = 2                           {{{...} strength 100} IQ 75}
relative.strength = 55                      {{{...} strength 55} IQ 75}
relative.IQ = 10                            {{{...} strength 55} IQ 10}
```

Figure 12-4. Seeing how inheritance works among properties stored in different classes

Understanding Polymorphism

When one class (subclass) inherits from another class (superclass), it contains all the properties and methods stored in the superclass. Although a subclass inherits all properties and methods from a superclass, those properties and methods aren't displayed inside the subclass. The only code that appears in each class are properties and methods unique to that class.

Properties inherited from another class retain the same name and data type. Methods inherited from another class retain the same method name and code that makes it do something useful.

The problem with inheriting methods is that you may want to modify the code in an inherited method. For example, suppose you had a video game where you have dogs running on the ground and birds flying in the air. You could create a basic class like this:

```
class gameObject {
    var speed : Int = 0
    var locationX : Int = 3
    var locationY : Int = 3
    func move (X: Int, Y: Int) {
        locationX += X + speed
        locationY += Y + speed
    }
}

var dog = gameObject()
```

Now the dog object, created from the gameObject class, has three properties (speed, locationX, and locationY) and one method (move) that change the locationX and locationY properties.

A dog can only run on the ground, but a bird can move in two dimensions, so it needs an additional height property. To move a flying object, the move method needs to change the height property. That means the move method needs to be different.

One clumsy way around this problem is to create a different name for the move method such as changing its name form "move" to "fly":

```
class flyingObject : gameObject {
    var height : Int = 0
      func fly (X: Int, Y: Int) {
        locationX += X + speed
        locationY += Y + speed
        height += (X + Y) / 2
    }
}

var bird = flyingObject()
```

The problem with this solution is that the bird object, created from the flyingObject class, now has two methods: the move method inherited from gameObject and the new fly method defined in flyingObject.

You could simply ignore the move method and use the fly method, but that risks creating errors if you accidentally use the move method to change the position of a bird instead of the correct fly method that moves a bird in two dimensions instead of one.

That's why polymorphism exists. Polymorphism basically lets you reuse a method name (such as move) but replace it with completely different code to make it work. To identify when you're using polymorphism to reuse a method name but modify its code, you must use the "override" keyword in front of the method you're changing such as:

```
override func move (X: Int, Y: Int) {
    locationX += X + speed
    locationY += Y + speed
    height += (X + Y) / 2
}
```

When you override a method (use polymorphism), you essentially have two identically named methods, but one version is defined in one class and the second version is defined in another class. The computer never gets confused because you can only run each method by specifying both the object name and the method name. Even though the method names are identical, the object names are not.

To see how polymorphism works, follow these steps:

1. Make sure your InheritPlayground file is loaded into Xcode.

2. Edit the code as follows:

```
import Cocoa

class gameObject {
    var speed : Int = 0
    var locationX : Int = 3
    var locationY : Int = 3
    func move (X: Int, Y: Int) {
        locationX += X + speed
        locationY += Y + speed
    }
}

var dog = gameObject()

class flyingObject : gameObject {
    var height : Int = 0
    override func move (X: Int, Y: Int) {
        locationX += X + speed
        locationY += Y + speed
        height += (X + Y) / 2
    }
}

var bird = flyingObject()

dog.move (4, Y: 7)
bird.move (4, Y: 7)
```

To override a method, the flying Object class must first inherit from another class. In this case flyingObject inherits from gameObject. Now the flyingObject class can use the "override" keyword to specify that it's changing the code that makes the move method work. In this case, the only change was adding code to modify the height property, but we could have added completely different code inside the overridden move method.

Notice that when you run the move method for the dog object (dog.move), the move method only changes the values of locationX and locationY, but when you run the move method for the bird object (bird.move), the overridden method runs and also changes the height property as shown in Figure 12-5.

```
class gameObject {
    var speed : Int = 0
    var locationX : Int = 3
    var locationY : Int = 3
    func move (X: Int, Y: Int) {
        locationX += X + speed
        locationY += Y + speed
    }
}

var dog = gameObject()                              {speed 0 locationX 3 locationY 3}

class flyingObject : gameObject {
    var height : Int = 0
    override func move (X: Int, Y: Int) {
        locationX += X + speed
        locationY += Y + speed
        height += (X + Y) / 2
    }
}

var bird = flyingObject()                           {{speed 0 locationX 3 locationY 3} height 0}

dog.move (4, Y: 7)                                  {speed 0 locationX 7 locationY 10}
bird.move (4, Y: 7)                                 {{speed 0 locationX 7 locationY 10} height 5}
```

Figure 12-5. Overridden methods can behave differently

When overriding methods, you can only change the code inside the method. You cannot change the parameter list of the method. For example, consider this class:

```
class basicDesign {
    var location : Int = 0
    func moveMe (X : Int) {
        location += X
    }
}
```

To override the moveMe method, this next class needs to inherit from the basicDesign class and change only the code inside the overridden method. The following would not work:

```
class newDesign : basicDesign {
    override func moveMe (X: Int, Y: Int) { // Does NOT work

    }
}
```

Notice that the original moveMe method only has one parameter (X : Int), but the moveMe method in the newDesign class has two parameters (X: Int, Y: Int). Despite having the same name, this method has a different parameter list so it won't work. When overriding methods, you can only change the code, not the parameter list.

Overriding Properties

Besides overriding methods, Swift also lets you override properties. When you override properties, you must keep the same property name and data type. What you can change are the getters and setters along with the property observers of a variable.

At the simplest level, a getter simply returns a value of a variable. On a more sophisticated level, a getter calculates a value. Consider the following:

```
class basicDesign {
    var location: Int {
        get {
            return 4
        }
    }
}
```

This basicDesign class defines a single property called location with a getter that returns the value 4 in the location property. To override this property, you need to retain the variable name and data type (Int), but you can change the getter code such as:

```
class newDesign : basicDesign {
    override var location: Int {
        get {
            return 7
        }
    }
}
```

This newDesign class inherits the location property from the basicDesign class. However it overrides the location property with a new getter that returns a value of 7.

To see how overriding properties work, follow these steps:

1. Make sure your InheritPlayground file is loaded into Xcode.

2. Edit the code as follows:

```
import Cocoa

class basicDesign {
    var location: Int {
        get {
            return 4
        }
    }
}
```

```
class newDesign : basicDesign {
    override var location: Int {
        get {
            return 7
        }
    }
}

var ant = basicDesign()
var fly = newDesign()
ant.location
fly.location
```

In this example, the ant object is based on the basicDesign class, which defines the location property with a value of 4. The fly object is based on the newDesign class, which inherits the location property. However, the newDesign class overrides the location property's getter code so instead of storing a value of 4 in the location property, it stores a value of 7, instead, as shown in Figure 12-6.

```
class basicDesign {
    var location: Int {
        get {
            return 4                                    4
        }
    }
}

class newDesign : basicDesign {
    override var location: Int {
        get {
            return 7                                    7
        }
    }
}

var ant = basicDesign()                                 __lldb_expr_1308.basicDesign
var fly = newDesign()                                   (__lldb_expr_1308.basicDesign)
ant.location                                            4
fly.location                                            7
```

Figure 12-6. *Overriding properties with new getter code*

Remember, when overriding methods and properties, you can only change:

- code in the method

- code in the property's getter/setter or property observer

You can never change the:

- method name

- method parameter list

- property name

- property data type

Preventing Polymorphism

In some cases, you may want to prevent a method, property, or even an entire class from being modified through polymorphism. To do this, you just need to insert the "final" keyword. If you wanted to prevent an entire class from being inherited, just put the "final" keyword in front of the class name like this:

```
final class className {
        var propertyName = initialValue
        func methodName() {

        }
}
```

> **Note**   If you place "final" in front of a class name, it automatically prevents that class's properties and methods from being overridden so you don't need to place "final" in front of each property or method name.

If you wanted to prevent an individual property or method from being overridden, just place the "final" keyword in front of the property or method like this:

```
class className {
        final var propertyName = initialValue
        func methodName() {

        }
}
```

The "final" keyword in the above example prevents the property from being overridden while allowing the method to be overridden. If you wanted to prevent the method from being overridden while allowing the property to be overridden, you would place the "final" keyword in front of the method like this:

```
class className {
        var propertyName = initialValue
        final func methodName() {

        }
}
```

Using Extensions

If there's a class that contains the properties and methods you need, the object-oriented approach is to inherit from that class (create a subclass). The problem with constantly creating subclasses is that it can get awkward to create objects from slightly different class files.

This can be especially true when you want to extend the features of classes that are part of the Cocoa framework. For example, if you're working with String data types, you probably don't want to create a subclass of the String data type and then create objects based on this new subclass. Ideally, you want to continue using String data types but have added features as well.

That's why Swift offers extensions. Extensions essentially let you add code to an existing class without creating a subclass. That way you can still get to use the original class but you also get to add new features to that class without going through inheritance, polymorphism, or subclasses. The structure of an extension looks like this:

```
extension className {

}
```

Extensions can define methods along with properties that contain code such as:

- getters and setters
- initializers
- property observers

While extensions add new properties methods to a class without inheritance, extensions cannot override existing methods or properties in a class. Extensions also can't create properties assigned an initial value such as:

```
var temperature : Int = 100        // Cannot be used in an extension
```

To see how to an extension can add properties and methods to a class, create a new playground by following these steps:

1. Start Xcode.

2. Choose File ➤ New ➤ Playground. (If you see the Xcode welcome screen, you can also click on Get started with a playground.) Xcode asks for a playground name and platform.

3. Click in the Name text field and type **ExtensionPlayground**.

4. Click in the Platform pop-up menu and choose OS X. Xcode asks where you want to save your playground file.

5. Click on a folder where you want to save your playground file and click the Create button. Xcode displays the playground file.

6. Edit the code as follows:

    ```
    import Cocoa

    class emptyClass {

    }
    ```

```
extension emptyClass {
    var age : Int {
        get {
            return 50
        }
    }
    func retire (testAge : Int) -> String {
        if testAge < 62 {
            return "Keep working"
        } else {
            return "Time to retire"
        }
    }
}

var aWorker = emptyClass ()
aWorker.retire(65)
aWorker.age
```

This code creates a completely empty class, then creates an extension that adds an "age" property and a "retire" method to the empty class. Finally, it creates an object from that empty class, calls the "retire" method (defined in the extension) and displays the value stored in the "age" property as shown in Figure 12-7.

```
class emptyClass {

}

extension emptyClass {
    var age : Int {
        get {
            return 50                                                    50
        }
    }
    func retire (testAge : Int) -> String {
        if testAge < 62 {
            return "Keep working"
        } else {
            return "Time to retire"                          "Time to retire"
        }
    }
}

var aWorker = emptyClass ()                              __lldb_expr_4143.emptyClass
aWorker.retire(65)                                            "Time to retire"
aWorker.age                                                   50
```

Figure 12-7. *Using an extension to add a property and method to an empty class*

You can see that the class itself does nothing, but with extensions, the class now gets added features that it didn't have before.

Using Protocols

In the beginning of this chapter, you were first introduced to something that appears in the class AppDelegate.swift file that you've been creating to learn the basic principles of each chapter. This class AppDelegate declaration looks like this:

```
class AppDelegate: NSObject, NSApplicationDelegate {
```

This line of code creates a class called AppDelegate, which inherits properties and methods from the NSObject class that's part of the Cocoa framework. However, the NSApplicationDelegate is the name of another file used to extend classes without going through inheritance or subclasses.

The NSApplicationDelegate file is a protocol file. The above Swift code creates a class called AppDelegate, inherits properties and methods from the NSObject class, and also inherits code from the NSApplicationDelegate file. (You can see more details about the NSApplicationDelegate protocol by viewing it in the Xcode Documentation window.)

The main difference between a class (such as NSObject) and a protocol (such as NSApplicationDelegate) is that a class defines properties and methods while a protocol only defines properties and method names without any code that actually implements them. A protocol is sometimes called an empty class because it never defines any Swift code to make anything actually work.

A protocol defines a group of property and method names for solving a particular type of problem. Now it's up to the class that adopts or conforms to this protocol to provide the actual Swift code that implements each method or property declaration.

A protocol declaration looks identical to a class or structure declaration. The only difference is that a protocol declaration uses the "protocol" keyword:

```
protocol protocolName {

}
```

Within this protocol declaration you can define properties and methods without implementing any Swift code like this:

```
protocol protocolName {
    var property1 : datatype { get }        // read-only
    var property2 : datatype { get set }    // read-write
    func methodName (parameters) -> datatype
}
```

When a protocol defines a property or method, any class that adopts that protocol must implement that property or method exactly as its defined in the protocol. In the above example, property1 is defined with a getter and property2 is defined with a getter and a setter.

That means when a class implements those two properties, it must define a getter only for property1 and both a getter and a setter for property2.

Likewise, the method defined in the protocol must be exact when adopted in the class file. That means if the method is defined in the protocol with two integer parameters, then the implementation of that method must also have the exact same two integer parameters.

Protocols are generally used when working with common user interface items that require specific types of methods to manipulate them, but can't define exactly how to manipulate them because the data may differ from one program to another.

For example, table views are a user interface item that displays a list of data in rows. The table view needs to know how many rows of data to hold and what type of data to display in each row. Since every table view needs to know this information, it makes sense to create standard methods to do this, but since every table view needs to contain different information, it also makes sense to avoid writing Swift code to actually fill a table view with data.

Any program that includes a table view can take advantage of predefined method names stored in a protocol for manipulating data. All you need to do is add Swift code to fill the table view with data.

By using protocols, you can manipulate table views using identical method names from one program to another. Without table view protocols, you'd be forced to make up your own method names for adding and displaying data in a table view. Thus protocols are typically used in the Cocoa framework to provide a consistent list of methods for performing common tasks.

To see how protocols work, follow these steps:

1. Make sure the ExtensionPlayground file is loaded into Xcode.

2. Edit the code as follows:

```
import Cocoa

protocol testMe {
    var cash : Int { get }
    var creditCheck : Int { get set }
    func purchase (price : Int) -> String
}

class windowShopper : testMe {
    var tempValue : Int = 0

    var cash : Int = 0
    var creditCheck : Int {
        get {
            return tempValue
        }
        set (newValue) {
            tempValue = newValue
            cash -= 10
        }
    }
}
```

```
        func purchase (price : Int) -> String {
            cash -= price
            return "Bought something!"
        }
    }

    var shopper = windowShopper ()
    shopper.cash = 450
    shopper.purchase (129)
    shopper.cash
```

Notice that the testMe protocol defines two properties and a method. The "cash" property is defined only with a getter. The "creditCheck" property is defined with both a getter and a setter. The "purchase" method only lists its parameters ("price" as an integer) and its return value, which is a String. Notice that the protocol doesn't actually implement any of the necessary Swift code.

When the windowShopper class is created, it adopts or conforms to the testMe protocol. That means it must provide Swift code to define the getter for the "cash" property and the getter and setter for the "creditCheck" property. It will also need to implement the Swift code for the "purchase" method.

If you fail to write Swift code for all the properties and methods defined in the testMe protocol, Xcode will give an error saying the windowShopper class failed to conform to the protocol. When adopting a protocol, make sure you implement all the necessary properties and methods.

Running the above code displays the results as shown in Figure 12-8.

```
protocol testMe {
    var cash : Int { get }
    var creditCheck : Int { get set }
    func purchase (price : Int) -> String
}

class windowShopper : testMe {
    var tempValue : Int = 0

    var cash : Int = 0
    var creditCheck : Int {
        get {
            return tempValue
        }
        set (newValue) {
            tempValue = newValue
            cash -= 10
        }
    }
    func purchase (price : Int) -> String {             "Bought something!"
        cash -= price
        return "Bought something!"
    }
}

var shopper = windowShopper ()                          {tempValue 0 cash 0}
shopper.cash = 450                                      {tempValue 0 cash 450}
shopper.purchase (129)                                  "Bought something!"
shopper.cash                                            321
```

Figure 12-8. A class conforming to a protocol

Defining Optional Methods and Properties in Protocols

When you create a protocol, every property and method you define must be implemented by any class that adopts that protocol. However, you can also make one or more properties and methods optional so they can be ignored. To define optional properties or methods, you need to identify the protocol with the @objc keyword and identify individual properties or methods with the "optional" keyword as well such as:

```
@objc protocol protocolName {
    var requiredProperty : dataType { get }
    optional var optionalProperty : dataType { get }
    optional func optionalMethod ()
}
```

To adopt or conform to this protocol, a class only needs to implement any property or method that is not identified by the "optional" keyword. To implement required properties or methods, you need to identify them with the @objc keyword such as:

```
class className : protocolName {
    @objc var requiredProperty : dataType = initialValue
}
```

However, if you want to implement an optional property or method, you can omit the @objc keyword like this:

```
class className : protocolName {
    @objc var requiredProperty : dataType = initialValue
        var optionalProperty : dataType = initialValue
}
```

To see how to create optional properties and methods in a protocol, follow these steps:

1. Make sure the ExtensionPlayground file is loaded into Xcode.

2. Edit the code as follows:

    ```
    import Cocoa

    @objc protocol person {
        var name : String { get }
        optional var age : Int { get }
        optional func move (X: Int) -> Int
    }

    class politician : person {
        @objc var name : String = ""
    }

    var candidate = politician ()
    candidate.name = "John Doe"
    ```

Notice that the only required item in the person protocol defined above is the property "name." That's why the politician class only needs to implement the "name" property, but it must identify it with the @objc keyword.

Try experimenting with making different properties and methods optional so you can see how they affect how you need to implement them in the class.

Using Inheritance with Protocols

Protocols can even inherit properties and methods from other protocols. This lets one protocol inherit properties and methods from multiple protocols. Now a class must adopt or conform to all the properties and methods defined in all the protocols.

To see how to inherit properties and methods from multiple protocols, follow these steps:

1. Make sure the ExtensionPlayground file is loaded into Xcode.

2. Edit the code as follows:

    ```
    import Cocoa

    protocol first {
        var name : String { get }
    }
    ```

```
protocol second {
    var ID : Int { get }
}

protocol third: first, second {
    var email : String { get }
}

class inheritProtocols : third {
    var name : String = ""
    var ID : Int = 0
    var email : String = ""
}

var friend = inheritProtocols()
friend.name = "Cindy Smith"
friend.ID = 12
friend.email = "cindysmith@isp.com"
```

In this example, the "name," "ID," and "email" properties are defined in three different protocols. The third protocol inherits from the first and second protocol.

Now when a class adopts the last protocol, it must implement the properties and methods stored in all the protocols. Even though the "name," "ID," and "email" properties were all declared in different protocols, the inheritProtocols class can access them all as shown in Figure 12-9.

Figure 12-9. Inheriting properties and methods from multiple protocols

Using Delegates

Protocols are closely related to delegation. The main idea behind delegation is for a class to hand off or delegate responsibility to code stored in another class. So rather than create a new subclass to add new features, you can use a delegate that contains additional features.

One common way to use delegates is to allow the view (the user interface) to communicate to the controller. Normally the controller communicates to the view through IBOutlets that allow the controller to display data on the user interface or retrieve data from the user interface.

However, the view can also communicate back to the controller through protocols. The protocol file defines methods and delegates the responsibility to the controller for implementing those methods. The most common types of methods the controller implements involve method names that include will, should, and did such as applicationDidFinishLaunching or applicationWillTerminate.

Figure 12-10 shows how the controller communicates to the view through IBOutlets and the view communicates with the controller through protocols.

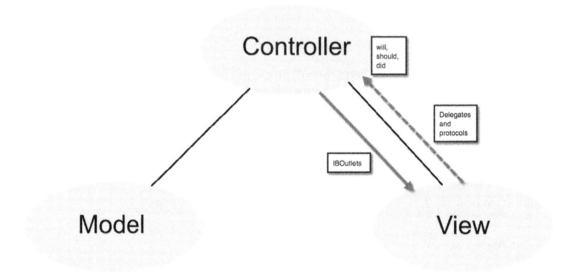

Figure 12-10. Views can communicate to controllers through protocols

To see how a view uses delegates to communicate with the controller, follow these steps:

1. From within Xcode choose File ➤ New ➤ Project.

2. Click Application under the OS X category.

3. Click Cocoa Application and click the Next button. Xcode now asks for a product name.

4. Click in the Product Name text field and type **DelegateProgram**.

5. Make sure the Language pop-up menu displays Swift and that no check boxes are selected.

6. Click the Next button. Xcode asks where you want to store the project.

7. Choose a folder to store your project and click the Create button.

8. Click the AppDelegate.swift file in the Project Navigator. The contents of the AppDelegate.swift file appears in the middle of the Xcode window. Look for the following line of code:

```
class AppDelegate: NSObject, NSApplicationDelegate {
```

This line defines a class called AppDelegate that inherits properties and methods from the NSObject class. In addition, it also adopts any properties and methods defined by the NSApplicationDelegate file.

9. Hold down the Option key and click the mouse over NSObject. When the mouse pointer turns into a question mark, click over NSObject to make a pop-up window appear as shown in Figure 12-11.

Figure 12-11. Option-clicking on a class name displays information about that class

10. Release the Option key and click the mouse over NSObject Class Reference at the bottom of the pop-up window. The Documentation window appears, showing details about the different properties and methods available in the NSObject class as shown in Figure 12-12. All those properties and methods are also available in your AppDelegate class as well.

Figure 12-12. The Documentation window displaying information about the NSObject class

11. Click the close button (the red dot) in the upper left corner of the Documentation window to make it go away.

12. Hold down the Option key and click the mouse over NSApplicationDelegate. When the mouse pointer turns into a question mark, click over NSApplicationDelegate to make a pop-up window appear as shown in Figure 12-13.

Figure 12-13. Option-clicking displays information about the NSApplication protocol

13. Release the Option key and click the mouse over NSApplicationDelegate Protocol Reference at the bottom of the pop-up window. The Documentation window appears, showing details about the NSApplicationDelegate Protocol as shown in Figure 12-14. Notice that two methods that the NSApplicationDelegate protocol defines are called applicationDidFinishLaunching and applicationWillTerminate.

Figure 12-14. Viewing the NSApplicationDelegate protocol in the Documentation window

14. Click the close button (the red dot) in the upper left corner of the Documentation window to make it go away. The Xcode window appears again. Notice that the AppDelegate.swift file contains two empty functions called applicationDidFinishLaunching and applicationWillTerminate. These are defined by the NSApplicationDelegate protocol file but implemented in the AppDelegate.swift file.

15. Modify both of these functions as follows:

```
func applicationDidFinishLaunching(aNotification: NSNotification) {
    print ("This line should print after the program runs")
}

func applicationWillTerminate(aNotification: NSNotification) {
    print ("This line should print before your program stops")
}
```

16. Choose Product ➤ Run. Xcode runs your DelegateProgram project and displays an empty user interface.

17. Choose DelegateProgram ➤ Quit DelegateProgram. The Xcode window appears. The Debug Area at the bottom of the Xcode window now displays the text that the two println commands printed. Notice that the println command inside the applicationDidFinishLaunching function ran first as shown in Figure 12-15.

```
This line should print after the program runs
This line should print before your program stops
```

All Output ↻

Figure 12-15. *The methods defined by the NSApplicationDelegate file tell the program what the user interface is doing*

Using Inheritance in an OS X Program

Inheritance lets you create method names that remain the same while the underlying code changes between two classes. In this sample program, you'll define one class and then inherit properties and methods for a second class. This second class will also override a method and add code to make that overridden method behave slightly differently.

To create the sample program that shows how inheritance works, follow these steps:

1. From within Xcode choose File ➤ New ➤ Project.

2. Click Application under the OS X category.

3. Click Cocoa Application and click the Next button. Xcode now asks for a product name.

4. Click in the Product Name text field and type **InheritProgram**.

5. Make sure the Language pop-up menu displays Swift and that no check boxes are selected.

6. Click the Next button. Xcode asks where you want to store the project.

7. Choose a folder to store your project and click the Create button.

8. Click the MainMenu.xib file in the Project Navigator.

9. Click on the StructureProgram icon to make the window of the user interface appear.

10. Choose View ➤ Utilities ➤ Show Object Library to make the Object Library appear in the bottom right corner of the Xcode window.

11. Drag one Push Button and two Labels on the user interface and double-click on the push buttons and labels to change the text that appears on them so that it looks similar to Figure 12-16.

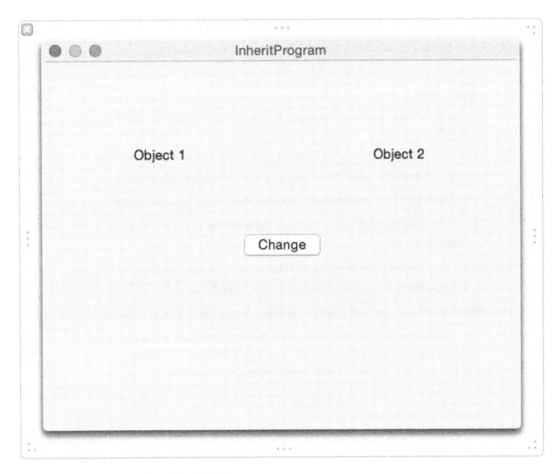

Figure 12-16. The user interface of the InheritProgram

This user interface displays two labels that represent two different objects. Object 1 only contains one property and a method to alter that property. Object 2 inherits from Object 1 and contains one additional property along with overriding the method defined in Object 1.

When you click the Change button, both labels will change their appearance based on the properties and method defined by each object. To connect your user interface to your Swift code, follow these steps:

1. With your user interface still visible in the Xcode window, choose View ➤ Assistant Editor ➤ Show Assistant Editor. The AppDelegate. swift file appears next to the user interface.

2. Move the mouse over the Change button, hold down the Control key, and drag just above the last curly bracket at the bottom of the AppDelegate.swift file.

3.   Release the mouse and the Control key. A pop-up window appears.

4.   Click in the Connection pop-up menu and choose Action.

5.   Click in the Name text field and type **changeButton**.

6.   Click in the Type pop-up menu and choose NSButton. Then click the Connect button. Xcode creates an empty IBAction method called changeButton.

7.   Move the mouse over the Object 1 label, hold down the Control key, and drag below the @IBOutlet line in the AppDelegate.swift file.

8.   Release the mouse and the Control key. A po-pup window appears.

9.   Click in the Name text field and type **ObjectOne** and click the Connect button.

10.   Move the mouse over the Object 2 label, hold down the Control key, and drag below the @IBOutlet line in the AppDelegate.swift file.

11.   Release the mouse and the Control key. A pop-up window appears.

12.   Click in the Name text field and type **ObjectTwo** and click the Connect button. You should now have the following IBOutlets that represent all the labels on your user interface:

```
@IBOutlet weak var window: NSWindow!
@IBOutlet weak var ObjectOne: NSTextField!
@IBOutlet weak var ObjectTwo: NSTextField!
```

13.   Type the following directly underneath the IBOutlet lines of code:

```
class one {
    var myColor : NSColor = NSColor.blackColor ()
    func change () {
        myColor = NSColor.redColor()
    }
}

class two : one {
    var myBackground : NSColor = NSColor.whiteColor()
    override func change() {
        myColor = NSColor.blueColor()
        myBackground = NSColor.greenColor()
    }
}
var ThingOne = one ()
var ThingTwo = two()
```

14.   Modify the IBAction changeButton method as follows:

```
@IBAction func changeButton(sender: NSButton) {
    ThingOne.change()
    ThingTwo.change()
    ObjectOne.textColor = ThingOne.myColor
    ObjectTwo.textColor = ThingTwo.myColor
    ObjectTwo.drawsBackground = true
    ObjectTwo.backgroundColor = ThingTwo.myBackground
}
```

This IBAction method runs the change method in both the ThingOne and ThingTwo objects, which are based on the one and two classes respectively. The two class inherits from the one class, but overrides the change method to modify an additional property called myBackground.

After both ThingOne and ThingTwo change their properties, the first label (represented by ObjectOne) assigns its text color to the myColor property from the ThingOne object. The second label (represented by ObjectTwo) changed its myColor and myBackground properties, so it sets those properties to the label.

The complete contents of the AppDelegate.swift file should look like this:

```
import Cocoa

@NSApplicationMain
class AppDelegate: NSObject, NSApplicationDelegate {

    @IBOutlet weak var window: NSWindow!
    @IBOutlet weak var ObjectOne: NSTextField!
    @IBOutlet weak var ObjectTwo: NSTextField!

    class one {
        var myColor : NSColor = NSColor.blackColor ()
        func change () {
            myColor = NSColor.redColor()
        }
    }

    class two : one {
        var myBackground : NSColor = NSColor.whiteColor()
        override func change() {
            myColor = NSColor.blueColor()
            myBackground = NSColor.greenColor()
        }
    }

    var ThingOne = one ()
    var ThingTwo = two()
```

```
func applicationDidFinishLaunching(aNotification: NSNotification) {
    // Insert code here to initialize your application
}

func applicationWillTerminate(aNotification: NSNotification) {
    // Insert code here to tear down your application
}

@IBAction func changeButton(sender: NSButton) {
    ThingOne.change()
    ThingTwo.change()
    ObjectOne.textColor = ThingOne.myColor
    ObjectTwo.textColor = ThingTwo.myColor
    ObjectTwo.drawsBackground = true
    ObjectTwo.backgroundColor = ThingTwo.myBackground
}
}
```

To see how this program works, follow these steps:

1.   Choose Product ➤ Run. Xcode runs your InheritProgram project. Notice that both labels look identical.

2.   Click the Change button. The Object 1 label only changes its text color because it represented a class that only has one property (myColor). The Object 2 label changes both its text color and its background color because it has two properties (myColor and myBackground). Even though the change method name is identical in both classes, it's been overridden in the second class to modify the myBackground property.

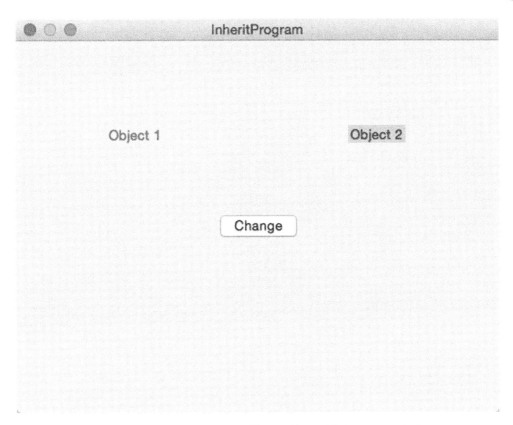

Figure 12-17. *Clicking the Change button modifies two different objects with the same method name*

3. Choose InheritProgram ➤ Quit InheritProgram.

Summary

Classes let you organize related code together where data (properties) and functions (methods) to manipulate that data are stored in the same place. The most straightforward way to extend the features of a class is through inheritance where you create a subclass.

Inheritance lets you inherit all the properties and methods of another class. A class can only inherit from one other class, but it's possible for that other class to inherit from another class as well, creating a daisy-chain effect of classes inheriting from other classes. The Cocoa framework is based on this idea of inheritance among daisy chains of classes.

To block inheritance, you can use the "final" keyword. To identify when you're overriding a property or method, you need to use the "override" keyword.

Beyond inheritance, you can also extend the features of a class through extensions and protocols. Protocols are commonly used with the Cocoa framework to extend the features of a class. Through inheritance, extensions, and protocols, you can extend the features of any class to make it easy to reuse existing code.

Chapter

13

Creating a User Interface

While it's possible to create programs that don't need to interact with a user at all (such as a program that controls a traffic light), it's far more common to create programs that display a user interface of some kind. Typically that means showing a window filled with different items such as labels to display text, text fields to allow the user to type something in, and buttons or pull-down menus to give the user control over the program.

Creating an effective user interface depends entirely on the purpose of your program. A business program typically follows standard conventions with pull-down menus and buttons, but a video game may create a custom interface that may not look anything like a standard OS X program. Ultimately a user interface needs to meet the needs of the user. Given a choice between following standard user interface design conventions or making a user interface easier for the user, focus on the user every time.

To help you better understand user interface design, Apple provides a free document called the OS X Human Interface Guidelines. This document gives a brief overview of what makes a typical OS X user interface work effectively with special emphasis on taking advantage of the latest features of OS X. By doing this, your OS X program will look modern and up to date. Failure to take advantage of the latest OS X features means your program could look dated even if it's brand new.

In previous chapters you've designed simple user interfaces using Xcode. In this chapter, we'll dig a little deeper into the different parts of Xcode that focus on helping you design user interfaces.

Remember, there is no "perfect" design for a user interface. The "perfect" user interface is one that makes tasks as simple and effortless as possible to the point where the user doesn't even notice interacting with any user interface whatsoever. A user interface acts as the middleman or translator between you and the program. The goal of any user interface is to make users feel as if they're communicating and manipulating a program directly.

Understanding User Interface Files

The Cocoa framework defines classes for creating every possible user interface item from a button (the NSButton class) and a text field (NSTextField) to a slider (NSSlider) or a date picker (NSDatePicker). Theoretically, it's possible to create an entire user interface using nothing but Swift code. However, this can be tedious because you can't see how your user interface looks until you actually run your program. This can be as clumsy as trying to paint a picture by describing exactly where you need to put a paintbrush on a canvas and the specific angle and direction to move your hand.

Rather than force you to write Swift code to define your user interface, Xcode offers a feature called Interface Builder. The idea behind Interface Builder is that you can design your user interface by dragging and dropping items on to a window.

The advantage of dragging and dropping items to create a user interface means you can see how your user interface looks so you can rapidly adjust and modify it. In addition, by separating the design of your user interface from your Swift code, you can now make changes to your user interface without affecting your Swift code and vice versa.

In the old days when programmers had to write code to create a user interface, modifying the user interface code risked affecting the code that made the program work (and vice versa). That meant modifying a program went slowly because you had to constantly test to make sure your changes didn't affect another part of your program.

By keeping your user interface isolated from your Swift code, Xcode lets you create reliable programs faster than before. Now you can swap out one user interface and replace it with another one without affecting your code, or you can modify your code without affecting your user interface.

Xcode gives you two choices for how to store your user interface:

- In an .xib file
- In a .storyboard file

An .xib file (which stands for Xcode Interface Builder) typically contains a single window or view of your user interface. A simple program might have one .xib file for its user interface, but a more sophisticated program would likely need several .xib files to store different windows.

A .storyboard file consists of one or more views and segues where a view typically represents a window that appears on the screen and a segue defines the transition from one view to the next.

You can actually combine both .xib and .storyboard files in a single project to create your program's user interface. Since .storyboard files are used to create iOS apps, .storyboard files are becoming more common for creating OS X user interfaces as well. (Chapter 14 explains more about storyboards and segues.)

The basic component of a user interface is a view, which displays information on the screen. A view can be an entire window or just a box that can display information such as a table, a scrolling list of text, or a picture. Whether you're using .xib or .storyboard files, user interfaces always consist of one or more views containing other user interface items, such as buttons and text fields.

Searching the Object Library

To display your program's user interface, you need to click on the .xib or .storyboard file in the Project Navigator pane. Once you've selected a user interface file to modify, you can then drag items from the Object Library (in the bottom right corner of the Xcode window) and place it anywhere on your user interface. To view the Object Library, choose View ➤ Utilities ➤ Show Object Library.

There are two ways to search the Object Library. One way is to simply scroll up and down until you find the item you want. Since the Object Library lists every possible user interface item available, scrolling can be clumsy and slow.

A faster method is to use the search field at the bottom of the Object Library pane as shown in Figure 13-1. Just type part of the name of the user interface item you want to use and the Object Library filters out every item that doesn't match what you typed.

Figure 13-1. *The search field lets you quickly find user interface items in the Object Library*

To see how to search the Object Library, follow these steps:

1.   From within Xcode choose File ➤ New ➤ Project.

2.   Click Application under the OS X category.

3.   Click Cocoa Application and click the Next button. Xcode now asks for a product name.

4.   Click in the Product Name text field and type **UIProgram**.

5. Make sure the Language pop-up menu displays Swift and that no check boxes are selected. Notice at this point you could choose to use storyboards by selecting the "Use Storyboards" check box as shown in Figure 13-2. Keep the "Use Storyboards" check box clear for now.

Choose options for your new project:

Product Name:	UIProgram
Organization Name:	Wallace Wang
Organization Identifier:	com.topbananas
Bundle Identifier:	com.topbananas.UIProgram
Language:	Swift
	☐ Use Storyboards
	☐ Create Document-Based Application
Document Extension:	super
	☐ Use Core Data

Cancel   Previous   Next

Figure 13-2. When creating a new project, you have the option of using storyboards for your user interface

6. Click the Next button. Xcode asks where you want to store the project.

7. Choose a folder to store your project and click the Create button.

8. Click the MainMenu.xib file in the Project Navigator. Your program's user interface appears.

9. Click the UIProgram icon, as shown in Figure 13-3, to display the window of your program's user interface.

Figure 13-3. The UIProgram icon represents your user interface window

10. Choose View ➤ Utilities ➤ Show Object Library. The Object Library appears in the bottom right corner of the Xcode window.

11. Scroll up and down through the Object Library. Notice the names and variety of different items you can add to your user interface.

12. Click in the search field at the bottom of the Object Library and type **text**. Notice that the Object Library now only shows those items that have "text" in their names or descriptions as shown in Figure 13-4.

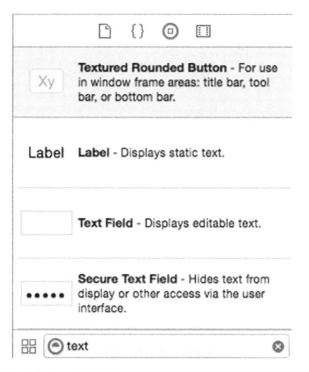

Figure 13-4. Searching the Object Library for "text"

13. Click in the search field at the bottom of the Object Library and click the close icon (the X inside the gray circle on the far right of the search field) to clear the search field.

14. Type **button**. Notice that the Object Library now only shows those items that have "button" in their names or descriptions. If you know all or even part of the name or purpose of the item you want, it's far faster to search for it in the Object Library than scrolling through the lengthy list of every user interface item available.

User Interface Items That Display and Accept Text

Although the Object Library contains a huge number of available items that you can place on a user interface, most items can be grouped into categories by function. Remember, a user interface has three functions:

▪ Display information to the user

▪ Accept data from the user

▪ Allow the user to control the program

The simplest way to display information on a user interface is through a label. In the Cocoa framework, a label is based on the NSTextField class. Essentially a label is a text field that you can't edit. To identify the class of any item in the Object Library, just click on it and a pop-up window appears that describes the item's purpose and the class it's based on as shown in Figure 13-5.

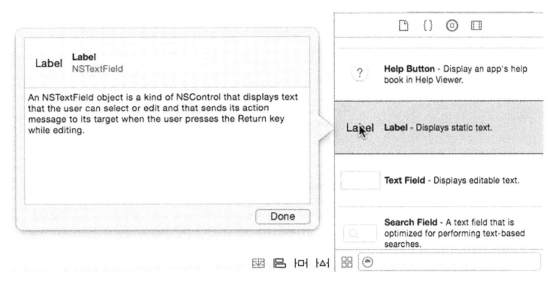

Figure 13-5. Identifying the class of a user interface item in the Object Library

Any user interface item based on the NSTextField can be used to display and accept text, although it's more common to use a label for displaying text and any other type of text field for letting the user type in text. The list of user interface items based on the NSTextField is shown in Figure 13-6:

- Label – Displays text but does not allow the user to enter or edit text.

- Text Field – Lets the user enter and edit text.

- Secure Text Field – Masks entered text with characters such as hiding typed passwords from view.

- Text Field with Number Formatter – Lets the user enter and edit formatted numbers easily.

- Wrapping Label – Displays text on multiple lines.

- Wrapping Text Field – Lets the user enter and edit text that appears on multiple lines.

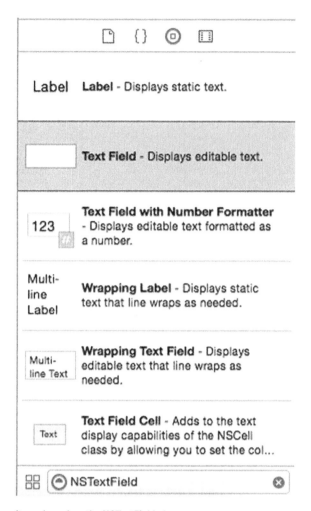

Figure 13-6. User interface items based on the NSTextField class

User Interface Items That Restrict Choices

Letting the user enter data in a text field provides maximum flexibility. However, this flexibility also means that your program has no idea what type of data the user might enter. If a program expects the user to type in a number for an age, but the user types in "forty-nine" instead, the program will likely crash because it expects a number but received a word.

Even worse, a program could ask for someone's age and a user could type a negative number or an outrageously high number such as 239, which is clearly impossible for someone's age. To ensure that users enter in correct data, you can use a variety of different user interface items that lets the user choose a range of valid options. User interface items that display text (including numbers) choices include:

- Pop Up Button (NSPopUpButton) – Displays a menu of valid options.
- Radio Group (NSMatrix) – Displays a list of radio buttons where only one can be chosen at any given time.

- Check Box (NSButton) – Displays one or more check boxes to let the user select multiple options.

- Combo Box (NSComboBox) – Acts like a combination text field and pop-up button where the user can either type in text or choose from a list of valid options.

User interface items that allow the user to select a range of valid numeric options include:

- Date Picker (NSDataPicker) – Lets the user choose a date including day, month, and year.

- Horizontal/Vertical/Circular Slider (NSSlider) – Lets the user move a slider to select a fixed range of valid numeric values.

- Stepper (NSStepper) – Increments or decrements a value by a fixed amount.

With text options, you need to list all valid options that the user can choose. With numeric options, you just need to list a range of all valid options such as letting the user choose a number between 1 and 100.

User Interface Items That Accept Commands

The most common user interface item is one that accepts commands so the user can control a program. The two most common types of user interface items that accept commands are buttons and menus. Each button or menu item represent a single command, so when the user clicks on a button or menu item, that command tells the program to do something.

Both buttons and menu items allow the view to communicate back to the controller using something called target-action as shown in Figure 13-7. The target is a button or menu item, which triggers an action back in the controller, such as running an IBAction method.

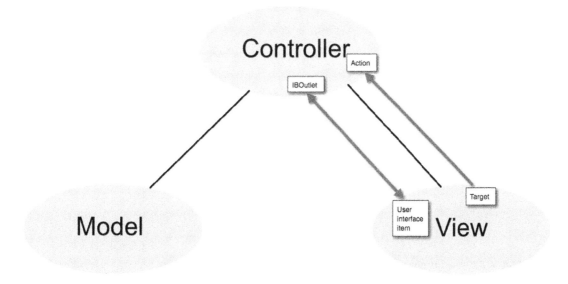

Figure 13-7. Buttons and menu items let a view communicate back to a controller

User interface buttons are based on the NSButton class. Menu items are based on the NSMenuItem class. The Object Library displays a variety of different types of buttons and menu items, but they all work alike where the button or menu item represents a command. To make that command work, you need to connect the button on the user interface to an IBAction method in a Swift file.

User Interface Items That Groups Items

One type of user interface item does nothing but group and organize other items on the user interface, such as displaying a box around related buttons or text. These user interface items are more decorative so you likely won't need to connect them to Swift code using IBOutlets or IBAction methods. Some examples of items that group and organize other user interface items include:

- Table View (NSTableView) – Displays data in rows.

- Collection View (NSCollectionView) – Displays data in rows and columns.

- Box (NSBox) – Displays a box that draws a border around related items.

- Tab View (NSTabView) – Displays a two or more tabs that can change the data that appears inside a box as shown in Figure 13-8.

Figure 13-8. A Tab View can group two or more groups of related items in the same box

■ Windows (NSWindow) – Displays a window that can hold other user interface items.

■ Toolbar (NSToolbar) – Displays icons that represent commands.

Although the Object Library contains many other items, they typically fall in one of these four categories:

■ Items that display or accept text.

■ Items that let the user choose from a limited range of valid options.

■ Items that let the user choose a command to control the program.

■ Items that group or organize other user interface items.

Using Constraints in Auto Layout

No matter what type of items you place on a user interface, you need to consider what happens if the user resizes the window. A window that's too big might leave too much empty space on the user interface. A window that's too small might cut off items as shown in Figure 13-9.

Figure 13-9. A user interface that doesn't adapt when the user resizes a window risks cutting off items

There are two ways to make sure a user interface remains usable when the user resizes a window. First, you can define minimum and maximum sizes for a window to keep a window from shrinking or expanding too much. Second, you can set constraints on individual items that define the distance between neighboring items and the edges of the window.

In most cases, you can use both methods. That way you can define a minimum and maximum size for a window, and define how items on your user interface should adapt to changes in the window size.

Defining Window Sizes

A window displays your program's user interface on the screen. Xcode lets you define the following for a window as shown in Figure 13-10:

- The initial size of the window.
- The minimum size of the window.
- The maximum size of the window.
- The initial position of the window on the screen.

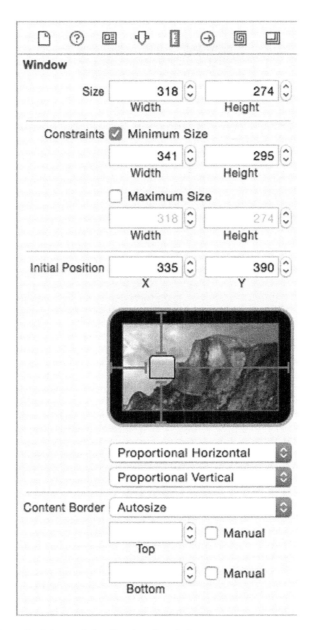

Figure 13-10. *The Size Inspector lets you define the size of a window*

To define the size of a window of an .xib file in Xcode, follow these steps:

1. Click on the .xib file in the Project Navigator pane. Xcode displays the user interface stored in the .xib file.

2. If necessary, click the Hide Document Outline icon that appears in the bottom left corner as shown in Figure 13-11.

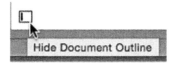

Figure 13-11. *The Hide Document Outline icon*

3. Click on the bottom icon that represents the window of your user
    interface as shown in Figure 13-12.

Figure 13-12. *The bottom icon represents your user interface window*

4. Choose View ➤ Utilities ➤ Show Size Inspector. The Size Inspector
    pane appears (see Figure 13-10).

Windows stored in .storyboard files work slightly differently than .xib files. To define the size
of a window of a .storyboard file in Xcode, follow these steps:

1. Click on the .storyboard file in the Project Navigator pane. Xcode
    displays the user interface stored in the .storyboard file.

2. Click on the View Controller of the window you want to modify as
    shown in Figure 13-13.

Figure 13-13. *The View Controller defines your user interface window*

3. Choose View ➤ Utilities ➤ Show Size Inspector. The Size Inspector
    pane appears (see Figure 13-10).

Xcode gives you two ways to change the size of a window. First, you can drag a side or
corner of the window (or view controller) using the mouse. Second, you can click in the
Width and Height text fields next to the Size label to choose a precise size for your window's
width and height as shown in Figure 13-14.

Figure 13-14. The View Controller defines your user interface window

To define the minimum and/or maximum size of a window involves a two-step process. First,
you need to select the Minimum Size and/or Maximum Size check box. Second, you need to
type or choose a width and height to define the minimum or maximum size for your window
as shown in Figure 13-15.

Figure 13-15. Defining the minimum and maximum size for a window

Finally, you can define the initial position of a window when it first appears. You can do this
by either dragging on the window icon on the simulated screen or by typing in an X and Y
value into the Initial Position text fields as shown in Figure 13-16.

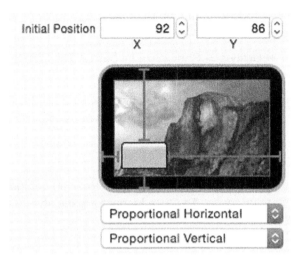

Figure 13-16. Defining the initial position of a window

The two pop-up menus underneath the simulated screen lets you define how to determine the initial position of a window:

- Fixed from Left/Right – Defines a fixed value between the window edge and the screen edge

- Proportional Horizontal/Vertical – Defines a proportional value between the window edge and the screen edge, based on the size of the screen

- Center Horizontally/Vertically – Defines the window to appear in the center of the screen

To see how you can specify a window's position and minimum/maximum size, let's create a simple program and modify its window.

1. From within Xcode choose File ➤ New ➤ Project.

2. Click Application under the OS X category.

3. Click Cocoa Application and click the Next button. Xcode now asks for a product name.

4. Click in the Product Name text field and type **WindowProgram**.

5. Make sure the Language pop-up menu displays Swift and that no check boxes are selected.

6. Click the Next button. Xcode asks where you want to store the project.

7. Choose a folder to store your project and click the Create button.

8. Click the MainMenu.xib file in the Project Navigator.

9. Click on the WindowProgram icon to make the window of the user interface appear.

10. Choose View ➤ Utilities ➤ Show Size Inspector. The Size Inspector pane appears.

11. Click the Minimum Content Size check box. Xcode displays the current width and height of the window, so keep those values.

12. Click the Maximum Content Size check box and change the Width and Height text fields to 600.

13. Drag the gray window rectangle in the Initial Position category to the far bottom right corner. The Size Inspector pane should look like Figure 13-17.

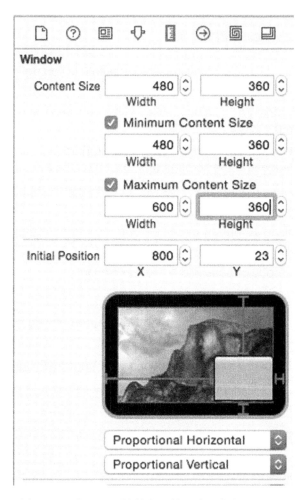

Figure 13-17. Specifying a minimum, maximum, and initial position of a window

14. Choose Product ➤ Run. Notice that the program's window appears in the bottom right corner since that's where you defined its initial position.

15. Move the mouse pointer over the left edge of the window, hold down the left mouse button, and drag the mouse left and right. Notice that you can only widen and shrink the window to a fixed size. That's because you defined both a minimum and maximum size for the window.

16. Choose WindowProgram ➤ Quit WindowProgram.

Placing Constraints on User Interface Items

Defining a minimum size for a window can keep the user from shrinking a window so small that it cuts off the items that appear on the user interface. However, what happens if the user expands a window? Then the items in the window should ideally adjust their position to adapt to the expanded window size.

Constraints define the distance between two items such as between a button and the edge of the window or between two buttons. Xcode gives you three ways to place constraints on a user interface item:

▪ Control-drag the mouse from a user interface item to another item or the edge of a window

▪ Choose Editor ➤ Pin or Resolve Auto Layout Issues

▪ Click the Pin or Resolve Auto Layout Issues icons in the bottom right corner as shown in Figure 13-18

Figure 13-18. The Align, Pin, and Resolve Auto Layout Issues icons

To use the Control-drag method to place a constraint, follow these steps:

1. Move the mouse pointer over the user interface item you want to constrain.

2. Hold down the Control key and drag the mouse toward another user interface item or the edge of the window.

3. Release the Control key and the mouse button when the mouse pointer appears near the other user interface item or window edge. A pop-up window appears similar to Figure 13-19.

Figure 13-19. *Releasing the Control key and the mouse displays a pop-up window*

Depending on the direction you Control-drag the mouse, you'll see different options in the pop-up window.

Direction to window edge	Constraint Option
Up	Top Space to Container
Bottom	Bottom Space to Container
Right	Trailing Space to Container
Left	Leading Space to Container

Besides Control-dragging to a window edge, you can also Control-drag from one user interface item over another user interface item. Doing this lets you define the distance between two items on the user interface such as the distance between two buttons or one button and a text field.

When you Control-drag the mouse over another user interface item, a pop-up window appears. If you're defining the distance between two items that are side by side, the pop-up window will display the Horizontal Spacing option. If you're defining the distance between two items that are stacked one on top of another, the pop-up window will display the Vertical Spacing option.

Direction to another item	Constraint Option
Left/Right	Horizontal Spacing
Up/Down	Vertical Spacing

The Control-drag method lets you place constraints visually on different user interface items. Another way to define constraints is to click on the user interface item you want to constrain, and then click on the Pin icon to display a pop-up window. To define constraints through the Pin icon, follow these steps:

1. Click on the user interface item that you want to constrain.

2. Click the Pin icon. A pop-up window appears, showing four constraints to the left, right, up, and down as shown in Figure 13-20.

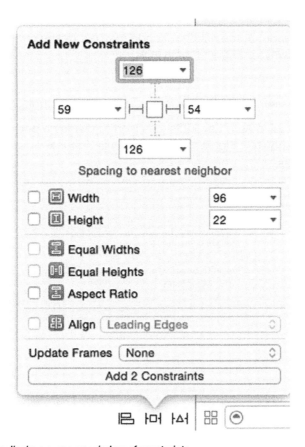

Figure 13-20. The Pin icon displays a pop-up window of constraints

3. Click on a constraint to select it (the left and right constraints are selected in Figure 13-20 so they're shown in red, but the up and down constraints are now selected so they appear as dotted lines).

4. Click in any of the additional check boxes.

5. Click on the Add X Constraints button at the bottom of the pop-up window to define a constraint.

The Pin pop-up window lets you define additional types of constraints for your selected user interface item:

- Width or Height – This keeps the size of your selected user interface item at a fixed size

- Equal Widths or Heights – This keeps two or more selected user interface items at the same fixed size

- Aspect Ratio – This keeps the ratio between the selected user interface item properly proportioned if it's resized

- Align – This aligns two or more selected user interface items

A third way to define constraints is to let Xcode choose constraints for you. This lets you add constraints quickly, but at the risk that Xcode may not define constraints correctly. Fortunately, you can always edit constraints later.

To let Xcode choose constraints, follow these steps:

1.   Click on the user interface item that you want to constrain.

2.   Click the Resolve Auto Layout Issues icon to display a pop-up window as shown in Figure 13-21 (or choose Editor ➤ Resolve Auto Layout Issues).

Figure 13-21. The Resolve Auto Layout Issues pop-up window

3.   Choose Add Missing Constraints or Reset to Suggested Constraints.

If you choose the options in the top half of the window, you'll affect only the selected user interface item. If you choose the options in the bottom half of the window, you'll affect all user interface items whether on the currently displayed window whether you selected them or not.

Remember, adding constraints can be a trial and error process of defining a constraint and seeing how it works before modifying or deleting it altogether. As you add constraints, Xcode displays constraint lines around your user interface item. If Xcode doesn't think you have enough constraints, all constraints on that item will appear as orange. The moment Xcode thinks you have enough constraints on an item, the constraints will appear in blue.

To see how constraints work with user interface items, follow these steps:

1.   Make sure your WindowProgram project is loaded in Xcode.

2.   Click the MainMenu.xib in the Project Navigator pane.

3.   Click the Window icon to make the user interface window visible.

4.   Choose View ➤ Utilites ➤ Show Object Library. The Object Library appears in the bottom right corner of the Xcode window.

5. Drag a Push Button item from the Object Library and place it anywhere on your window.

6. Move the mouse pointer over the Push Button that you just placed on the window.

7. Hold down the Control key and drag the mouse to the right until the entire window turns blue. Then let go of the Control key and the mouse. A pop-up menu appears (see Figure 13-19).

8. Choose Trailing Space to Container. Xcode displays a constraint between the edge of the window and the right edge of the push button as shown in Figure 13-22.

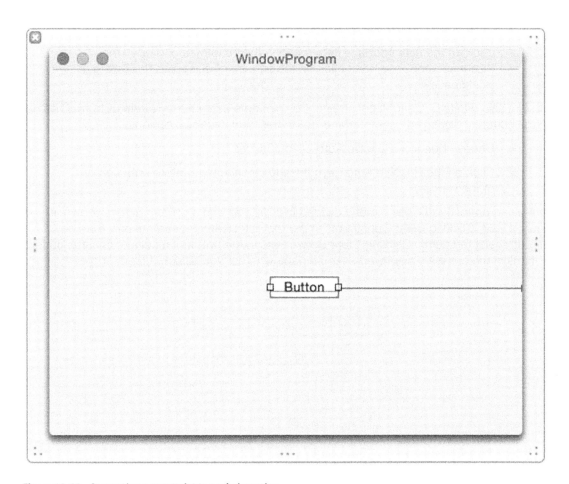

Figure 13-22. Connecting a constraint to a window edge

9.   Choose Product ➤ Run. Your window appears in the initial position you defined earlier.

10. Move the window to the center of the screen and resize the right edge. Notice that when you resize the right edge of the window, the button moves its position at the same time.

11. Choose WindowProgram ➤ Quit WindowProgram.

Editing Constraints

Once you've defined one or more constraints, you can always delete or edit existing constraints. To delete a constraint, you have several options:

- Click on the constraint and then press the Delete or Backspace key

- Click on the user interface item that has the constraint and open the Size Inspector pane, then click on the constraint and press the Delete or Backspace key

You can also delete or clear all constraints from a single user interface item or from all items on the currently displayed user interface. To do this, you have two options:

- Choose Editor ➤ Resolve Auto Layout Issues

- Click on the Resolve Auto Layout Issues icon in the bottom right corner of the window

With either option, you'll see a menu divided in a top half and a bottom half as shown in Figure 13-23. Clicking Clear Constraints in the top half clears constraints only from any currently selected items. Clicking Clear Constraints in the bottom half clears constraints from all items in the currently displayed user interface whether you selected them or not.

Figure 13-23. *A pop-up window lets you modify a constraint*

Rather than delete a constraint, you can edit it. Editing lets you modify how it behaves. Three values you can modify about a constraint include:

- Constant – A fixed value that defines the value of the constraint

- Priority – A numeric value that determines which constraints must be followed first

- Modifier – A numeric value that defines a ratio that affects two values such as an item's height to its width or one item's width to a second item's width

To edit a constraint, follow these steps:

1. Click on the user interface item that contains the constraint you want to edit.

2. Choose View ➤ Utilities ➤ Show Size Inspector. The Size Inspector pane lists all defined constraints as shown in Figure 13-24.

Figure 13-24. Viewing a list of defined constraints in the Size Inspector pane

3. Click the Edit button on the far right of the constraint you want to modify. A pop-up window appears as shown in Figure 13-25.

Figure 13-25. *A pop-up window lets you modify a constraint*

Notice that to the right of the Constant: label, there's a pop-up menu showing an equal sign (=). If you click on this pop-up menu, you can select greater than or equal to, less than or equal to, or equal to.

Further to the right of the Constant: label is a drop-down field that displays a number. If you click on the downward-pointing arrow, you'll be able to choose between three options:

- A numeric value that you can type or edit

- Use Standard Value – Lets Xcode decide the best value

- Use Canvas Value – Uses the current distance on the screen to define a fixed value

Keep in mind that a fixed value or Canvas Value may behave differently on different size monitors. You may need to experiment until you find the right value for your particular user interface.

Priorities are used to resolve conflicts between two or more constraints that may contradict each other, such as one constraint keeping a button pinned to the right edge of a window and a second constraint keeping the same button pinned to the left edge of a window while a third constraint keeps the button a fixed width. By modifying priorities, you can make sure your constraints don't conflict.

Finding the right combination of constraints can be tedious and frustrating at times. To simplify setting constraints, Xcode offers two ways to define constraints for you:

- Add Missing Constraints – Keeps any existing constraints you've defined and adds new ones Xcode thinks you're missing

- Reset to Suggested Constraints – Deletes all constraints you may have set for an item and replaces it with its own constraints

When you first define constraints, Xcode displays them in orange to let you know that you don't have enough constraints to define the position of an item on your user interface. Once you've defined enough constraints to specify a position, then Xcode displays constraints in blue.

If you define constraints, you may see a dotted orange line that represents the outline of your currently selected item. This dotted line is a frame and shows where your item will appear when you actually run your program.

To move an item into its proper location, you need to choose either Editor ➤ Resolve Auto Layout Issues ➤ Update Frames, or click on the Resolve Auto Layout Issues icon in the bottom right corner of the Xcode window and choose Update Frames (see Figure 13-23).

To see how Xcode can automatically define constraints, follow these steps:

1. Make sure your WindowProgram project is loaded in Xcode.

2. Click the MainMenu.xib in the Project Navigator pane.

3. Click the Window icon to make the user interface window visible.

4. Click on the Push Button your program's window to select that button.

5. Choose Editor ➤ Resolve Auto Layout Issues. A pop-up menu appears (see Figure 13-23).

6. Choose Clear Constraints in the top half of the menu. (The top half of the menu affects only the selected item, which is the push button. The bottom half of the menu affects all items on the window. In this case, the only item is the push button, so you could actually select Clear Constraints in the top or bottom half of the menu.) Xcode removes the constraint from the button.

7. Choose Editor ➤ Resolve Auto Layout Issues. A pop-up menu appears (see Figure 13-23).

8. Choose Add Missing Constraints in the top half of the menu. Xcode adds constraints that it thinks the push button needs as shown in Figure 13-26.

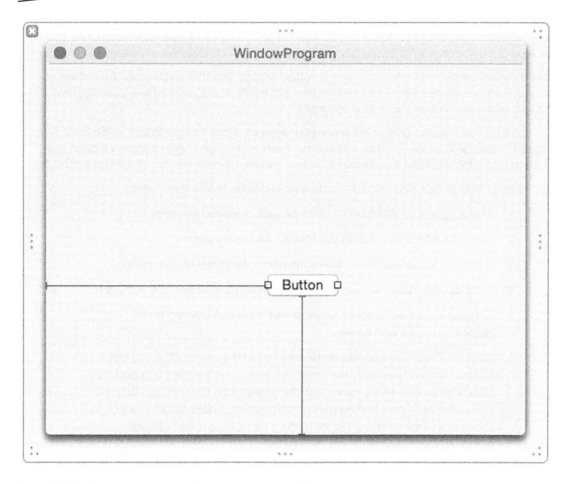

Figure 13-26. Xcode automatically adds all necessary constraints

9.   Choose Product ➤ Run. Your window appears in the initial position you defined earlier.

10. Move the window to the center of the screen and resize the left edge. Notice that when you resize the left edge of the window, the button moves its position at the same time.

11. Choose WindowProgram ➤ Quit WindowProgram.

Defining Constraints in an OS X Program

To fully understand how constraints work, you need to see how they work in an actual program. Then you can see how your user interface adjusts each time you resize its window. In this sample program, we'll define relationships constraints for a push button and a text field, and also define an aspect ratio for an image.

Earlier in this chapter you created an OS X project called UIProgram so we'll use that to see how constraints work:

1. Make sure your UIProgram project is loaded in Xcode.

2. Click the MainMenu.xib file in the Project Navigator.

3. Click on the UIProgram icon to make the window of the user interface appear.

4. Choose View ➤ Utilities ➤ Show Object Library to make the Object Library appear in the bottom right corner of the Xcode window.

5. Drag one Push Button, one Text Field, and one Text View on the user interface so that it looks similar to Figure 13-27.

Figure 13-27. The user interface of the InheritProgram

While this user interface may look fine right now, it will look awful as soon as the user resizes the window. Choose Product ➤ Run and then resize the window to see how shrinking the window cuts off or hides items on the user interface. Now expand the size of the window and notice all the empty space inside the expanded window. Exit out of your program by choosing UIProgram ➤ Quit UIProgram.

First, let's define the window's minimum size by following these steps:

6. Move the mouse pointer over the bottom right corner of the frame that surrounds your user interface window.

7. Drag the mouse until you see blue guidelines showing the boundary between your button and window edge as shown in Figure 13-28.

Figure 13-28. Adjusting the size of the user interface window

8. Click the frame surrounding the user interface window and choose View ➤ Utilities ➤ Show Size Inspector to display the window constraints (see Figure 13-16).

9. Click the Minimum Size check box to define the current window size as its minimum size.

10. Choose Product ➤ Run. Resize the user interface window. Notice that you can only shrink the window to a certain size.

11. Choose UIProgram ➤ Quit UIProgram.

By defining a minimum window size, you've kept your user interface from getting cut off or having items disappear if the user shrinks the window too small. Now let's add constraints to make the user interface adapt if the user expands the window size.

1. Move the mouse pointer over the button, hold down the Control key, and drag the mouse to the right and stop right before the window's right edge as shown in Figure 13-29.

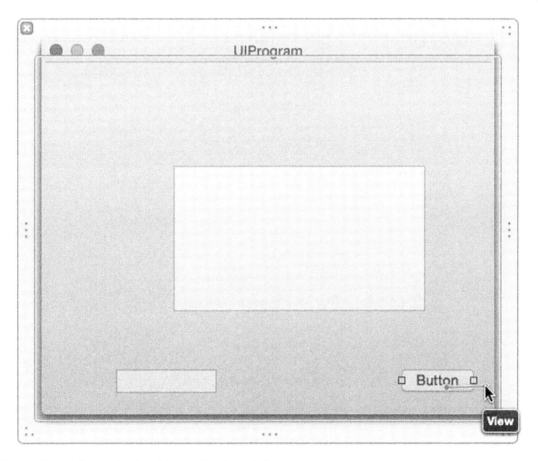

Figure 13-29. Adjusting the size of the user interface window

2. Release the Control key and the mouse. A pop-up window appears.

3. Choose Trailing Space to Container. Notice that the constraints appear in orange to show that you don't have enough constraints on the button yet.

4. Move the mouse pointer over the button, hold down the Control key, and drag the mouse down and stop right before the window's bottom edge.

5. Release the Control key and the mouse. A pop-up window appears.

6. Choose Bottom Space to Container.

7. Click on the text field to select it.

8. Choose Editor ➤ Resolve Auto Layout Issues ➤ Add Missing Constraints. Xcode adds constraints automatically as shown in Figure 13-30.

Figure 13-30. Constraints on the text field

9. Move the mouse pointer anywhere over the Text View.

10. Hold down the Control key and drag the mouse at a 45 degree angle up or down as shown in Figure 13-31.

Figure 13-31. *Defining an aspect ratio constraint*

11. Release the Control key and the mouse. A pop-up window appears.

12. Choose Aspect Ratio to keep the width and height in proportion. Xcode displays orange constraints around the Text View to indicate that you don't have enough constraints on the Text View.

13. Click the Resolve Auto Layout Issues icon in the bottom right corner and choose Add Missing Constraints. Xcode adds missing constraints so they now appear in blue.

14. Choose Product ➤ Run.

15. Resize the window. Notice how the user interface items adjust when you expand the window size. As you can see, constraints keep user interface items in their proper place and size no matter how the user resizes the window. Feel free to experiment with editing your constraints to see how they work.

16. Choose UIProgram ➤ Quit UIProgram.

Summary

Your program's user interface determines how people interact with your program. Every user interface needs to display information, retrieve information from the user, and allow the user to choose commands. Ideally a user interface should focus more on using your program and less on figuring out how the user interface works.

The Object Library displays all possible items you can add to your user interface whether you use .xib or .storyboard files. To help you find items in the Object Library, you can type all or part of a word in the search field at the bottom of the Object Library.

Constraints help keep your user interface looking good no matter how the user resizes your program's windows. The two basic types of constraints involve the following:

- Relationship constraints that define the distance between neighboring items such as between two buttons or a button and the edge of a window.

- Size constraints that define the height, width, or aspect ratio of an item.

You can define constraints on your own, let Xcode define constraints, or use a combination of both. Defining constraints may be a trial and error process until your user interface adapts to resizing windows exactly the way you want.

Working with Views and Storyboards

The most common part of every program's user interface is a window that displays items such as buttons and text fields. In Xcode, windows are called views. In all but the simplest programs, a user interface will likely consist of two or more windows or views. That means your program needs to know how to open additional windows and close them again.

The two ways to create and store views are .xib files and .storyboard files. An .xib file holds one view so if you need to display multiple views, you'll need to create multiple .xib files. A .storyboard file can hold one or more views.

You can create user interfaces with either .xib or .storyboard files, or a combination of both. Generally, .storyboard files are best for windows that logically link together. The biggest advantage of .storyboard files is that they link multiple views together in a logical sequence. The biggest disadvantage of .storyboard files is that if you have multiple views in your program, there may not be a logical sequence between displaying different views in a particular order. In that case, a .storyboard file can appear cluttered and be difficult to organize.

Whether you use .xib or .storyboard files is less important than knowing how to design a good user interface that makes performing tasks as easy as possible for the user.

Creating User Interface Files

When you create a project, Xcode gives you a choice between using storyboards or not as shown in Figure 14-1. If you choose not to use storyboards, then Xcode will create and store your user interface in an .xib file. If you choose to use storyboards, then Xcode will store your user interface in a .storyboard file.

Choose options for your new project:

Product Name:	
Organization Name:	Wallace Wang
Organization Identifier:	com.topbananas
Bundle Identifier:	com.topbananas.ProductName
Language:	Swift

☑ Use Storyboards
☐ Create Document-Based Application

Document Extension: super

☐ Use Core Data

Cancel   Previous   Next

Figure 14-1. *When creating an OS X project, Xcode gives you a choice of choosing storyboards or not*

After you've created a project, you can always add additional .xib or .storyboard files no matter if you initially started with storyboards or not.

Adding an .xib or .storyboard File

To add an .xib or .storyboard file to a project, follow these steps:

1. From within Xcode choose File ➤ New ➤ File.

2. Click User Interface under the OS X category.

3. Click on Window (.xib) or Storyboard (.storyboard) as shown in Figure 14-2.

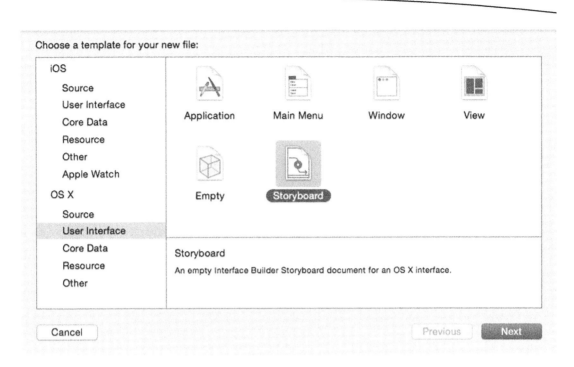

Choose a template for your new file:

iOS
  Source
  User Interface
  Core Data
  Resource
  Other
  Apple Watch
OS X
  Source
  User Interface
  Core Data
  Resource
  Other

Application   Main Menu   Window   View

Empty   Storyboard

Storyboard
An empty Interface Builder Storyboard document for an OS X interface.

Cancel   Previous   Next

Figure 14-2. Adding an .xib or .storyboard file to a project

4. Click the Next button. Xcode asks where you want to store the project.

5. Choose a folder to store your project and click the Create button. Your .xib or .storyboard user interface file appears in the Project Navigator pane.

If you create an .xib file using the above steps, you may still need to create a Swift file called a view controller to manage the view. To create a view controller Swift file and an .xib file at the same time, follow these steps:

1. From within Xcode choose File ➤ New ➤ File.

2. Click Source under the OS X category and click Cocoa Class as shown in Figure 14-3.

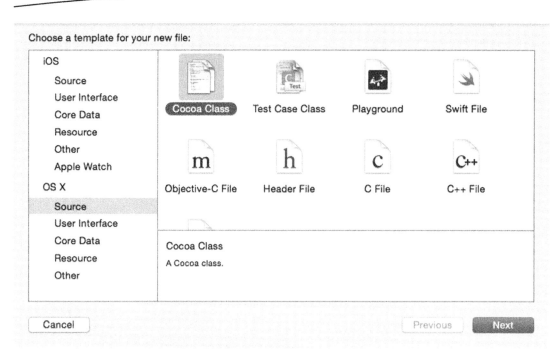

Choose a template for your new file:

iOS
  Source
  User Interface
  Core Data
  Resource
  Other
  Apple Watch
OS X
  Source
  User Interface
  Core Data
  Resource
  Other

Cocoa Class   Test Case Class   Playground   Swift File

m   h   c   C++

Objective-C File   Header File   C File   C++ File

Cocoa Class
A Cocoa class.

Cancel   Previous   Next

Figure 14-3. Choosing Cocoa Class under the Source category

3. Click the Next button. Xcode now asks for a class name, subclass, and whether you want to create an accompanying .xib file.

4. Type any name in the Name text field.

5. Click in the Subclass of: pop-up menu and choose NSViewController.

6. Select the "Also create XIB file for user interface" check box and make sure the Language pop-up menu displays Swift as shown in Figure 14-4.

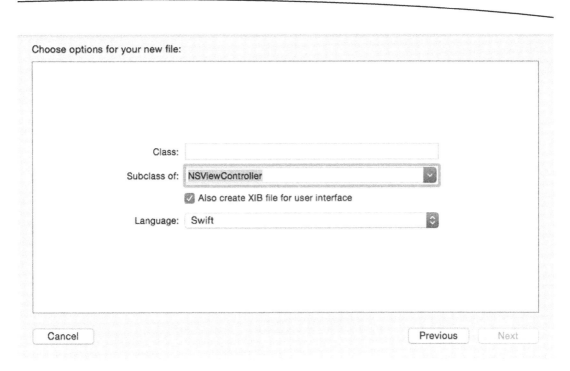

Figure 14-4. Defining a class name, subclass, and .xib file

7. Click the Next button. Xcode asks where you want to store your new file.

8. Click the Create button. Xcode creates an .xib and accompanying .swift file in the Project Navigator pane.

Defining the Main User Interface

If your project only consists of a single .xib or .storyboard file, Xcode uses that one file as your program's main user interface. However, if you have multiple user interface files (such as two .xib or .storyboard files, or a combination of both .xib and .storyboard files), you need to define which file should be your main user interface.

To define a main user interface file, follow these steps:

1. Click on the project name in the top of the Project Navigator pane. Xcode displays a list of settings you can define for your project.

2. Click the Main Interface pop-up menu and choose the user interface file (.xib or .storyboard) that you want to use as shown in Figure 14-5.

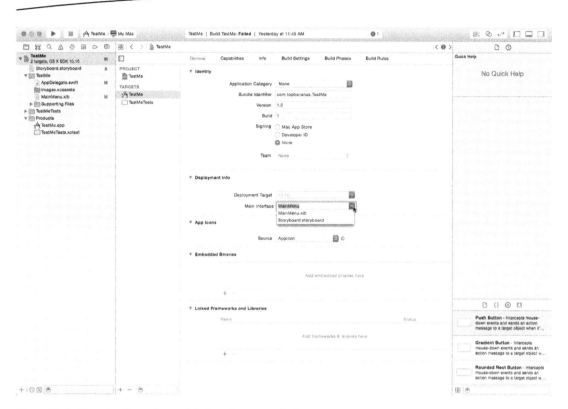

Figure 14-5. *Choosing the main user interface for your project*

3. Click on the .xib or .storyboard file in the Project Navigator pane that
    you chose in step 2 so you can edit your main user interface.

Displaying Multiple .xib Files

If you have multiple .xib files in a project, you need to designate one .xib file as your main
user interface. That means the other .xib files won't be visible until you specifically make
them appear. To open one .xib file from another one, there are three steps you need to take:

- Create a view controller and .xib file

- Create an object to represent your view controller

- Use the showWindow and close commands to open the .xib file and
  close it afterwards

To see how to open and close an .xib file, follow these steps:

1. From within Xcode choose File ➤ New ➤ Project.

2. Click Application under the OS X category.

3. Click Cocoa Application and click the Next button. Xcode now asks
    for a product name.

4. Click in the Product Name text field and type **XIBProgram**.

5. Make sure the Language pop-up menu displays Swift and that no check boxes are selected.

6. Click the Next button. Xcode asks where you want to store the project.

7. Choose a folder to store your project and click the Create button.

8. Click the MainMenu.xib file in the Project Navigator. Your program's user interface appears.

9. Click the XIBProgram icon to display the window of your program's user interface.

10. Choose View ➤ Utilities ➤ Show Attributes Inspector. The Attributes Inspector pane appears as shown in Figure 14-6. The Attributes Inspector gives you options for modifying the appearance of each window of your user interface. For now, don't change anything.

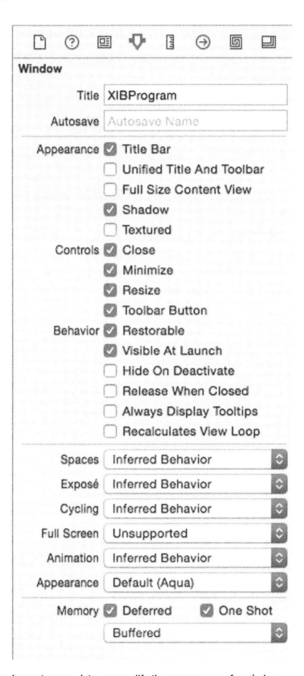

Figure 14-6. The Attributes Inspector pane lets you modify the appearance of a window

11. Choose View ➤ Utilities ➤ Show Object Library. The Object Library appears in the bottom right corner of the Xcode window.

12. Drag a Push Button on the window of your user interface and change its label to read "Open Window."

At this point, your program consists of a MainMenu.xib file that displays a single window with a push button on it. Now we need to create a view controller (containing Swift code) and an accompanying .xib file by following these steps:

1. Choose File ➤ New ➤ File. A template dialog appears.

2. Choose Source under the OS X category and click Cocoa Class (see Figure 14-3). Click the Next button. Another dialog appears, asking for a class name.

3. Type secondView in the Class Name text field.

4. Click in the Subclass of: pop-up menu and choose NSWindowController.

5. Select the "Also create XIB file for user interface" check box.

6. Make sure the Language pop-up menu displays Swift as shown in Figure 14-7.

Choose options for your new file:

Class:	secondView
Subclass of:	NSWindowController
	☑ Also create XIB file for user interface
Language:	Swift

Cancel   Previous   Next

Figure 14-7. Defining the features of a second. xib file and its view controller

7. Click the Next button. Xcode asks where you want to store your file.

8. Click the Create button. Xcode displays a secondView.swift and a secondView.xib file in the Project Navigator pane.

At this point, you've created a second. xib file and an accompanying view controller file. Now it's time to write Swift code to make everything work by following these steps:

1. Click in the MainMenu.xib file in the Project Navigator pane.

2. Choose View ➤ Assistant Editor ➤ Show Assistant Editor. Xcode shows the AppDelegate.swift file to the right of the MainMenu.xib file.

3. Move the mouse pointer over the Open Window button, hold down the Control key and drag the mouse above the last curly bracket in the AppDelegate.swift file.

4. Release the Control key and the mouse button. A pop-up window appears.

5. Click the Connection pop-up menu and choose Action.

6. Click in the Name text field and type openWindow.

7. Click in the Type pop-up menu and choose NSButton as shown in Figure 14-8.

Figure 14-8. Creating an IBAction method for the Open Window button

8. Click the Connect button. Xcode creates an empty IBAction method.

9. Underneath the @IBOutlet line, type the following:

    ```
    var windowController = secondView(windowNibName: "secondView")
    ```

10. Modify the IBAction method as follows:

    ```
    @IBAction func openWindow(sender: NSButton) {
        windowController.showWindow(sender)
    }
    ```

11. Click on the secondView.xib file. The Assistant Editor should stay open and show the secondView.swift file to the right.

12. Drag a Push Button on to the window of the secondView.xib file and label this button Back.

13. Move the mouse button over this Back button you just created, hold down the Control key, and drag the mouse above the last curly bracket in the secondView.swift file.

14. Release the Control key and the mouse. A pop-up window appears.

15. Click the Connection pop-up menu and choose Action.

16. Click in the Name text field and type closeWindow.

17. Click in the Type pop-up menu and choose NSButton.

18. Click the Connect button.

19. Modify the IBAction method closeWindow as follows:

```
@IBAction func closeWindow(sender: NSButton) {
    self.close()
}
```

20. Choose Product ➤ Run. Your program appears.

21. Click the Open Window button. The second window appears as shown in Figure 14-9.

Figure 14-9. Running the XIBProgram

22. Click the Back button to close the second window defined by your secondView.xib file.

23. Choose XIBProgram ➤ Quit XIBProgram.

What you did was create a second .xib file with a view controller. Then you created an object in the AppDelegate.swift file called windowController, based on the secondView class that loads the secondView.xib file.

Inside the openWindow IBAction method, you used the showWindow method to open the .xib file stored in the windowController object, which is the secondView class.

When this second window appears, you clicked on the Back button, which ran the self. close() command that closed the window.

As you can see, opening and closing multiple .xib files requires Swift code. To make transitioning from one window to another easier, Xcode also offers storyboards.

Using Storyboards

Storyboards consist of two parts:

- Scenes – Display the windows of your user interface
- Segues – Define the transitions between scenes

You create scenes and place items on scenes such as buttons and text fields. Then you connect scenes using segues. By doing this, you can define how your user interface displays information on the screen.

To experiment with storyboards, you'll need to create a project that uses storyboards by following these steps:

1. From within Xcode choose File ➤ New ➤ Project.

2. Click Application under the OS X category.

3. Click Cocoa Application and click the Next button. Xcode now asks for a product name.

4. Click in the Product Name text field and type **StoryProgram**.

5. Make sure the Language pop-up menu displays Swift and that only the "Use Storyboards" check box is selected.

6. Click the Next button. Xcode asks where you want to store the project.

7. Choose a folder to store your project and click the Create button.

When you create a project that uses storyboards, you'll see two boxes where one box represents your window or view (labeled Window Controller) and the second box represents that window's contents (labeled View Controller in its title bar) as shown in Figure 14-10. The second box (that has an arrow pointing to it) is where you can place additional user interface items such as buttons, text fields, and labels.

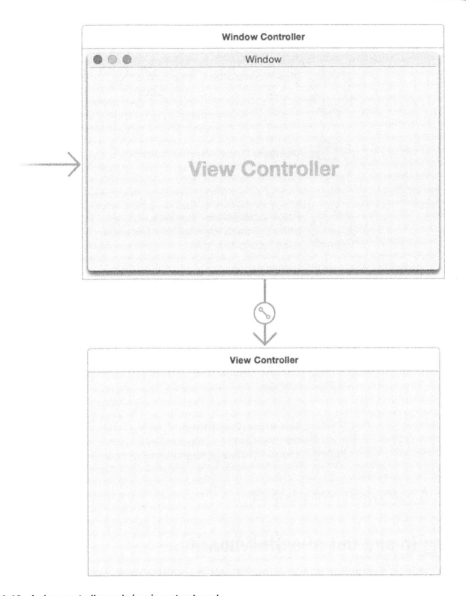

Figure 14-10. *A view controller and view in a storyboard*

You place items from the Object Library onto the bottom window (labeled View Controller). To add additional windows to a storyboard, you use the Object Library and drag different controller objects into your storyboard as shown in Figure 14-11.

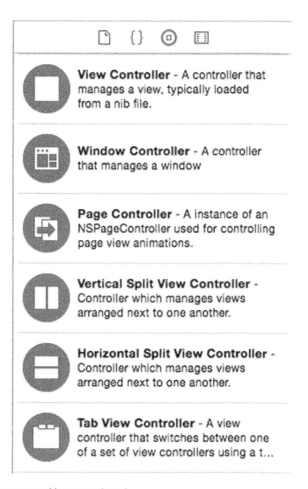

Figure 14-11. *Controllers you can add to a storyboard*

Zooming In and Out of a Storyboard

When you click on a .storyboard file in the Project Navigator pane, Xcode displays your storyboard. The problem with storyboards is that they tend to consist of multiple scenes and segues, which you can't easily see.

To help you see your entire storyboard or just a part of it, you can zoom magnification in and out. Xcode offers two ways to zoom in and out:

- Double-click on the blank space away from anything on the storyboard (this toggles the storyboard between zooming in and zooming out).

- Right-click on the blank space on the storyboard and choose a magnification level from a pop-up menu as shown in Figure 14-12.

Figure 14-12. *Right-clicking displays a magnification pop-up menu*

The lower to zoom magnification, the more of the storyboard you'll be able to see, so a zoom magnification of 25% displays more of the storyboard than a zoom magnification of 50%.

> **Note**   You'll need to change the storyboard magnification to 100% when you want to place different items on the user interface such as buttons or text fields.

Adding Scenes to a Storyboard

You can add scenes to a storyboard at any magnification. Lower magnifications (such as 25% or 50%) just make it easier to see how the individual scenes in your storyboard are connected. To place a new scene on a storyboard, follow these steps:

1. Click on the .storyboard file in the Project Navigator pane.

2. Choose View ➤ Utilities ➤ Show Object Library.

3. Drag any blue controller from the Object Library (see Figure 14-11) anywhere on the storyboard.

The five types of controllers you can place on a storyboard include:

- View Controller – Controls an .xib file so you can include it with a storyboard

- Window Controller – Controls a single window or view

- Page Controller – Defines the animation between views

- Vertical/Horizontal Split View Controller – Displays two views side by side or stacked on top of each other

- Tab View Controller – Displays a tabbed interface that controls two or more views

You can think of a Window Controller as a window that contains a view. The view displayed inside the window is identified by an arrow pointing from the Window Controller to the view as shown in Figure 14-13.

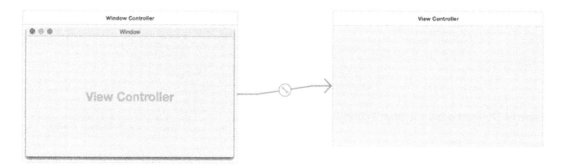

Figure 14-13. *A Window Controller contains a single view*

On the other hand, a Vertical/Horizontal Split View Controller acts like a window that holds two views either side by side or stacked on top of each other as shown in Figure 14-14.

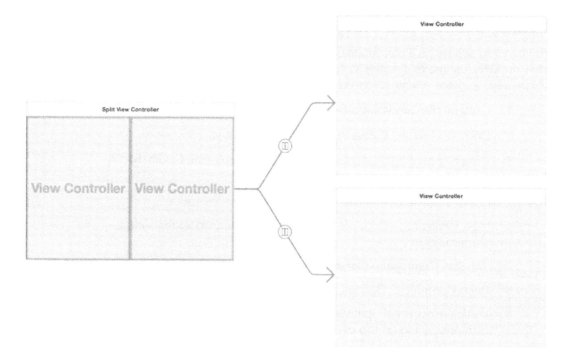

Figure 14-14. *A Split View Controller contains two views*

The Tab View Controller also consists of a single window that can contain two or more views. The difference is that it can display tabs where each tab represents a different view as shown in Figure 14-15. You can also add more than two views to a Tab View Controller.

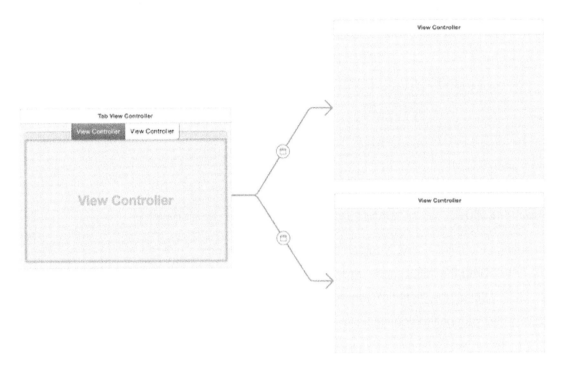

Figure 14-15. A Tab View Controller displays two or more views in one window identified by tabs

Defining the Initial Scene in a Storyboard

In every storyboard, one scene must be designated as the initial scene, which is the first window or view that appears when your program runs. Xcode identifies the initial scene with an arrow pointing to the right.

Another way to identify the initial scene is to click on the blue icon in the top middle part of the controller and open the Show Attributes Inspector pane. If the "Is Initial Controller" check box is selected, then the currently selected window is the initial scene as shown in Figure 14-16.

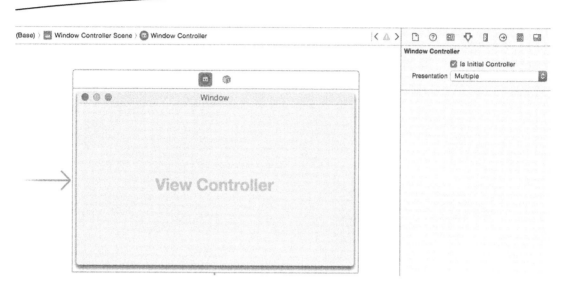

Figure 14-16. *An arrow and the "Is Initial Controller" check box identifies the initial scene*

To change the initial scene, you can do one of the following:

■ Drag the initial scene arrow and make it point to a different scene

■ Select the "Is Initial Controller" check box for a different scene

Note: There can only be one initial scene at a time.

Connecting Scenes with Segues

When a storyboard consists or two or more scenes, you need a way to display those other scenes. First, you need a way to switch from one scene to another. Second, you need a way to go back. Third, you may need to pass data from one scene to another.

Moving from one scene to another involves creating a segue between scenes. To create a segue between scenes, follow these steps:

1. Make sure your StoryProgram project is loaded in Xcode and click on the Main.storyboard file in the Project Navigator pane.

2. Place a button on the first scene.

3. Move the mouse pointer over this button, hold down the Control key, and drag the mouse from this button over the second scene. Xcode highlights the second scene as shown in Figure 14-17.

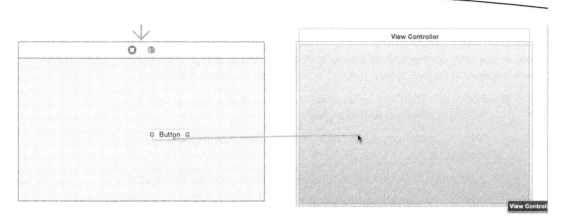

Figure 14-17. *Control-dragging the mouse from a button to another scene creates a segue*

4. Release the Control key and the mouse. Xcode displays a pop-up menu as shown in Figure 14-18.

Figure 14-18. *A pop-up menu lets you define how to display the scene*

5. Choose an option such as popover or sheet. Xcode creates a segue between the two scenes. If you click on a segue, Xcode highlights the button that runs the segue. If you open the Show Attributes Inspector pane, you can give the segue an identifying name and also change the segue style as shown in Figure 14-19.

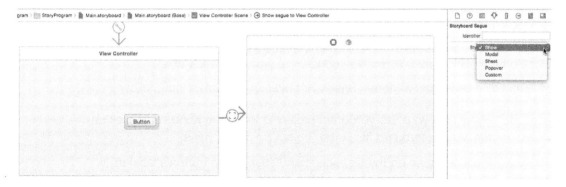

Figure 14-19. *Clicking on a segue lets you edit its attributes and identify the user interface item that runs that segue*

Displaying Scenes From a Segue

A segue not only connects one scene to another scene, but also defines how that second scene appears. The five different ways a scene can appear include:

- Popover – Displays a scene as a window that pops up over or under the button connected to the segue

- Show – Displays a scene as a separate window that can be moved and resized

- Custom – Lets you create a custom appearance for the scene

- Modal – Displays a scene as a dialog that won't let the user do anything else until dismissing this scene

- Sheet – Displays a scene that slides down from the title bar of the window

When you first create a segue, you can define how the segue should display the scene. However, you can always change this by following these steps:

1. Make sure your StoryProgram project is loaded in Xcode and click on the Main.storyboard file in the Project Navigator pane.

2. Click on the segue that you want to modify. Xcode highlights your chosen segue.

3. Choose View ➤ Utilities ➤ Show Attributes Inspector. The Attributes Inspector pane lets you modify the Identifier and Style properties (see Figure 14-19).

4. Click in the Style pop-up menu in the Show Attributes Inspector pane and choose a different style such as Modal or Sheet.

Removing a Scene After a Segue

A segue works in one direction from one scene to a second scene. When you create a second scene using the Modal, Sheet, Popover, or Custom segue, you can close this second scene using Swift code. To do this, you need to create a Swift controller file for your scene. Then connect a user interface item from that scene (such as a button) to define an IBAction method where you can use Swift code to close a scene.

If you open a scene using a Show segue, then the user can close the scene by clicking the close button, which doesn't require you to write any Swift code at all.

To remove a scene after a Modal, Sheet, Popover, or Custom segue, follow these steps:

1. Make sure your StoryProgram project is loaded in Xcode and click on the Main.storyboard file in the Project Navigator pane.

2. Place a button on the first scene and change the button's label to Open Scene.

3. Click on the segue, choose View ➤ Utilities ➤ Show Attributes Inspector, and make sure the Style pop-up menu displays Modal, Sheet, Popover, or Custom.

4. Choose File ➤ New ➤ File. Xcode displays different templates you can use.

5. Choose Source under OS X and click the Cocoa Class icon. Then click the Next button. Another dialog appears, asking for a name and a subclass.

6. Click in the Name text field and type a descriptive name for your class to control your scene.

7. Click in the Subclass of: pop-up menu and choose NSViewController.

8. Clear the "Also create XIB file for user interface" check box.

9. Make sure the Language pop-up menu displays Swift as shown in Figure 14-20. Click the Next button. Xcode asks where you want to save your new Swift class.

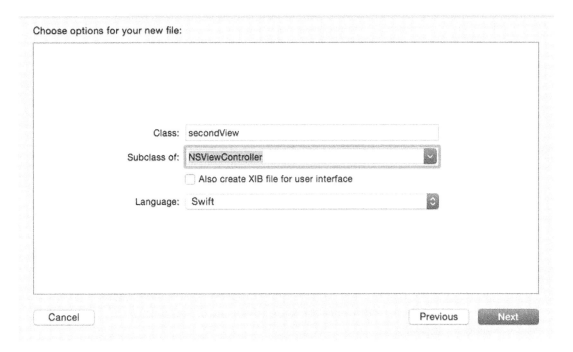

Figure 14-20. Creating a Swift class to control a scene in a storyboard

10. Choose a folder and click the Create button. Xcode displays your Swift class in the Project Navigator pane. At this point, the Swift class and the scene aren't connected so we have to fix this by making the scene's view controller a class of the Swift file we just created.

11.   Click on the Main.storyboard file to display your user interface.

12.   Click on the blue View Controller icon on the scene that has a segue pointing to it. This should be the scene that you want to go away.

13.   Choose View ➤ Utilities ➤ Show Identity Inspector.

14.   Click in the Class pop-up menu and choose secondView, the view controller you created earlier as shown in Figure 14-21.

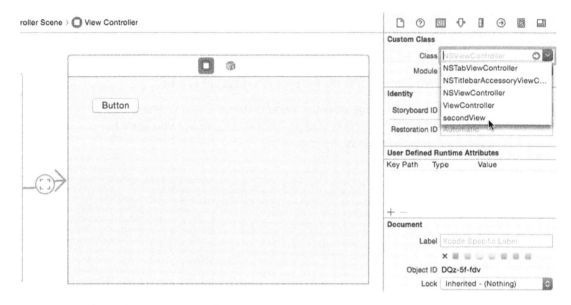

Figure 14-21. Connecting a scene to a Swift view controller file

15.   Drag a push button on to this second scene and change its label to Close Scene.

16.   Choose View ➤ Assistant Editor ➤ Show Assistant Editor. The Assistant Editor displays the secondView Swift file you just created.

17.   Move the mouse pointer over the push button on this second scene, hold down the Control key, and drag the mouse just above the last curly bracket in the bottom of the secondView.swift file. A pop-up window appears.

18.   Click in the Connection pop-up menu and choose Action.

19.   Click in the Name text field and type closeScene.

20.   Click in the Type pop-up menu and choose NSButton. Then click the Connect button. Xcode displays an empty IBAction method.

21. Modify the IBAction method as follows:

```
@IBAction func closeScene(sender: NSButton) {
    self.dismissController(self)

}
```

22. Choose Product ➤ Run. Your program's initial scene appears with the button Open Scene.

23. Click the Open Scene. Your second scene appears in the way you defined the segue such as Modal, Sheet, Popover, or Custom.

24. Click the Close Scene button on this second scene. The second scene goes away.

25. Choose StoryProgram ➤ Quit StoryProgram.

Passing Data Between Scenes

When you make changes on one scene and then open another scene, you may want that second scene to know of any changes you made earlier on the previous scene. To do this, you need to do the following:

▨ In the first scene, create a prepareForSegue method that uses the segue.destinationViewController command to identify the name of the second scene's view controller and assign a value to the representedObject property.

▨ In the second scene's view controller, declare a variable to hold the data you want to receive from the first scene and unwrap the value from representedObject.

To see how to pass data from one scene to another, follow these steps:

1. Make sure your StoryProgram project is loaded in Xcode and click on the Main.storyboard file in the Project Navigator pane.

2. Drag a text field and widen it on the scene that contains the Open Scene button as shown in Figure 14-22.

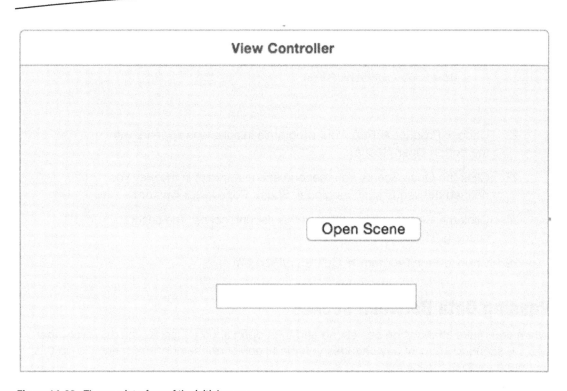

Figure 14-22. The user interface of the initial scene

3. Choose View ➤ Assistant Editor ➤ Show Assistant Editor to display the ViewController.swift file that controls the initial scene.

4. Move the mouse pointer over the text field, hold down the Control key, and drag the mouse from the text field to under the class ViewController line.

5. Release the Control key and mouse. A pop-up menu appears.

6. Click in the Name text field, type passedText, and click the Connect button. Xcode creates an IBOutlet like this:

```
@IBOutlet weak var passedText: NSTextField!
```

7. Write a prepareForSegue method so the entire code in the ViewController.swift file looks like this:

```
import Cocoa

class ViewController: NSViewController {

    @IBOutlet weak var passedText: NSTextField!

    override func viewDidLoad() {
        super.viewDidLoad()
```

```
        // Do any additional setup after loading the view.
    }

    override func prepareForSegue(segue: NSStoryboardSegue, sender: AnyObject?) {
        let secondScene = segue.destinationController as! secondView
        secondScene.representedObject = passedText.stringValue
    }

    override var representedObject: AnyObject? {
        didSet {
        // Update the view, if already loaded.
        }
    }

}
```

The passedText IBOutlet retrieves the text that the user types into the text field. Then the prepareForSegue method creates a constant called "secondScene" that represents the segue's destination, which is the secondView class. Then it takes the text from the passedText IBOutlet and stores it into the representedObject property.

8. Click on the second scene in your storyboard, place a Label on there and make it wider as shown in Figure 14-23.

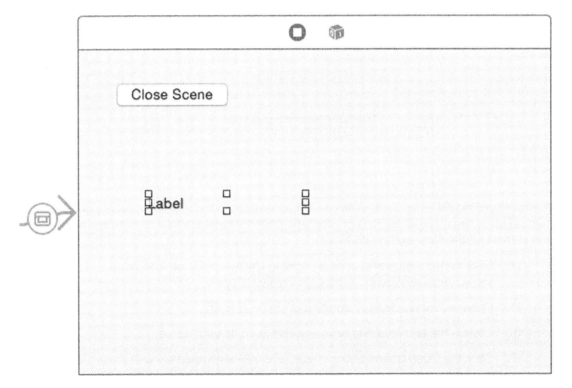

Figure 14-23. The user interface of the second scene

9.   Choose View ➤ Assistant Editor ➤ Show Assistant Editor. If the assistant editor does not display the secondView.swift file, click Automatic in the upper left corner of the assistant editor to display a menu. From this menu, choose Manual ➤ StoryProgram ➤ StoryProgram and then click on the secondView.swift file.

10. Move the mouse pointer over the label, hold down the Control key, and drag the mouse from the label to under the class secondView line.

11. Release the Control key and mouse. A pop-up menu appears.

12. Click in the Name text field, type receivedText, and click the Connect button. Xcode creates an IBOutlet like this:

```
@IBOutlet weak var receivedText: NSTextField!
```

13. Modify the viewDidLoad method so the entire code in the secondView.swift file looks like this:

```
import Cocoa

class secondView: NSViewController {

    @IBOutlet weak var receivedText: NSTextField!

    override func viewDidLoad() {
        super.viewDidLoad()
        // Do view setup here.
                receivedText.stringValue = self.representedObject! as! String
    }

    @IBAction func closeScene(sender: NSButton) {
        self.dismissController(self)
    }

}
```

The receivedText IBOutlet displays the text that appears in the label. Then the viewDidLoad method takes the representedObject property, casts or turns it into a String data type, and stores this into the receivedText IBOutlet.

14. Click on the segue and choose View ➤ Utilities ➤ Show Attributes Inspector to display the Attributes Inspector pane.

15. Choose Product ➤ Run. Your initial scene appears.

16. Click in the text field and type any text such as your name.

17. Click the Open Scene button. Your second scene appears with the text you typed now displayed in the label.

18. Click the Close Scene button to make the second scene go away.

19. Choose StoryProgram ➤ Quit StoryProgram.

Summary

You create your user interface and store them in multiple .xib files or a single .storyboard file that contains multiple scenes. To open and close different .xib files, you have to write Swift code. To open a scene in a storyboard, you just need to Control-drag from a button on one scene to another scene.

To make a second scene close after opening it, you have to write Swift code. You also need to use Swift code to transfer data from one scene to another. When you transfer data from one scene to another, you use the representedObject property. To access any value in the representedObject property, you must unwrap it and cast or turn it into a specific data type.

Storyboards let you define the order that scenes appear that make up your program's user interface. To make it easy to see your entire storyboard, you can adjust the magnification to shrink or enlarge the storyboard. However when you want to place items on a storyboard scene, you must enlarge the magnification to 100%.

When you add additional scenes in a storyboard, you'll need to create Swift files that control those scenes. These Swift files need to be of the NSViewController class, and then you must connect your scene to that Swift file.

Designing your program's user interface involves using .xib or .storyboard files, or a combination of both. Storyboards reduce the need to write Swift code, but with both types of files, you'll still need to write Swift code to make your user interface work completely.

Choosing Commands with Buttons

Every program needs to give the user a way to control the computer. In the old days, that meant knowing how to type the proper commands to make a program work, but with today's graphical user interfaces, the easier way to control a program is to choose from a list of available commands. The simplest way to give a command to a program is through a button.

By displaying multiple buttons on the screen, a user interface offers multiple choices for the user at all times. Instead of memorizing cryptic commands, the user just needs to select a command by pointing at it with the mouse and clicking on it to choose it.

Xcode provides a variety of different types of buttons you can place on a user interface, but they all work the same way. A button represents a single command, and clicking on that button runs Swift code stored in an IBAction method.

To use buttons, just place them on a user interface (either a .xib or .storyboard file), modify the label to display the command you want the button to represent, and connect your button to Swift code through an IBAction method.

All buttons are based on the NSButton class defined in the Cocoa framework. While most buttons display text that can contain the command the button represents, some buttons don't display text at all. Despite the differences in appearance, all buttons work the same and can be changed into another button type at any time. The different button types available are shown in Figure 15-1:

- Push Button
- Gradient Button
- Rounded Rect Button
- Rounded Textured Button
- Textured Button

- Recessed Button
- Disclosure Triangle (does not display text)
- Square Button (does not display text)
- Help Button (does not display text)
- Disclosure Button (does not display text)
- Round Button (does not display text)
- Bevel Button (does not display text)
- Inline Button

Figure 15-1. The different types of buttons you can place on a user interface

Buttons without titles take up less space but may appear cryptic because the user has no idea what that button might do. The square and bevel buttons are often used to display images that represent commands.

Modifying Text on a Button

For those buttons that display text, Xcode gives you two ways to modify a button's text:

- Double-click directly on the button's text and edit the text.

- Click on a button to select it, choose View ➤ Utilities ➤ Show Attributes Inspector, and edit the Title property as shown in Figure 15-2.

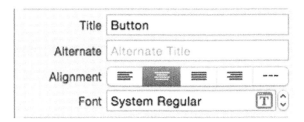

Figure 15-2. *The Show Attributes Inspector pane lets you edit the title of a button*

To modify text on a button, you can open the Show Attributes Inspector pane and edit the Title property, or you can directly modify the title property in Swift code. To do this, you must first create an IBOutlet that represents your user interface button. Then modify the Title property in Swift using code like this:

```
@IBOutlet weak var myButton: NSButton!
myButton.Title = "New Text"
```

Underneath the Title property is an Alternate property, which you can also adjust using Swift code by storing text in a button's alternateTitle property. The Alternate Title text only appears if a button's Type property is set to Toggle or Switch as shown in Figure 15-3.

Figure 15-3. *Changing the Type property of a button*

When a button's Alternate Title text is non-empty and the button's Type property is Toggle or Switch, clicking on a Toggle or Switch button alternates between showing the Title text and the Alternate Title text. To see how the Title and Alternate Title properties of a button work, follow these steps:

1. From within Xcode choose File ➤ New ➤ Project.

2. Click Application under the OS X category.

3. Click Cocoa Application and click the Next button. Xcode now asks for a product name.

4. Click in the Product Name text field and type **ButtonProgram**.

5. Make sure the Language pop-up menu displays Swift and that no check boxes are selected.

6. Click the Next button. Xcode asks where you want to store the project.

7. Choose a folder to store your project and click the Create button.

8. Click the MainMenu.xib file in the Project Navigator. Your program's user interface appears.

9. Click the ButtonProgram icon to display the window of your program's user interface.

10. Choose View ➤ Utilities ➤ Show Object Library. The Object Library appears in the bottom right corner of the Xcode window.

11. Drag a Push Button and a Text Field on to the user interface window and resize both items so it looks like Figure 15-4.

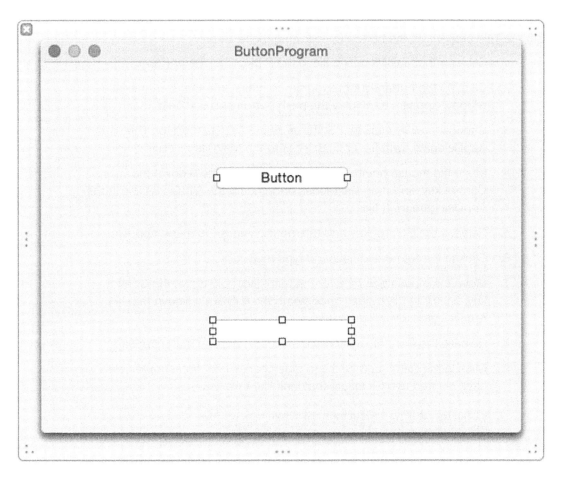

Figure 15-4. *The user interface of the ButtonProgram*

12. Click on the Push Button and choose View ➤ Utilities ➤ Show Attributes Inspector. The Show Attributes Inspector pane appears in the upper right corner of the Xcode window.

13. Click on the Type pop-up menu and choose Toggle.

14. Click in the Title text field and type **Change Me**.

15. Click in the Alternate text field and type **Alternate Text**.

16. Choose Product ➤ Run. Your user interface appears.

17. Click on the Change Me button. Notice that the text on the button now displays Alternate Text.

18. Click on the same button again. Notice that the text alternates between Change Me and Alternate Text.

19. Choose ButtonProgram ➤ Quit ButtonProgram.

Now let's see how to modify the Title of a button by taking text from the text field and storing it in the Title property of the button by following these steps:

1. Click on the MainMenu.xib file in the Project Navigator Pane.

2. Click on the button ButtonProgram to make sure the user interface window appears to display the push button and text field.

3. Choose View ➤ Assistant Editor ➤ Show Assistant Editor. The AppDelegate.swift file appears next to the MainMenu.xib file.

4. Move the mouse pointer over the push button, hold down the Control key, and drag the mouse underneath the @IBOutlet line in the AppDelegate.swift file.

5. Release the Control key and the mouse. A pop-up menu appears.

6. Click in the Name text field and type myButton.

7. Move the mouse pointer over the text field, hold down the Control key, and drag the mouse underneath the @IBOutlet line in the AppDelegate.swift file.

8. Release the Control key and the mouse. A pop-up menu appears.

9. Click in the Name text field and type changeText. You should now have created two IBOutlets that look like this:

```
@IBOutlet weak var myButton: NSButton!
@IBOutlet weak var changeText: NSTextField!
```

10. Move the mouse pointer over the push button, hold down the Control key, and drag the mouse above the last curly bracket in the bottom of the AppDelegate.swift file.

11. Release the Control key and the mouse. A pop-up menu appears.

12. Click in the Connection pop-up menu and choose Action.

13. Click in the Name text field and type changeTitle.

14. Click in the Type pop-up menu and choose NSButton, then click the Connect button. Xcode creates an empty IBAction method.

15. Modify this IBAction method as follows:

```
@IBAction func changeTitle(sender: NSButton) {
    myButton.title = changeText.stringValue
    }
```

This Swift code retrieves the text in the text field (the IBOutlet changeText) and stores it in the Title property of the button (the IBOutlet myButton).

16.   Choose Product ➤ Run. Your user interface appears.

17.   Click in the text field and type **Hello there!**

18.   Click on the Change Me button. The Alternate Text appears on the button.

19.   Click the button again. The text from the text field now appears.

20.   Choose ButtonProgram ➤ Quit ButtonProgram.

Adding Images and Sounds to a Button

Buttons typically display text that lists the command that the button represents. However, you can also display images on a button. This can be useful to create toolbar icons that display a descriptive icon that represents a command (such as showing a printer to represent the Print command). Images can appear on a button by themselves or with descriptive text.

Besides displaying images, buttons can also play sounds to give the user audio feedback. While most people might click a button using the mouse (or trackpad), some people might prefer using keystroke shortcuts, so you can also assign keystrokes to run an IBAction method linked to a particular button.

To add images to a button, you just need to modify the Image and/or the Alternate property directly underneath the Image property as shown in Figure 15-5.

Figure 15-5. The Image and Alternate pop-up menus let you choose from a list of predefined images

You can also define an image to display on a button using the image and alternateImage properties of an NSButton. When defining an image to appear on a button, you can also choose the position of that image relative to any text that also appears on that image.

The Position property defines how an image appears with text where text is represented by a horizontal line and the image is represented by a square as shown in Figure 15-6.

Figure 15-6. The Position property lets you align text and images on a button

The seven different positions from left to right are:

- Text only
- Image only
- Image on the left and text on the right
- Text on the left and image on the right
- Text overlapping the middle of the image
- Text underneath the image
- Text above the image

To define a sound to play when the user clicks on a button, you can modify the Sound property as shown in Figure 15-7. (You may need to adjust the volume of your computer to hear the sound played when you click on a button.)

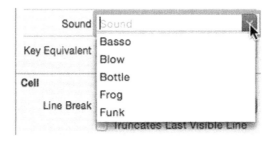

Figure 15-7. The Sound property lets you choose a sound to play

To see how to add images and a sound to a button, follow these steps:

1. Click in the MainMenu.xib file in the Project Navigator pane.

2. Click on the push button on your user interface to select it.

3. Choose View ➤ Utilities ➤ Show Attributes Inspector. The Show Attributes Inspector pane appears in the upper right corner of the Xcode window.

4. Click in the Image pop-up menu and choose NSCaution.

5. Click in the Alternate pop-up menu and choose NSComputer (see Figure 15-5).

6. Click in the Position property to choose the icon (third from the left) that displays the image on the left and the text on the right (see Figure 15-6).

7. Click in the Sound pop-up menu and choose a sound such as Frog.

8. Choose Product ➤ Run. Your program appears. Notice that the caution icon appears on the button.

9. Click in the text field and type **Hello there!**

10. Click the button. The text on the button displays the alternate text and plays your chosen sound. Each time you click on the button, it alternates between showing the Title and Image properties and the Alternate (Text and Image) properties.

11. Choose ButtonProgram ➤ Quit ButtonProgram.

Connecting Multiple User Interface Items to IBAction Methods

Typically you link one IBAction method to one user interface item such as a button. However, it's possible to connect multiple items to a single IBAction method. When doing this, the IBAction method needs to know what user interface item called the IBAction method to run.

To identify a particular user interface item, you need to change the Tag property of each item linked to the same IBAction method. The Tag property can hold an integer value so you can use distinct Tag values to identify different user interface items.

Once you've given each user interface item a distinct Tag value, you can create an IBAction method normally using the Control-drag method from one user interface item into your Swift file. Then you use the same Control-drag method to connect the remaining user interface items to that existing IBAction method.

There's no limit to the number of items you can link to the same IBAction method just as long as you use the Tag property to identify which user interface item called the IBAction method.

To see how to connect multiple items to a single IBAction method, follow these steps:

1. From within Xcode choose File ➤ New ➤ Project.

2. Click Application under the OS X category.

3. Click Cocoa Application and click the Next button. Xcode now asks for a product name.

4.   Click in the Product Name text field and type **MultipleProgram**.

5.   Make sure the Language pop-up menu displays Swift and that all check boxes are clear and not selected.

6.   Click the Next button. Xcode asks where you want to store the project.

7.   Choose a folder to store your project and click the Create button.

8.   Click on the MainMenu.xib file in the Project Navigator Pane.

9.   Click on the MultipleProgram icon to make the window of the user interface appear.

10.   Drag a Push Button, Recessed Button, Inline Button, and Label on to the user interface and resize with width of the label as shown in Figure 15-8.

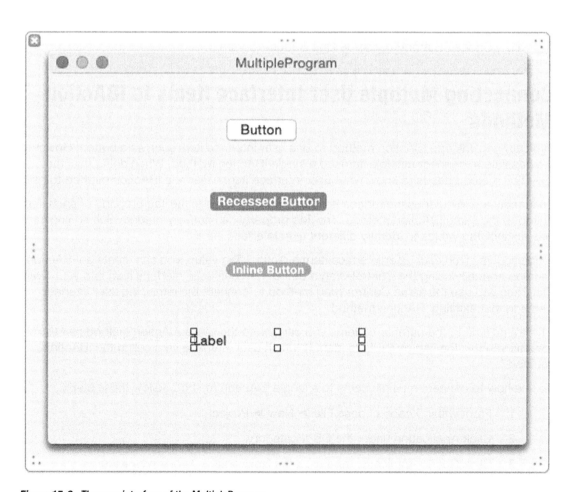

Figure 15-8. The user interface of the MultipleProgram

At this point you have three different types of buttons on the window and a label. We'll create a single IBAction method that all three buttons can run. When you click on a button, the label will display the button title to show you which button you just clicked on.

First, we'll need to modify the Tag property of each button. The top button will have a Tag value of 0, the middle button will have a Tag value of 1, and the lowest button will have a Tag value of 2.

Then we'll create an IBAction method that identifies the Tag property and displays the button's title in the label. To do this, follow these steps:

1. Click on the MainMenu.xib file in the Project Navigator pane.

2. Choose View ➤ Assistant Editor ➤ Show Assistant Editor. Xcode displays the AppDelegate.swift file next to the user interface.

3. Move the mouse pointer over the Label, hold down the Control key, and drag the mouse under the IBOutlet line in the AppDelegate.swift file.

4. Release the Control key and the mouse button. A pop-up window appears.

5. Click in the Name text filed, type displayLabel, and click the Connect button. You should have an IBOutlet as follows:

    ```
    @IBOutlet weak var displayLabel: NSTextField!
    ```

6. Move the mouse pointer over the Push Button, hold down the Control key, and drag the mouse above the last curly bracket at the bottom of the AppDelegate.swift file.

7. Release the Control key and the mouse button. A pop-up window appears.

8. Click in the Connection pop-up menu and choose Action.

9. Click in the Name text field and type displayButton.

10. Make sure the Type pop-up menu displays AnyObject. If we wanted to limit the IBAction method only to buttons, we could change this to NSButton, but we want to let other user interface items connect to this IBAction method later.

11. Click the Connect button. Xcode displays an empty IBAction method.

12. Move the mouse pointer over the Recessed Button, hold down the Control key, and drag the mouse over the IBAction method until Xcode highlights the entire IBAction method as shown in Figure 15-9.

Figure 15-9. *Connecting to an existing IBAction method*

13. Release the Control key and the mouse button. Xcode connects the Recessed Button to the IBAction method.

14. Move the mouse pointer over the Inline Button, hold down the Control key, and drag the mouse over the IBAction method until Xcode highlights the entire IBAction method.

15. Release the Control key and the mouse button. Xcode connects the Inline Button to the IBAction method.

16. Click the Recessed Button to select it and choose View ➤ Utilities ➤ Show Attributes Inspector. The Show Attributes Inspector pane appears in the upper right corner of the Xcode window.

17. Scroll down to the View category, click in the Tag text field and type 1. (The Push Button has the default Tag value of 0, the Recessed Button will have a Tag value of 1, and the Inline Button will have a Tag value of 2.)

18. Click on the Inline Button to select it.

19. Scroll down to the View category, click in the Tag text field and type 2.

20. Modify the IBAction method as follows:

```
@IBAction func displayButton(sender: AnyObject) {
    if sender is NSButton {
        let whichObject = sender as! NSButton
        switch whichObject.tag {
        case 0:
            displayLabel.stringValue = "Clicked Push Button"
        case 1:
            displayLabel.stringValue = "Clicked Recessed Button"
        case 2:
            displayLabel.stringValue = "Clicked Inline Button"
        default:
            displayLabel.stringValue = "Unknown"
        }
    }
}
```

The sender: AnyObject code means that the IBAction method can connect to any type of user interface item. First, we'll check if the sender (the user interface item that called the IBAction method) is an NSButton. If so, then we'll cast the sender as an NSButton and assign that button to whichObject.

Now we'll use the tab property of whichObject to determine which button the user clicked using a switch statement. We'll display the proper message in the label depending on which button the user clicked.

21. Choose Product ➤ Run. Your program's user interface appears.

22. Click on the three different buttons to see the proper message appear in the label.

23. Choose MultipleProgram ➤ Quit Multiple Program.

In this example, you connected multiple buttons to a single IBAction method. However, you can connect different user interface items to the same IBAction method as long as that IBAction method has (sender: AnyObject) as its parameter.

To see how another user interface item can connect to an IBAction method, follow these steps:

1. Drag a Vertical Slider and place it anywhere on your user interface.

2. Move the mouse pointer over the Vertical Slider, hold down the Control key, and drag the mouse over the IBAction displayButton method until Xcode highlights the entire IBAction method.

3. Release the Control key and the mouse button. The IBAction method is now linked to the Vertical Slider.

4. Modify the IBAction method so it looks like this:

```
@IBAction func displayButton(sender: AnyObject) {
    if sender is NSButton {
        let whichObject = sender as! NSButton
        switch whichObject.tag {
        case 0:
            displayLabel.stringValue = "Clicked Push Button"
        case 1:
            displayLabel.stringValue = "Clicked Recessed Button"
        case 2:
            displayLabel.stringValue = "Clicked Inline Button"
        default:
            displayLabel.stringValue = "Unknown"
        }
    } else if sender is NSSlider {
        displayLabel.stringValue = "Dragged slider"
    }
}
```

The last else-if portion of the code checks if the sender is an NSSlider, which means the user dragged the vertical slider, which called the IBAction method. If the user dragged the vertical slider, then the code puts the string "Dragged slider" into the label.

5. Choose Product ➤ Run. Your user interface appears.

6. Drag the vertical slider. Notice that "Dragged slider" appears in the label.

7. Click on any button. Notice that the label now identifies which button you clicked. The buttons and vertical slider are all linked to the same IBAction method, which must determine which user interface item called the IBAction method to run.

8. Choose MultipleProgram ➤ Quit MultipleProgram.

Working with Pop-Up Buttons

Buttons can be handy for displaying commands on the screen, but if you need to offer several options, then having each button represent one command can get cumbersome and crowded. One option is to condense multiple options into a single pop-up button. A pop-up button takes less space and can provide a large number of options for the user to select.

To see how pop-up buttons work, follow these steps:

1. From within Xcode choose File ➤ New ➤ Project.

2. Click Application under the OS X category.

3. Click Cocoa Application and click the Next button. Xcode now asks for a product name.

4. Click in the Product Name text field and type **PopupProgram**.

5. Make sure the Language pop-up menu displays Swift and that no check boxes are selected.

6. Click the Next button. Xcode asks where you want to store the project.

7. Choose a folder to store your project and click the Create button.

8. Click the MainMenu.xib file in the Project Navigator. Your program's user interface appears.

9. Click the PopupProgram icon to display the window of your program's user interface.

10. Choose View ➤ Utilities ➤ Show Object Library. The Object Library appears in the bottom right corner of the Xcode window.

11. Drag a Popup Button and a Label on to the user interface window and resize the width of the Label so it looks like Figure 15-10.

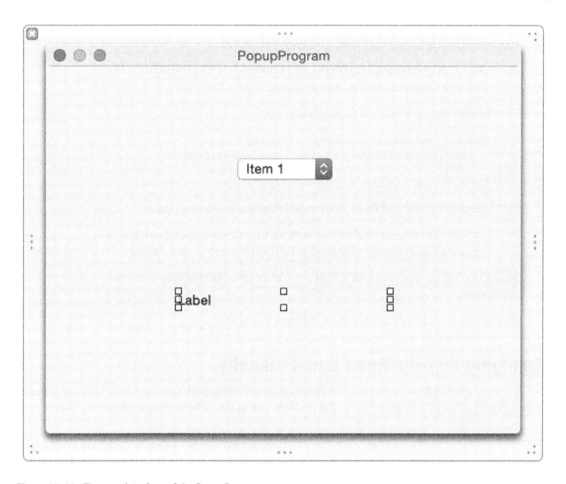

Figure 15-10. The user interface of the PopupProgram

12. Choose View ➤ Assistant Editor ➤ Show Assistant Editor. Xcode displays the AppDelegate.swift file next to your user interface.

13. Move the mouse pointer over the label, hold down the Control key, and drag underneath the IBOutlet line in the AppDelegate.swift file.

14. Release the Control key and the mouse. A pop-up window appears.

15. Click in the Name text field, type labelChoice, and click the Connect button. Xcode creates an IBOutlet as follows:

```
@IBOutlet weak var labelChoice: NSTextField!
```

16. Move the mouse pointer over the pop-up button, hold down the Control key, and drag the mouse above the last curly bracket in the bottom of the AppDelegate.swift file.

17. Release the Control key and the mouse. A pop-up window appears.

18. Click in the Connection pop-up menu and choose Action.

19. Click in the Name text field and type showChoice.

20. Click in the Type pop-up menu and choose NSPopUpButton. Then click the Connect button. Xcode displays an empty IBAction method.

21. Modify the IBAction method as follows:

    ```
    @IBAction func showChoice(sender: NSPopUpButton) {
        labelChoice.stringValue = sender.titleOfSelectedItem!
    }
    ```

22. Choose Product ➤ Run. Your user interface window appears.

23. Click on the pop-up button. Notice that by default, a pop-up button contains three generic items labeled Item 1, Item 2, and Item 3.

24. Click on an option. Notice that your chosen option appears in the label.

25. Choose PopupProgram ➤ Quit PopupProgram.

Modifying Pop-Up Menu Items Visually

A pop-up button contains a default list of three items. However, you can add, edit, or delete items from that list at any time. To edit a pop-up menu list, follow these steps:

1. Double-click on the pop-up button on the user interface. The current list of menu items appears as shown in Figure 15-11.

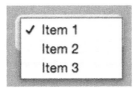

Figure 15-11. *Double-clicking on a pop-up button displays its list of menu items*

2. Double-click on the menu item you want to edit. Xcode highlights the text of your chosen menu item as shown in Figure 15-12.

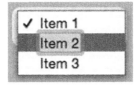

Figure 15-12. *Double-clicking on a menu item lets you edit the text*

> **Note**   You can also choose View ➤ Utilities ➤ Show Attributes Inspector and edit the text of a menu item by editing the Title property of the selected menu item.

3. Use the arrow keys, Backspace, or Delete key to edit the text and type any new text.

4. Press Return. Xcode saves your edited text for the menu item.

To delete a menu item from a pop-up button, follow these steps:

1. Double-click on the pop-up button on the user interface. The current list of menu items appears (see Figure 15-11).

2. Click on the menu item that you want to delete. Xcode highlights your chosen menu item.

3. Press the Backspace or Delete key. Your chosen menu item disappears.

> **Note**   If you delete a menu item by mistake, just press Command+Z or choose Edit ➤ Undo to reverse the delete command.

To add a menu item to a pop-up button, follow these steps:

1. Double-click on the pop-up button on the user interface. The current list of menu items appears (see Figure 15-11).

2. Choose View ➤ Utilities ➤ Show Object Library. The Object Library appears in the bottom right corner of the Xcode window.

3. Type **menu item** and press Return in the search field at the bottom of the Object Library. The Object Library displays a list of menu items as shown in Figure 15-13.

Figure 15-13. The list of menu items in the Object Library

4. Drag the Menu Item from the Object Library over the list of menu items stored in the pop-up button on the user interface.

5. Release the mouse button. Xcode adds a menu item to the pop-up button list.

Adding Pop-Up Menu Items with Swift Code

As an alternative to modifying menu items in a pop-up button visually, you can also use Swift code to add, delete, or change a menu item. Pop-up button menu items are based on the NSMenuItem class, but you can find the methods you need to manipulate a list of pop-up button menu items in the NSMenu class.

If you want to add just one new menu item to a pop-up button, you can use the addItemWithTitle method and specify a string such as:

```
myPopUp.addItemWithTitle("New Item")
```

You can also add a list of new menu items by storing them in an array and using the addItemsWithTitles method such as:

```
myPopUp.addItemsWithTitles(["Cat", "Dog", "Bird", "Fish", "Reptile"])
```

You can remove individual menu items using the removeItemAtIndex method that needs an Int value to define which item to remove. The first item in a pop-up menu list is at index 0, the second at index 1, and so on.

To remove all items in a pop-up button's menu list, just use the removeAllItems() method, which clears out the entire list no matter how many (or how few) items may be currently stored in that list.

To see how to use Swift code to add and delete items from a pop-up button menu list, follow these steps:

1. From within Xcode choose File ➤ New ➤ Project.

2. Click Application under the OS X category.

3. Click Cocoa Application and click the Next button. Xcode now asks for a product name.

4. Click in the Product Name text field and type **EditPopProgram**.

5. Make sure the Language pop-up menu displays Swift and that no check boxes are selected.

6. Click the Next button. Xcode asks where you want to store the project.

7. Choose a folder to store your project and click the Create button.

8. Click the MainMenu.xib file in the Project Navigator. Your program's user interface appears.

9. Click the EditPopProgram icon to display the window of your program's user interface.

10. Choose View ➤ Utilities ➤ Show Object Library. The Object Library appears in the bottom right corner of the Xcode window.

11. Drag a PopUp Button, three Push Buttons, and a Text Field on to the user interface window and edit the titles on both push buttons so it looks like Figure 15-14.

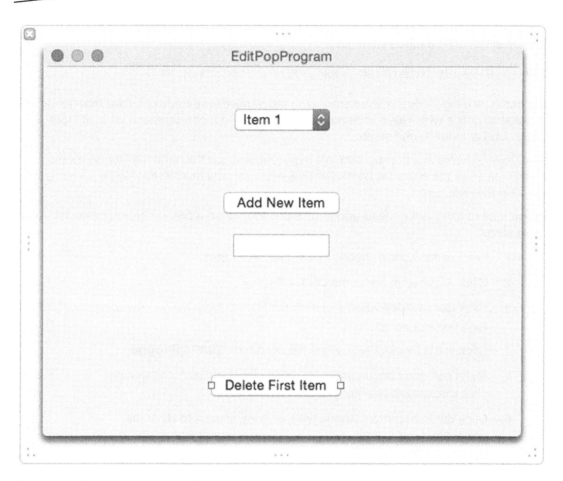

Figure 15-14. The user interface of the EditPopProgram

12.   Choose View ➤ Assistant Editor ➤ Show Assistant Editor. Xcode displays the AppDelegate.swift file next to your user interface.

13.   Move the mouse pointer over the pop-up button, hold down the Control key, and drag the mouse underneath the IBOutlet line near the top of the AppDelegate.swift file.

14.   Release the Control key and the mouse. A pop-up window appears.

15.   Click in the Name text field and type myPopUp. Then click the Connect button. Xcode creates an IBOutlet.

16.   Move the mouse pointer over the text field, hold down the Control key, and drag the mouse underneath the IBOutlet line near the top of the AppDelegate.swift file.

17. Release the Control key and the mouse. A pop-up window appears.

18. Click in the Name text field and type newItem. Then click the Connect button. Xcode creates another IBOutlet so you should have two IBOutlets that look like this:

```
@IBOutlet weak var myPopUp: NSPopUpButton!
@IBOutlet weak var newItem: NSTextField!
```

19. Move the mouse pointer over the Add New Item button, hold down the Control key, and drag the mouse above the last curly bracket at the bottom of the AppDelegate.swift file.

20. Release the Control key and the mouse. A pop-up window appears.

21. Click in the Connection pop-up menu and choose Action.

22. Click in the Name text field and type addNewItem.

23. Click in the Type pop-up menu and choose NSButton. Then click the Connect button. Xcode creates an empty IBAction method.

24. Move the mouse pointer over the Delete First Item button, hold down the Control key, and drag the mouse above the last curly bracket at the bottom of the AppDelegate.swift file.

25. Release the Control key and the mouse. A pop-up window appears.

26. Click in the Connection pop-up menu and choose Action.

27. Click in the Name text field and type deleteFirstItem.

28. Click in the Type pop-up menu and choose NSButton. Then click the Connect button. Xcode creates an empty IBAction method.

29. Move the mouse pointer over the Add New List button, hold down the Control key, and drag the mouse above the last curly bracket at the bottom of the AppDelegate.swift file.

30. Release the Control key and the mouse. A pop-up window appears.

31. Click in the Connection pop-up menu and choose Action.

32. Click in the Name text field and type addList.

33. Click in the Type pop-up menu and choose NSButton. Then click the Connect button. Xcode creates another empty IBAction method.

34.   Modify all three IBAction methods as follows:

```
@IBAction func addNewItem(sender: NSButton) {
    myPopUp.addItemWithTitle(newItem.stringValue)
}

@IBAction func deleteFirstItem(sender: NSButton) {
    myPopUp.removeItemAtIndex(0)
}
@IBAction func addList(sender: NSButton) {
    myPopUp.removeAllItems()
    myPopUp.addItemsWithTitles(["Cat", "Dog", "Bird", "Fish", "Reptile"])
}
```

The addNewItem IBAction method takes text from the text field and uses the addItemWithTitle method to add that text as a new menu item in the pop-up button list. The deleteFirstItem IBAction method uses the removeItemAtIndex method to delete the first menu item in the pop-up button's list. The addList IBAction method uses the removeAllItems method to clear out the current list in the pop-up button, then replaces it with a new array of strings.

35.   Choose Product ➤ Run. Your user interface appears.

36.   Click on the pop-up button. Notice that the menu item list displays three items labeled Item 1, Item 2, and Item 3.

37.   Click the Delete First Item button.

38.   Click on the pop-up button. Notice that the menu item list now displays only two items labeled Item 2 and Item 3.

39.   Click in the text field and type **My Item.**

40.   Click the Add New Item button.

41.   Click on the pop-up button. Notice that now the menu item list displays three items labeled Item 2, Item 3, and My Item.

42.   Click the Add New List button.

43.   Click on the pop-up button. Notice that now the menu item list displays the array of strings defined inside the addList IBAction method.

44.   Choose EditPopProgram ➤ Quit EditPopProgram.

Summary

Buttons represent commands that users can click on to choose an option. Xcode offers several different types of buttons you can place on a user interface, but they're all based on the same NSButton class defined in the Cocoa frameworks.

Not all buttons display text, but those buttons that do display text use a Title property to hold text. If you want to display an image on a button, you can define an image using the Image property. If you change the Type property of a button to Switch or Toggle, then you can make a button display text stored in the Title property along with text displayed in the Alternate Text property and/or the Alternate Image property as well.

If you need to offer multiple options to the user, placing more than a handful of buttons on the user interface can get messy and cluttered. A simpler alternative is to use a pop-up button instead that displays a list of options that you can modify visually or through Swift code.

Buttons often connect to a single IBAction method, but you can link multiple buttons (or other user interface items) to a single IBAction method. When connecting multiple user interface items to an IBAction method, you need to use Swift code to identify the user interface item that called the IBAction method. Buttons represent the most straightforward way to offer users an option to select.

Making Choices with Radio Buttons, Check Boxes, Date Pickers, and Sliders

Rather than let the user choose a specific command through a button, user interfaces often give choices to pick. Such choices let the user pick one or more options, such as customizing the way a program works. When a user interface needs to offer multiple choices, the two most common ways to offer options are through radio buttons and check boxes.

Radio buttons get their name from car radios that let you press a button to switch to a different radio station. Since you can only listen to one radio station at a time, radio buttons give you multiple options but limit you to choosing only one button. The moment you select a different button, your previous choice is no longer selected. With radio buttons, you can either select zero buttons or select exactly one button at a time.

Check boxes work slightly differently. Like radio buttons, check boxes offer multiple choices. The main difference is that with a group of check boxes, you can select zero or more check boxes at the same time so you can choose multiple options at once.

When you need to limit the user to zero or one choices, use radio buttons. When you need to let the user choose zero or more choices, use check boxes. Figure 16-1 shows the Xcode Preferences dialog that uses both radio buttons and a check box to let the user customize how Xcode behaves.

Figure 16-1. The Xcode Preferences dialog uses both radio buttons and check boxes for the user to select options

While radio buttons and check boxes are commonly used to display choices displayed as text, a date picker displays different types of dates for the user to choose. Then the date picker stores the user's choice in a special date format (rather than separate text representing months or numbers representing days or years).

By storing dates in a special format, your program can properly display dates according to the user's settings on their computer. For example, in some parts of the world, they display dates like this: mm/dd/yyyy. Yet in other parts of the world they display dates like this: dd/mm/yyyy.

Rather than worry about a particular date format setting on each user's computer, a date picker uses a special date format so that way the computer can properly display the correct format based on the user's current settings.

Date pickers, like radio buttons, and check boxes give users a fixed but limited range of valid options to select. This ensures that whatever choice the user makes, the choice will be acceptable to your program.

Check boxes and radio buttons are good for offering users a limited range of choices that are usually text options. For offering users a range of numeric values to select, you can use a slider. Sliders let the user visually select a range of valid options.

Using Check Boxes

You can use a check box by itself or grouped together with other check boxes. A check box is actually based on the NSButton class although it looks and behaves much differently than a typical button. For a check box, the three most important properties include:

- Title – The text that appears next to a check box that describes an option for the user to choose.
- State – Determines if the check box is selected (1) or clear (0).
- Alternate – Text that appears when the check box is clear. (The Title text appears when the check box is selected.)

To see how check boxes work, follow these steps:

1. From within Xcode choose File ➤ New ➤ Project.

2. Click Application under the OS X category.

3. Click Cocoa Application and click the Next button. Xcode now asks for a product name.

4. Click in the Product Name text field and type **CheckProgram**.

5. Make sure the Language pop-up menu displays Swift and that no check boxes are selected.

6. Click the Next button. Xcode asks where you want to store the project.

7. Choose a folder to store your project and click the Create button.

8. Click the MainMenu.xib file in the Project Navigator. Your program's user interface appears.

9. Click the CheckProgram icon to display the window of your program's user interface.

10. Choose View ➤ Utilities ➤ Show Object Library. The Object Library appears in the bottom right corner of the Xcode window.

11. Drag a Push Button, three Check Boxes, and a Wrapping Text Field on to the user interface window. Make sure you resize Wrapping Text Field and all the check box widths so it looks like Figure 16-2.

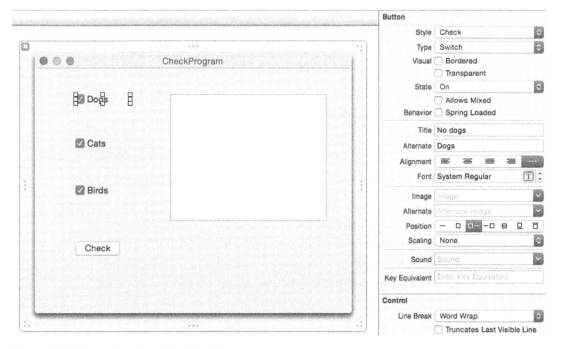

Figure 16-2. The user interface of the CheckProgram.

12. Choose View ➤ Utilities ➤ Show Attributes Inspector. The Show Attributes Inspector pane appears in the upper right corner of the Xcode window.

13. Click on the top check box and in the Show Attributes Inspector pane, change its Title to "No dogs" and its Alternate to "Dogs."

14. Click on the middle check box and in the Show Attributes Inspector pane, change its Title to "No cats" and its Alternate to "Cats."

15. Click on the top check box and in the Show Attributes Inspector pane, change its Title to "No birds" and its Alternate to "Birds."

16. Double-click on the Push Button and change its Title to "Check."

17. Choose View ➤ Assistant Editor ➤ Show Assistant Editor. Xcode displays the AppDelegate.swift file next to the user interface.

18. Move the mouse pointer over the Dogs check box, hold down the Control key, and drag the mouse under the IBOutlet line in the AppDelegate.swift file.

19. Release the Control key and the mouse. A pop-up window appears.

20. Click in the Name text field, type dogBox, and click the Connect button.

21. Move the mouse pointer over the Cats check box, hold down the Control key, and drag the mouse under the IBOutlet line in the AppDelegate.swift file.

22. Release the Control key and the mouse. A pop-up window appears.

23. Click in the Name text field, type catBox, and click the Connect button.

24. Move the mouse pointer over the Birds check box, hold down the Control key, and drag the mouse under the IBOutlet line in the AppDelegate.swift file.

25. Release the Control key and the mouse. A pop-up window appears.

26. Click in the Name text field, type birdBox, and click the Connect button.

27. Move the mouse pointer over the Wrapping Text Field, hold down the Control key, and drag the mouse under the IBOutlet line in the AppDelegate.swift file.

28. Release the Control key and the mouse. A pop-up window appears.

29. Click in the Name text field, type messageBox, and click the Connect button. You should now have four new IBOutlets that look like this:

```
@IBOutlet weak var dogBox: NSButton!
@IBOutlet weak var catBox: NSButton!
@IBOutlet weak var birdBox: NSButton!
@IBOutlet weak var messageBox: NSTextField!
```

30. Move the mouse pointer over the Check Push Button, hold down the Control key, and drag the mouse over the last curly bracket in the bottom of the AppDelegate.swift file.

31. Release the Control key and the mouse. A pop-up window appears.

32. Click in the Connection pop-up menu and choose Action.

33. Click in the Name text field and type checkBoxes.

34. Click in the Type pop-up menu and choose NSButton. Xcode creates an empty IBAction method.

35. Modify this check boxes IBAction method as follows:

```
@IBAction func checkBoxes(sender: NSButton) {
    let nextLine = "\r\n"
    var message : String = ""
    if dogBox.state == 1 {
        message = "Dog check box selected" + nextLine
    } else {
        message = "Dog check box NOT selected" + nextLine
    }

    if catBox.state == 1 {
        message = message + "Cat check box selected" + nextLine
    } else {
        message = message + "Cat check box NOT selected" + nextLine
    }

    if birdBox.state == 1 {
        message = message + "Bird check box selected" + nextLine
    } else {
        message = message + "Bird check box NOT selected" + nextLine
    }

    messageBox.stringValue = message
}
```

This code creates a constant that represents a carriage return "\r" and a new line "\n" character. It declares a message variable that can hold String data types and initially contains "", which is an empty string. The multiple if-else statements check the State property of each check box to determine if it's selected (state = 1) or clear (state = 0). Then it displays the results in the Wrapping Text Field, which is represented by an IBOutlet variable called messageBox.

36. Choose Product ➤ Run. Your user interface appears.

37. Click on the different check boxes. Notice that each time you select or clear a check box, the Title or Alternate text appears.

38. Click the Check push button. The Wrapping Text Field identifies which check boxes you selected and which ones are clear.

39. Choose CheckProgram ➤ Quit CheckProgram.

Using Radio Buttons

Unlike check boxes that allow the user to select multiple options, radio buttons display multiple options but only let the user select one at a time. The moment the user selects another radio button, the currently selected radio button gets cleared.

Radio buttons are defined by the NSMatrix class in the Cocoa frameworks. That means when you create a group of radio buttons, you need to define how many you want by defining the number of rows and columns as shown in Figure 16-3.

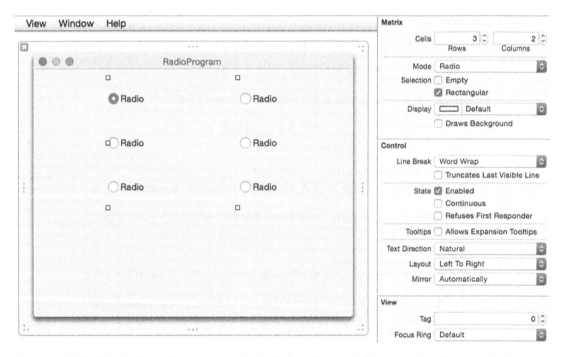

Figure 16-3. The Show Attributes Inspector pane of a Radio Group lets you define the number of rows and columns to display radio buttons

To add or remove radio buttons, just adjust the number of rows and columns under the Matrix category in the Show Attributes Inspector pane. If you need to create an odd number of radio buttons, select the radio button you don't want and select its Transparent property as shown in Figure 16-4.

Figure 16-4. The Transparent property lets you hide a radio button from a group

To identify which radio button a user selected, you need to change the Tag property of each radio button individually. Then you can retrieve the selected radio button by using the selectedTag() method.

To see how to use radio buttons, follow these steps:

1. From within Xcode choose File ➤ New ➤ Project.

2. Click Application under the OS X category.

3. Click Cocoa Application and click the Next button. Xcode now asks for a product name.

4. Click in the Product Name text field and type **RadioProgram**.

5. Make sure the Language pop-up menu displays Swift and that no check boxes are selected.

6. Click the Next button. Xcode asks where you want to store the project.

7. Choose a folder to store your project and click the Create button.

8. Click the MainMenu.xib file in the Project Navigator. Your program's user interface appears.

9. Click the RadioProgram icon to display the window of your program's user interface.

10. Choose View ➤ Utilities ➤ Show Object Library. The Object Library appears in the bottom right corner of the Xcode window.

11. Drag a Push Button and a Radio Group on to the user interface window.

12. Click on the Radio Group and choose View ➤ Utilities ➤ Show Attributes Inspector to open the Show Attributes Inspector pane in the upper right corner of the Xcode window.

13. Modify the Rows and Columns to display three Rows and two Columns so it looks like Figure 16-5.

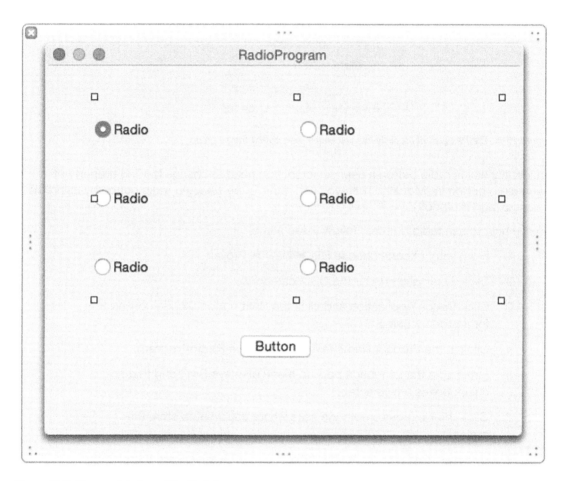

Figure 16-5. The user interface of the RadioProgram

14. Click on the radio button that appears in the bottom right corner of the Radio Group. Xcode highlights your chosen radio button as shown in Figure 16-6.

Figure 16-6. *Selecting a radio button to modify*

15. Select the Transparent check box under the Button Cell category in the Show Attributes Inspector pane (see Figure 16-4). Your chosen radio button disappears.

16. Click on the top radio button in the upper left corner and make sure its Tag property in the Show Attributes Inspector pane is set to 0.

17. Click on the middle radio button in the left column and make sure its Tag property in the Show Attributes Inspector pane is set to 1.

18. Click on the bottom radio button in the left column and make sure its Tag property in the Show Attributes Inspector pane is set to 2.

19. Click on the top radio button in the right column and make sure its Tag property in the Show Attributes Inspector pane is set to 3.

20. Click on the middle radio button in the right column and make sure its Tag property in the Show Attributes Inspector pane is set to 4.

21. Choose View ➤ Assistant Editor ➤ Show Assistant Editor. The AppDelegate.swift file appears next to your user interface.

22. Move the mouse pointer over the Radio Group, hold down the Control key, and drag underneath the IBOutlet line.

23. Release the Control key and the mouse. A pop-up window appears.

24. Click in the Name text field and type radioMatrix. An IBOutlet appears as follows:

```
@IBOutlet weak var radioMatrix: NSMatrix!
```

25. Move the mouse pointer over the Push Button, hold down the Control key, and drag the mouse over the last curly bracket at the bottom of the AppDelegate.swift file.

26. Release the Control key and the mouse. A pop-up window appears.

27. Click in the Connect pop-up menu and choose Action.

28. Click in the Name text field and type whichButton.

29. Click in the Type pop-up menu and choose NSButton. Xcode creates an empty IBAction method.

30. Modify the IBAction method as follows:

```
@IBAction func whichButton(sender: NSButton) {
    var myAlert = NSAlert()
    myAlert.messageText = "You clicked the radio button with a Tag \(radioMatrix.
    selectedTag())"
    myAlert.runModal()
}
```

31. Choose Product ➤ Run. Your user interface appears.

32. Click on a radio button and then click on the Push Button. An alert dialog appears, displaying the Tag number of the radio button you selected.

33. Click the OK button to make the alert dialog go away.

34. Choose RadioProgram ➤ Quit RadioProgram.

Using a Date Picker

A Date Picker makes it easy for users to choose a date and/or time in a proper format. The three types of date picker appearances are shown in Figure 16-7:

- Textual – Displays a date in a text field that requires the user to type in a proper date.

- Textual with Stepper – Displays a date in a text field that the user can change by clicking on a stepper to modify the currently selected part of the date.

- Graphical – Displays a calendar so the user can click on a date.

Figure 16-7. *The three variations of a date picker*

Some of the properties to modify in a date picker are shown in Figure 16-8:

- Style – Determines the date picker's appearance.

- Selects – Determines whether the user can select a single date or a range of dates.

- Elements – Determines what date and time elements to display such as Month, Day, Year, Hour, Minute, and Second.

- Minimum Date – Defines the earliest date possible.

- Maximum Date – Defines the latest date possible.

- Date – Defines the currently displayed date and/or time.

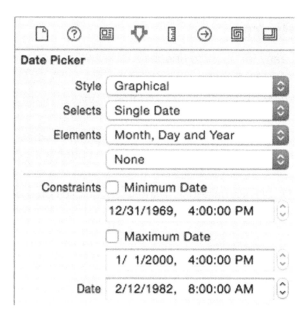

Figure 16-8. The date picker properties in the Show Attributes Inspector pane

To retrieve the user's chosen date from a date picker, you need to access the dateValue property, which represents an NSDate type.

To see how to use a date picker, follow these steps:

1. From within Xcode choose File ➤ New ➤ Project.

2. Click Application under the OS X category.

3. Click Cocoa Application and click the Next button. Xcode now asks for a product name.

4. Click in the Product Name text field and type **DateProgram**.

5. Make sure the Language pop-up menu displays Swift and that all check boxes are clear and not selected.

6. Click the Next button. Xcode asks where you want to store the project.

7. Choose a folder to store your project and click the Create button.

8. Click on the MainMenu.xib file in the Project Navigator Pane.

9. Click on the DateProgram icon to make the window of the user interface appear.

10. Drag a Push Button and Date Picker on to the user interface.

11. Click on the Date Picker and choose View ➤ Utilities ➤ Show Attributes Inspector.

12. Click in the Style pop-up menu and choose Graphical to make the date picker look like a monthly calendar as shown in Figure 16-9.

Figure 16-9. The user interface of the DateProgram

13. Choose View ➤ Assistant Editor ➤ Show Assistant Editor. Xcode displays the AppDelegate.swift file next to the user interface.

14. Move the mouse pointer over the date picker, hold down the Control key, and drag the mouse under the IBOutlet line in the AppDelegate.swift file.

15. Release the Control key and the mouse button. A pop-up window appears.

16. Click in the Name text field, type chooseDate, and click the Connect button. Xcode creates an IBOutlet like this:

```
@IBOutlet weak var chooseDate: NSDatePicker!
```

17. Move the mouse pointer over the Push Button, hold down the Control key, and drag the mouse over the last curly bracket in the bottom of the AppDelegate.swift file.

18. Release the Control key and the mouse. A pop-up window appears.

19. Click in the Connect pop-up menu and choose Action.

20. Click in the Name text field and type showDate.

21. Click in the Type pop-up menu and choose NSButton. Then click the Connect button. Xcode creates an IBAction method.

22. Modify this IBAction method as follows:

```
@IBAction func showDate(sender: NSButton) {
            var myAlert = NSAlert()
    myAlert.messageText = "You chose this date =  \(chooseDate.dateValue)"
    myAlert.runModal()
}
```

23. Choose Product ➤ Run. Your user interface appears.

24. Choose a date on the date picker and click the push button. An alert dialog appears, displaying the date you chose.

25. Click the OK button to make this alert dialog go away.

26. Choose DateProgram ➤ Quit DateProgram.

Using Sliders

A slider can appear vertically or horizontally. Sliders visually represent a range of values that the user can select by dragging the slider back and forth (or up and down). One end represents the minimum value (left or bottom) while the other end represents the maximum value (right or top). To help users understand the different values a slider represents, you can also choose to display tick marks as shown in Figure 16-10.

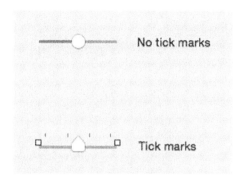

Figure 16-10. *The appearance of a slider with and without tick marks*

Some of the more important properties to define on a slider include:

- Tick Marks – Defines the position of tick marks and how many tick marks to display.

- Minimum – Defines the smallest value possible.

- Maximum – Defines the largest value possible.

- Current – Identifies the initial value of the slider when it first appears on the user interface.

You can use the integerValue property to retrieve the current value of the slider and display this value in another user interface item such as a text field. To see how to do this, follow these steps:

1. From within Xcode choose File ➤ New ➤ Project.

2. Click Application under the OS X category.

3. Click Cocoa Application and click the Next button. Xcode now asks for a product name.

4. Click in the Product Name text field and type **SliderProgram**.

5. Make sure the Language pop-up menu displays Swift and that all check boxes are clear and not selected.

6. Click the Next button. Xcode asks where you want to store the project.

7. Choose a folder to store your project and click the Create button.

8. Click on the MainMenu.xib file in the Project Navigator Pane.

9. Click on the SliderProgram icon to make the window of the user interface appear.

10. Drag a Horizontal Slider and a Text Field on to the user interface so it looks like Figure 16-11.

Figure 16-11. The user interface of the SliderProgram

11. Choose View ➤ Assistant Editor ➤ Show Assistant Editor. Xcode shows the AppDelegate.swift file next to the user interface.

12. Move the mouse pointer over the Horizontal Slider, hold down the Control key, and drag the mouse under the IBOutlet line in the AppDelegate.swift file.

13. Release the Control key and the mouse. A pop-up window appears.

14. Click in the Name text field, type mySlider, and click the Connect button.

15. Move the mouse pointer over the text field, hold down the Control key, and drag the mouse under the IBOutlet line in the AppDelegate. swift file.

16. Release the Control key and the mouse. A pop-up window appears.

17. Click in the Name text field, type sliderValue, and click the Connect button. You should now have these two IBOutlets:

```
@IBOutlet weak var mySlider: NSSlider!
@IBOutlet weak var sliderValue: NSTextField!
```

18. Move the mouse pointer over the Horizontal Slider, hold down the Control key, and drag the mouse just above the last curly bracket at the bottom of the AppDelegate.swift file.

19. Release the Control key and the mouse. A pop-up window appears.

20. Click in the Connection pop-up menu and choose Action.

21. Click in the Name text field and type getValue.

22. Click in the Type pop-up menu and choose NSSlider. Then click the Connect button. Xcode creates an empty IBAction method.

23. Modify this IBAction method as follows:

```
@IBAction func getValue(sender: NSSlider) {
    sliderValue.integerValue = mySlider.integerValue
}
```

24. Choose Product ➤ Run. Your user interface appears.

25. Drag the slider left and right. Notice that each time you drag the slider and release the mouse button, the slider's current value appears in the text box.

26. Choose SliderProgram ➤ Quit SliderProgram.

Summary

Check boxes, radio buttons, and date pickers let you provide the user with a range of valid options to select. This ensures that the user can't give a program invalid data by mistake (or deliberately).

Check boxes allow the user to choose zero or more options. A group of radio buttons only allow the user to choose one option. A date picker allows the user to choose a correctly formatted date.

To identify which check boxes a user selected, examine the State property of each check box. If the State value is 1, the check box is selected. If the State value is 0, the check box is clear.

It's possible to display alternate text on a check box and radio button. That way one text appears when the check box or radio button is selected, and different text appears when the check box or radio button is clear.

To identify which radio button a user may have selected, you need to use the Tag property. Each radio button needs a unique Tag value, which can be an integer. By identifying the Tag value, you can identify the radio button that the user selected.

The date picker makes it easy for the user to choose a date and/or a time. The date picker stores the selected date/time in a special NSDate format that you can access through the dateValue property of the date picker.

Sliders let users choose from a range of valid numeric values. By using check boxes, radio buttons, date pickers, and sliders, a program ensures that users can only choose from a range of valid options.

Using Text with Labels, Text Fields, and Combo Boxes

When a program can offer a limited range of valid options to the user, that's when you want to use check boxes, radio buttons, date pickers, or sliders. However, sometimes a program needs to allow the user to type in data that can never be predicted ahead of time, such as a person's name. When a program needs to allow the user to type in data, that's when you need to use a text field or a combo box.

A text field lets the user type in anything he or she wants including numbers, unusual characters, or ordinary letters. That means a program needs to verify that the user typed in valid data.

Sometimes a program can offer the user both the option of choosing from a limited selection of valid options or typing in data instead. For example, a program might ask the user to choose a country. Then the program can offer a limited range of likely options or give the user the freedom to type something else.

This ability to either choose from a limited range of options or type something in is the main advantage of a combo box. The combo box gets its name because it combines the features of a pop-up button (displaying a list of valid options) with the freedom to type anything in (like a text field).

While text fields and combo boxes are used to accept data from the user, labels are used to display information to the user. When you just need to display information such as displaying instructions or identifying the purpose of a text field (such as telling a user to type a name or address), you'll want to use a label. Together, labels, text fields, and combo boxes work to accept and display text on a user interface.

Using Text Fields

Since a user can type anything into a text field, a text field stores data as a string, which you can retrieve using the stringValue property. However, since users can type in integer or decimal numbers, a text field is versatile enough to recognize such numbers.

If the user types in an integer, you can retrieve that value by accessing the intValue property. If the user types in a decimal number, you can retrieve that value by accessing either the floatValue or doubleValue properties.

No matter what the user types into a text field, you can retrieve the proper value. Since text fields can accept strings or numbers, your program can retrieve the proper value by accessing one of the following properties:

- intValue – Retrieves an integer value. If the user types a string, this property stores 0. If the user types a decimal number such as 10.9, it stores only the integer value such as 10.

- floatValue or doubleValue – Retrieves a floating-point or double value. If the user types a string, this property stores 0.0. If the user types an integer such as 4, the floatValue and doubleValue properties store it as a decimal such as 4.0.

- stringValue – Retrieves a string value. If the user types a number, it stores that number as a string (such as "4.305").

> **Note**   When the user types text into a text field, that typed text gets stored in all four properties: intValue, floatValue, doubleValue, and stringValue.

Beyond the standard text field, Xcode offers several text field variations for handling different types of text entry:

- Text Field with Number Formatter – Defines the type of numbers that can be typed in

- Secure Text Field – Masks typed text

- Search Field – Stores a list of previously entered text

- Token Field – Allows the user to enter tokens of content in addition to typing ordinary text

Using a Number Formatter

A number formatter lets you define valid numeric values the user can type into the text box such as a minimum or maximum value, or a specific way to enter data such as with a % sign or by typing the number out as "four" instead of typing 4.

Xcode gives you two ways to create a text field with a number formatter. First, you can drag and drop the Text Field with Number Formatter from the Object Library and place it on your user interface. Second, you can drag and drop the Number Formatter from the Object Library and place it on an existing text field on your user interface.

To quickest way to find both of these items is to type "Number Formatter" in the search text field at the bottom of the Object Library as shown in Figure 17-1.

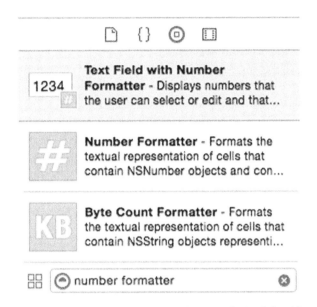

Figure 17-1. The Text Field with Number Formatter and Number Formatter in the Object Library

Whether you create a new text field with the Text Field with Number Formatter item or apply Number Formatter to an existing text field, you'll need to define the number formatter settings. To do this, you need to follow several steps:

1. Click the Show Document Outline icon to display the Document Outline.

2. Click on the disclosure triangle to the left of the Text Field that uses the Number Formatter.

3. Click on the disclosure triangle that appears to the left of the Text Field Cell underneath the text field.

4. Click on the Number Formatter as shown in Figure 17-2.

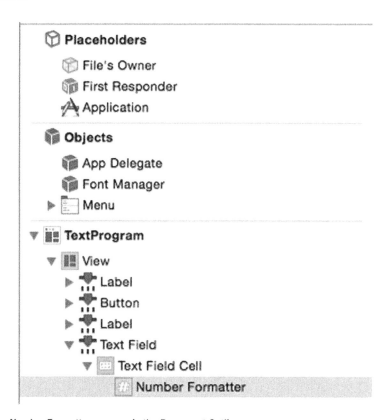

Figure 17-2. *The Number Formatter appears in the Document Outline*

5. Choose View ➤ Utilities➤ Show Attributes Inspector. The Show
    Attributes Inspector pane appears in the upper right corner of the
    Xcode window as shown in Figure 17-3.

Figure 17-3. *The Show Attributes Inspector pane*

The Minimum and Maximum check boxes let you define a minimum and/or maximum value that the text field will accept. If you define a minimum value of 10 and the user types in a number less than 10, the text field won't accept the number.

The Localize check box tells Xcode to use the user's local settings to determine the appearance of a decimal point and currency symbol. In some parts of the world, they use a period for a decimal point while in others they use a comma.

Likewise for currency, Europeans would use the Euro symbol, Americans would use the dollar symbol, and British users would use the British pound symbol. Selecting the Localize check box ensures that your text field number formatter works no matter what part of the world the program may be used.

The Style pop-up menu lets you define different ways to format numbers. When you choose a Style, the Unformatted and Formatted text fields under the Sample category shows you how your numbers may look.

For example, in Figure 17-3, choosing the None Style means that if the user types in 1,234.75 into a text field with a number formatter and presses Return, the text field formats that number as simply 1235.

However, if the Style is Currency, Percent, Scientific, or Spell Out, that means the user can enter a number as defined by the Formatted example, and the text field will store the number as shown in the Unformatted example.

To see how to use these different number formatters, follow these steps:

1. From within Xcode choose File ➤ New ➤ Project.

2. Click Application under the OS X category.

3. Click Cocoa Application and click the Next button. Xcode now asks for a product name.

4. Click in the Product Name text field and type **NumberProgram**.

5. Make sure the Language pop-up menu displays Swift and that no check boxes are selected.

6. Click the Next button. Xcode asks where you want to store the project.

7. Choose a folder to store your project and click the Create button.

8. Click the MainMenu.xib file in the Project Navigator. Your program's user interface appears.

9. Click the NumberProgram icon to display the window of your program's user interface.

10. Choose View ➤ Utilities ➤ Show Object Library. The Object Library appears in the bottom right corner of the Xcode window.

11. Drag a Pop-Up Button, a Push Button, and a Text Field with Number Formatter on to the user interface window so it looks like Figure 17-4.

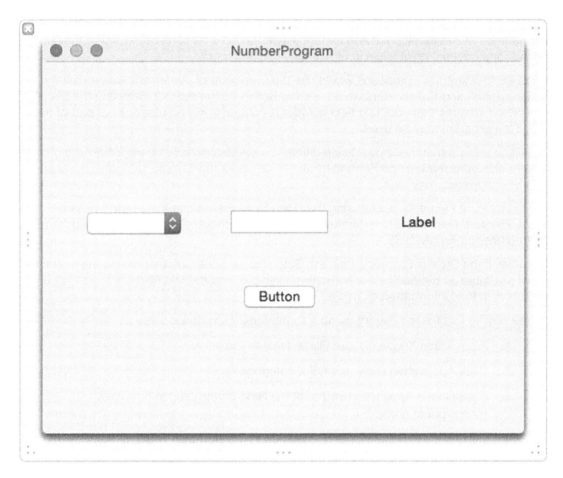

Figure 17-4. *The user interface of the NumberProgram*

12. Double-click on the pop-up button. Xcode displays a list of three choices labeled Item 1, Item 2, and Item 3 as shown in Figure 17-5.

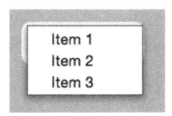

Figure 17-5. *Modifying a pop-up button*

13. Double-click on Item 1 and when Xcode highlights it, type None.

14. Double-click on Item 2 and when Xcode highlights it, type Decimal.

15. Double-click on Item 3 and when Xcode highlights it, type Currency.

16. Drag three Menu Items from the Object Library to the bottom of the pop-up button list.

17. Double-click on each of these three new menu items and modify the name so it displays Percent, Scientific, and Spell Out.

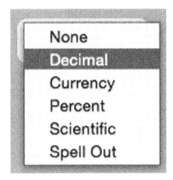

Figure 17-6. The modified pop-up button menu

18. Choose View ➤ Assistant Editor ➤ Show Assistant Editor. The AppDelegate.swift file appears next to your user interface.

19. Move the mouse pointer over the pop-up button, hold down the Control key, and drag underneath the IBOutlet line.

20. Release the Control key and the mouse. A pop-up window appears.

21. Click in the Name text field, type popUpChoice, and click the Connect button. An IBOutlet appears.

22. Move the mouse pointer over the text field, hold down the Control key, and drag the mouse under the IBOutlet line.

23. Release the Control key and the mouse. A pop-up window appears.

24. Click in the Name text field, type textBox, and click the Connect button.

25. Move the mouse pointer over the label, hold down the Control key, and drag the mouse under the IBOutlet line.

26. Release the Control key and the mouse. A pop-up window appears.

27. Click in the Name text field, type labelResult, and click the Connect button.

28. Click the Show Document Outline icon to reveal the Document Outline.

29. Move the mouse pointer over Number Formatter, hold down the Control key, and drag the mouse under the IBOutlet line.

30. Release the Control key and the mouse. A pop-up window appears.

31. Click in the Name text field, type numberFormat, and click the Connect button. You should have four IBOutlet lines as follows:

```
@IBOutlet weak var popUpChoice: NSPopUpButton!
@IBOutlet weak var textBox: NSTextField!
@IBOutlet weak var labelResult: NSTextField!
@IBOutlet weak var numberFormat: NSNumberFormatter!
```

32. Click the Hide Document Outline icon to hide the document outline.

33. Move the mouse pointer over the push button, hold down the Control key, and drag the mouse above the last curly bracket in the bottom of the AppDelegate.swift file.

34. Release the Control key and the mouse button. A pop-up window appears.

35. Click in the Connect pop-up menu and choose Action.

36. Click in the Name text field and type showResults.

37. Click in the Type pop-up menu, choose NSButton, and click the Connect button. Xcode creates an empty IBAction method.

38. Modify the IBAction method as follows:

```
@IBAction func showResults(sender: NSButton) {
    if popUpChoice.titleOfSelectedItem! == "None" {
        numberFormat.numberStyle = NSNumberFormatterStyle.NoStyle
    } else if popUpChoice.titleOfSelectedItem! == "Decimal" {
        numberFormat.numberStyle = NSNumberFormatterStyle.DecimalStyle
    } else if popUpChoice.titleOfSelectedItem! == "Currency" {
        numberFormat.numberStyle = NSNumberFormatterStyle.CurrencyStyle
    } else if popUpChoice.titleOfSelectedItem! == "Percent" {
        numberFormat.numberStyle = NSNumberFormatterStyle.PercentStyle
    } else if popUpChoice.titleOfSelectedItem! == "Scientific" {
        numberFormat.numberStyle = NSNumberFormatterStyle.ScientificStyle
    } else if popUpChoice.titleOfSelectedItem! == "Spell Out" {
        numberFormat.numberStyle = NSNumberFormatterStyle.SpellOutStyle
    }
    labelResult.stringValue = String(stringInterpolationSegment: textBox.doubleValue)
}
```

39. Choose Product ➤ Run. Your user interface appears.

40. Click on the pop-up button, choose Decimal, type a decimal number into the text field, and then click on the Push Button. The label displays the result that the text field's number formatter contains.

41. Click on the pop-up button, choose Currency, type $4.56 into the text field, and then click on the Push Button. The label displays 4.56.

42. Click on the pop-up button, choose Percent, type 25% into the text field, and then click on the Push Button. The label displays 0.25.

43. Click on the pop-up button, choose Scientific, type 1.2E3 into the text field, and then click on the Push Button. The label displays 1200.0.

44. Click on the pop-up button, choose Spell Out, type **forty-five** into the text field, and then click on the Push Button. The label displays 45.0.

45. Choose NumberProgram ➤ Quit NumberProgram.

The above Swift code in the IBAction method uses the titleOfSelectedItem property to determine which option the user chose. Then it uses multiple if-else if statements to change the number Style property of the number formatter.

The pop-up button lets you choose different number formatting styles so you can see how they work when you type a formatted number into the text field. By choosing different formatting styles, you can see how the text field lets you type in differently formatted numbers such as 25% (which gets converted into 0.25) or 1.2E3 (which gets converted into 1200.0).

Using a Secure Text Field, a Search Field, and a Token Field

A secure text field simply hides text behind bullets when the user types. This can be handy for masking actual text such as passwords, credit card numbers, or other sensitive information from view. Beyond masking anything typed in, a secure text field works exactly like a regular text field where you can retrieve the value typed using the intValue, floatValue, doubleValue, or stringValue properties.

A search text field looks like a typical search field you might find in a browser that displays a magnifying glass icon and close icon that can delete the text in the search field with one click. Each time the user types something in the search field and presses Return, the search field stores the text as a list stored in the recentSearches property.

By accessing this recentSearches property, you can view a list of everything the user previously typed in that search field.

A token field lets you type text and then it encloses that text inside a token. Despite the appearance of tokens, you can still retrieve the text of a token field by accessing the stringValue property.

To see how to use a secure text field, a search field and a token field, follow these steps:

1. From within Xcode choose File ➤ New ➤ Project.

2. Click Application under the OS X category.

3. Click Cocoa Application and click the Next button. Xcode now asks for a product name.

4. Click in the Product Name text field and type **TextProgram**.

5. Make sure the Language pop-up menu displays Swift and that all check boxes are clear and not selected.

6. Click the Next button. Xcode asks where you want to store the project.

7. Choose a folder to store your project and click the Create button.

8. Click on the MainMenu.xib file in the Project Navigator Pane.

9. Click on the TextProgram icon to make the window of the user interface appear.

10. Drag a three Push Buttons, a Search Field, a Token Field, a Secure Text Field, and three labels resized to expand their width on to the user interface as shown in Figure 17-7.

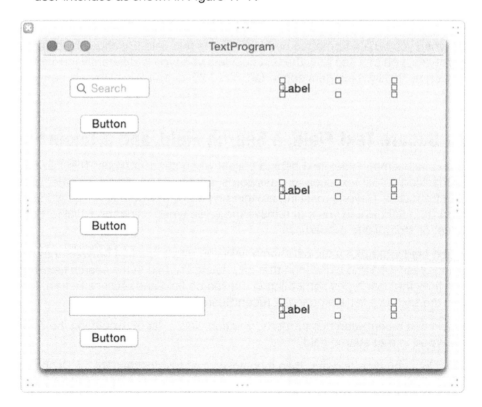

Figure 17-7. The user interface of the TextProgram

11. Choose View ➤ Assistant Editor ➤ Show Assistant Editor. Xcode displays the AppDelegate.swift file next to the user interface.

12. Move the mouse pointer over the Search Field, hold down the Control key, and drag the mouse under the IBOutlet line in the AppDelegate.swift file.

13. Release the Control key and the mouse button. A pop-up window appears.

14. Click in the Name text field, type searchBox, and click the Connect button.

15. Move the mouse pointer over the label to the right of the Search Field, hold down the Control key, and drag the mouse under the IBOutlet line.

16. Release the Control key and the mouse button. A pop-up window appears.

17. Click in the Name text field, type historyBox, and click the Connect button. You should have two IBOutlets like this:

```
@IBOutlet weak var searchBox: NSSearchField!
@IBOutlet weak var historyBox: NSTextField!
```

18. Move the mouse pointer over the Token Field, hold down the Control key, and drag the mouse under the IBOutlet line in the AppDelegate. swift file.

19. Release the Control key and the mouse button. A pop-up window appears.

20. Click in the Name text field, type tokenBox, and click the Connect button.

21. Move the mouse pointer over the label to the right of the Search Field, hold down the Control key, and drag the mouse under the IBOutlet line.

22. Release the Control key and the mouse button. A pop-up window appears.

23. Click in the Name text field, type tokenResult, and click the Connect button. You should have two more IBOutlets like this:

```
@IBOutlet weak var tokenBox: NSTokenField!
@IBOutlet weak var tokenResult: NSTextField!
```

24. Move the mouse pointer over the Secure Text Field, hold down the Control key, and drag the mouse under the IBOutlet line in the AppDelegate.swift file.

25. Release the Control key and the mouse button. A pop-up window appears.

26. Click in the Name text field, type secureBox, and click the Connect button.

27. Move the mouse pointer over the label to the right of the Search Field, hold down the Control key, and drag the mouse under the IBOutlet line.

28. Release the Control key and the mouse button. A pop-up window appears.

29. Click in the Name text field, type secureResults, and click the Connect button. You should have two more IBOutlets like this:

```
@IBOutlet weak var secureBox: NSSecureTextField!
@IBOutlet weak var secureResults: NSTextField!
```

30. Move the mouse pointer over the Push Button under the Search Field, hold down the Control key, and drag the mouse over the last curly bracket in the bottom of the AppDelegate.swift file.

31. Release the Control key and the mouse. A pop-up window appears.

32. Click in the Connect pop-up menu and choose Action.

33. Click in the Name text field and type showHistory.

34. Click in the Type pop-up menu and choose NSButton. Then click the Connect button. Xcode creates an IBAction method.

35. Move the mouse pointer over the Push Button under the Token Field, hold down the Control key, and drag the mouse over the last curly bracket in the bottom of the AppDelegate.swift file.

36. Release the Control key and the mouse. A pop-up window appears.

37. Click in the Connect pop-up menu and choose Action.

38. Click in the Name text field and type showToken.

39. Click in the Type pop-up menu and choose NSButton. Then click the Connect button. Xcode creates an IBAction method.

40. Move the mouse pointer over the Push Button under the Secure Text Field, hold down the Control key, and drag the mouse over the last curly bracket in the bottom of the AppDelegate.swift file.

41. Release the Control key and the mouse. A pop-up window appears.

42. Click in the Connect pop-up menu and choose Action.

43. Click in the Name text field and type showSecret.

44. Click in the Type pop-up menu and choose NSButton. Then click the Connect button. Xcode creates an IBAction method.

45. Modify these IBAction methods as follows:

```
@IBAction func showHistory(sender: NSButton) {
    historyBox.stringValue = String(stringInterpolationSegment: searchBox.
recentSearches)
}

@IBAction func showToken(sender: NSButton) {
    tokenResult.stringValue = tokenBox.stringValue
}

@IBAction func showSecret(sender: NSButton) {
    secureResults.stringValue = secureBox.stringValue
}
```

46. Choose Product ➤ Run. Your user interface appears.

47. Click in the Search Field, type Yahoo, and press Return.

48. Click the close icon (the X in the gray circle) to clear the Search Field, type Google, and press Return.

49. Click the push button underneath the Search Field. Notice that the label to the right displays the two search results.

50. Click in the Token field, type Yahoo, and press Return. Notice that the token field displays your typed text as a token.

51. Click in the Token field and next to the Yahoo token, type Google and press Return.

52. Click the push button underneath the Token field. Notice that the label to the right displays your two token texts.

53. Click in the Secure Text Field and type password. Notice that the Secure Text Field masks the text.

54. Click the push button underneath the Secure Text Field. Notice the label to the right displays the text from the Secure Text Field as shown in Figure 17-8.

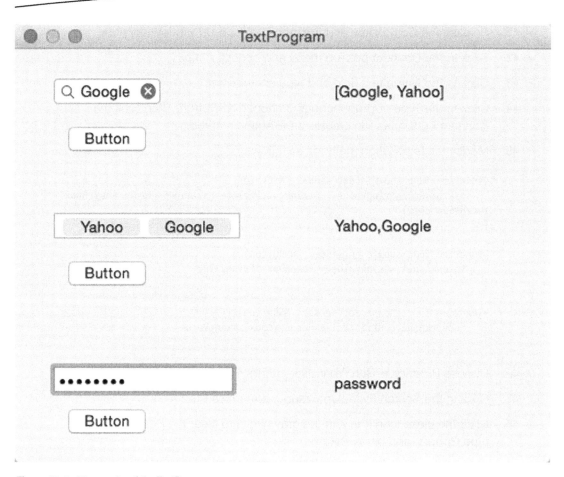

Figure 17-8. *The results of the TextProgram*

55.   Choose TextProgram ➤ Quit TextProgram.

Although Search Fields, Token Fields, and Secure Text Fields look differently, they behave exactly like a text field when you need to access the values stored inside them.

Using Combo Boxes

A text field lets the user type in anything while a pop-up button displays a fixed range of options. When you want to display a fixed range of options and let the user type in text, that's when you can use a combo box.

A combo box is based on the NSComboBox class, which is based on the NSTextField class that defines all text fields. As a result, you can retrieve values from a combo box using the intValue, floatValue, doubleValue, or stringValue properties.

When using a combo box, you have two ways to fill its pop-up list of options. First, you can create an internal list using the Show Attributes Inspector pane. Second, you can use an external data source so the combo box retrieves data from a database file or over the Internet.

Creating an Internal List

An internal list is best when you know ahead of time exactly how many and which items you want to store in a combo box, such as a list of countries or product names. To create an internal list, follow these steps:

1. Place a combo box on your program's user interface.

2. Click to select that combo box.

3. Choose View ➤ Utilities ➤ Show Attributes Inspector. The Items list appears as shown in Figure 17-9.

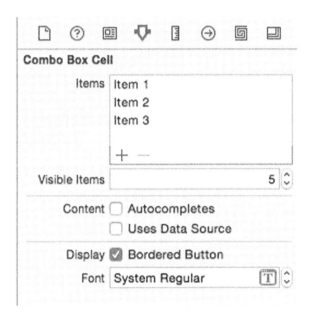

Figure 17-9. The Items list lets you define items to appear in a combo box

To edit an existing item in the list, click on that item to select it and press Return. Now you can edit the text.

To remove an existing item, click on that item to select it and click the minus sign icon.

To add a new item, click on the plus sign icon. Then click on the newly added item, press Return, and edit the text.

The Visible Items text field defines how many items the combo box menu displays.

The Autocompletes check box lets the combo box displays items in its list that matches what the user started to type in. So if the user types one letter, autocomplete displays a list of all items in the combo box list that begins with the same letter the user typed.

The Uses Data Source check box determines if the combo box uses its internal Items list to display menu items, or retrieves data from another source. If the Uses Data Source check box is selected, then you'll need to write Swift code to fill a combo box with data.

To see how to fill a combo box using an internal list, follow these steps:

1. From within Xcode choose File ➤ New ➤ Project.

2. Click Application under the OS X category.

3. Click Cocoa Application and click the Next button. Xcode now asks for a product name.

4. Click in the Product Name text field and type **ComboProgram**.

5. Make sure the Language pop-up menu displays Swift and that all check boxes are clear and not selected.

6. Click the Next button. Xcode asks where you want to store the project.

7. Choose a folder to store your project and click the Create button.

8. Click on the MainMenu.xib file in the Project Navigator Pane.

9. Click on the ComboProgram icon to make the window of the user interface appear.

10. Drag a Combo Box, Push Button, and a Label on to the user interface, and widen the label so it looks like Figure 17-10.

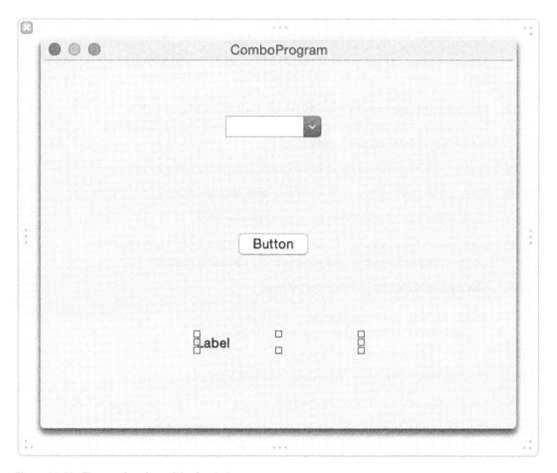

Figure 17-10. *The user interface of the ComboProgram*

11. Choose View ➤ Assistant Editor ➤ Show Assistant Editor. Xcode
     shows the AppDelegate.swift file next to the user interface.

12. Move the mouse pointer over the Combo Box, hold down the
     Control key, and drag the mouse under the IBOutlet line in
     the AppDelegate.swift file.

13. Release the Control key and the mouse. A pop-up window appears.

14. Click in the Name text field, type myCombo, and click the Connect
     button.

15. Move the mouse pointer over the Label, hold down the Control key,
     and drag the mouse under the IBOutlet line in the AppDelegate.swift
     file.

16. Release the Control key and the mouse. A pop-up window appears.

17. Click in the Name text field, type comboResult, and click the Connect button. You should now have these two IBOutlets:

```
@IBOutlet weak var myCombo: NSComboBox!
@IBOutlet weak var comboResult: NSTextField!
```

18. Move the mouse pointer over the Push Button, hold down the Control key, and drag the mouse just above the last curly bracket at the bottom of the AppDelegate.swift file.

19. Release the Control key and the mouse. A pop-up window appears.

20. Click in the Connection pop-up menu and choose Action.

21. Click in the Name text field and type showResult.

22. Click in the Type pop-up menu and choose NSButton. Then click the Connect button. Xcode creates an empty IBAction method.

23. Modify this IBAction method as follows:

```
@IBAction func showResult(sender: NSButton) {
    comboResult.stringValue = myCombo.stringValue
}
```

24. Choose Product ➤ Run. Your user interface appears.

25. Click in the combo box and type Hello.

26. Click the push button. The word Hello appears in the label.

27. Click in downward-pointing arrow on the right edge of the combo box to display its list of items. Since we didn't modify the default list, the combo box list contains three items labeled Item 1, Item 2, and Item 3.

28. Click on Item 3 and then click the push button. The label underneath displays Item 3.

29. Choose ComboProgram ➤ Quit ComboProgram.

This example used the default item list for the combo box. Experiment by adding or modifying this combo box item list and select the Autocompletes check box to see how these options modify the combo box.

Using a Data Source

A data source is best when a combo box needs to display data that may change over time, such as displaying a list of information from a database. To use a data source, you need to write Swift code. First, you need to adopt the NSComboBoxDataSource protocol in a class like this:

```
class AppDelegate: NSObject, NSApplicationDelegate, NSComboBoxDataSource {
```

Next, you need to write two functions. One function needs to count the number of items to display in the combo box. The second function needs to retrieve data to insert in the combo box's list of items.

Finally, you need to specify a data source (the file that contains the data you want to display in the combo box) and make sure the usesDataSource property for the combo box is selected in the Show Attributes Inspector pane or set to true using Swift code.

To see how a data source works to fill a combo box with a list of items, follow these steps:

1. Make sure the ComboProgram project is loaded in Xcode.

2. Modify the class name to include the NSComboBoxDataSource protocol as follows:

```
class AppDelegate: NSObject, NSApplicationDelegate, NSComboBoxDataSource {
```

3. Click on the AppDelegate.swift file in the Project Navigator pane.

4. Underneath the IBOutlet lines, add the following line to create an array of strings that will fill the combo box's item list:

```
let myArray = ["Sandwich", "Chips", "Soda", "Salad"]
```

5. Modify the applicationDidFinishLaunching function as follows:

```
func applicationDidFinishLaunching(aNotification: NSNotification) {
    // Insert code here to initialize your application
    myCombo.dataSource = self
    myCombo.usesDataSource = true

    numberOfItemsInComboBox(myCombo)
    comboBox(myCombo, objectValueForItemAtIndex: 0)
}
```

This Swift code defines the data source for the combo box (identified by the myCombo IBOutlet) as self, which means the same class is also the data source. It makes sure the usesDataSource property is true to use a data source. Then it calls two functions defined by the NSComboBoxDataSource protocol.

6. Above the IBAction method, add the following two function implementations:

```
func numberOfItemsInComboBox(aComboBox: NSComboBox) -> Int {
    return myArray.count
}

func comboBox(aComboBox: NSComboBox, objectValueForItemAtIndex index: Int) ->
AnyObject {
    return myArray[index]
}
```

The numberOfItemsInComboBox function counts all the items in the myArray array and returns that integer. The comboBox function places each array item in the combo box's item list.

7. Choose Product ➤ Run.

8. Click on the downward-pointing arrow of the combo box. Notice that its item list contains the items defined in myArray ("Sandwich," "Chips," "Soda," and "Salad").

9. Click on Sandwich in the combo box to select it and then click the push button. Notice that the label underneath displays Sandwich.

10. Choose ComboProgram ➤ Quit ComboProgram.

This simple program shows how to retrieve a list of items from another data source (in this case an array called myArray) to fill an item list for a combo box. The complete code for the AppDelegate.swift file should look like this:

```swift
import Cocoa

@NSApplicationMain
class AppDelegate: NSObject, NSApplicationDelegate, NSComboBoxDataSource {

    @IBOutlet weak var window: NSWindow!
    @IBOutlet weak var myCombo: NSComboBox!
    @IBOutlet weak var comboResult: NSTextField!

    let myArray = ["Sandwich", "Chips", "Soda", "Salad"]

    func applicationDidFinishLaunching(aNotification: NSNotification) {
        // Insert code here to initialize your application
        myCombo.usesDataSource = true
                myCombo.dataSource = self

        numberOfItemsInComboBox(myCombo)
        comboBox(myCombo, objectValueForItemAtIndex: 0)
    }

    func applicationWillTerminate(aNotification: NSNotification) {
        // Insert code here to tear down your application
    }

    func numberOfItemsInComboBox(aComboBox: NSComboBox) -> Int {
        return myArray.count
    }
```

```
    func comboBox(aComboBox: NSComboBox, objectValueForItemAtIndex index: Int) -> AnyObject
{

        return myArray[index]
    }

    @IBAction func showResult(sender: NSButton) {
        comboResult.stringValue = myCombo.stringValue
    }


}
```

Summary

Text fields allow the user to type anything such as numbers or strings, so a text field offers multiple properties (intValue, floatValue, doubleValue, and stringValue) to store typed information in the proper data type. To restrict numeric information the user may type, you can use a number formatter to define minimum and/or maximum values along with defining different ways the user can enter numeric data such as with a percentage sign or a currency sign.

Besides ordinary text fields, Xcode offers several variations of text fields for specialized purposes. Labels are designed for simply displaying text without allowing the user to edit the displayed text. A secure text field masks typed in data to keep it safe from prying eyes. A token field displays typed in data as groups or tokens while a search field offers a property to remember previously typed in data.

Combo boxes combine the features of a text field with a pop-up button. A combo box can display a list of valid options that the user can click on, or the user can type in data. You can define a combo box's list of options in the Show Attributes Inspector pane, or you can retrieve data from another source such as from an array.

The main purpose of text fields and combo boxes is to allow the user to type in any type of data. When the user types in data, you may need to write Swift code to verify that the entered data is actually valid for your program.

Using Alerts and Panels

With every program, you'll need to design the unique features of your program while letting the Cocoa framework worry about making your program look and behave like a standard OS X program. Two common features of nearly every OS X program are alerts and panels.

An alert typically pops up on the screen to inform the user such as asking the user to verify the deletion of a file or to alert the user of a problem. A panel displays common user interface items such as a print panel that OS X programs typically display to give you options for printing, or an open panel for selecting a file.

By using alerts and panels, you can add common OS X user interface elements without having to create your own user interface or without needing to write Swift code. Alerts and panels are part of the Cocoa framework that your OS X programs can use to create a standard OS X user interface.

Using Alerts

An alert is based on the NSAlert class in the Cocoa framework. At the simplest level, you can create an alert with two lines of Swift code:

```
var myAlert = NSAlert()
    myAlert.runModal()
```

The first line declares an object called myAlert that is based on the NSAlert class. Then the second line uses the runModal() method to display the alert. When an alert appears, it's considered modal, which means the alert won't let the user do anything until the user dismisses the alert.

The above two lines of code creates a generic alert that displays an OK button, a generic graphic image, and a generic text message as shown in Figure 18-1.

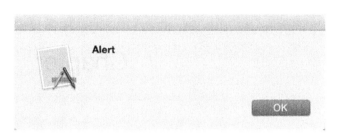

Figure 18-1. Creating a generic alert

To customize an alert, you can modify the following properties:

- messageText – Displays the main alert message in bold. In Figure 18-1, **Alert** is the messageText.

- informativeText – Displays non-bold text directly underneath the messageText. In Figure 18-1, there is no informativeText.

- icon – Displays an icon. By default, the icon is the program's icon.

- alertStyle – Displays a critical icon when set to NSAlertStyle. CriticalAlertStyle. Otherwise displays the default alert icon.

- showsSuppressionButton – Displays a check box with the default text of "Do not show this message again" unless the suppressionButton?.title is defined.

- suppressionButton?.title – Replaces the default text ("Do not show this message again") with custom text for the check box.

To see how to customize an alert, follow these steps:

1. From within Xcode choose File ➤ New ➤ Project.

2. Click Application under the OS X category.

3. Click Cocoa Application and click the Next button. Xcode now asks for a product name.

4. Click in the Product Name text field and type **AlertProgram**.

5. Make sure the Language pop-up menu displays Swift and that no check boxes are selected.

6. Click the Next button. Xcode asks where you want to store the project.

7. Choose a folder to store your project and click the Create button.

8. Click the MainMenu.xib file in the Project Navigator. Your program's user interface appears.

9. Click the AlertProgram icon to display the window of your program's user interface.

10. Choose View ➤ Utilities ➤ Show Object Library. The Object Library appears in the bottom right corner of the Xcode window.

11. Drag a Push Button on to the user interface window.

12. Choose View ➤ Assistant Editor ➤ Show Assistant Editor. The AppDelegate.swift file appears next to your user interface.

13. Move the mouse pointer over the push button, hold down the Control key, and drag the mouse above the last curly bracket in the bottom of the AppDelegate.swift file.

14. Release the Control key and the mouse button. A pop-up window appears.

15. Click in the Connect pop-up menu and choose Action.

16. Click in the Name text field and type showAlert.

17. Click in the Type pop-up menu, choose NSButton, and click the Connect button. Xcode creates an empty IBAction method.

18. Modify the IBAction method as follows:

```
@IBAction func showAlert(sender: NSButton) {
    var myAlert = NSAlert()
    myAlert.messageText = "Warning!"
    myAlert.informativeText = "Zombies approaching"
    myAlert.alertStyle = NSAlertStyle.CriticalAlertStyle
    myAlert.showsSuppressionButton = true
    myAlert.suppressionButton?.title = "Stop scaring me"
    myAlert.runModal()
}
```

19. Choose Product ➤ Run. Your user interface appears.

20. Click on the push button. An alert appears as shown in Figure 18-2.

Figure 18-2. Displaying a customized alert

21. Click the OK button on the alert to make it go away.

22. Choose AlertProgram ➤ Quit AlertProgram.

Getting Feedback from an Alert

An alert typically displays a single OK button so the user can dismiss the alert. However, an alert can get feedback from the user in one of two ways:

- Selecting the suppression check box

- Clicking on a button other than the OK button

To determine if the user selected the suppression check box or not, you need to access the suppressionButton!.state property. If the check box is selected, the suppressionButton!.state property is 1. If the check box is clear, the suppressionButton!.state property is 0.

The second way to get feedback from an alert is by displaying two or more buttons on an alert. To add more buttons to an alert, you need to use the addButtonWithTitle method. Then to determine which button the user selected, you need to use the NSAlertFirstButtonReturn, NSAlertSecondButtonReturn, or NSAlertThirdButtonReturn constants.

If you have four or more buttons on an alert, you can check for the fourth button by using NSAlertThirdButtonReturn + 1, a fifth button by using NSAlertThirdButtonReturn + 2, and so on for each additional button beyond the third one.

To see how to identify what options the user chose in an alert, follow these steps:

1. Make sure your AlertProgram project is loaded in Xcode.

2. Click on the AppDelegate.swift file in the Project Navigator pane.

3. Modify the IBAction showAlert method as follows:

```
@IBAction func showAlert(sender: NSButton) {
    var myAlert = NSAlert()
    myAlert.messageText = "Warning!"
    myAlert.informativeText = "Zombies approaching"
    myAlert.alertStyle = NSAlertStyle.CriticalAlertStyle
    myAlert.showsSuppressionButton = true
    myAlert.suppressionButton?.title = "Stop scaring me"

    myAlert.addButtonWithTitle("Ignore it")
    myAlert.addButtonWithTitle("Run")
    myAlert.addButtonWithTitle("Panic")
    myAlert.addButtonWithTitle("Do nothing")

    let choice = myAlert.runModal()

    switch choice {
    case NSAlertFirstButtonReturn:
        print ("User clicked Ignore it")
    case NSAlertSecondButtonReturn:
        print ("User clicked Run")
    case NSAlertThirdButtonReturn:
        print ("User clicked Panic")
```

```
        case NSAlertThirdButtonReturn + 1:
            print ("User clicked Do nothing")
        default: break
        }

        if myAlert.suppressionButton!.state == 1 {
            print ("Checked")
        } else {
            print ("Not checked")
        }

    }
```

The addButtonWithTitle methods create buttons on the alert where the first addButtonWithTitle method creates a default button and the other addButtonWithTitle methods create additional buttons. To capture the button that the user clicked on, the above code creates a constant called "choice."

Then it uses a switch statement to identify which button the user clicked. Notice that the fourth button is identified by adding 1 to the NSAlertThirdButtonReturn constant.

The suppressionButton!.state property checks if the user selected the check box that appears on the alert. If its value is 1, then the user selected the check box. Otherwise if its value is 0, the check box is clear.

4. Choose Product ➤ Run. Your user interface appears.

5. Click the button. The alert appears as shown in Figure 18-3.

Figure 18-3. The alert created by Swift code

6. Click in the Stop scaring me check box to select it.

7. Click on one of the buttons such as Panic or Run. No matter which button you click, the alert goes away.

8. Choose AlertProgram ➤ Quit AlertProgram. Xcode appears again and displays text in the Debug Area such as User clicked Panic and Checked.

Displaying Alerts as Sheets

Alerts typically appear as a modal dialog that creates another window that you can move separately from the main program window. Another way to display alert is as a sheet that appears to scroll down from the title bar of the currently active window.

To make an alert appear as a sheet, you need to use the beginSheetModalForWindow method like this:

```
alertObject.beginSheetModalForWindow(window, completionHandler: closure)
```

The first parameter defines the window where you want the sheet to appear. In the AlertProgram project, the IBOutlet representing the user interface window is called a window. The second parameter is the completion handler label, which identifies the name of a special function called a closure.

A closure represents a shorthand way of writing a function. Instead of writing a function the traditional way like this:

```
func functionName(parameters) -> Type {
    // Insert code here
            return value
}
```

You can write a closure like this:

```
    let closureName = { (parameters) -> Type in
    // Insert code here
}
```

To see how to turn an alert into a sheet and use closures, follow these steps:

1. Make sure your AlertProgram project is loaded in Xcode.

2. Click on the AppDelegate.swift file in the Project Navigator pane.

3. Modify the IBAction showAlert method as follows:

```
@IBAction func showAlert(sender: NSButton) {
    var myAlert = NSAlert()
    myAlert.messageText = "Warning!"
    myAlert.informativeText = "Zombies approaching"
    myAlert.alertStyle = NSAlertStyle.CriticalAlertStyle
    myAlert.showsSuppressionButton = true
    myAlert.suppressionButton?.title = "Stop scaring me"

    myAlert.addButtonWithTitle("Ignore it")
    myAlert.addButtonWithTitle("Run")
    myAlert.addButtonWithTitle("Panic")
    myAlert.addButtonWithTitle("Do nothing")
```

```
let myCode = { (choice:NSModalResponse) -> Void in
    switch choice {
    case NSAlertFirstButtonReturn:
        print ("User clicked Ignore it")
    case NSAlertSecondButtonReturn:
        print ("User clicked Run")
    case NSAlertThirdButtonReturn:
        print ("User clicked Panic")
    case NSAlertThirdButtonReturn + 1:
        print ("User clicked Do nothing")
    default: break
    }

    if myAlert.suppressionButton!.state == 1 {
        print ("Checked")
    } else {
        print ("Not checked")
    }
}
myAlert.beginSheetModalForWindow(window, completionHandler: myCode)
}
```

4. Choose Product ➤ Run. The user interface appears.

5. Click on the button. Notice that now the alert drops down as a sheet as shown in Figure 18-4.

Figure 18-4. The alert as a sheet

6. Click in the Stop scaring me check box to select it.

7. Click on one of the buttons such as Panic or Run. No matter which button you click, the alert goes away.

8. Choose AlertProgram ➤ Quit AlertProgram. Xcode appears again and displays text in the Debug Area such as User clicked Run and Checked.

In the above Swift code, the closure is defined as follows:

```
let myCode = { (choice:NSModalResponse) -> Void in
    switch choice {
    case NSAlertFirstButtonReturn:
        print ("User clicked Ignore it")
    case NSAlertSecondButtonReturn:
        print ("User clicked Run")
    case NSAlertThirdButtonReturn:
        print ("User clicked Panic")
    case NSAlertThirdButtonReturn + 1:
        print ("User clicked Do nothing")
    default: break
    }

    if myAlert.suppressionButton!.state == 1 {
        print ("Checked")
    } else {
        print ("Not checked")
    }
}
```

However, you can also place closures inline, which means instead of the completion handler identifying the closure name, you simply put the closure itself in that location. So in the above code, the beginSheetModalForWindow method calls the closure by name like this:

```
myAlert.beginSheetModalForWindow(window, completionHandler: myCode)
```

You could replace the closure name of "myCode" with the actual closure code in its place like this:

```
myAlert.beginSheetModalForWindow(window, completionHandler: { (choice:NSModalResponse) ->
Void in
    switch choice {
    case NSAlertFirstButtonReturn:
        print ("User clicked Ignore it")
    case NSAlertSecondButtonReturn:
        print ("User clicked Run")
    case NSAlertThirdButtonReturn:
        print ("User clicked Panic")
```

```
    case NSAlertThirdButtonReturn + 1:
        print ("User clicked Do nothing")
    default: break
    }

    if myAlert.suppressionButton!.state == 1 {
        print ("Checked")
    } else {
        print ("Not checked")
    }
})
```

Putting closures inline directly within a method shortens the amount of code you need to write, but at the possible expense of making the overall code harder to understand. Separating the closure by name and then calling it by name makes it easier to reuse that closure elsewhere in your program if necessary, but also makes your code clearer at the expense of forcing you to write more code.

Choose whatever method you like best but as in all aspects of programming, stick to one style to make it easy for other programmers to understand your code later if you're not around to explain how it works.

Using Panels

Panels represent common user interface elements that OS X programs need such as displaying an Open panel to let users select a file to open and a Save panel to let users choose a folder to store a file. The Open panel is based on the NSOpenPanel class while the Save panel is based on the NSSavePanel class.

Creating an Open Panel

An Open panel let the user select a file to open. The Open panel needs to return a file name if the user selected a file. Some properties that the Open panel uses include:

- canChooseFiles – Lets the user select a file.

- canChooseDirectories – Lets the user select a folder or directory.

- allowsMultipleSelection – Lets the user select more than one item.

- URLs – Holds the name of the chosen item. If the allowsMultipleSelection property is set to true, then the URLs property holds an array of items. Otherwise it holds a single item.

To see how to use an Open panel, follow these steps:

1. From within Xcode choose File ➤ New ➤ Project.

2. Click Application under the OS X category.

3. Click Cocoa Application and click the Next button. Xcode now asks for a product name.

4. Click in the Product Name text field and type **PanelProgram**.

5. Make sure the Language pop-up menu displays Swift and that no check boxes are selected.

6. Click the Next button. Xcode asks where you want to store the project.

7. Choose a folder to store your project and click the Create button.

8. Click the MainMenu.xib file in the Project Navigator. Your program's user interface appears.

9. Click the PanelProgram icon to display the window of your program's user interface.

10. Choose View ➤ Utilities ➤ Show Object Library. The Object Library appears in the bottom right corner of the Xcode window.

11. Drag a Push Button on to the user interface window and double-click on it to change its title to Open.

12. Choose View ➤ Assistant Editor ➤ Show Assistant Editor. The AppDelegate.swift file appears next to your user interface.

13. Move the mouse pointer over the push button, hold down the Control key, and drag the mouse above the last curly bracket in the bottom of the AppDelegate.swift file.

14. Release the Control key and the mouse button. A pop-up window appears.

15. Click in the Connect pop-up menu and choose Action.

16. Click in the Name text field and type openPanel.

17. Click in the Type pop-up menu, choose NSButton, and click the Connect button. Xcode creates an empty IBAction method.

18. Modify the IBAction method as follows:

```
@IBAction func openPanel(sender: NSButton) {
    var myOpen = NSOpenPanel()
    myOpen.canChooseFiles = true
    myOpen.canChooseDirectories = true
    myOpen.allowsMultipleSelection = true

    myOpen.beginWithCompletionHandler { (result) -> Void in
        if result == NSFileHandlingPanelOKButton {
            print (myOpen.URLs)
        }
    }

}
```

19.   Choose Product ➤ Run. The user interface appears.

20.   Click on the button. An Open panel appears as shown in Figure 18-5.

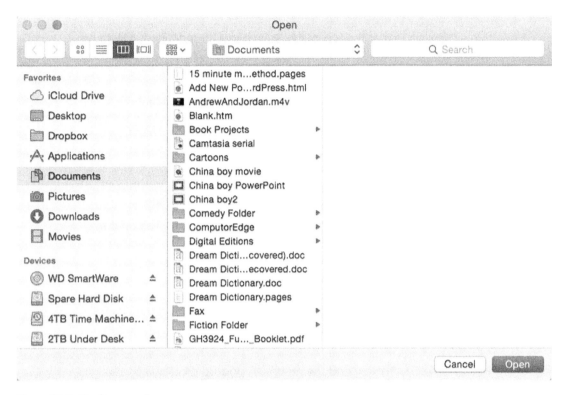

Figure 18-5. *The Open panel*

21.   Hold down the Command key and click on two different items such as two different files or a file and a folder.

22.   Click the Open button.

23.   Choose PanelProgram ➤ Quit PanelProgram. Xcode appears again. In the Debug area, you should see a list of the files/folders you chose.

Note   The Open panel only selects a file/folder, but you'll still need to write Swift code to actually open any file the user selects.

Creating a Save Panel

A Save panel looks similar to an Open panel, but its purpose is to let the user select folder and define a file name to save. The Save panel needs to return a file name if the user selected a file. Some properties that the Open panel uses include:

- title – Displays text at the top of the Save panel. If undefined, it defaults to displaying "Save".

- prompt – Displays text on the default button.

- URL – Holds the path name and file name of the user's selection.

- nameFieldStringValue – Holds just the file name the user chose.

To see how to use a Save panel, follow these steps:

1. Make sure the PanelProgram is loaded in Xcode.

2. Click on the MainMenu.xib file in the Project Navigator pane.

3. Drag a Push Button on to the user interface and double-click on it to change its title to Save.

4. Choose View ➤ Assistant Editor ➤ Show Assistant Editor. Xcode shows the AppDelegate.swift file next to the user interface.

5. Move the mouse pointer over the Save button, hold down the Control key, and drag the mouse under the IBOutlet line in the AppDelegate. swift file.

6. Release the Control key and the mouse. A pop-up window appears.

7. Click in the Connection pop-up menu and choose Action.

8. Click in the Name text field, type savePanel, and click the Connect button.

9. Click in the Type pop-up menu and choose NSButton. Then click the Connect button. Xcode creates an empty IBAction method.

10. Modify this IBAction method as follows:

```
@IBAction func savePanel(sender: NSButton) {
    var mySave = NSSavePanel()
    mySave.title = "Save a File Here"
    mySave.prompt = "Save Me"

    mySave.beginWithCompletionHandler { (result) -> Void in
        if result == NSFileHandlingPanelOKButton {
            print (mySave.URL)
            print (mySave.nameFieldStringValue)
        }
    }
}
```

11. Choose Product ➤ Run. Your user interface appears.

12. Click the Save button. A Save panel appears as shown in Figure 18-6. Notice that the title property creates the text that appears at the top of the Save panel while the prompt property creates the text that appears on the default button in the bottom right corner of the Save panel.

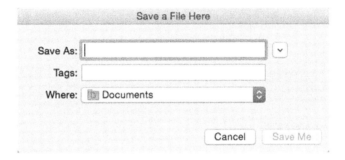

Figure 18-6. *The condensed Save panel*

13 Click the Expand button that appears to the far right of the Save As text field. The Save panel expands as shown in Figure 18-7.

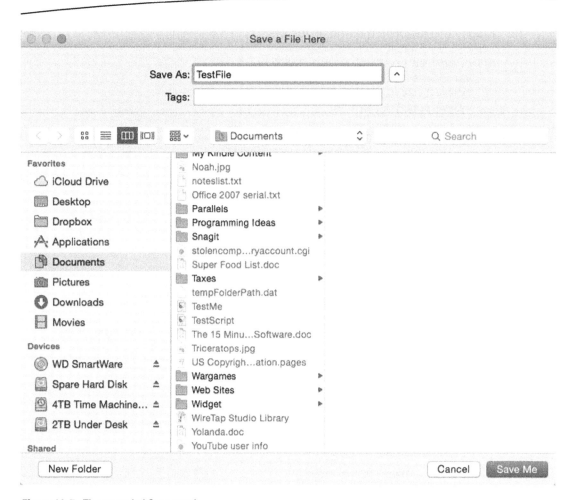

Figure 18-7. *The expanded Save panel*

14.   Click in Save As text field and type TestFile.

15.   Click the Save Me button.

16.   Choose PanelProgram ➤ Quit PanelProgram. The Xcode window
      appears again. In the Debug Area at the bottom of the Xcode
      window, you should see the full path name of the file and folder you
      chose, and just the file name you typed.

Summary

When designing a standard OS X user interface, you don't have to create everything yourself. By taking advantage of the Cocoa framework, you can create alerts and panels that look and behave like other OS X programs with little extra coding on your own part.

Alerts let you display brief messages to the user such as warnings. You can customize an alert with text and graphics, and place two or more buttons on the alert. If you place two or more buttons on an alert, you'll need to write Swift code to identify which button the user clicked.

An alert typically appears as a separate window, but you can also make it appear as a sheet that drops down from a window's title.

Panels display commonly used user interface items such as an Open panel to select a file to open, and a Save panel to select a folder and a file name to save data. The Open and Save panels are part of the Cocoa framework, but you'll need to write additional Swift code to make the Open and Save panels actually open or save a file to a hard disk.

Alerts and panels let you create standard OS X user interface elements with little additional coding. By using these features of the Cocoa framework, you can create standard OS X programs that work reliably and behave how users expect an OS X program to look and behave.

Creating Pull-Down Menus

Pull-down menus represent the standard way to interact with an OS X program. While your program may display buttons to represent commands, too many buttons can clutter the screen. To avoid trying to cram multiple buttons on the screen, you can group related commands in multiple pull-down menus. By default, Xcode creates every OS X project with the following pull-down menu titles:

- File – Displays commands for opening, saving, creating, and printing.
- Edit – Displays commands for copying, cutting, pasting, undoing, and redoing commands.
- Format – Displays commands for modifying text or graphics such as changing fonts or aligning text.
- View – Displays commands for changing the way data appears in the window such as zooming in and out or displaying other user interface items such as toolbars.
- Window – Displays commands for manipulating document windows such as switching between multiple open windows.
- Help – Displays commands for getting help using a program.

Besides using the standard pull-down menu titles, you can add your own or delete the existing ones. To organize commands within a pull-down menu, you can use horizontal lines to group similar commands together or store them in submenus. For the user's convenience, you can also assign keystroke shortcuts to commands.

Pull-down menus represent a standard way for users to control a program. By creating pull-down menus for your own programs, you can create a familiar user interface so others can learn and use your program quickly with little or no additional training.

Editing Pull-Down Menus

Each time you create a Cocoa Application project, Xcode creates a default pull-down menu that contains common menu titles and commands. Without writing a single line of Swift code, many of these commands already work. For example, the Quit command under the application menu (the name of your program such as MenuProgram) knows how to quit your program, and the Zoom and Minimize commands under the Window menu title know how to zoom and minimize the user interface window.

In most cases, you'll need to customize these pull-down menus by editing existing commands, adding new commands, and deleting existing commands. To modify a program's pull-down menus, you have two options:

- Edit the pull-down menus directly
- Open the Document Outline and edit the menus

To edit pull-down menus directly, click on the .xib or .storyboard file in the Project Navigator pane and then click directly on your program's pull-down menus as shown in Figure 19-1.

Figure 19-1. You can click directly on a program's pull-down menus to select individual items

A second way to edit pull-down menus is to open the Document Outline by clicking on the Show Document Outline icon as shown in Figure 19-2.

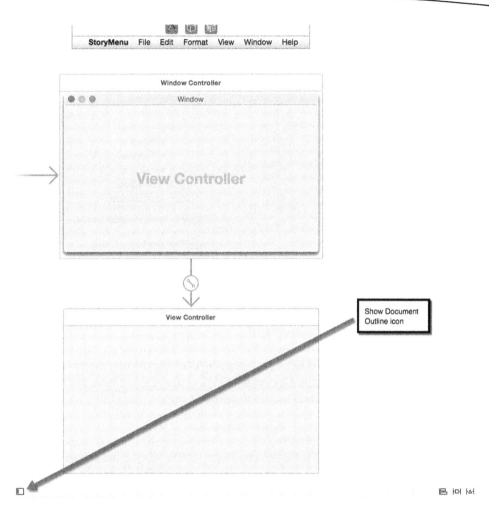

Figure 19-2. *The Show Document Outline icon*

With the Document Outline open, you can click on the disclosure triangles to view the different pull-down menus and their commands as shown in Figure 19-3.

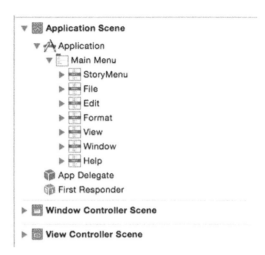

Menus in the Document
Outline of a .xib file

Menus in the Document
Outline of a .storyboard file

Figure 19-3. Viewing menus in the Document Outline pane

To delete a menu item, click on it to select it (either by clicking directly on the pull-down menu item or on the menu item in the Document Outline pane) and press the Backspace or Delete key. This lets you delete individual menu items or entire menu titles such as the File or Edit pull-down menu title.

> **Note**   If you delete a menu item or entire pull-down menu title by mistake, just choose Edit ➤ Undo or press Command+Z to recover it right away.

To add items to a program's pull-down menus, you have two choices:

- Add a new menu item to an existing pull-down menu title such as File or Edit

- Add a new pull-down menu title that lists its own commands

Adding New Pull-Down Menu Titles to the Menu Bar

You can add menu items and pull-down menu titles either directly on the pull-down menu, or inside the Document Outline.

The Object Library displays the following pull-down menu titles that you can add to a program's menu bar as shown in Figure 19-4:

- Application Menu Item – Contains typical commands found in an application pull-down menu title such as About, Preferences, and Services.

- File Menu Item – Contains typical commands found in a File pull-down menu title such as Open, New, and Save.

- Edit Menu Item – Contains typical commands found in the Edit pull-down menu title such as Cut, Copy, and Paste.

- Font Menu Item – Contains typical commands found in a Font pull-down menu title such as Bold, Bigger, and Copy Style.

- Format Menu Item – Contains typical commands found in a Format pull-down menu title such as Font and Text.

- Text Menu Item – Contains typical commands found in a Text pull-down menu title such as Center, Writing Direction, and Show Ruler.

- Find Menu Item – Contains typical commands found in a Find pull-down menu title such as Find, Find and Replace, and Find Next.

- Window Menu Item – Contains typical commands found in a Window pull-down menu title such as Minimize, Bring to Front, and Zoom.

- Help Menu Item – Contains typical commands found in a Help pull-down menu title such as Application Help.

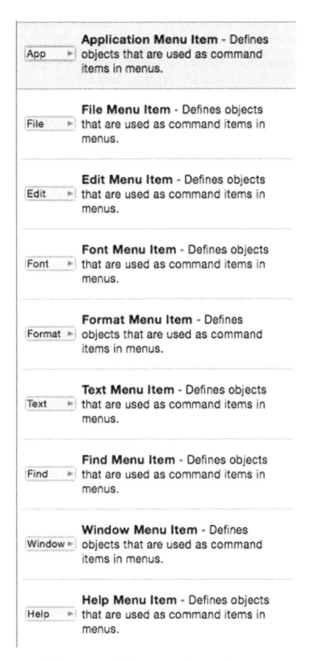

Figure 19-4. *The pull-down menu titles you can add to a program's menu bar*

To add a pull-down menu title to a program's menu bar, follow these steps:

1.   Click on the .xib or .storyboard file in the Project Navigator pane.

2.   Choose View ➤ Utilities ➤ Show Object Library to display the Object Library in the bottom right corner of the Xcode window.

3. Drag a pull-down menu item (see Figure 19-4) from the Object Library and move the mouse over the program's menu bar until a vertical blue line appears to show you where the pull-down menu title will appear as shown in Figure 19-5.

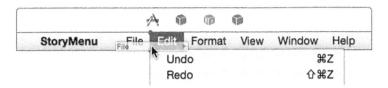

Figure 19-5. Adding a new pull-down menu title to a menu bar

Instead of dragging the mouse over the program's menu bar, you can also drag the mouse in between pull-down menu titles in the Document Outline until a horizontal blue line appears to show where your menu title will appear as shown in Figure 19-6.

Figure 19-6. Adding a new pull-down menu title to a menu bar using the Document Outline

4. Release the mouse. Your new pull-down menu title appears on the menu bar.

To rearrange the pull-down menu titles, move the mouse pointer over the menu title you wish to move (either on the menu bar or in the Document Outline), and drag the mouse to move the menu title to a new location.

Adding New Commands to a Pull-Down Menu

You can always delete, rearrange, and add commands on any pull-down menu. To delete a command, simply select it and press the Backspace or Delete key. To rearrange a command, drag and drop it to a new location.

To add a new command to a pull-down menu, you need to use the following three items from the Object Library as shown in Figure 19-7:

- Menu Item – Represents a single command.
- Submenu Menu Item – Represents a submenu of additional commands.
- Separate Menu Item – Displays a horizontal line to separate commands on a pull-down menu.

Figure 19-7. Three items for modifying commands on a pull-down menu

To add a new command to a pull-down menu, follows these steps:

1. Click on the .xib or .storyboard file in the Project Navigator pane.

2. Choose View ➤ Utilities ➤ Show Object Library to display the Object Library in the bottom right corner of the Xcode window.

3. Click on the pull-down menu where you want to add a new command. You can either click directly on the pull-down menu title on the menu bar or click on a disclosure triangle to open a pull-down menu title in the Document Outline as shown in Figure 19-8.

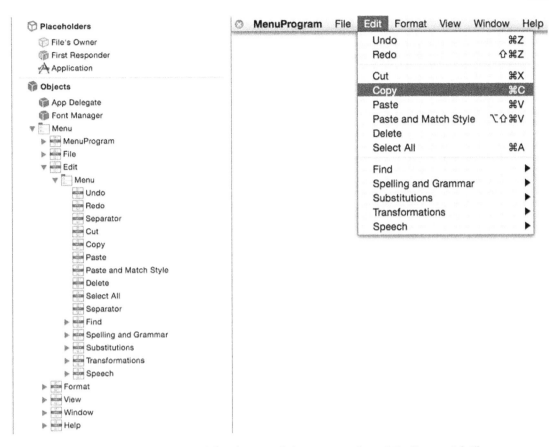

Figure 19-8. You can add a new command directly on a pull-down menu or through the Document Outline

4.   Drag a menu item (see Figure 19-7) from the Object Library and move the mouse in the pull-down menu list until a horizontal blue line appears to show you where the command will appear as shown in Figure 19-9.

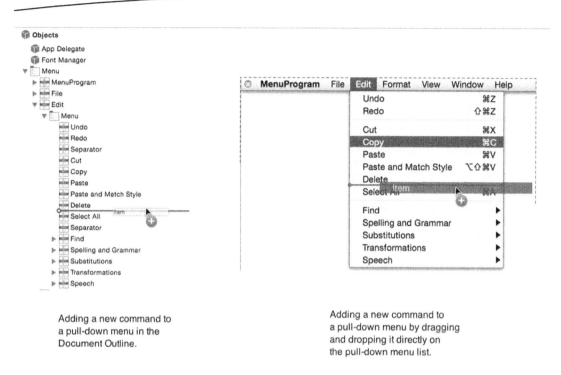

Adding a new command to a pull-down menu in the Document Outline.

Adding a new command to a pull-down menu by dragging and dropping it directly on the pull-down menu list.

Figure 19-9. Dragging and dropping a new command in a pull-down menu list

5. Release the mouse. Xcode adds your new menu item to the pull-down menu. If you added a Submenu Menu Item, you can now edit the commands stored on its submenu.

Editing Commands

Once you've modified the pull-down menu titles that appear on a menu bar and modified the commands that appear on each pull-down menu, you may want to further edit each individual command using the Inspector pane. The Inspector pane can be useful to modify the following properties:

- Title – Displays the text of the menu command.

- Key Equivalent – Defines a keystroke shortcut for a command.

To edit a command (or a pull-down menu title), follow these steps:

1. Click on the .xib or .storyboard file in the Project Navigator pane.

2. Click on the pull-down menu command (or pull-down menu title) that you want to edit either in the Document Outline or directly on the pull-down menu itself.

3. Choose View ➤ Utilities ➤ Show Attributes Inspector. The Show Attributes Inspector pane appears as shown in Figure 19-10.

Figure 19-10. Dragging and dropping a new command in a pull-down menu list

4.   Click in the Title text field in the Inspector pane to edit the text of the command.

5.   Click in the Key Equivalent text field and press (not type) the keystroke shortcut you want to assign to your command. Make sure this keystroke shortcut isn't used by another command (such as Command+X for the Cut command). Xcode displays your keystroke shortcut to the right of the command on the pull-down menu.

Connecting Menu Commands to Swift Code

Once you've modified your pull-down menu titles and filled them with the proper commands, you'll eventually need to make those commands actually do something. That means linking your menu commands to IBAction methods much like connecting buttons or other user interface items to a file containing Swift code. You can Control-drag from either the menu command on the pull-down menu itself or from the menu command displayed in the Document Outline.

When you create a Cocoa Application project, you'll find that many menu commands already work such as the File ➤ Print, Window ➤ Minimize, and application name ➤ About commands. These features are provided by the NSApplication, NSWindow, NSView, and NSResponder classes in the Cocoa framework.

If you click on a menu command in a Cocoa Application project, and then choose View ➤ Utilities ➤ Show Connections Inspector, you'll see the Connections Inspector pane in the upper right corner of the Xcode window.

The Connections Inspector pane lets you see what the selected user interface item (such as a command on a pull-down menu) is connected to as shown in Figure 19-11.

Figure 19-11. The Connections Inspector pane shows what IBAction method a user interface is connected to

Normally when you view the Connections Inspector for a user interface item, you'll see the name of the IBAction method on the left side (such as print) with a line connecting it to the file where the IBAction method is actually stored (such as AppDelegate).

In Figure 19-11, the Print menu command on the File menu is connected to the print IBAction method, but this IBAction method isn't stored in a specific file. Instead, it's connected to something called First Responder, which is defined by the NSResponder class.

A user interface consists of several objects based on NSApplication, NSWindow, and NSView so First Responder simply points to the first object that should respond to the user clicking on a user interface item (such as the Print command on the File menu). If this first object doesn't have a print IBAction method, then it searches for this IBAction method in the next object.

So if you had a text field on a window and clicked the Print command on the File menu, the Print command would look for the print IBAction method in the text field (based on NSTextfield, which is based on NSView) first. If it fails to find the print IBAction method in the NSTextfield class, it would look next in the window (based on NSWindow) or the application itself (based on NSApplication).

If you click on the First Responder icon and then choose View ➤ Utilities ➤ Show Connections Inspector, you can see the Connections Inspector pane for the First Responder, which identifies all the IBAction methods connected to the default pull-down menus of a typical Cocoa Application project as shown in Figure 19-12.

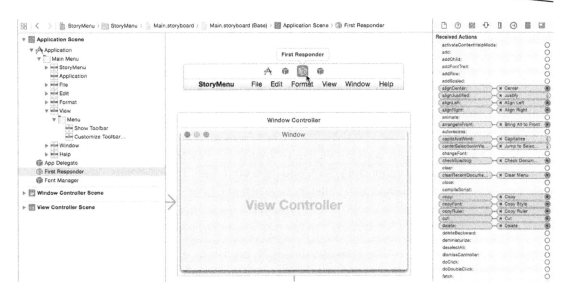

Figure 19-12. The First Responder Connections Inspector pane lists all the IBAction methods connected to the default pull-down menus of a Cocoa Application project

Note   Another way to view the Connections Inspector is to right-click on the First Responder icon.

Although the Cocoa Application template creates standard pull-down menus and commands, you'll still need to write Swift code to make many of these commands actually work. For example, the Save command doesn't know what to save or how to save it and the New command doesn't know what type of document to create.

To see how menu commands work with IBAction methods like other user interface items, follow these steps:

1. From within Xcode choose File ➤ New ➤ Project.

2. Click Application under the OS X category.

3. Click Cocoa Application and click the Next button. Xcode now asks for a product name.

4. Click in the Product Name text field and type **MenuProgram**.

5. Make sure the Language pop-up menu displays Swift and that no check boxes are selected.

6. Click the Next button. Xcode asks where you want to store the project.

7. Choose a folder to store your project and click the Create button.

8. Click the MainMenu.xib file in the Project Navigator. Your program's user interface appears.

9. Click the MenuProgram icon to display the window of your program's user interface.

10. Choose View ➤ Utilities ➤ Show Object Library. The Object Library appears in the bottom right corner of the Xcode window.

11. Drag a Text Field on to the user interface window. You may want to widen the width of the text field.

12. Drag a Menu Item from the Object Library to the bottom of the File menu. You can either drag the Menu Item on to the File pull-down menu or in the Document Outline as shown in Figure 19-13.

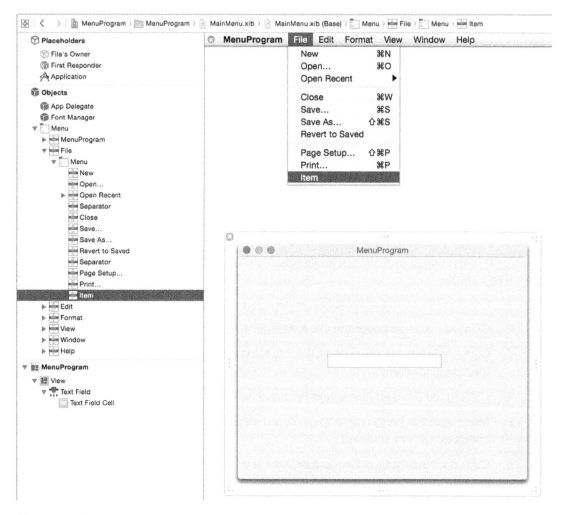

Figure 19-13. Drag a Menu Item to the bottom of the File pull-down menu

13. Choose View ➤ Assistant Editor ➤ Show Assistant Editor. The AppDelegate.swift file appears next to your user interface.

14. Move the mouse pointer over the text field, hold down the Control key, and drag the mouse under the IBOutlet line in the AppDelegate. swift file.

15. Release the Control key and the mouse button. A pop-up window appears.

16. Click in the Name text field, type textResult, and click the Connect button so your IBOutlet looks like this:

```
@IBOutlet weak var textResult: NSTextField!
```

17. Move the mouse pointer over the Menu Item you just added to the bottom of the File pull-down menu (either on the pull-down menu or in the Document Outline), hold down the Control key, and drag the mouse above the last curly bracket in the bottom of the AppDelegate.swift file.

18. Release the Control key and the mouse button. A pop-up window appears.

19. Click in the Connection pop-up menu and choose Action.

20. Click in the Name text field and type myMenu.

21. Click in the Type pop-up menu, choose NSMenuItem, and click the Connect button. Xcode creates an empty IBAction method.

22. Modify the IBAction method as follows:

```
@IBAction func myMenu(sender: NSMenuItem) {
        textResult.stringValue = "Clicked on = " + sender.title     }
```

23. Click on the Save command on the File pull-down menu.

24. Choose View ➤ Utilities ➤ Show Connections Inspector. The Connections Inspector pane shows that the Save command is connected to the saveDocument IBAction method in the First Responder as shown in Figure 19-14.

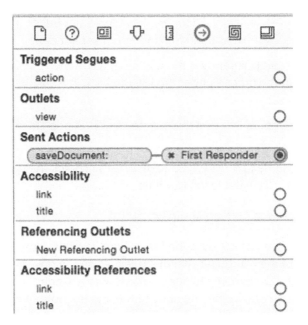

Figure 19-14. The Connections Inspector for the Save command in the File pull-down menu

25. Click the close icon (the X) that appears to the left of First Responder. This cuts the connection between the Save command and the saveDocument IBAction method.

26. Move the mouse pointer over the Save command on the File pull-down menu, hold down the Control key, and drag the mouse over the myMenu IBAction method you created in step 22. Make sure Xcode highlights the entire IBAction method and displays Connect Action as shown in Figure 19-15.

Figure 19-15. *Connecting the Save command to an existing IBAction method*

27.   Release the Control key and the mouse button. Xcode connects the
      Save command to the myMenu IBAction method.

28.   Choose Product ➤ Run. The user interface appears.

29.   Click on the File menu title. Notice that your Menu Item (labeled Item)
      appears at the bottom of the File pull-down menu.

30.   Click on the Save command. The text field displays "Clicked on =
      Save…"

31.   Click on the File menu title and click on Item, which is the Menu Item
      you added. The text field displays "Clicked on = Item."

32.   Choose MenuProgram ➤ Quit MenuProgram.

The MenuProgram project shows how to connect a menu command to text field so the text
field displays the name of the menu command that the user clicked on. However, when
working with storyboards, connecting menu commands works a little differently.

The main difference is that in a storyboard, the pull-down menus are stored in a separate
scene from the actual user interface as shown in Figure 19-16.

Figure 19-16. *Pull-down menus appear in a separate scene from the user interface in a storyboard*

That means when you Control-drag on a pull-down menu command, Xcode stores your Swift code in the AppDelegate.swift file, but if you Control-drag on a user interface item such as a text field, Xcode stores your Swift code in the ViewController.swift file.

Essentially this means if you create an IBOutlet for a text field, it's stored in the ViewController.swift file while your IBAction method for your pull-down menu commands are stored in the AppDelegate.swift file, which means the IBOutlet doesn't know the IBAction method exists (and vice versa).

The way around this problem is to connect your pull-down menu commands to the First Responder icon. This means that your program will first look for an IBAction method in its AppDelegate.swift file, but then will also look for the same IBAction method in other files as well.

So the trick is to create an empty IBAction method in the AppDelegate.swift file and an identical IBAction method in the ViewController.swift file, except you fill this second IBAction method with Swift code to make it retrieve the title of the selected menu command.

To see how menu commands work with storyboards, follow these steps:

1. From within Xcode choose File ➤ New ➤ Project.

2. Click Application under the OS X category.

3. Click Cocoa Application and click the Next button. Xcode now asks for a product name.

4. Click in the Product Name text field and type **StoryMenu**.

5. Make sure the Language pop-up menu displays Swift and that only the "Use storyboards" check box is selected.

6. Click the Next button. Xcode asks where you want to store the project.

7. Choose a folder to store your project and click the Create button.

8. Click the Main.storyboard file in the Project Navigator. Your program's user interface appears.

9. Choose View ➤ Utilities ➤ Show Object Library and drag a Text Field on to the user interface (identified by View Controller in its title bar). You may want to widen the text field width.

10. Choose View ➤ Assistant Editor ➤ Show Assistant Editor. Xcode shows the ViewController.swift file next to your user interface.

11. Move the mouse pointer over the text field, hold down the Control key, and drag the mouse under the class ViewController line.

12. Release the Control key and the mouse. A pop-up window appears.

13. Click in the Name text field, type textResult, and then click the Connect button. Xcode creates the following IBOutlet:

```
@IBOutlet weak var textResult: NSTextField!
```

14. Click the File pull-down menu to display its entire list. The Assistant Editor should now display the AppDelegate.swift file.

15. Drag a Menu Item from the Object Library to the bottom of the File pull-down menu.

16. Move the mouse pointer over the new Menu Item you just added to the bottom of the File pull-down menu, hold down the Control key, and drag the mouse above the last curly bracket at the bottom of the AppDelegate.swift file. A pop-up window appears.

17. Click in the Connection pop-up menu and choose Action.

18. Click in the Name text field and type myMenu.

19. Click in the Type pop-up menu, choose NSMenuItem, and click the Connect button. Xcode creates an empty IBAction method.

20. Select this empty IBAction method and choose Edit ➤ Copy.

21. Move the mouse pointer over the new Menu Item you just added at the bottom of the File menu, hold down the Control key, and drag the mouse over the First Responder icon as shown in Figure 19-17.

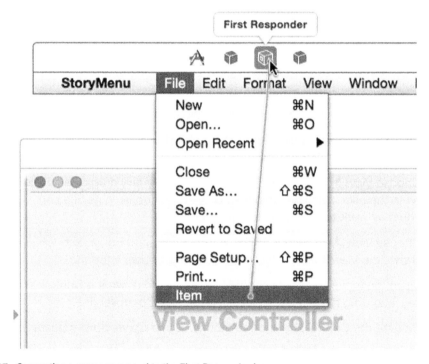

Figure 19-17. Connecting a menu command to the First Responder icon

22. Release the Control key and the mouse. A pop-up menu appears as shown in Figure 19-18.

Figure 19-18. *Connecting a menu command to the First Responder icon*

23. Click myMenu.

24. Move the mouse pointer over the Save command in the File pull-down menu.

25. Control-drag from the Save command over the First Responder icon.

26. Release the Control key and the mouse. A pop-up menu appears (see Figure 19-18).

27. Click myMenu

28. Choose View ➤ Standard Editor ➤ View Standard Editor to display just one file in the Xcode window.

29. Click the ViewController.swift file in the Project Navigator pane.

30. Move the cursor above the last curly bracket in the ViewController. swift file and choose Edit ➤ Paste. Xcode pasts your IBAction method from step 20.

31. Modify this IBAction method as follows:

```
@IBAction func myMenu(sender: NSMenuItem) {
    textResult.stringValue = "Clicked on = " + sender.title
}
```

32. Choose Product ➤ Run. Your user interface appears.

33. Choose File ➤ Save on your StoryMenu menu bar. Notice that the text field displays "Clicked on = Save…"

34.   Choose File ➤ Item on your StoryMenu menu bar. Notice that the text field now displays "Clicked on = Item-."

35.   Choose StoryMenu ➤ Quit StoryMenu.

Summary

When you create a Cocoa Application project, Xcode automatically creates pull-down menus for your program. You can add, delete, or rearrange menu titles on the menu bar or menu commands on the pull-down menus. For the user's convenience, you can even assign keystroke shortcuts to menu commands.

To edit a pull-down menu, you can either edit it directly on the pull-down menu or open the Document Outline. You can Control-drag from either the pull-down menu commands or the Document Outline to connect menu commands to IBAction methods.

When working with .storyboard files, you typically connect menu commands to the First Responder icon. Then you can implement the IBAction method in the correct Swift file to make that menu command work. When working with .xib files, you can directly connect menu commands to IBAction methods.

When Xcode creates pull-down menus for your Cocoa Application, many of those menu commands already know how to work such as Window ➤ Zoom and File ➤ Close. However, most of the menu commands won't do anything at all until you write Swift code of your own to make them work properly in your particular program.

Menu commands on pull-down menus give you one more way to connect commands to IBAction methods. Since most OS X programs rely on pull-down menus, focus first on organizing your program commands into pull-down menus, then write the Swift code to make each menu command actually work.

20

Protocol-Oriented Programming

When Apple introduced Swift during their Worldwide Developer's conference in 2014, they promoted it as an easier, safer, and faster programming language for iOS, OS X, and watchOS development than Objective-C. While both Swift and Objective-C allow object-oriented programming, Swift goes one step further and offers protocol-oriented programming as well.

One of the biggest problems with pure object-oriented programming languages is that extending the capabilities of a class means creating additional subclasses. Then you have to create objects based on those new subclasses. This can be a clumsy solution since you now have to keep track of one or more subclasses where each subclass has a different name and may only offer only minor differences between them.

Even worse, Swift (unlike some object-oriented programming languages) only allows single inheritance. That means a class can only inherit from exactly one other class. If you'd really like to inherit properties and methods from two different classes, you can't.

To get around this problem of inheritance and multiple subclasses, Swift offers protocols. Protocols work much like object-oriented programming but with some additional advantages:

- Protocols can extend features of classes, structs, and enums. Inheritance can only extend features of classes.

- A single class, struct, or enum can be extended by one or more protocols. Inheritance can only extend a single class.

This means that protocols are more flexible and versatile than classes while giving you the advantages of object-oriented programming without its disadvantages. Instead of using classes (object-oriented programming), you can use protocols (protocol-oriented programming), or mix both object-oriented programming and protocol-oriented programming so you can get the best of both worlds.

Understanding Protocols

Like a class, a protocol can define properties (variables) and methods (functions). The main difference is that unlike a class, a protocol can't set an initial value for a property and can't implement a method. A protocol simply defines a property and its data type. When defining a property in a protocol, you need to define the following three items:

- The property name, which can be any arbitrary, descriptive name.

- The data type of the property such as Int, Double, String, etc.

- Whether a property is gettable { get } or gettable and settable { get set }

> **Note**   A gettable/settable { get set } property cannot be assigned to a constant stored property (defined with the "let" keyword) or a read-only computed property. A gettable { get } property has no such limitations.

Consider the following protocol:

```
protocol Cat {
    var name: String { get set }
    var age: Int { get }
}
```

Now you can create a structure based on this protocol such as:

```
struct pet : Cat {
    var name : String
    //let name : String -- Invalid since "let" defines a constant stored property
    //var name : String { return "Fred" } -- Invalid since this is a read-only computed
property
    let age : Int
}
```

The above code defines a structure called "pet" that adopts the Cat protocol. That means it needs to declare the name property as a string and the age property as an integer.

Notice that because the age property is defined as gettable { get } by the Cat protocol, you can implement that property as a constant with the "let" keyword. You could also compute the age property by returning a value like this:

```
struct pet : Cat {
    var name : String
        var age : Int { return 4 }
}
```

To see how to use protocols and structures with different types of properties, follow these steps:

1. From within Xcode choose File ➤ New ➤ Playground. Xcode now asks for a playground name.

2. Click in the Name text field and type **ProtocolPlayground**.

3. Make sure the Platform pop-up menu displays OS X.

4. Click the Next button. Xcode asks where you want to store the playground.

5. Choose a folder to store your project and click the Create button.

6. Edit the playground code as follows:

```
import Cocoa

protocol Cat {
    var name: String { get set }
    var age: Int { get }
}

// Using a computed property
struct pet : Cat {
    var name : String
    var age : Int { return 4 }
}

var animal = pet(name: "Taffy")
print (animal.name)
print (animal.age)

// Using a constant stored property with "let"
struct feral : Cat {
    var name : String
    let age : Int
}

var pest = feral (name: "Stinky", age: 2)
print (pest.name)
print (pest.age)
```

Notice the differences when you declare a variable based on a structure. With computed properties for age, you don't need to create an initial value when declaring the variable such as:

```
// Using a computed property { return 4 }
struct pet : Cat {
    var name : String
    var age : Int { return 4 }
}
var animal = pet(name: "Taffy")
```

However if you don't have computed properties, then you must specifically initialize it when creating a variable such as:

```
// Using a constant stored property with "let"
struct feral : Cat {
    var name : String
    let age : Int
}
var pest = feral (name: "Stinky", age: 2)
```

Figure 20-1 shows how you can define two structures based on the same protocol.

```
import Cocoa

protocol Cat {
    var name: String { get set }
    var age: Int { get }
}

// Using a computed property {| return 4 }
struct pet : Cat {
    var name : String
    var age : Int { return 4 }                              4
}

var animal = pet(name: "Taffy")                             pet
print (animal.name)                                         "Taffy\n"
print (animal.age)                                          "4\n"


// Using a constant stored property with "let"
struct feral : Cat {
    var name : String
    let age : Int
}

var pest = feral (name: "Stinky", age: 2)                   feral
print (pest.name)                                           "Stinky\n"
print (pest.age)                                            "2\n"
```

Figure 20-1. Two different structures can adopt the same protocol

Using Methods in Protocols

When a protocol defines a method, it only defines the method name, any parameters, and any data type it returns, but it does not include any Swift code that actually implements that method such as:

```
protocol Cat {
    var name: String { get set }
    var age: Int { get }
        func meow (sound: String)
}
```

If a class, struct, or enum adopts this Cat protocol, it must not only define a name and age property, but it must also implement the protocol method with Swift code such as:

```
struct pet : Cat {
    var name : String
    var age : Int
    func meow (sound : String) {
        print (sound)
    }
}
```

Even though a class, structure, or enum might adopt the exact same protocol, the actual implementation of a method can be wildly different such as:

```
struct feral : Cat {
    var name : String
    var age : Int
    func meow (sound : String) {
        print ("Hear me roar")
        print (sound.uppercaseString)
    }
}
```

To see how to define methods in protocols and implement them in different structures, follow these steps:

1. Make sure the ProtocolPlayground file is loaded in Xcode.

2. Edit the playground code as follows:

```
import Cocoa

protocol Cat {
    var name: String { get set }
    var age: Int { get }
    func meow (sound : String)
}

// One way to implement the meow method
struct pet : Cat {
    var name : String
    var age : Int
    func meow (sound : String) {
        print (sound)
    }
}

var animal = pet(name: "Taffy", age: 16)
print (animal.name)
print (animal.age)
animal.meow("Feed me")methods

// A second way to implement the same meow method
struct feral : Cat {
    var name : String
    var age : Int
    func meow (sound : String) {
        print ("Hear me roar")
        print (sound.uppercaseString)
    }
}

var pest = feral(name: "Stinky", age: 2)
print (pest.name)
print(pest.age)
pest.meow("Growl")
```

Figure 20-2 shows how the two different implementations of the same protocol method work.

```
import Cocoa

protocol Cat {
    var name: String { get set }
    var age: Int { get }
    func meow (sound : String)
}

// Using a computed property { return 4 }
struct pet : Cat {
    var name : String
    var age : Int
    func meow (sound : String) {
        print (sound)                                        "Feed me\n"
    }
}

var animal = pet(name: "Taffy", age: 16)                     pet
print (animal.name)                                          "Taffy\n"
print (animal.age)                                           "16\n"
animal.meow("Feed me")                                       pet


struct feral : Cat {
    var name : String
    var age : Int
    func meow (sound : String) {
        print ("Hear me roar")                               "Hear me roar\n"
        print (sound.uppercaseString)                        "GROWL\n"
    }
}

var pest = feral(name: "Stinky", age: 2)                     feral
print (pest.name)                                            "Stinky\n"
print(pest.age)                                              "2\n"
pest.meow("Growl")                                           feral
```

Figure 20-2. *Method implementations can be different despite adopting the same protocol*

Adopting Multiple Protocols

One huge advantage protocols have over object-oriented programming is that a single class, structure, or enum can adopt one or more protocols. To do this, you just need to specify the name of each protocol to adopt such as:

```
struct structureName : protocolName1, protocolName2, protocolNameN {
```

By letting you adopt multiple protocols, Swift makes coding more flexible since you can pick and choose the protocols you want to use. To see how adopting multiple protocols works, follow these steps:

1. Make sure the ProtocolPlayground file is loaded in Xcode.

2. Edit the playground code as follows:

```
import Cocoa

protocol Cat {
    var name: String { get }
    var age: Int { get }
}

protocol CatSounds {
    func meow (sound : String)
}

struct pet : Cat, CatSounds {
    var name : String
    var age : Int
    func meow (sound : String) {
        print (sound)
    }
}

var animal = pet(name: "Fluffy", age: 6)
print (animal.name)
print (animal.age)
animal.meow("Wake up!")
```

Figure 20-3 shows how this code works by having a structure adopt two protocols. Notice that this code works exactly the same as if the name and age properties were defined in the same protocol as the meow method. By separating different properties and methods in multiple protocols, you don't have to implement properties and/or methods you don't need.

```
import Cocoa

protocol Cat {
    var name: String { get }
    var age: Int { get }
}

protocol CatSounds {
    func meow (sound : String)
}

struct pet : Cat, CatSounds {
    var name : String
    var age : Int
    func meow (sound : String) {
        print (sound)                                          "Wake up!\n"
    }
}

var animal = pet(name: "Fluffy", age: 6)                       pet
print (animal.name)                                            "Fluffy\n"
print (animal.age)                                             "6\n"
animal.meow("Wake up!")                                        pet
```

Figure 20-3. *A structure can adopt two or more protocols*

Since you can adopt multiple protocols, it's generally best to keep each protocol as short and simple as possible. This makes it easier to use only the protocols you need without being forced to implement additional properties and/or methods you may not need or want.

Protocol Extensions

In the world of object-oriented programming, you can extend a class through inheritance, which inherits every property and method that class may have inherited from other classes. In the world of protocol-oriented programming, you can extend a protocol through protocol extensions.

One purpose for protocol extensions is to define default values for properties. You could define default values by simply assigning values to one or more properties such as:

```
protocol Cat {
    var name: String { get }
    var age: Int { get }
}
```

This code defines a protocol called Cat, which defines a name and age property as gettable { get }. Then you can create a structure that adopts the Cat protocol and assigns an initial value to each property such as:

```
struct pet : Cat {
    var name : String = "Frank"
    var age : Int = 2
}
```

Now if you declare a variable based on this structure, the variable contains those initial values. Despite having an initial value, you can always store new data in those properties. To see how to define initial values for protocol properties without using extensions, follow these steps:

1. Make sure the ProtocolPlayground file is loaded in Xcode.

2. Edit the playground code as follows:

   ```
   import Cocoa

   protocol Cat {
       var name: String { get }
       var age: Int { get }
   }

   struct pet : Cat {
       var name : String = "Frank"
       var age : Int = 2
   }

   var animal = pet()
   print (animal.name)
   print (animal.age)

   animal.name = "Joey"
   animal.age = 13
   print (animal.name)
   print (animal.age)
   ```

When you first create the animal variable based on the pet structure, the initial name property value is "Frank" and the initial age property value is 2. At any time, you can store a new value in both properties as shown in Figure 20-4.

CHAPTER 20: Protocol-Oriented Programming   461

```
import Cocoa

protocol Cat {
    var name: String { get }
    var age: Int { get }
}

struct pet : Cat {
    var name : String = "Frank"
    var age : Int = 2
}

var animal = pet()                                  pet
print (animal.name)                                 "Frank\n
print (animal.age)                                  "2\n"

animal.name = "Joey"                                pet
animal.age = 13                                     pet
print (animal.name)                                 "Joey\n"
print (animal.age)                                  "13\n"
```

Figure 20-4. *You can assign initial values to gettable properties defined by a protocol*

If you want to set (and keep) an initial value for a property, that's when you can use protocol extensions. Protocol extensions can only work for gettable { get } properties. A protocol extension just uses the extension keyword followed by the name of the protocol you want to extend such as:

```
extension Cat {
    // Set one or more default values for gettable properties here
}
```

Inside the extension you can compute a default value for one or more gettable properties by using the return keyword such as:

```
extension Cat {
    var name : String { return "Frank" }
}
```

Not only does the protocol extension define the name property to hold the string "Frank," but it also eliminates the need to define the name property within a class, structure, or enum such as:

```
extension Cat {
    var name : String { return "Frank" }
}
```

```
struct pet : Cat {
    var age : Int = 2
}
```

The above protocol extension and structure is essentially equivalent to this:

```
struct pet : Cat {
    var name : String = "Frank"
    var age : Int = 2
}
```

The main difference is that when the name property is declared inside the structure, you can assign new strings to the name property later. When the name property is declared and set to a value inside a protocol extension, you cannot assign a new string to the name property later. To see how protocol extensions define a default value, follow these steps:

1. Make sure the ProtocolPlayground file is loaded in Xcode.

2. Edit the playground code as follows:

```
import Cocoa

protocol Cat {
    var name: String { get }
    var age: Int { get }
}

extension Cat {
    var name : String { return "Frank" }
}

struct pet : Cat {
    //var name : String = "Frank"
    var age : Int = 2
}

var animal = pet()
print (animal.name)
print (animal.age)

//animal.name = "Joey"
animal.age = 13
print (animal.name)
print (animal.age)
```

In the above code, the two commented lines show you what the protocol extension eliminates. Once you define the name property inside the protocol extension, you no longer need to declare that name property inside the pet structure. You also can't assign a new string (such as "Joey") to the name property after it's been assigned a default value in the protocol extension. Figure 20-5 shows the results of the above code.

```
import Cocoa

protocol Cat {
    var name: String { get }
    var age: Int { get }
}

extension Cat {
    var name : String { return "Frank" }                    (2 times)
}

struct pet : Cat {
    //var name : String = "Frank"
    var age : Int = 2
}

var animal = pet()                                          pet
print (animal.name)                                        "Frank\n"
print (animal.age)                                         "2\n"

//animal.name = "Joey"
animal.age = 13                                            pet
print (animal.name)                                        "Frank\n"
print (animal.age)                                         "13\n"
```

Figure 20-5. Defining a default value with a protocol extension

One problem with defining a default value in a protocol extension is that anything that adopts that protocol is forced to also adopt that protocol's extension. That means everything based on that protocol and extension will have the same default value that can't be changed.

In case you want the flexibility of defining default values, but only for certain classes, structures, or enums, you can create a protocol extension that only applies to any class, structure, or enum that also adopts a second protocol:

```
extension protocol2Extend where Self: protocol2Use {
    // Set one or more default values for gettable properties here
}
```

The above Swift code extends a protocol defined by "protocol2Extend." However the "where Self:" keywords identify a second protocol defined by "protocol2Use."

That means if a class, structure, or enum adopts the protocol defined by "protocol2Extend," then the extension only sets a default value if the class, structure, or enum also adopts the second protocol defined by "protocol2Use."

Suppose you created the following protocol extension:

```
extension Cat where Self: CatType {
    var name : String { return "Frank" }
}
```

This would define a default value of "Frank" to the name property to any class, structure, or enum that adopts the Cat protocol and the CatType protocol. If a class, structure, or enum only adopts the Cat protocol, its name property won't be assigned a default value of "Frank."

To see how this version of a protocol extension only works when a class, structure, or enum adopts a specific protocol, follow these steps:

1. Make sure the ProtocolPlayground file is loaded in Xcode.

2. Edit the playground code as follows:

```
import Cocoa

protocol Cat {
    var name: String { get }
    var age: Int { get }
}

protocol CatType {
    var species: String { get }
}

extension Cat where Self: CatType {
    var name : String { return "Frank" }
}

struct pet : Cat {
    var name : String = "Max"
    var age : Int = 2
}

var animal = pet()
print (animal.name)
print (animal.age)
```

```
    animal.name = "Joey"
    animal.age = 13
    print (animal.name)
    print (animal.age)

    // New structure that adopts two protocols
    struct wild : Cat, CatType {
        var age : Int = 2
        var species : String = "Lion"
    }

    var beast = wild()
    print (beast.name)
    print (beast.age)
    print (beast.species)
```

Notice that pet structure adopts the Cat protocol but since it doesn't adopt the CatType protocol as well, you can assign an initial value of "Max" to its name property, and you can later assign "Joey" to that same name property.

However the wild structure adopts both the Cat and CatType protocols, so it also adopts the protocol extension, which assigns "Frank" as a default value to the wild structure's name property as shown in Figure 20-6.

```
import Cocoa

protocol Cat {
    var name: String { get }
    var age: Int { get }
}

protocol CatType {
    var species: String { get }
}

extension Cat where Self: CatType {                              "Frank"
    var name : String { return "Frank" }
}

struct pet : Cat {
    var name : String = "Max"
    var age : Int = 2
}

var animal = pet()                                              pet
print (animal.name)                                            "Max\n"
print (animal.age)                                             "2\n"

animal.name = "Joey"                                           pet
animal.age = 13                                                pet
print (animal.name)                                           "Joey\n"
print (animal.age)                                            "13\n"


// New structure that adopts two protocols
struct wild : Cat, CatType {
    var age : Int = 2
    var species : String = "Lion"
}

var beast = wild()                                             wild
print (beast.name)                                            "Frank\n"
print (beast.age)                                             "2\n"
print (beast.species)                                         "Lion\n"
```

Figure 20-6. *Protocol extensions can selectively assign default values to a structure that adopts a specific protocol*

Using Protocol Extensions to Extend Common Data Types

Perhaps the most interesting use for protocol extensions is to add properties to common data types such as String, Int, and Double. A protocol extension for extending data types looks like this:

```
extension dataType {
  // New property {
        // return computed value
  }
}
```

When you extend a common data type with a protocol, you must create a variable that represents the data type followed by a period and the property name. So if you created an extension for the Int data type like this:

```
extension Int {
    var name : String {
       return text
      }
}
```

You could store a string value like this:

```
var status = 25.name    // represents a String
```

To see how to use protocol extensions to extend common data types, follow these steps:

1. Make sure the ProtocolPlayground file is loaded in Xcode.

2. Edit the playground code as follows:

   ```
   import Cocoa

   func checkMe (myAge : Int) -> String {
       if myAge >= 21 {
           return "Legal"
       } else {
           return "Underage"
       }
   }

   var text : String
   var myAge : Int

   myAge = 32
   text = checkMe (myAge)

   extension Int {
       var name : String {
           return text
         }
   }
   ```

```
        var status = myAge.name
        print (myAge)
        print (status)

        myAge = 16
        text = checkMe (myAge)
        status = myAge.name
        print (myAge)
        print (status)
```

Figure 20-7 shows the result of running this code. As you can see, when the myAge variable is greater than 21, its name property stores a string, which gets stored in the status variable. Depending on the value of the myAge variable, the name property stores either the string "Legal" or the string "Underage."

```
import Cocoa

func checkMe (myAge : Int) -> String {
    if myAge >= 21 {
        return "Legal"                              "Legal"
    } else {
        return "Underage"                           "Underage"
    }
}

var text : String
var myAge : Int

myAge = 32                                          32
text = checkMe (myAge)                              "Legal"

extension Int {
    var name : String {
        return text                                 (2 times)
    }
}

var status = myAge.name                             "Legal"
print (myAge)                                       "32\n"
print (status)                                      "Legal\n"

myAge = 16                                          16
text = checkMe (myAge)                              "Underage"
status = myAge.name                                 "Underage"
print (myAge)                                       "16\n"
print (status)                                      "Underage\n"
```

Figure 20-7. Protocol extensions can extend common data types

Summary

Protocols offer an alternate way to extend existing code. Just like a class, a protocol can define properties and methods. The main difference is that a protocol only defines a method's name and parameters, but does not actually include Swift code that implements that method.

Another difference is that when a protocol defines properties, it must also define whether that property is gettable { get } or gettable and settable { get set }.

Protocols work much like inheritance. While inheritance only allows classes to inherit from exactly one other class, protocols can extend classes, structures, and enums using one or more protocols.

Protocol extensions let you define default values for properties. When combined with common data types such as Int, String, and Double, protocol extensions allow a data type to store additional information.

Just remember that you can mix object-oriented programming with protocol-oriented programming so you don't have to choose between one or the other. Both objects and protocols can be useful depending on what you need to accomplish in your particular program. Make sure you understand how to define protocols, use them, and extend them because protocols will be a common feature of Swift programming.

Chapter 21

Chapter **21**

Defensive Programming

Programmers tend to be optimistic because when they write code, they assume that it will work correctly. However, it's often better to be more pessimistic when it comes to programming. Instead of assuming your code will work the first time, it's safer to assume your code won't work at all. This forces you to be extra careful when writing Swift code to make sure it does exactly what you want and doesn't do anything unexpected.

No program is error-free. Rather than waste time hunting down problems, it's far better to anticipate them and do your best to prevent them from creeping into your code in the first place. While it's not possible to write error-free code 100 percent of the time, the more defensive you are in writing code, the less likely you'll need to spend time hunting down errors that keep your code from working properly.

In general, assume nothing. Assumptions will surprise you every time, and rarely for the better. By anticipating problems ahead of time, you can plan for them so they won't wreck your program and force you to spend countless hours trying to fix a problem that you assumed should never have existed at all.

Test with Extreme Values

The simplest way to test your code is to start with extreme values to see how your program handles data way out of range from the expected. When working with numbers, programs often assume that the user will give it valid data within a fixed range, but what happens if the user types a letter or a symbol such as a smiley face instead of a number? What if the user types an integer instead of a decimal number (or vice versa)? What if the user types an extreme number such as 42 billion or -0.00000005580?

When working with strings, do the same type of test. How does your program react when it expects a string but receives a number instead? What happens if it receives a huge string consisting of 3,000 characters? What happens if it receives foreign language symbols with accent marks or unusual letters?

By testing your program with extreme values, you can see if your program responds gracefully or simply crashes. Ultimately the goal is to avoid crashes and respond gracefully. That might mean asking the user for valid data over and over again, or at least warn the user when the program receives invalid data. Reliable programs need to guard against anything that threatens to keep it from working properly.

Be Careful with Language Shortcuts

Every programming language offers shortcuts to make programming faster by requiring less code. However, those language shortcuts can often trip up even the most experienced programmers so use shortcuts with care.

One simple mistake is mixing up prefix and postfix operators such as counter++ or ++counter. Although the postfix and prefix increment operators look nearly identical, they create two completely different results as shown in Figure 21-1.

```
import Cocoa

var counter : Int

counter = 20                                                20
print (counter++)                                          "20"
print (++counter)                                          "22"
```

Figure 21-1. *Using the prefix and postfix increment shortcut*

Notice that the postfix increment operator (counter++) first uses the value of counter and then adds 1 to it. That's why the print (counter++) line prints 20. Right after it prints 20, the postfix increment operator adds 1 to the counter variable.

On the other hand, the prefix increment operator (++counter) adds 1 first and then uses the value of the counter. After the counter++ operator adds 1 to 20 and gets 21, the ++counter prefix increment operator adds 1 to it before using it. That's why it prints 22.

Depending on what you need, mixing these two increment operators up can give you slightly different results, which can keep your program from working properly. If you're not sure how these increment operators work, just play it safe and use counter = counter + 1 instead. Clarity is always better than confusion even if it means writing additional lines of code.

To see how the postfix increment operator differs from the prefix increment operator, follow these steps:

1. From within Xcode choose File ➤ New ➤ Playground. Xcode now asks for a playground name.

2. Click in the Name text field and type **DefensePlayground**.

3. Make sure the Platform pop-up menu displays OS X.

4. Click the Next button. Xcode asks where you want to store the playground.

5. Choose a folder to store your project and click the Create button.

6. Edit the playground code as follows:

```
import Cocoa

var counter : Int

counter = 20
print (counter++)
print (++counter)
```

The postfix increment operator and the prefix increment operator can be a shortcut, but could have unintended consequences if used incorrectly. Another shortcut is Swift's if-else statement. Normally it looks like this:

```
if Booleancondition {
    // Do something if true
} else {
    // Do something if false
}
```

However, Swift also offers an if-else shortcut that looks like this:

```
Booleancondition ? Result1 : Result2
```

Unless you're familiar with this shortcut version of the if-else statement, it can be confusing even though it's shorter. Any time code is confusing, there's a risk you'll use it incorrectly. To see how this if-else statement works, follow these steps:

1. Make sure the **DefensePlayground** is loaded into Xcode.

2. Edit the playground code as follows:

```
import Cocoa

var i : Int

i = 1

// Normal if-else statement
if i < 5 {
    print ("Less than 5")
} else {
    print ("Greater than 5")
}
```

```
i = 1

// Ternary operator version of if-else statement
print ((i < 5) ? "Less than 5" : "Greater than 5"
)
```

Notice that both if-else statements work exactly alike as shown in Figure 21-2, but the shortcut version is much harder to understand in exchange for typing less code. Any time code is hard to understand, there's always the risk that you'll use it incorrectly. When in doubt, don't use shortcuts.

```
import Cocoa

var i : Int

i = 1                                                    1

// Normal if-else statement
if i < 5 {
    print ("Less than 5")                        "Less than 5"
} else {
    print ("Greater than 5")
}

i = 1                                                    1

// Ternary operator version of if-else statement
print ((i < 5) ? "Less than 5" : "Greater than 5"    "Less than 5"
)
```

Figure 21-2. *The shortcut version of the if-else statement*

Working with Optional Variables

One of Swift's most powerful features is optional variables. An optional variable can contain a value or nothing at all (identified with a nil value). However, you must use optional variables with care because if you try using them when they contain a nil value, your program could crash.

When working with optional variables, you need to worry about the following:

- Whether the optional variable holds a nil value or not
- Unwrapping an optional variable to retrieve its actual value

Normally you can access the value stored inside an optional by using the exclamation mark, which is called unwrapping an optional. The big problem with unwrapping an optional is if you assume its value is not nil. Suppose you had the following:

```
var test : String?

print (test)
print (test!)
```

Since the "test" optional variable hasn't been assigned a value, its default value is nil. The first print command simply prints nil. However the second print command tries to unwrap the optional, but since its value is nil, this causes an error as shown in Figure 21-3.

```
import Cocoa

var test : String?                                              nil

print (test)                                                    "nil"

print (test!)                                                   ① error
    ① Execution was interrupted, reason: EXC_BAD_INSTRUCTION (code=EXC_I3...
```

Figure 21-3. Unwrapping an optional that has a nil value causes an error

When working with optionals, always test to see if they're nil before you try using them. One way to test for a nil value is to simply test if the optional is equal to nil such as:

```
import Cocoa

var test : String?

if test == nil {
    print ("Nil value")
} else {
    print (test!)
}
```

In this example, the if-else statement first checks if the "test" optional is equal to nil. If so, then it prints "Nil value." If not, then it can safely unwrap the optional using the exclamation mark.

Another way to check for a nil value is to assign a constant to an optional, which is known as optional binding. Instead of using the optional variable, you assign or bind its value to a constant such as:

```
if let constant = optionalVariable {
    // Optional is not nil
} else {
    // Optional is a nil value
}
```

If you need to test several optional variables, you can list them on a single line like this:

```
if let constant = optionalVariable, constant2 = optionalVariable2 {
    // No optionals are nil
} else {
    // One or more optionals are nil
}
```

If the constant holds a value, then the if-else statement can use the constant value. If the constant does not hold a value (contains nil), then the if-else statement does something else to avoid using a nil value. By using a constant to store the value of an optional variable, you avoid unwrapping an optional variable using the exclamation mark.

Let's see how to use optional binding:

1. Make sure the **DefensePlayground** is loaded into Xcode.

2. Edit the playground code as follows:

    ```
    import Cocoa

    var test : String?
    var final : String?

    if let checkMe = test, let checkMe2 = final {
        print (checkMe)
    } else {
        print ("Nil value in one or both optionals")
    }

    test = "Hello"
    if let checkMe = test, let checkMe2 = final {
        print (checkMe)
    } else {
        print ("Nil value in one or both optionals")
    }

    final = "Bye"
    if let checkMe = test, let checkMe2 = final {
        print (checkMe + " & " + checkMe2)
    } else {
        print ("Nil value in one or both optionals")
    }
    ```

The above code assigns two different optional variable values to two different constants. Only if both constants contain a non-nil value will the first part of the if-else statement run. If one or both constants contain a nil value, then the else part of the if-else statement runs as shown in Figure 21-4. Also notice that none of the code unwraps any optional variable using the exclamation mark.

```
import Cocoa

var test : String?                                        nil
var final : String?                                       nil

if let checkMe = test, let checkMe2 = final {
    print (checkMe)
} else {
    print ("Nil value in one or both optionals")          "Nil value in one or both optionals"
}

test = "Hello"                                            "Hello"
if let checkMe = test, let checkMe2 = final {
    print (checkMe)
} else {
    print ("Nil value in one or both optionals")          "Nil value in one or both optionals"
}

final = "Bye"                                             "Bye"
if let checkMe = test, let checkMe2 = final {
    print (checkMe + " & " + checkMe2)                    "Hello & Bye"
} else {
    print ("Nil value in one or both optionals")
}
```

Figure 21-4. *Using optional binding to assign an optional variable value to a constant*

Working with Optional Chaining

When dealing with optionals, you typically declare an optional variable with a question mark ? such as Int?, String?, Float?, and Double? Besides using common data types, you can declare any type as an optional variable including classes.

To declare an ordinary data type as an optional variable, you just add a question mark to the data type name like this:

```
var myNumber : String?
```

Normally properties in a class hold a common data type such as String, Int, or Double. However, a class property can also hold another class. If you can declare a class as a type, you can also declare a class as an optional variable, too, like this:

```
class Dreamer {
    var candidate: Politician?
}

class Politician {
    var name = ""
}
```

Now if you create an object based on the Dreamer class, you'll wind up with a candidate property that holds an optional variable.

```
let person = Dreamer()
```

The person object is based on the Dreamer class, which means it also holds a property called candidate. However the candidate property is also an optional variable object based on the Politician class. At this point the candidate property has an initial value of nil.

To see how an object can have another object as an optional variable, follow these steps:

1. Make sure the **DefensePlayground** is loaded into Xcode.

2. Edit the playground code as follows:

```
import Cocoa

class Dreamer {
    var candidate: Politician?
}

class Politician {
    var name : String = ""
}

let person = Dreamer()

if let check = person.candidate?.name {
    print ("Name = \(check)")
}
else {
    print ("Nil value here")
}
```

This code fails to create an object from the Politician class, so the candidate property is nil. Because we declared the candidate property as an optional variable, we can use what's called optional chaining to access its name property in the if-else statement as shown in Figure 21-5.

```
import Cocoa

class Dreamer {
    var candidate: Politician?
}

class Politician {
    var name : String = ""
}

let person = Dreamer()                                              {nil}

if let check = person.candidate?.name {
    print ("Name = \(check)")
}
else {
    print ("Nil value here")                                    "Nil value here"
}
```

Figure 21-5. Optional chaining can access an optional variable property of a class

To store a value in the candidate property, we need to create another object like this:

```
person.candidate = Politician ()
```

Then we need to store data in the Politician class's name property. To do this, we need to unwrap the optional variable (the Politician class) to access its name property like this:

```
person.candidate!.name = "Sally"
```

Remember, unwrapping optionals with the exclamation mark should only be done when you're absolutely sure the optional variable contains a value. In this case, we're assigning a value ("Sally") to the optional variable so it's safe to unwrap the optional variable.

Let's see how to modify our previous code to store a value in an optional variable property:

1. Make sure the **DefensePlayground** is loaded into Xcode.

2. Edit the playground code as follows:

    ```
    import Cocoa

    class Dreamer {
        var candidate: Politician?
    }

    class Politician {
        var name : String = ""
    }

    let person = Dreamer()

    if let check = person.candidate?.name {
        print ("Name = \(check)")
    }
    else {
        print ("Nil value here")
    }

    person.candidate = Politician ()
    person.candidate!.name = "Sally"

    if let check = person.candidate?.name {
        print ("Name = \(check)")
    }
    else {
        print ("Nil value here")
    }
    ```

Notice that the candidate optional variable (Politician) is undefined or nil until we specifically store a value in it. As soon as we store a string ("Sally") into the name property, it no longer holds a nil value as shown in Figure 21-6.

```
import Cocoa

class Dreamer {
    var candidate: Politician?
}

class Politician {
    var name : String = ""
}

let person = Dreamer()                              {nil}

if let check = person.candidate?.name {
    print ("Name = \(check)")
}
else {
    print ("Nil value here")                        "Nil value here"
}



person.candidate = Politician ()                    {{{name ""}}}
person.candidate!.name = "Sally"                    {name "Sally"}

if let check = person.candidate?.name {
    print ("Name = \(check)")                        "Name = Sally"
}
else {
    print ("Nil value here")
}
```

Figure 21-6. *You need to unwrap an optional variable to store a value in it*

The key when working with optional variables is to make sure you use the question mark ? and exclamation mark ! symbols correctly. Fortunately if you omit either symbol, Xcode can often prompt you to choose the right symbol as shown in Figure 21-7.

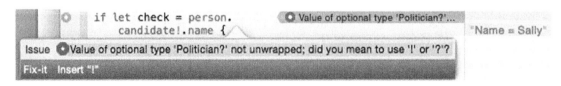

Figure 21-7. *Xcode's editor can prompt you when to use the ? or ! symbols when working with optional variables*

The question mark ? symbol is used to create optional variables or safely access optional variables. The exclamation mark ! symbol is used to unwrap optional variables, so make sure those unwrapped optional variables hold a non-nil value.

In general, any time you see a question mark ? used with optional variables, your code is likely safe when dealing with nil values. However, any time you see an exclamation mark ! with optional variables, make sure the optional variable holds a value because if it holds a nil value, your code may be unsafe and could crash.

Error Handling

Since you can't expect to write bug-free code every time, Swift offers a feature called error handling. The idea behind error handling is to identify and catch likely errors so your program handles them gracefully rather than let the program crash or act unpredictably. To handle errors, you need to go through several steps:

- Define descriptive errors that you want to identify
- Identify one or more functions to detect an error and identify the type of error that occurred
- Handle the error

Defining Errors with enum and ErrorType

In the old days, programs often displayed cryptic error messages filled with hexadecimal numbers and odd symbols. Those type of error messages are generally useless to identify the problem that may have occurred. That's why the first step to handling errors is creating a list of descriptive error types.

The names you give different errors are completely arbitrary, but you should give meaningful names to different types of error messages. To create a list of descriptive error types, you need to create an enum that uses the ErrorType protocol like this:

```
enum enumName : ErrorType {
    case descriptiveError1
    case descriptiveError2
    case descriptiveError3
}
```

Replace enumName with a descriptive name that identifies the type of error you want to identify. Then type a descriptive error name as one word (without spaces) using the case keyword. Your list of possible errors can range from one to as many errors as you wish to describe so you're not limited to a fixed number. If you wanted to create an enum that lists three error types, you might use code like this:

```
enum ageError : ErrorType {
    case negativeAge // Negative numbers
    case unrealAge   // Numbers > 140
    case underAge    // Under 21
}
```

Creating a Function to Identify Errors

Once you've created a list of descriptive error types, you now need to create one or more functions where you think the error might occur. Normally you would define a function like this:

```
func functionName () {
      // Code goes here
}
```

To make a function identify errors, you need to insert the throws keyword like this:

```
func functionName () throws {
      // Code goes here
}
```

If the function returns a value, the "throws" keyword appears before the return data type like this:

```
func functionName () throws -> dataType {
      // Code goes here
}
```

The throws keyword means that the function "throws" the error for some other part of your code to handle. Inside a function with the throws keyword, you need to use one or more guard statements.

A guard statement identifies what's allowed and works similar to an if-else statement. If the guard statement's Boolean condition is true, then nothing happens. However if the guard statement is false, then the guard statement can use the throw keyword to identify a specific type of error like this:

```
guard Booleancondition else {
      throw enumName.descriptiveError
}
```

If you wanted to allow only values greater than 21, you could create a guard statement like this:.

```
guard myAge > 21 else {
      throw ageError.underAge
}
```

This guard statement would do nothing if the Boolean condition (myAge > 21) is true. Otherwise it would throw the ageError.underAge error where "ageError" is the name of the enum that lists different errors to identify and "underAge" is one of the possible errors likely to occur.

The guard statement always defines acceptable behavior (myAge > 21) or else it identifies an error with the throw keyword. A function (identified with the throws keyword) can have one or more guard statements.

Handling the Error

When you've identified one or more functions with the throws keyword where it uses one or more guard statements to identify possible errors, you finally need a way to handle those errors. In Swift you do that using a do-try-catch statement like this:

```
do {
    try callFunctionThatThrows
} catch enumName.descriptiveError {
    // Code to handle the error
}
```

The do-try-catch statement tries to run a function that can identify errors using the throws keyword. If the function doesn't identify any errors with one or more guard statements, then the do-try-catch statement works exactly like a normal function call.

However if the function identifies an error, the do-try-catch statement is where you need to write code to handle that error. How you handle this error can be as simple as printing a message to let you know of a problem or as complicated as running an entirely new set of code just to deal with the problem.

The point is that if you anticipate possible errors and write code to handle those errors, your program will be less likely to crash. If your program does crash, simply find out why (which may not be easy), create a new descriptive error name to identify it, and then create a new catch statement to deal with that error.

Let's see how error handling works:

1. Make sure the **DefensePlayground** is loaded into Xcode.

2. Edit the playground code as follows:

```
import Cocoa

enum ageError : ErrorType {
    case negativeAge // Negative numbers
    case unrealAge   // Numbers > 140
    case underAge    // Under 21
}
```

```
func checkAge(myAge : Int) throws {
    print (myAge)

    guard myAge > 0 else {
        throw ageError.negativeAge
    }

    guard myAge <= 140 else {
        throw ageError.unrealAge
    }

    guard myAge > 21 else {
        throw ageError.underAge
    }

}

var oldAge = -9

do {
    try checkAge (oldAge)
} catch ageError.negativeAge {
    print ("An age can't be a negative number")
} catch ageError.unrealAge {
    print ("An age can't be greater than 140")
} catch ageError.underAge {
    print ("Sorry, you have to be 21 or older")
}

print (oldAge)
```

Notice how a negative number gets identified and handled with a simple message as shown in Figure 21-8.

```
import Cocoa

enum ageError : ErrorType {
    case negativeAge // Negative numbers
    case unrealAge   // Numbers > 140
    case underAge    // Under 21
}

func checkAge(myAge : Int) throws {
    print (myAge)                                          "-9\n"

    guard myAge > 0 else {
        throw ageError.negativeAge
    }

    guard myAge <= 140 else {
        throw ageError.unrealAge
    }

    guard myAge > 21 else {
        throw ageError.underAge
    }

}

var oldAge = -9                                            -9

do {
    try checkAge (oldAge)
} catch ageError.negativeAge {
    print ("An age can't be a negative number")            "An age can't be a negative number\n"
} catch ageError.unrealAge {
    print ("An age can't be greater than 140")
} catch ageError.underAge {
    print ("Sorry, you have to be 21 or older")
}

print (oldAge)                                            "-9\n"
```

Figure 21-8. Error handling involves an enum, a function with guard statements, and a do-try-catch statement

Change the value of the oldAge variable to 250 to see how the do-try-catch statement catches that number as higher than 140, which makes it unrealistic. Change the value of the oldAge variable to 15 to see how the do-try-catch statement identifies an age under 21.

To use error handling in your programs, you must first identify possible problems, then you need to decide how to handle these problems. Error handling can only identify errors you already know about, but it can make your programs less fragile when confronted with common types of problems your program may face.

Summary

No matter how talented, skilled, or educated you may be as a programmer, you will make mistakes occasionally. Sometimes those mistakes will be simple errors you can easily correct, but sometimes you'll make mistakes that cause a variety of subtle problems that will challenge and frustrate you to find and fix. That's just the nature of programming.

However, any problems you accidentally create are also problems you can learn to discover and fix. Once you learn how one mistake works, you'll likely remember how to fix those types of mistakes in the future if you or someone else makes them again. That frees you up to make new mistakes you'll likely never have experience facing again.

The best way to reduce errors in your program is to examine your code carefully and assume nothing will go right. Then look for every possible way to make sure it can't go wrong. The more you code with a defensive mindset, the more likely you'll prevent problems before they occur.

Programming is more of an art than a science, so learn the best ways that work for you to reduce introducing errors in your programs. When experimenting with new code, it's usually safer to test it out in a Swift playground or in a simple program separate from your real program.

That way you can isolate and test your code safely. When it works, then you can copy and paste it into your program.

Errors are a way of life in the world of programming. Ideally you want to spend more time writing code and less time debugging it.

Simplifying User Interface Design

Designing a user interface can be challenging. Not only do you need to design a user interface that's easy to use, but you also need to design an adaptive user interface that can respond to any changes the user might make to a window's size. If the user shrinks a window, your user interface must shrink accordingly without cutting any items off. If the user enlarges a window, your user interface must expand accordingly to maintain a consistent appearance.

To help create adaptive user interfaces, Xcode provides constraints that fix the edges of various user interface items to a window's edge or the edge of other user interface items. In this chapter, you'll learn more about constraints and storyboards to help make user interface design easier than ever before.

Using Stack View

If your user interface contains a handful of items such as a text field, a button, and a label, it's fairly straightforward to place constraints on these items so they stay in the correct place. However, if your user interface contains multiple items, then it can get messy to place so many constraints on each item. Change one constraint and your entire user interface can fail to adapt properly, which often means wasting time trying to get your multiple constraints working. Figure 22-1 shows how messy multiple constraints can look on a crowded user interface.

Figure 22-1. Multiple constraints make it hard to correctly lay out a user interface

To solve this problem, Xcode offers a feature called Stack View. The idea behind stack view is that groups of user interface items often need to stay together. Rather than set constraints for each item individually, you group them together in a stack view, then set constraints for that single stack view.

To see how to create and use a stack view, follow these steps:

1. From within Xcode choose File ➤ New ➤ Project.

2. Click Application under the OS X category.

3. Click Cocoa Application and click the Next button. Xcode now asks for a product name.

4. Click in the Product Name text field and type **StackViewProgram**.

5. Make sure the Language pop-up menu displays Swift and that no check boxes are selected.

6. Click the Next button. Xcode asks where you want to store the project.

7. Choose a folder to store your project and click the Create button.

8. Click the MainMenu.xib file in the Project Navigator.

9. Click on the window icon in the pane that appears to the right of the Project Navigator pane. Your program's user interface appears.

10. Choose View ➤ Utilities ➤ Show Object Library. The Object Library appears in the bottom right corner of the Xcode window.

11. Drag three check boxes on to the user interface window so they appear stacked on top of each other. Notice that unless you precisely align each check box, they won't appear organized.

12. Drag the mouse to select all three check boxes as shown in Figure 22-2. (Another way to select multiple items is to hold down the Shift key and click on each item you want to select.)

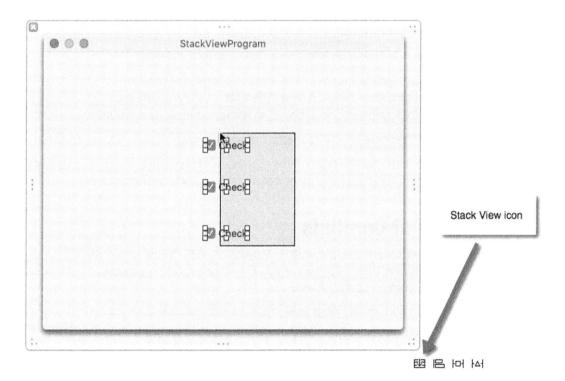

Stack View icon

Figure 22-2. Dragging is a fast way to select multiple items

13. Choose Editor ➤ Embed In ➤ Stack View (or click the Stack View icon in the bottom right corner of the middle Xcode pane). Xcode groups your selected items inside a single stack view.

14. Move the mouse pointer over the stack view of three check boxes, hold down the Control key, and drag the mouse toward the right edge of the window.

15. Release the Control key and the mouse button. A pop-up window appears.

16. Choose Trailing Space to Container. Xcode displays the constraint for the entire stack view.

17. Move the mouse pointer over the stack view of three check boxes, hold down the Control key, and drag the mouse toward the bottom edge of the window.

18. Release the Control key and the mouse button. A pop-up window appears.

19. Choose Bottom Space to Container. Xcode displays the constraint for the entire stack view.

20. Choose Product ➤ Run. The program's user interface appears.

21. Drag the bottom right corner of the window to shrink and enlarge the window. Notice that as you change the width and height of the window, the stack of three check boxes all move together as a group.

22. Choose StackViewProgram ➤ Quit StackViewProgram.

By using a stack view, you can keep grouped items together and only use one set of constraints for the entire group rather than exhaustively place constraints on each item individually.

Fixing Constraint Conflicts

Ideally, constraints should keep items a specific distance from the edge of the window or the edge of another user interface item. However if you shrink or expand a window, it's possible for constraints to create unexpected problems.

Let's see how setting two constraints on a user interface item can create a problem:

1. Make sure the StackViewProgram project is loaded in Xcode.

2. Click on the MainMenu.xib file in the Project Navigator pane.

3. Click on the window icon in the pane that appears to the right of the Project Navigator pane. Your program's user interface appears.

4. Choose Edit ➤ Select All (or press Command+A). Xcode selects your stack view that's currently on the user interface window.

5. Press the Delete key on your keyboard, or choose Edit ➤ Delete to delete all user interface items from the window.

6. Choose View ➤ Utilities ➤ Show Object Library.

7. Drag a single text field in the middle of the user interface window. (Don't worry about the exact positioning.)

8. Move the mouse pointer over the text field, hold down the Control key, and drag the mouse to the right edge of the window.

9. Release the Control key and the mouse. A pop-up window appears.

10. Choose Trailing Space to Container. Xcode creates a constraint from the right edge of the text field to the right edge of the window.

11. Move the mouse pointer over the text field, hold down the Control key, and drag the mouse to the left edge of the window.

12. Release the Control key and the mouse. A pop-up window appears.

13. Choose Leading Space to Container. Xcode creates a constraint from the left edge of the text field to the left edge of the window.

14. Choose Product ➤ Run. The user interface window appears.

15. Move the mouse pointer over the right edge of the window and expand the window width by dragging the mouse to the right. Notice that the text field expands to the right.

16. Move the mouse pointer over the right edge of the window and shrink the window width by dragging the mouse to the left. Notice that the text field shrinks. If you keep shrinking the window width, the text field eventually disappears altogether, which is probably not what you want.

17. Choose StackViewProgram ➤ Quit StackViewProgram.

Right now we have two constraints that keep the text field a fixed distance from the two window edges, but they do nothing to keep the text field from disappearing if the window shrinks too much. One way to fix this is to create a compression constraint.

A compression constraint keeps a user interface item from shrinking or expanding too much. To create a compression constraint, you hold down the Control key and drag the mouse within the boundaries of that user interface element.

1. Make sure the StackViewProgram project is loaded in Xcode.

2. Click on the MainMenu.xib file in the Project Navigator pane.

3. Move the mouse pointer over the text field.

4. Hold down the Control key and drag the mouse to the left or right, keeping the mouse pointer within the boundary of the text field.

5. Release the Control key and the mouse. A pop-up menu appears as shown in Figure 22-3.

Figure 22-3. Defining a compression constraint

6. Choose Width. Xcode displays a compression constraint underneath the text field as shown in Figure 22-4.

Compression constraint

Figure 22-4. A compression constraint appears underneath a user interface item

7. Choose Product ➤ Run. The user interface window appears.

8. Move the mouse pointer over the right edge of the window and try dragging the window to expand or shrink its width. Notice that you can't do that because of the compression constraint.

9. Choose StackViewProgram ➤ Quit StackViewProgram.

The compression constraint tells Xcode to keep the text field a fixed width, and the left and right constraints tell Xcode to keep the text field a fixed distance from the left and right edges of the window. To satisfy all of these constraints, the window can no longer be resized in width.

What if we want to keep the text field width no smaller than its current width, but allow the window to resize? One solution is to use constraint priorities.

Priorities define which constraints must be satisfied first. Each time you create a constraint, Xcode gives it a priority of 1000, which is the highest priority possible. If you give a constraint a lower priority, then that constraint will allow constraints with higher priorities to take precedence. Let's see how changing priorities on constraints works:

1. Make sure the StackViewProgram project is loaded in Xcode.

2. Click on the MainMenu.xib file in the Project Navigator pane.

3. Click on the text field to select it.

4. Chose View ➤ Utilities ➤ Show Size Inspector. The Size Inspector pane appears in the upper right corner of the Xcode window.

5. Click Edit to the right of the Width constraint. A pop-up window appears as shown in Figure 22-5.

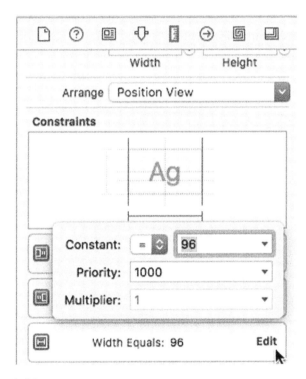

Figure 22-5. Editing a constraint

6. Click on the downward-pointing arrow to the right of the Priority text field. A pop-up menu appears as shown in Figure 22-6.

Figure 22-6. *Changing the priority of a constraint*

7. Choose Low (250). Notice that Xcode now displays the width constraint as a dotted line to visually show you that its priority is lower than the constraints with a solid line as shown in Figure 22-7.

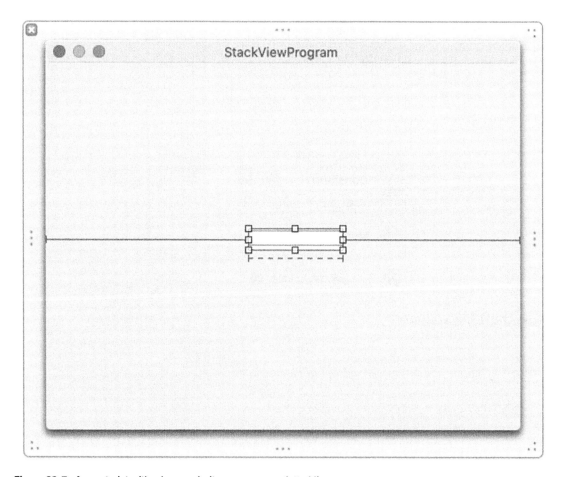

Figure 22-7. *A constraint with a lower priority appears as a dotted line*

8. Choose Product ➤ Run. The user interface window appears.

9. Move the mouse pointer over the right edge of the window and try dragging the window to expand or shrink its width. Notice that if you shrink the window width, the text field disappears again.

10. Choose StackViewProgram ➤ Quit StackViewProgram.

Changing constraint priorities may not always give you the result you want so you may need to change how the constraint works. Most constraints define a fixed value that the constraint must satisfy. For more flexibility, you can also change this equal constraint to a greater than or equal or a less than or equal constraint.

1. Make sure the StackViewProgram project is loaded in Xcode.

2. Click on the MainMenu.xib file in the Project Navigator pane.

3. Click on the text field to select it.

4. Chose View ➤ Utilities ➤ Show Size Inspector. The Size Inspector pane appears in the upper right corner of the Xcode window.

5. Click Edit to the right of the Width constraint. A pop-up window appears (see Figure 22-5).

6. Click on the pop-up menu to the right of the Constant label. A pop-up menu appears as shown in Figure 22-8.

Figure 22-8. Changing an equal sign to a greater than or equal to or less than or equal to sign

7. Choose the Greater than or equal to sign.

8. Click on the downward-pointing arrow to the right of the Priority text field so a menu appears, and choose High (750).

9. Choose Product ➤ Run. Notice that if you shrink the width of the window, the compression constraint will only shrink the text field a limited distance before stopping the text field from disappearing altogether. If you expand the width of the window, the text field expands.

10. Choose StackViewProgram ➤ Quit StackViewProgram.

When your user interface doesn't adapt correctly, try one or more of the following options:

- Add or delete constraints

- Change constraint priorities

- Change constraints from equaling a fixed value to greater than or equal or less than or equal relationships

Each user interface problem with adapting to window resizing can be different, so solving that problem could be as simple as modifying one constraint or as complicated as modifying multiple constraints. If groups of user interface items move together, group them in a stack view for simplicity.

Often times you may need to experiment with modifying different constraints to see how they work in various combinations. Just be aware of your options for modifying constraints, and you'll eventually find the best solution for your particular user interface.

Working with Storyboard References

The two ways to design user interfaces involve .xib files and .storyboard files. Storyboard files represent scenes (windows) connected by segues. For a simple program that consists of a handful of windows, a storyboard may be fine, but if your program's user interface consists of many windows, then a storyboard can get clumsy and cluttered with multiple segues linking scenes.

The more scenes your user interface needs, the more complicated your storyboard can be to understand as shown in Figure 22-9.

Figure 22-9. Large storyboards can look cluttered and hard to understand

To avoid storing your entire user interface in a single, cluttered storyboard, Xcode lets you divide a storyboard into parts using storyboard references. A storyboard reference lets you store scenes and segues in a separate storyboard file.

A storyboard reference replaces one or more scenes and segues with a storyboard reference box as shown in Figure 22-10. You can have multiple storyboard reference boxes where each one represents a separate storyboard file.

Figure 22-10. Storyboard references represent multiple scenes and segues stored in another storyboard file

You can create a storyboard reference in two ways:

- Select the storyboard scenes you want to separate from a storyboard file and choose Editor ➤ Refactor to Storyboard

- Drag a Storyboard Reference from the Object Library and connect it to an existing scene in a storyboard

To see how to use storyboard references, follow these steps:

1. From within Xcode choose File ➤ New ➤ Project.

2. Click Application under the OS X category.

3. Click Cocoa Application and click the Next button. Xcode now asks for a product name.

4. Click in the Product Name text field and type **StoryProgram**.

5. Make sure the Language pop-up menu displays Swift and that Use Storyboards check box is selected.

Note   If you fail to select the Use Storyboards check box, Xcode will store your user interface in a .xib file instead of a .storyboard file.

6. Click the Next button. Xcode asks where you want to store the project.

7. Choose a folder to store your project and click the Create button.

8. Click the Main.storyboard file in the Project Navigator. Your program's user interface appears displaying a single view.

9. Choose View ➤ Utilities ➤ Show Object Library.

10. Drag a Push Button and place it on the View Controller window.

11. Drag a Tab View Controller into your storyboard to the right of the View Controller window that contains the push button.

12. Move the mouse pointer over the push button, hold down the Control key, and drag the mouse over the Tab View Controller as shown in Figure 22-11.

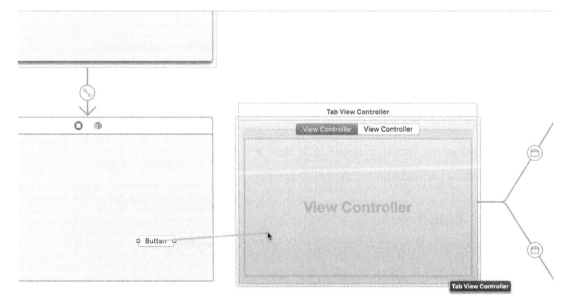

Figure 22-11. Control-dragging creates a segue between view controllers

13. Release the Control key and the mouse. A pop-up window appears.

14. Choose show. Xcode draws a segue between the two view controllers.

15. Click on the Tab View Controller to select it.

16. Choose Editor ➤ Refactor to Storyboard. A sheet drops down to ask the name you want to give your storyboard as shown in Figure 22-12.

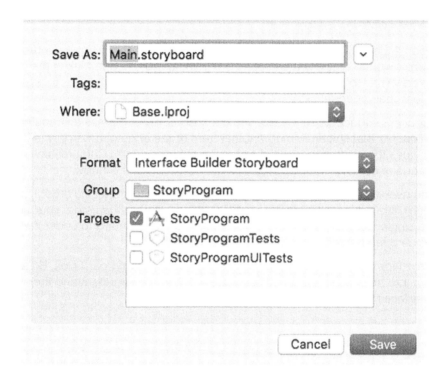

Figure 22-12. Control-dragging creates a segue between view controllers

17. Click in the Save As text field and type Tab.storyboard

18. Click the Save button. Xcode saves the Tab View Controller in a Tab.storyboard file and displays a storyboard reference box in the Main.storyboard file.

19. Click on the Tab.storyboard file in the Project Navigator pane. Xcode shows the Tab View Controller.

Summary

Every program's user interface is crucial to letting users control a program. It doesn't matter how powerful your program may be if the user interface frustrates users and discourages them from using the program.

Since every user interface needs to respond to changes the user might make to the size of a window, stack views let you group related items together and apply constraints on that entire stack view. Without grouping related items together, you would have to apply constraints to each item individually, which could get messy and be difficult to fix if they don't respond the way you expect.

If you have constraint conflicts, you can modify priorities of each constraint and/or modify how a constraint works. When you create a constraint initially, Xcode makes the constraint equal to a fixed value. To provide flexibility, you can change this equal sign to a greater than or equal, or less than or equal sign.

To keep your user interface items visible, you can also apply compression constraints. Unlike ordinary constraints that link an item to another item or the edge of a window, a compression constraint defines the width and/or height of a user interface item. Compression constraints keep user interface items from disappearing if the user resizes a window.

For designing user interfaces that display windows or views in a specific order, you might find storyboard files easier to use than multiple .xib files. Rather than store your entire user interface in a single storyboard file (which can get cluttered and hard to understand), you can create storyboard references.

A storyboard reference divides a user interface into multiple storyboard files. By separating a user interface into multiple storyboard files, you can design and understand the structure of your user interface much easier.

Chapter **23**

Debugging Your Programs

In the professional world of software, you'll actually spend more time modifying existing programs than you ever will creating new ones. When writing new programs or editing existing ones, it doesn't matter how much experience or education you might have because even the best programmers can make mistakes. In fact, you can expect that you will make mistakes no matter how careful you may be. Once you accept this inevitable fact of programming, you can learn how to find and fix your mistakes.

In the world of computers, mistakes are commonly called "bugs," which gets its name from an early computer that used physical switches to work. One day the computer failed and when technicians opened the computer, they found that a moth had been crushed within a switch, preventing the switch from closing. From that point on, programming errors have been called bugs and fixing computer problems has been known as debugging.

Three common types of computer bugs are:

- Syntax errors – Occurs when you misspell something such as a keyword, variable name, function name, or class name, or use a symbol incorrectly.

- Logic errors – Occurs when you use commands correctly, but the logic of your code doesn't do what you intended.

- Runtime errors – Occurs when a program encounters unexpected situations such as the user entering invalid data or when another program somehow interferes with your program unexpectantly.

Syntax errors are the easiest to find and fix because they're merely misspellings of variable names that you created or misspelling of Swift commands that Xcode can help you identify. If you type a Swift keyword such as "var" or "let," Xcode displays that keyword in pink (or whatever color you specify for displaying keywords in the Xcode editor).

Now if you type a Swift keyword and it doesn't appear in its usual identifying color, then you know you probably typed it wrong somehow. By coloring your code, Xcode's editor helps you visually identify common misspellings or typos.

Besides using color, the Xcode editor provides a second way to help you avoid mistakes when you need to type the name of a method or class defined in the Cocoa framework. As soon as Xcode recognizes that you might be typing something from the Cocoa framework, it displays a pop-up menu of possible options. Now instead of typing the entire command yourself, you can simply click on your choice in the pop-up menu and press the Tab key one or more times to let Xcode type your chosen command correctly as shown in Figure 23-1.

Figure 23-1. Xcode displays a menu of possible commands that you might want to use

Syntax errors often keep your program from running at all. When a syntax error keeps your program from running, Xcode can usually identify the line (or the nearby area) of your program where the misspelled commands appears so you can fix it as shown in Figure 23-2.

Figure 23-2. Syntax errors often keep a program from running, which allows Xcode to identify the syntax error

Logic errors are much harder to find and detect than syntax errors. Xcode can identify syntax errors because it recognizes the differences between a properly spelled Swift keyword (such as "var") compared to a similar misspelled Swift keyword (such as "varr" instead of "var").

However, logic errors occur when you use Swift code correctly, but it doesn't do what you intended it to do. Since your code is actually valid, Xcode has no way of knowing that it's not working the way you intended. As a result, logic errors can be difficult to debug because you think you wrote your code correctly but you (obviously) did not.

How do you find a mistake in code that you thought you wrote correctly? Finding your mistake can often involve starting from the beginning of your program and exhaustively searching each line all the way until the end. (Of course there are faster ways than searching your entire program, line by line, which you'll learn about later in this chapter.)

Finally, the hardest errors to find and debug are runtime errors. Syntax errors usually keep your program from running so if your program actually runs, you can assume that you have eliminated most, if not all, syntax errors in your code.

Logic errors can be tougher to find, but they're predictable. For example, if your program asks the user for a password but fails to give the user access even though the user types a correct password, you know you have a logic error. Each time you run your program, you can reliably predict when the logic error will occur.

Runtime errors are more insidious because they don't always occur predictably. For example, your program may run perfectly well on your computer, but the moment you run the same program on an identical computer, the program may fail. That's because conditions between two different computers will never be exactly the same.

As a result, the same program can run fine on one computer but fail on the exact same type of computer somewhere else. The problem is that unexpected, outside circumstances can affect your program's behavior. For example, your program may run just fine until the user presses a number key on the numeric keypad instead of the number key at the top of the alphanumeric keys.

Even though the user may be typing the exact same number (such as 5), the program may treat the 5 key above the R and T keys as a completely different key as the 5 key on the numeric keypad. As subtle as that may be, it could be enough to cause a program to fail or crash.

Because runtime errors can't always be duplicated, they can be frustrating to find and even harder to fix since you can't always examine every possible condition your program might face when running on other computers. Some programs have been known to work perfectly – except if the user accidentally presses two keys at the same time. Other programs work just fine – until the user happens to save a file at the exact moment that another program tries to receive e-mail over the Internet.

Usually you can eliminate most syntax errors and find and fix most logic errors. However, it may not be possible to find and completely eliminate all runtime errors in a program. The best way to avoid spending time hunting for bugs is to strive to write code and test it carefully to make sure it's as error-free as possible.

Simple Debugging Techniques

When your program isn't working, you often have no idea what could be wrong. While you could tediously examine your code from beginning to end, it's often faster to simply guess where the mistake might be.

Once you have a rough idea what part of your program might be causing the problem, you have two choices. First, you can delete the suspicious code and run your program again. If the problem magically goes away, then you'll know that the code you deleted was likely the culprit.

However if your program still doesn't work, you have to retype your deleted code back into your program. A simpler solution might be to cut and paste code out of Xcode and store it in a text editor such as the TextEdit program that comes with every Macintosh, but this can be tedious.

That's why a second solution is to just temporarily hide code that you suspect might be causing a problem. Then if the problem persists, you can simply unhide that code and make it visible again. To do this in Xcode, you just need to turn your code into comments.

Remember, comments are text that Xcode completely ignores. You can create comments in three ways:

- Add the // symbols at the beginning of each line that you want to convert into a comment. This method lets you convert a single line into a comment.

- Add the /* symbols at the beginning of code and add the */ at the end of code you want to convert into a comment. This method lets you convert one or more lines into a comment.

- Select the lines of code you want to turn into a comment and choose Editor ➤ Structure ➤ Comment Selection (or press Command + /). This method lets you convert one or more lines into a comment by placing the // symbols at the beginning of each line of code you selected.

> **Note**   Xcode color codes comments in green (or whatever color you may have defined to identify comments). After creating a comment, make sure Xcode color codes it properly to ensure you have created a comment. If Xcode fails to recognize your comments, it will treat your text as a valid Swift command, which will likely keep your program from running properly.

By turning code into comments, you essentially hide that code from Xcode. Now if you want to turn that comment back into code again, you just remove the // or /* and */ symbols that defines your commented out code.

If you commented out code by choosing Editor ➤ Structure ➤ Comment Selection (or pressing Command + /), just choose Editor ➤ Structure ➤ Uncomment Selection (or press Command + / again) to convert that commented code back to working code once more.

Besides turning your code into comments to temporarily hide it, a second simple debugging technique is to use the print command. The idea is to put the print command in your code to print out the values of a variable.

By doing this, you can see what values one or more variables may contain. Putting multiple print commands throughout your program gives you a chance to make sure your program is running correctly.

To see how using the print command along with commenting out code can work to help you debug a program, follow these steps

1. From within Xcode choose File ➤ New ➤ Project.

2. Click Application under the OS X category.

3. Click Cocoa Application and click the Next button. Xcode now asks for a product name.

4. Click in the Product Name text field and type **DebugProgram**.

5. Make sure the Language pop-up menu displays Swift and that no check boxes are selected.

6. Click the Next button. Xcode asks where you want to store the project.

7. Choose a folder to store your project and click the Create button.

8. Click the AppDelegate.swift file in the Project Navigator. The contents of the AppDelegate.swift file appears.

9. Edit the applicationDidFinishLaunching method as follows:

```
func applicationDidFinishLaunching(aNotification: NSNotification) {
    var myMessage = "Temperature in Celsius:"
    let temp = 100.0
    print (myMessage + "\(temp)")
    myMessage = "Temperature in Fahrenheit:"
    print (myMessage + "\(C2F(temp))")
}
```

10. Directly above this function, add the following code:

```
func C2F (tempC : Double) -> Double {
    var tempF : Double
    tempF = tempC + 32 * 9/5
    return tempF
}
```

11. Choose Product ➤ Run. Your program's user interface appears (which is blank).

12. Choose DebugProgram ➤ Quit DebugProgram. Xcode appears. If you look in the bottom of the Xcode window in the Debug Area, you can see what your two print commands printed, which is "Temperature in Celsius: 100.0" and "Temperature in Fahrenheit: 157.6" as shown in Figure 23-3.

Figure 23-3. The print command displays text in the Debug Area of the Xcode window

To view or hide the Debug Area, you have three options:

- Click the View/Hide Debug Area icon in the upper right corner of the Xcode window.

- Choose View ➤ Debug Area ➤ Show/Hide Debug Area.

- Press Shift+Command+Y.

By peeking in the Debug Area, we can see what the print commands have displayed. If you know anything about temperatures in Fahrenheit and Celsius, you know that the boiling point in Celsius is 100 degrees and the boiling point in Fahrenheit is 212 degrees. Yet our temperature conversion program calculates that 100 degrees Celsius is equal to 157.6 degrees in Fahrenheit, which means the Fahrenheit temperature should be 212 instead of 157.6. Obviously something is wrong, so let's use the print command and comments to help debug the problem.

1. Make sure the DebugProgram project is loaded in Xcode.

2. Click the AppDelegate.swift file in the Project Navigator pane.

3. Edit the C2F function by typing the // symbols to the left of the * symbol (multiplication sign) as follows:

```
func C2F (tempC : Double) -> Double {
    var tempF : Double
    tempF = tempC + 32 //* 9/5
    return tempF
}
```

This comment will let us check if the tempC parameter is properly coming into the C2F function and getting stored in the tempF variable.

4. Add a "print (tempC)" command above the return statement as follows:

```
func C2F (tempC : Double) -> Double {
    var tempF : Double
    tempF = tempC + 32 //* 9/5
    print (tempF)
    return tempF
}
```

5. Choose Product ➤ Run. The blank user interface of your program appears.

6. Choose DebugProgram ➤ Quit DebugProgram. Xcode appears again, displaying the result in the Debug Area, which prints:

Temperature in Celsius: 100.0 132.0 Temperature in Fahrenheit: 132.0

By commenting out the calculation part of the code and using the "print (tempF)" command, we can see that the C2F function is storing 100.0 correctly in the tempC variable and adding 32 to this value before storing it in the tempF variable. Because we commented out the calculation part of the code, we can assume that the error must be in our commented out portion of the code.

Although the formula might look correct, the error occurs because of the way Swift (and most programming languages) calculate formulas. First, they start from left to right. Second, they calculate certain operations such as multiplication before addition.

The error occurs because our conversion formula first multiples 32 by 9 (288), and then divides the result (288) by 5 to get 57.6. Finally, it adds 57.6 to 100.0 to get the incorrect result of 157.6. What it should really be doing is multiplying 9/5 by the temperature in Celsius and then adding 32 to the result.

7. Modify the C2F function as follows:

```
func C2F (tempC : Double) -> Double {
    var tempF : Double
    tempF = tempC * (9/5) + 32
    print (tempF)
    return tempF
}
```

8. Choose Product ➤ Run. Your program's blank user interface appears.

9. Choose DebugProgram ➤ Quit DebugProgram. Xcode appears again.

10. Look in the Debug Area and you'll see that the program now correctly converts 100 degrees Celsius to 212 degrees Fahrenheit.

For simple debugging, turning code temporarily into comments and using the print command can work, but it's fairly clumsy to keep adding and removing comment symbols and print commands. A much better solution is to use breakpoints and variable watching, which essentially duplicates using comments and print commands.

Using the Xcode Debugger

While comments and the print command can help you isolate problems in your code, they can be clumsy to use. The print command can be especially tedious since you have to type it into your code and then remember to remove it later when you're ready to ship your program.

Although leaving one or more print commands buried in your program won't likely hurt your program's performance, it's poor programming practice to leave code in your program that no longer serves any purpose.

As an alternative to typing the print command throughout your program, Xcode offers a more convenient alternative using the Xcode debugger. The debugger gives you two ways to hunt out and identify bugs in your program:

- Breakpoints
- Variable watching

Using Breakpoints

Breakpoints let you identify a specific line in your code where you want your program to stop. Once your program stops, you can step through your code, line by line. As you do so, you can also peek at the contents of one or more variables to check if the variables are holding the right values.

For example, if your program converts Celsius to Fahrenheit, but somehow converts 100 degrees Celsius into -41259 degrees Fahrenheit, you know your code isn't working right. By inserting breakpoints in your code and examining the values of your variables at each breakpoint, you can identify where your code calculates its values. The moment you spot the line where it miscalculates a value, you know the exact area of your program that you need to fix.

You can set a breakpoint by doing one of the following:

- Clicking to the left of the code where you want to set the breakpoint

- Moving the cursor to a line where you want to set the breakpoint and pressing Command + \

- Moving the cursor to a line where you want to set the breakpoint and choosing Debug ➤ Breakpoints ➤ Add Breakpoint at Current Line

Stepping Through Code

Once a breakpoint has stopped your program from running, you can step through your code line by line using the Step command. Xcode offers a variety of different Step commands but the three most common are:

- Step Over
- Step Into
- Step Out

The Step Over command examines the next line of code, treating function or method calls as a single line of code.

The Step Into command works exactly like the Step Over command until it highlights a function or method call. Then it jumps to the first line of code in that function or method.

The Step Out command is used to prematurely exit out of a function or method that you entered using the Step Into command. The Step Out command returns to the line of code where a function or method was called.

All three Step commands are used after a program temporarily stops at a breakpoint. By using a Step command, you can examine your code, line by line, and see how values stored in different variables may change.

Such variable watching lets you examine the contents of one or more variables to verify if it's holding the correct data. The moment you spot a variable holding incorrect data, you can zero in on the line of code that's creating that error.

The best part about breakpoints is that you can easily add and remove them since they don't modify your code at all, unlike comments and multiple print commands. Xcode can remove all breakpoints for you automatically so you don't have to hunt through your code to remove them one by one.

To see how to use breakpoints, step commands, and variable watching, follow these steps:

1. Make sure the DebugProgram project is loaded in Xcode.

2. Click the AppDelegate.swift file in the Project Navigator pane.

3. Modify the C2F function as follows:

```
func C2F (tempC : Double) -> Double {
    var tempF : Double
    tempF = tempC + 32 * 9/5
    return tempF
}
```

4. Move the cursor anywhere inside the following line inside the applicationDidFinishLaunching function:

```
var myMessage = "Temperature in Celsius:"
```

5. Choose Debug ➤ Breakpoints ➤ Add Breakpoint at Current Line.
    Xcode displays a breakpoint as a blue arrow as shown in Figure 23-4.

Breakpoint

```
func applicationDidFinishLaunching(aNotification: NSNotification) {
    // Insert code here to initialize your application
    var myMessage = "Temperature in Celsius:"
    let temp = 100.0
    print (myMessage + "\(temp)")
    myMessage = "Temperature in Fahrenheit:"
    print (myMessage + "\(C2F(temp))")
}

func applicationWillTerminate(aNotification: NSNotification) {
    // Insert code here to tear down your application
}
```

Figure 23-4. A breakpoint appears to the left of your Swift code

6. Choose Product ➤ Run. Notice that Xcode highlights the line where
    your breakpoint appears as shown in Figure 23-5. Notice that initially
    the value of the myMessage variable is not defined.

Figure 23-5. A breakpoint halts program execution so you can examine its current state

7. Choose Debug ➤ Step Over (or press F6). Xcode highlights the next line under your breakpoint. The information in the left-hand side of the Debug Area displays the current values that your program is using as shown in Figure 23-6. Notice that after the breakpoint code runs, the value of the myMessage variable is now defined as the string "Temperature in Celsius:".

```
func applicationDidFinishLaunching(aNotification: NSNotification) {
    // Insert code here to initialize your application
    var myMessage = "Temperature in Celsius:"
    let temp = 100.0                                                         Thread 1: step over
    print (myMessage + "\(temp)")
    myMessage = "Temperature in Fahrenheit:"
    print (myMessage + "\(C2F(temp))")
}

func applicationWillTerminate(aNotification: NSNotification) {
    // Insert code here to tear down your application
}
}
```

```
0 StackViewProgram.AppDelegate.applicationDidFinishLaunchin...StackViewProgram.AppDelegate)(ObjectiveC.NSNotification) -> ()
▶ aNotification = (NSNotification) "NSApplicationDidFinishLaunchingNotification"    (lldb)
▶ self = (StackViewProgram.AppDelegate) 0x000060000002fba0
▶ myMessage = (String) "Temperature in Celsius:"
   temp = (Double) 0

Auto ◇                                                                    All Output ◇
```

Figure 23-6. By watching how variables change, you can see how each line of code affects each variable

8. Choose Debug ➤ Step Over (or press F6) several more times until Xcode highlights the following line:

```
print (myMessage + "\(C2F(temp))")
```

9. Choose Debug ➤ Step Into (or press F7). Xcode now highlights the first line of code in the C2F function as shown in Figure 23-7.

```
func C2F (tempC : Double) -> Double {
    var tempF : Double
    tempF = tempC + 32 * 9/5                                                 Thread 1: step in
    return tempF
}

func applicationDidFinishLaunching(aNotification: NSNotification) {
    // Insert code here to initialize your application
    var myMessage = "Temperature in Celsius:"
    let temp = 100.0
    print (myMessage + "\(temp)")
    myMessage = "Temperature in Fahrenheit:"
    print (myMessage + "\(C2F(temp))")
}

func applicationWillTerminate(aNotification: NSNotification) {
    // Insert code here to tear down your application
}
}
```

```
Stack...rogram ▶ Thread 1 ▶ 0 StackViewProgram.AppDelegate.C2F (StackViewProgram.AppDelegate)(Swift.Double) -> Swift.Double
   tempC = (Double) 100                              Temperature in Celsius:100.0
▶ self = (StackViewProgram.AppDelegate) 0x00006080000271a0    (lldb)
   tempF = (Double) 0

Auto ◇                                                                    All Output ◇
```

Figure 23-7. The Step Into command lets you step through the code stored in a function or method

10. Choose Debug ➤ Step Out (or press F8). Xcode now highlights the line that called the C2F function.

11. Choose Debug ➤ Continue to continue running the program until the next breakpoint. In this program there's only one breakpoint so the program displays its empty user interface.

12. Choose DebugProgram ➤ Quit DebugProgram. The Xcode window appears again.

13. Debug ➤ Deactivate Breakpoints. Xcode dims the breakpoint. Xcode will ignore deactivated breakpoints.

14. Choose Product ➤ Run. Notice that because you deactivated the breakpoint, Xcode ignores it and runs your program by displaying its empty user interface.

15. Choose DebugProgram ➤ Quit DebugProgram. The Xcode window appears again.

Managing Breakpoints

There's no limit to the number of breakpoints you can put in a program so feel free to place as many as you need to help you track down an error. Of course if you place breakpoints in a program, you may lose track of how many breakpoints you've set and where they might be set. To help you manage your breakpoints, Xcode offers a Breakpoint Navigator.

You can open the Breakpoint Navigator in one of three ways:

▪ Choose View ➤ Navigators ➤ Show Breakpoint Navigator

▪ Press Command+7

▪ Click the Show Breakpoint Navigator icon in the Navigator pane

The Breakpoint Navigator lists all the breakpoints set in your program, identifies the files the breakpoints are in, and the line number of each breakpoint as shown in Figure 23-8.

Figure 23-8. *The Breakpoint Navigator identifies all your breakpoints*

Since the Breakpoint Navigator identifies breakpoints by line number, you might want to display line numbers in the Xcode editor (see Figure 23-8). To turn on line numbers, follow these steps:

1. Choose Xcode ➤ Preferences. The Xcode Preferences window appears.

2. Click the Text Editing icon. The Text Editing options appear.

3. Select the "Line numbers" check box as shown in Figure 23-9.

Figure 23-9. The Line numbers check box lets you show or hide line numbers in the Xcode editor

Click on the close button (the red button) in the upper left corner of the Xcode Preferences window. Xcode now displays line numbers in the left margin of the editor.

To see how to use the Breakpoint Navigator, follow these steps:

1. Make sure the DebugProgram project is loaded in Xcode.

2. Turn on line numbers in Xcode.

3. Click on the AppDelegate.swift file in the Project Navigator pane.

4. Place three breakpoints anywhere in your code using whatever method you like best such as clicking in the left margin of the Xcode editor, pressing Command+\, or choosing Debug ➤ Breakpoints ➤ Add Breakpoint at Current Line). (The exact location doesn't matter.)

5. Click on the MainMenu.xib file in the Project Navigator pane. Xcode displays the user interface of your program.

6. Choose View ➤ Navigators ➤ Show Breakpoint Navigator. The Breakpoint Navigator displays your three breakpoints.

7. Click on any breakpoint. Xcode displays the file containing your chosen breakpoint.

8. Right-click on any breakpoint in the Breakpoint Navigator pane. A pop-up menu appears as shown in Figure 23-10.

Figure 23-10. *The Breakpoint Navigator lets you see where you have placed breakpoints*

9. Choose Disable Breakpoint. Notice this lets you deactivate or disable breakpoints individually instead of deactivating all of them at once through the Debug ➤ Deactivate Breakpoints command.

10. Right-click on any breakpoint in the Breakpoint Navigator pane and choose Delete Breakpoint. (Another way to delete a breakpoint is to drag the breakpoint away from your code and release the left mouse button.)

11. Delete all your breakpoints until no more breakpoints are left.

Using Symbolic Breakpoints

When you create a breakpoint, you must place it on the line where you want your program's execution to temporarily stop. However, this often means guessing where the problem might be and then using the various step commands to examine your code line by line.

To avoid this problem, Xcode offers a symbolic breakpoint. A symbolic breakpoint stops program execution only when a specific function or method runs. In case you don't want your program's execution to stop every time a particular function or method runs, you can tell Xcode to ignore it a certain number of times such as ten. That means the function or method will run up to ten times and then on the eleventh time it's called, the symbolic breakpoint will temporarily halt execution so you can step through your code line by line.

To create a symbolic breakpoint, you can define the following:

- ▨ Symbol – The name of the function or method to halt program execution.

- ▨ Module – The file name containing the function or method defined by the Symbol text field.

- ▨ Ignore – The number of times from 0 or more that you want the function or method to run before temporarily halting program execution.

To see how a Symbolic breakpoint works, follows these steps:

1. Make sure the DebugProgram project is loaded in Xcode.

2. Choose Debug ➤ Breakpoints ➤ Create Symbolic Breakpoint. A Symbolic Breakpoint pop-up window appears as shown in Figure 23-11.

Figure 23-11. The Symbolic Breakpoint pop-up window lets you define a breakpoint

3. Click in the Symbol text field and type C2F, which is the name of the function or method you want to examine.

4. (Optional) If the function or method name you specified in the Symbol text field is used in other files, click in the Module text field and type a file name. This file name will limit the symbolic breakpoint only to that function or method in that particular file. Since the C2F function is only used once, you can leave the Module text field empty.

5. (Optional) Click in the Ignore text field and type a number to specify how many times to ignore a function or method being called before halting program execution. In this case, leave 0 in the Ignore text field.

6. Click anywhere away from the Symbolic Breakpoint pop-up window to make it disappear.

7. Choose Product ➤ Run. The C2F Symbolic breakpoint causes the program to temporarily halt execution on the first line of code in the C2F function that calculates a result as shown in Figure 23-12.

Figure 23-12. The Symbolic breakpoint halts program execution in the C2F function defined by the Symbol text field

8. Choose Product ➤ Stop to make your program stop running.

9. Choose View ➤ Navigators ➤ Show Breakpoint Navigator. The Breakpoint Navigator pane appears.

10. Right-click on the C2F breakpoint in the Breakpoint Navigator pane and when a pop-up menu appears, choose Delete Breakpoint. There should be no breakpoints displayed in the Breakpoint Navigator pane.

Note   Another way to set a breakpoint without specifying a specific line of code is to create an Exception breakpoint. Normally if your program crashes, Xcode displays a bunch of cryptic error messages and you have no idea what caused the error. If you set an Exception breakpoint, Xcode can identify the line of code that created the crash so you can fix it.

Using Conditional Breakpoints

Breakpoints normally stop program execution at a specific line every time. However, you may want to stop program execution on a particular line only if a certain condition holds true, such as if a variable exceeds a certain value, which can signal when something has gone wrong.

To see how a Conditional breakpoint works, follow these steps:

1. Make sure the DebugProgram project is loaded in Xcode.

2. Click on the AppDelegate.swift file in the Project Navigator pane.

3. Place a breakpoint on the following line by clicking in the left margin or moving the cursor in the line and pressing Command+\ or choosing Debug ➤ Breakpoints ➤ Add Breakpoint at Current Line:

```
print (myMessage + "\(C2F(temp))")
```

4. Choose View ➤ Navigators ➤ Show Breakpoint Navigator. The Breakpoint Navigator pane appears, showing the breakpoint you just created.

5. Right-click on the breakpoint in the Breakpoint Navigator pane and choose Edit Breakpoint. A pop-up window appears as shown in Figure 23-13.

Figure 23-13. *The Symbolic breakpoint halts program execution in the C2F function defined by the Symbol text field*

6. Click in the Condition text field and type C2F(temp) > 200 and press Return.

7. Choose Product ➤ Run. Xcode highlights your breakpoint to temporarily stop program execution, which means that the condition (C2F(temp) > 200) must be true.

8. Choose Product ➤ Stop to halt and exit out of your program and return back to Xcode.

9. Choose View ➤ Navigators ➤ Show Breakpoint Navigator, right-click on the breakpoint you created, and choose Edit Breakpoint. The pop-up window appears.

10. Click in the Condition text field and edit the text so it reads C2F(temp > 500). Press Return.

11. Choose Product ➤ Run. Notice that this time your breakpoint does not stop program execution because its condition (C2F(temp) > 500) is not true. Because the breakpoint didn't stop your program, your program's blank user interface appears.

12. Choose DebugProgram ➤ Quit DebugProgram.

13. Drag the breakpoint away from the left margin and release the left mouse button to delete the breakpoint. (You can also right-click on the breakpoint in the Breakpoint Navigator pane and choose Delete Breakpoint.)

Troubleshooting Breakpoints in Xcode

Bugs occur in every program from operating systems and games to spreadsheets and word processors. Keep in mind that because Xcode is a program, it also has bugs in it, which can sometimes frustrate you until Apple updates and fixes these bugs in another version of Xcode.

One common problem with using breakpoints in Xcode is that they may not always work. A breakpoint is supposed to stop program execution, but if Xcode seems to be ignoring your breakpoints, there may be several reasons why this is occurring that doesn't involve possible bugs in Xcode.

First, make sure you didn't accidentally deactivate all your breakpoints by pressing Command+Y or choosing Debug ➤ Deactivate Breakpoints.

Second, Xcode can compile your program with or without debugging information. Usually you want debugging information turned on so you can debug your program. However, when your program is ready to ship, you want to strip debugging information out to make your program take up less memory and storage space. If you accidentally turn off debugging information, then Xcode will ignore any breakpoints you may have set.

To make sure debugging information is turned on, follow these steps:

1. Choose Product ➤ Scheme ➤ Edit Scheme. A window sheet appears.

2. Click on Run in the left pane as shown in Figure 23-14.

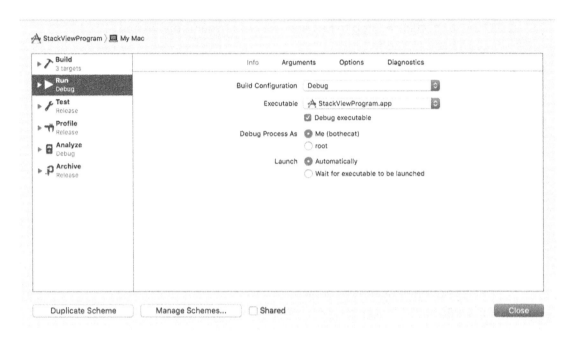

Figure 23-14. Turning on debugging information

3. Make sure the Debug executable check box is selected.

4. Make sure the Build Configuration pop-up menu shows Debug (and not Release).

5. Click the Close button.

Summary

Errors or bugs are unavoidable in any program. While syntax errors are easy to find and fix, logic errors can be tougher to find because you thought your code would create one type of result but it winds up creating a different result. Now you're left trying to figure out what you did wrong when you thought you were doing everything right. Even harder errors to track down are runtime errors that occur seemingly at random because of unknown conditions that affect a program

To help you track down and eliminate most bugs, you can use the print command along with comments, but for most robust debugging, you should use Xcode's built-in debugger. With the debugger you can set breakpoints in your code and watch how values get stored in one or more variables.

A conditional breakpoint only stops program execution when a certain condition occurs. A symbolic breakpoint only stops program execution when a specific function or method gets called. Once a breakpoint stops a program, you can continue examining your code line by line using various step commands. The Step Into command lets you view code stored inside a function or method while the Step Out command lets you prematurely exit out of a function or method and jump back to the function or method call.

By using breakpoints and step commands, you can exhaustively examine how your program works, line by line, to eliminate as many errors as possible. The fewer errors your program contains, the happier your users will be.

Planning a Program Before and After Coding

Before you invest days, weeks, months, or years working on a program, make sure the world even wants your program in the first place. If you're writing a program for yourself, then you can ignore what the rest of the world thinks. However, if you plan on selling your programs to others, make sure your program has a future before you even begin.

Here's one way to determine if there's a market for your program. Look for competition. Most people think it's better to target a market with no competition, but if there's no competition, this could be a big clue that there's also no market.

However, if you look for a market loaded with lots of competitors, this means there's a thriving market for that type of program. Just do a quick search for lottery-picking software or astrology programs and you'll find plenty of competition. The more competition, the more active the market.

If only one or two big companies dominate a particular market, chances are good that the opportunity in that market has already passed. For example, despite the availability of OS X and Linux, Windows is still the dominant operating system for PCs. That means you'll probably waste your time trying to write a rival operating system to compete against Windows.

Likewise, there are only a handful of major word processors, spreadsheets, and presentation programs on the market today, which means trying to write another general word processor, spreadsheet, or presentation program will likely be an exercise in futility.

Lots of competition means an active market. Little or no competition means that the market has probably already settled on a leader, and your program likely will never be able to overthrow that leader. Trying to convince people to buy your word processor instead of using Microsoft Word or Pages will likely be a waste of time.

However, look for niche markets. For example, the word processor market may already be dominated by Microsoft Word, but specialized word processors are still in demand. Although Microsoft Word can be used to write screenplays and novels, it's not optimized for that purpose. That's why other companies can successfully sell screenplay writing word processors or novel writing word processors that help you organize your ideas.

Such specialized niches are too small for big companies to worry about, which means you'll never have to compete directly against any of these big companies. Besides targeting niche markets that big companies ignore, a second approach is to find out what the big companies are lacking in their software, and then write a program that solves that missing need.

For example, Microsoft Office offers a password protection feature to lock files. However, Microsoft's encryption feature is weak and easily broken. As a result, there's a market for software that can encrypt files much better than what Microsoft Office does, while offering a similar user interface as Microsoft Office.

Most important, write a program because you're interested in that particular field, not because you think it will make you a lot of money. There may be money selling real estate management software or software for controlling drones, but unless you're interested in those fields, you likely won't have the passion or long-term interest to spend the long hours needed to develop and market a program for those users.

As a general rule, avoid competing directly against a big company. Even Apple couldn't compete against Microsoft Windows for the PC operating system market, and a free offering such as Linux hasn't succeeded much against Windows either.

Instead of directly competing against a big company, look for niche markets that are too small for big companies to tackle, or look for ways to supplement a big company's existing programs. Above all, look for a problem in a field that you're passionately committed to solving, and this will give you the motivation to create the best program possible.

Identifying the Purpose of Your Program

When programmers first get an idea, their natural tendency is to rush to the computer and start writing code. However this is like living in Los Angeles, getting an idea to visit New York, and hopping in your car to drive there. You may get there eventually, but without a plan, you'll likely waste time by not planning which roads to take or what to bring with to make your trip more enjoyable.

Just as you should take your time and plan ahead before rushing off to visit another city, so you should also take your time and plan ahead when developing a new program. If you start writing Swift code in a flurry of inspiration, you'll likely run out of energy and ideas long before you finish your program. That will likely create a half-completed, poorly designed program that will need to be heavily modified or dumped completely to make it work.

Writing code is actually the most straightforward part of creating any program. The hardest part of programming can be deciding what you hope to get out of a program when it's finished.

For example, if you're learning and experimenting with Swift, you might want to create programs just to learn a specific feature such as how to retrieve data from a stock market web site or how to create animation for a game. In this case, your goal is just to create short, disposable programs that let you understand how to use specific programming features.

If you're planning to create programs for other people to use, then you need to do some additional planning. First of all, why do you want to create a program for other people? Perhaps you want to create a custom program for a particular person. Maybe you want to create a program that offers features that current programs lack. Whatever the reason, every program must ultimately satisfy the user.

If you're creating a program for your own use, then you're the user. However if you're creating programs for other people, then the user can be a specific person and computer (such as one dentist in your neighborhood dental office), or a general group of users (any dentist who needs to manage a dental office). Whoever the user might be, identify the single most important task your program must solve for that user. Then make sure your program accomplishes that one crucial task correctly.

> **Note**   Between 2000 and 2005, the FBI spent $170 million dollars creating a program called Virtual Case File. The government eventually abandoned the entire project because of constantly changing specifications for what the program was supposed to do and how it was supposed to work. If you don't know what a program is supposed to do, you won't know how it's supposed to achieve that result.

Before writing any program, identify the following:

- Who is the user of the program?
- What is the program supposed to do for the user?
- How will the program achieve that result for the user?

The user of your program completely determines the design of your program's user interface. Compare the cockpit of a 777 jet airliner to the dashboard of a typical car. To the average person, a 777 cockpit may look intimidating, but to an experienced pilot, everything is within arm's reach and easy to understand. If your program caters to specialists, your user interface can rely on the user's knowledge to work. If your program caters to the general public, your user interface may need to guide the user more often.

Every program must create a useful result for the user. Word processors organize text into neatly formatted pages, spreadsheets automatically and accurately calculate mathematical formulas, and even games provide entertainment. Imagine your program giving the user superpowers that the user can't achieve any other way. What superpower will your program give to the user?

Once you know what your program should do for the user, the final step is determining how it will achieve that result. Programs typically accept input from the user, manipulate that input somehow, and provide a new result. As a programmer, you need to determine how to achieve that new result, step by step. Then you need to translate those steps into a programming language such as Swift.

Ultimately, programming is a creative talent that requires clear, specific goals and methodical persistence to succeed.

Designing the Structure of a Program

Once you know what your program needs to do and how it can do it, the next step is to design how your program will actually work. There's no single "best" way to write a program since you can write the same program a million different ways. However, you need to design a program that not only works, but is also easy to understand and modify in the future.

Every program can always be improved. Sometimes that improvement means optimizing the program so it runs faster or uses less memory. Other times improvement means adding new features to the program. In either case, every program will likely go through several modifications during its lifetime, so it's crucial that you design your program from the start so it's easy to understand and modify.

In the world of object-oriented programming, the common way to design a program is to separate a large program into multiple objects that represent logical features. For example, if you were designing a program to control a car, you could divide the program into the following objects:

- Engine object
- Steering object
- Stereo object
- Transmission object

Now if you needed to improve the program's steering ability, you could just replace the steering object with a new steering object without the risk that your changes would affect the rest of the program.

How you divide a program into objects is completely arbitrary. You could just as well design the same car program into the following objects:

- Front object
- Back object
- Inside object
- Undercarriage object

If you design your program well from the start, you'll make it easy for you or other programmers to modify that program easily in the future.

Designing the User Interface of a Program

Besides the structure of your program's design, the other crucial element of your program is the user interface. With Xcode, you can design the structure of your program (its various objects) in complete isolation from the user interface (and vice versa). This gives you the freedom to easily design and modify the structure of your program or the user interface without affecting the other part of your program.

The user interface defines how your user sees your program. A poor user interface makes a program hard to use. A good user interface makes a program easy to use. Even if the underlying structure of a program is poor, a good user interface can make that program appear responsive, elegant, and well-designed.

So what is a good user interface? Ideally a user interface dissolves in the background to the point where the user isn't even aware that it exists. When you pinch two fingers on the screen of an iPhone or iPad, you can make an image appear larger or smaller.

From the user's point of view, the user interface doesn't even exist because the user gets the sensation of directly manipulating an image. In reality, the user interface translates the user's fingertip positions into magnifying an image's appearance. The user interface is still there, but the user doesn't need to read a thick training manual and follow multiple steps to manipulate it. A good user interface essentially melts into the background.

Here's how a clumsy user interface would accomplish the exact same task. First, the user would have to tap a button on the screen to display a menu. Second, the user would have to choose a Zoom command from that menu. Third, the user would have to type in a number that represents the magnification percentage such as 50 percent or 125 percent. Fourth, the user would have to tap an OK button to finally complete the task and change the magnification of an image.

Which user interface would you rather use?

As a general rule, the more steps needed to accomplish a task, the harder the user interface will be to use because if the user omits one step or does one step out of order, the entire task fails. Oftentimes programmers try to fix poor user interface designs by simply adding more ways to accomplish the same task through keystroke shortcuts or toolbar icons. Unfortunately if you have a poor user interface, adding more ways to accomplish the same task won't necessarily make your user interface easier to use.

If you have a poor user interface, it may be easier to redesign the whole interface rather than try to fix a faulty design.

Design a User Interface with Paper and Pencil

As a general rule, your first idea for a user interface will rarely be the final design. That's because what you think will work won't work, and what you may not even consider could be vitally important to your users. So rather than design your user interface and be forced to change it later, it's far faster and simpler to design your user interface with paper and pencil instead.

Once you have a rough design on paper, show it to your eventual users to get their feedback. Even though looking at static images of crudely drawn user interfaces might seem pointless, it can give you feedback on the general design of your user interface. When evaluating a preliminary user interface, ask your users:

- What's missing? Are there commands or features that need to be displayed but aren't?

- What's not needed? Are there commands or features that are currently displayed but aren't necessary?

- What could be easier? How can the user interface be rearranged or organized to make it simpler?

- What's confusing? Is there anything that users don't understand? Help menus and descriptive tool tips can never substitute for cleaner user interface designs.

- What's intuitive? What will users expect to do with your user interface? Does your user interface support or frustrate users' expectations?

Designing user interfaces on paper is quick, fast, and easy. Since you don't have much time invested in any particular user interface design, it's much easier to throw away bad designs rather than try to defend and justify keeping them.

In addition, paper designs make it easy for you or others to scribble on them to redesign them. Because paper user interface designs are so fast and simple for anyone to make, feel free to experiment. The more user interface designs you can create, the more likely you'll stumble across one that will work.

Study existing programs and see what you like best and what you like least. Then put both features (the ones you like and the ones you dislike) into different user interface designs. The design you may think is best may be the ones that others like the least, and the design you like the least may be the ones others find are the best.

Design a User Interface with Software

Once you've experimented with different user interface designs and found one or more that seem promising, it's time to move beyond paper and pencil and create a user interface prototype that people can actually see on a computer screen.

What may look nice on paper may not work on a computer screen. More importantly, a computer screen can create a simple form of interaction. When the user clicks on a button, a new screen can appear just like the real user interface would work. This interactivity is something you can only poorly mimic with paper and pencil designs.

A fast way to create an interactive user interface prototype is to use presentation software such as PowerPoint or Keynote. Presentation software lets you create slides where each slide can represent a window of your user interface. You can place buttons and graphics to create rough user interface designs, then create links between those buttons and slides to create a limited form of interactivity.

An interactive user interface prototype lets you test how users expect the user interface to respond. For example, users might expect to see a certain window after clicking a command. If your interactive prototype shows users a different window, then you'll know what you need to fix.

Like paper and pencil designs, the goal of a user interface prototype is to find out what works and what doesn't work while spending as little time designing your prototype. The less time you spend designing your prototype, the more time you can spend coming up with alternate ideas and testing them.

In addition to creating user interface prototypes using presentation software, you can also buy special mock-up software that contains common user interface elements such as buttons, windows, and check boxes that you can quickly drag and drop to create a simulated user interface as shown in Figure 24-1.

Figure 24-1. Balsamiq Mockups is a specialized program for creating user interface prototypes

A software version of your user interface prototype provides interactivity. When you're satisfied with your user interface design as a prototype, the final step is to convert your prototype into an actual Xcode user interface.

Remember, Xcode lets you create your Swift code completely separate from your user interface. That means you can create user interfaces in Xcode without writing a single line of code. When you're happy with the appearance and design of your user interface, you can connect its various items (buttons, menus, etc.) to IBOutlets and IBAction methods to link your user interface to your Swift code.

Marketing Your Software

Once you create a program, you'll need to test it to make sure it works. Such early testers (known as alpha and beta testers) can help spot bugs in your program so you can fix them right away. When your program is as bug-free as possible, that's the time to release your software on the market.

Here's the biggest mistake most people make. They write a program, put up a web site advertising the program or their company, and wait for the orders to roll in. In the OS X world, Apple offers a special Mac App Store that gives every Macintosh user potential access to your software.

However, it's never enough to advertise your software on a web site or the Mac App Store and wait for people to buy it. To maximize sales, you also have to promote your software.

To many people, marketing means spending money advertising. While you could do that, it's always best to spend as little as possible. It's easy to spend money on advertising and marketing, but unless your advertising and marketing expenses are less than the sales that advertising and marketing generates, you risk going bankrupt slowly. Where most people go wrong is that they spend money on advertising and marketing, but they have no idea if all that advertising and marketing is generating enough sales to justify the expense.

That's why you should focus on free ways to advertise and market your software so you can find out what people like about your software, what types of people are more likely to buy your software, and the best ways to reach your potential users, all without going broke to do it.

For example, suppose you sell software that makes video look aged as if it had been filmed decades ago on film complete with scratches, faded images, and sound effects of film threading through a movie projector. You might initially target people who want to turn their videos into older movies for fun, but you may find that your actual market is Hollywood studios who need to create visual effects to simulate older films.

Your initial market may not care about your software but an entirely different market just might. If you spent money advertising to your initial market, you would have wasted money targeting people who didn't really want your program after all. Only later might you find the real market for your software, and it could come from an unexpected niche that you never thought about before.

So don't substitute spending money for doing market research. It's easy to spend more money. It's harder to take the time to determine how effective your marketing and advertising really is and whether you're even targeting the most lucrative market for your software in the first place.

Beyond spending a minimal amount of money promoting your software through a web site, here are some other ways to promote your software for little or no cost:

- Start a blog.
- Give away free software.
- Post videos of your software on video sharing sites such as YouTube.
- Create and give away free information stored in PDF files offering tips for people who are potential customers of your software.
- Find the social networks where your potential customers gather and participate in discussions to answer their questions.

Blogging About Your Software

A web site is like putting a billboard in the middle of the desert and hoping people will magically find it. While search engines can help people find your web site, it's far better to include a blog on your website as well.

A blog serves several purposes. First, by constantly blogging at least once a week, you generate new content for your web site. New content tells search engines that your site is active, and thus search engines will rank them as more relevant than a site that hasn't been updated in months or even years. So blogs increase your search engine rank, thereby increasing the chance that potential customers can find your product.

Second, a blog puts a human face behind your software. By discussing the challenges you faced creating the software and responding to questions from people about your software, you demonstrate that there's someone who cares and is willing to respond to questions about that software. Given a choice between buying from a faceless corporation or someone who seems like a real person, this subtle difference can increase the likelihood that potential customers will buy your software.

Third, each blog post acts like another miniature ad for your software. Most people create a web site describing their software and hope that will convince people to buy it. However, a blog lets you focus on a different aspect of your software. One blog post might talk about a special feature that you're particularly proud to highlight. A second blog post might tell a story of a happy customer who used your software to solve a problem. A third blog post might explain why you designed your program the way you did.

Since each blog post is slightly different, you avoid repetition. Yet since each blog post continually promotes your software, you're constantly advertising your software from different points of view. This increases the chance that one of your blog posts will convince someone to buy your software.

Blogging simply costs time, yet provides higher search engine rankings while promoting your software over and over again. Think of blogs as a free way to advertise on the Internet.

Giving Away Free Software

There's a reason companies give away free samples of everything from food to toothpaste. They know once you try a product and like it, you'll be far more likely to buy it. If you never try a product, it's much harder for a company to convince you to buy it.

Giving away free software works the same way. Some companies give away free "lite" versions of their software that's fully functional. This lets customers try and use your software at no cost. A certain percentage of people will eventually want more advanced features, and those people will translate into paying customers.

The more people you get using your free software, the more people you'll get paying for the advanced version.

For example, assume 1 percent of all people trying your free software decide to buy your advanced version. If you can get your free software in the hands of 100 people, that translates into one sale. However, if you can get your free software in the hands of 10,000 people, that translates into 100 sales.

Since distributing free software doesn't cost you anything to duplicate or distribute, your advertising and marketing costs are essentially zero.

Besides offering a free "lite" version of your program, you could also offer free software related to your main program. For example, suppose you sell a word processor targeted for scientists to write complex mathematical and chemical formulas. Rather than give away a free "lite" version of your program, you could give away free software that your target audience (engineers and scientists) might like such as an interactive periodic table of elements or a simple equation solving program.

Such free software simply gives potential customers something for free. Now if they like your free software, they'll be far more likely to trust your commercial software. If your free software is well-designed and useful, potential customers will believe your commercial software must also be just as well-designed and useful. Free software lets potential customers sample your products without risk.

Posting Videos About Your Software

Blogging about your software can be great for people who like reading. Unfortunately, in today's busy world, many people don't have time to read. That's why you can make short videos demonstrating how your software works so people can see what problems your software solves and how it does it.

In general, nobody wants to buy or use your software. What they really want are the solutions your software offers, and that's what you need to emphasize in your videos. Don't explain the menu system or the organization of your user interface. Focus on solving a single problem and emphasize something unique about your software.

For example, suppose your software is designed to help real estate agents. Your potential customers will either want to save time or make money, so show how your software can help real estate agents do both. Show a feature that simplifies an existing, time-consuming process. Show another feature that increases the number of potential buyers of a property with little additional work. Always focus on how your software benefits the user.

Keep your videos short and to the point. More people will watch a video demonstrating a single feature that runs under a minute. Far fewer people will watch a thirty-minute video demonstrating multiple features. With many video sharing sites like YouTube, you can even link multiple videos together so when one video ends, a second one begins. Now each video acts like another advertisement for your product and by linking each video to another one, each new video increases the chance that someone will find and watch at least one of them.

Give Away Free Information

People tend to buy more from people they trust, so one way to get people to trust you is to give out free, useful information. For example, if your software helps edit photographs, write up a list of tips for capturing better pictures. Now share that list of tips as a PDF file and give it away for free, with a link back to your web site promoting your software.

Free, useful information acts as a subtle advertisement. Traditional ads blatantly promote a product, which can immediately turn off even your best potential customers. Free information subtly promotes a product. Since the free information is useful to your potential customer, they'll be more willing to look at it and even share it with others. If they want more information, they can visit your web site.

One visually appealing way to provide free information is through a combination of text and graphics known as infographics. An infographic presents information in a colorful manner so it's easy to read and understand without wading through large amounts of text. As Figure 24-2 shows, even IBM creates and distributes free infographics to promote their services and products.

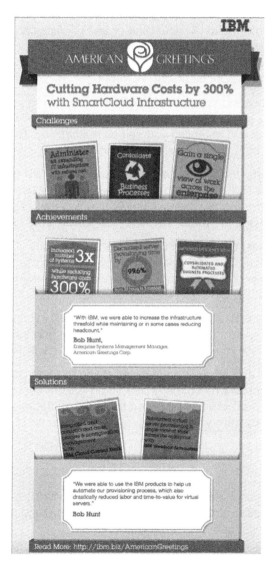

Figure 24-2. IBM provides an infographic as a PDF file to promote how their services helped American Greetings

By providing free, useful information, you establish yourself as an authority. If you can provide free, useful information as PDF files and blog posts on your web site, you'll give people additional reasons to keep coming back to your web site/blog over and over again. The more times people visit, the more likely they'll eventually buy your software or tell others about your web site/blog.

Free, useful information establishes you as trustworthy, which lowers the barrier to buying your software. The more people trust you, the more likely they'll believe your product will do what you claim it does.

Join Social Networks

Giving away free, useful information in your blog or as PDF files can help establish you as an authority in your field. However, a blog requires that someone visits your site and a PDF file requires someone download that file. Another way to share useful information for free is to stay in constant contact with popular social networks.

Find out which social networks your potential customers visit and join those networks. Now as people post questions, jump in and answer them with useful advice. The purpose is to answer people's questions and establish yourself as trustworthy. Then make sure each post you make includes a link back to your web site or blog.

Visiting social networks lets you reach potential customers far faster than hoping they'll visit your blog or find your PDF file. Just make sure you provide useful information instead of thinly disguised advertising copy that will simply annoy others. The more people learn to trust you on a social network, the more likely they'll also visit your web site/blog.

With all of these techniques, the goal isn't to get someone to buy your product right away (although that's always nice). The real goal is to draw them one step closer toward learning more about you and your product. The more people know about your product, the more likely they'll buy from you.

Advertising and marketing is basically a numbers game. Keep helping others for free in ways that don't take up much time or money, and you'll eventually find that others will find you and buy your software. The more you help others, the more others will trust and buy from you.

The old way of marketing and advertising involves trying to force people to listen to ads and buy against their will (which is why so many people dislike marketing and advertising). The new way of marketing and advertising is to give potential customers something of value before you ask them to buy from you.

Summary

Most programmers focus on increasing their technical knowledge of programming. While knowing as much as possible about Swift's features and the Cocoa framework can always be helpful, technical knowledge alone is rarely enough.

Programming involves more than just writing code. Before you even start writing Swift code, you need to make sure there's a market for your program. Rather than try to compete against big companies, look for niche markets that big companies are ignoring, or look for ways your program can supplement programs offered by a big company. Big companies have far more resources that they can use to crush any direct competitors, so by targeting a niche market or a way to supplement their own products, you can avoid directly competing with a much bigger company.

Before you start writing Swift code, create prototypes of your software's user interface. Although user interface design may not sound as appealing to programmers as digging into the intricacies of writing code, it's a vital part of any software project. The user interface determines how people view your program. A well-designed user interface can make your program easier to use. A poorly designed user interface can make a program seem harder to use, despite any technical features it may offer.

Test your user interface designs as quickly and cheaply as possible using paper and pencil. When you need to create an interactive version of your user interface, create simple mock-ups using presentation software such as Keynote or PowerPoint, or consider buying special mock-up construction software.

When you have a final user interface design, create it in Xcode. Just remember that as your program continues to evolve, you'll likely still need to make changes to your user interface.

Finally, when your program is complete, your work still isn't done. You'll still need to advertise and market your software. Rather than spend money buying ads, it's far less expensive and often more effective to pursue free options instead.

Start a blog, give away free information, and provide something of value to others. The more you give to others, the more likely others will be attracted to your product and buy from you.

As you can see, coding is just one stage of creating and marketing software. Technical knowledge can create software, but you still need additional skills before and after coding to properly design your program and successfully sell it afterwards.

Index

Get the eBook for only $5!

Why limit yourself?

Now you can take the weightless companion with you wherever you go and access your content on your PC, phone, tablet, or reader.

Since you've purchased this print book, we're happy to offer you the eBook in all 3 formats for just $5.

Convenient and fully searchable, the PDF version enables you to easily find and copy code—or perform examples by quickly toggling between instructions and applications. The MOBI format is ideal for your Kindle, while the ePUB can be utilized on a variety of mobile devices.

To learn more, go to www.apress.com/companion or contact support@apress.com.

Lightning Source UK Ltd.
Milton Keynes UK
UKOW05f1145031115

261990UK00009B/120/P